A
THOUSAND
HILLS

A THOUSAND HILLS

Rwanda's Rebirth and
the Man Who Dreamed It

Stephen Kinzer

WILEY

John Wiley & Sons, Inc.

Published by John Wiley & Sons, Inc., Hoboken, New Jersey
Published simultaneously in Canada

Published in association with the literary agency of Alive Communications, Inc., 7680 Goddard Street, Suite 200, Colorado Springs, Colorado, 80920, www.alivecommunications.com.

For general information about our other products and services, please contact our Customer Care Department within the United States at (800) 762–2974, outside the United States at (317) 572–3993 or fax (317) 572–4002.

Wiley also publishes its books in a variety of electronic formats. Some content that appears in print may not be available in electronic books. For more information about Wiley products, visit our web site at www.wiley.com.

Library of Congress Cataloging-in-Publication Data:

Kinzer, Stephen.
A thousand hills: Rwanda's rebirth and the man who dreamed it / Stephen Kinzer.
   p. cm.
Includes bibliographical references and index.
   ISBN 978–0–470–12015–6 (cloth)
   1. Kagamé, Paul, 1957– 2. Presidents—Rwanda—Biography. 3. Rwanda—Politics and government—1994– 4. Political leadership—Rwanda. 5. Rwanda—History—Civil War, 1994—Atrocities. 6. Genocide—Rwanda. I Title.
   DT450.437.K37K56 2008
   967.57104′3—dc22

                                                                                    2007041613

Printed in the United States of America

10 9 8 7 6 5 4 3 2 1

To the people of Rwanda

Though we seemed dead, we did but sleep.

—Shakespeare

Contents

ACKNOWLEDGMENTS

This book could not have been written without the cooperation of its main character, President Paul Kagame. During 2006 and 2007 he generously sat for more than thirty hours of interviews. He did not ask for any control over the manuscript, nor was he given any.

All italicized quotes from President Kagame that appear in this book, along with others that are not otherwise sourced, come from my interviews with him. Those that come from other sources are footnoted. Quotes from other Rwandans that are not otherwise sourced also come from my interviews.

Every quote in this book is rendered verbatim, but with three adjustments to assure consistency and avoid confusion.

People from Rwanda are usually called Rwandan, but some use the word "Rwandese" instead. I have rendered it as "Rwandan" in every case.

Guerrillas of the Rwandan Patriotic Front who fought from 1990 to 1994 officially composed the Rwandan Patriotic Army, or RPA. Most people, however, continued to refer to both this force and its political umbrella organization as the RPF. In this narrative, I do the same.

There is no fixed rule about the plural of the words "Hutu" and "Tutsi." I have chosen the more common usage, which does not place an "s" at the end of these designations.

Insightful readers, especially Laura Hoemeke, Richard Orth, Karen Schmidt, and James Stone, made valuable comments on portions of this manuscript. The accomplished *editrice* Elmira

Bayrasli deftly helped shape it. Sierra Millman provided valuable research help. None of these readers saw the final draft, however, and therefore are not responsible for any errors.

Grace Lewis and others at the Oak Park Public Library in Oak Park, Illinois, helped me find books and articles from obscure sources.

Davinah Milenge was the always-patient presidential aide who served as my intermediary with President Kagame.

Joseph Bideri, George Baryamwisaki, Patricia Kanyiginya, and Frederick Munyarubuga helped me find images for the photo insert.

Wherever I traveled in Rwanda, people willingly spoke with me, guided me, and helped me. Rwandans living abroad also shared valuable perspectives. Their generosity led me to whatever understanding of their country is reflected in this book.

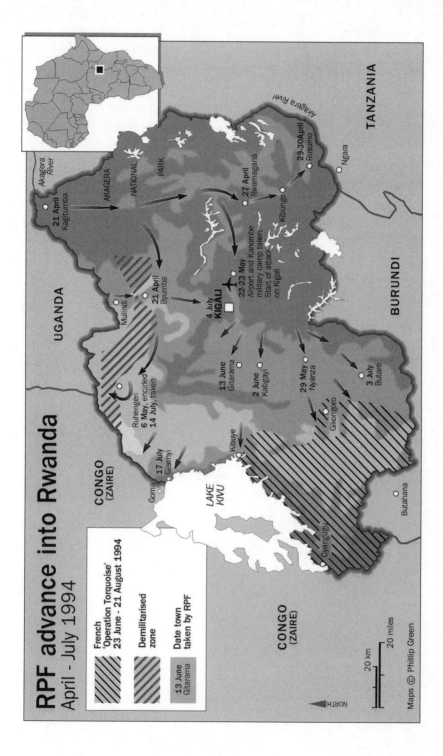

RPF advance into Rwanda
April - July 1994

French 'Operation Torquoise' 23 June - 21 August 1994

Demilitarised zone

Date town taken by RPF 13 June Gitarama

Maps © Phillip Green

NORTH

20 km

20 miles

CONGO (ZAIRE)

UGANDA

TANZANIA

BURUNDI

CONGO (ZAIRE)

AKAGERA NATIONAL PARK

Akagera River

21 April Kagitumba

Mulindi

21 April Byumba

Ruhengeri 6 May, encircled 14 July, taken

17 July Gisenyi

Goma

LAKE KIVU

Kibuye

Cyangugu

Butahana

Gikongoro

29 May Nyanza

3 July Butare

2 June Kabgayi

13 June Gitarama

4 July KIGALI

22-23 May Airport and Kanombe military camp taken. Start of attack on Kigali

27 April Rwamagana

Kibungo

29-30April Rusumo

Ngara

Akagera River

A
THOUSAND
HILLS

Why wouldn't you find it despicable to live in this situation? Why should we be a country that depends on other people? What's wrong with us? Why do we live off other people's money, off the taxpayers of other countries? How can it be that people who lived in this country two hundred years ago were better off than we are today? What happened? We are descendants of people with integrity, people who were hardworking, people who stood up and fought for their rights. We have been put in a position of being despised, of being held in contempt. We don't deserve that, and we have within ourselves what we need to stand up to these challenges.*

*This passage and all other italic passages in this book are from President Paul Kagame.

INTRODUCTION

D
URING ONE OF MY STAYS IN RWANDA, an unlikely visitor
turned up. He was the luckless fellow whom fate had
temporarily made president of Somalia, one of the
world's most chaotic states. Warlords control large regions of
Somalia, terror is a way of life in much of the country, and most
citizens dare not even dream of peace, safety, or fulfilling lives.

The president of this benighted country came to Rwanda begging for alms. What he wanted most was a contingent of soldiers
from the crack Rwandan army to help him stabilize Mogadishu.
He also asked President Paul Kagame for whatever other aid
might be available, anything at all that might help him confront
the overwhelming challenge of reviving his shattered nation.

Within this encounter lies the essence of what makes modern Rwanda so fascinating. In the mid-1990s, both Rwanda and
Somalia lay in ruins. The Rwandan genocide had taken as many as
a million lives or more, and Somali warlords were tearing their
country apart. These were probably the two most devastated
countries on earth. The phrase "failed state" barely hints at the hell
into which they had fallen. Both seemed headed for either ethnic
dictatorship or endless turmoil.

Somalia, as most people predicted, continued its free fall into
chaos and anarchy. Rwanda, however, rebelled against its destiny.

1

It has recovered from civil war and genocide more fully than anyone imagined possible and is united, stable, and at peace. Its leaders are boundlessly ambitious. Rwandans are bubbling over with a sense of unlimited possibility. Outsiders, drawn by the chance to help transform a resurgent nation, are streaming in.

Why did Rwanda recover from its catastrophe while Somalia did not? That question leaped to my mind as I watched their presidents shake hands. Barely a decade after its cataclysm, Rwanda is not only peaceful but exciting and full of promise. How did this happen?

Around the same time Somalia's president visited Rwanda with palm outstretched, another story burst onto Africa's front pages. This one was from Kenya, which like other African nations once seemed full of promise but is staggering under the weight of violence and corruption. An elderly American missionary who had spent most of her life in Africa, together with her fifty-two-year-old daughter, were murdered by carjackers on the outskirts of Nairobi. Senseless killings like these have become common in some parts of Africa. Because the victims of this one were white, it sent a wave of horror through the expatriate community. Among those it shocked was one of my friends, who ran an aid program in Nairobi. Before she could recover her equilibrium, her own gated compound, where guards are on constant duty and there is an alarm button in every room of every house, was invaded by a rampaging gang armed with assault rifles. The next day my friend decided she could no longer subject her family to such danger. She quit her job and made plans to leave the country.

This story too has a special resonance for Rwandans and their friends. In Rwanda there are no carjackers or armed gangs. People walk the streets at all hours carrying money, cell phones, and other valuables. If police officers stop a car, it is to check whether seat belts are fastened, not to threaten, extort, or kidnap.

Rwanda is not being torn apart by unending civil war, like Somalia, or by criminal violence, like Kenya. Instead, it is stable, its people groping their way toward modernity and liberation. I spent months traveling in Rwanda, and wherever I stopped, I asked people how this had come to pass. Nearly all gave me the same answer. Many even used the same words.

"In the end," they told me, "it's all about leadership."

The central figure in Rwanda's rebirth, Paul Kagame, emerged during the first decade of the twenty-first century as one of the most intriguing leaders in Africa. He preaches a doctrine of security, guided reconciliation, honest governance, and, above all, self-reliance. Already, he has brought Rwanda much that was inconceivable in the wake of the 1994 genocide: law and order, the beginnings of economic growth and social transformation, a cooling of sectarian passions, and, most astonishing of all, a pulsating sense of enthusiasm and optimism.

During one of my stays in Rwanda, Bill Clinton dropped in to visit a hospital that his foundation supports near Rwinkwavu on the rich eastern savannah. A few days later, Bill Gates showed up and announced that *his* foundation would spend $900,000 to build a medical center where doctors and technicians from across Africa will be trained in treating infectious diseases. Then came Howard Schultz, chairman of Starbucks, who was so impressed that he brought President Kagame to his company's next annual meeting in Seattle. Andrew Young, the former Atlanta mayor and UN ambassador, passed through with a delegation of African American leaders, and after returning home marveled, "Something great is happening in Rwanda!"

These are not the only outsiders who have been captivated by Rwanda's sudden emergence. Wherever I stopped, I found others just as convinced that this tiny country—about the size of Maryland or Belgium—may be poised for a historic leap toward prosperity. Their admiration for Kagame springs from the pages of my notebooks.

Kevin Terry, British-born mining engineer: "I consider myself an African. I've seen so many promising leaders come and go. Paul Kagame—I am so impressed with him. When you think of what this country has gone through and look at where it is now, it's something you can hardly believe. There's a future here. This is a place that people from all over Africa are starting to look at.

They're saying, 'Look what's happening there—why can't we do that where we are?' And you have to say that most of this is because of Paul Kagame. Problems that Africa has never seemed able to solve, he is solving."

Tim Schilling, agronomist from Texas who works with coffee farmers in southern Rwanda: "Kagame is the key. He's holding it all together. If Rwanda stays on track the way it's going now, this guy is really going to be the star of Africa."

Peter Schonherr, ambassador of the Netherlands: "What these people have achieved in the short time since the genocide is unbelievable. . . . This is a terrific country. You can work with these people. They have drive. They want to get things done. It's not like countries where the government promises the world and nothing happens. They work very hard, they know what they're doing, and they're smart. . . . They want to play in a very high league, and if they continue like they are now, I'm sure they can get there."

Alicea Lilly, director of a project to protect Rwanda's mountain gorillas: "The things I see in Rwanda are incredible. It's so positive. This place is moving ahead in spectacular ways. This president is doing incredible things."

Raj Rajendran, Indian-born businessman: "Things happen much faster here than in other places in this region. We have a sister company in Uganda, and we work with suppliers in Kenya, South Africa, and a lot of other countries. You see comparatively that this country is moving forward much faster. . . . I would give all the credit to the president. His personal traits made this whole project successful."

Despite this enthusiasm, there is good reason to doubt Rwanda's prospects. It faces daunting challenges. Most of the population lives in extreme poverty. The country is landlocked and overpopulated. Citizens are required to repeat platitudes about reconciliation, but hatred festers in many hearts.

The greatest enigma to those who wonder about Rwanda's prospects is President Kagame himself. He is a visionary endowed with enormous energy and ambition. Yet he can also be an angry, vengeful authoritarian. Because he so totally dominates Rwandan life, his choices will decisively shape the country's future.

No one who sees great potential in any African leader can ignore the abysmal record of former heroes. Many of the most revered founding fathers of postindependence Africa, like Kwame Nkrumah and Jomo Kenyatta, came to power amid limitless hopes but left their countries poorer, weaker, and more divided than they found them. Leaders of anticolonial revolutions, most vividly Robert Mugabe of Zimbabwe, were hailed as liberators but became oppressors. Yoweri Museveni, the Ugandan leader who was Kagame's mentor for years and was considered one of the "dashing warrior princes" who would revolutionize Africa, clung to power for decades and fell into the familiar vices of corruption, nepotism, and egomania.

Naïve outsiders, eager for success stories from Africa, are quick to praise any promising leader. Sometimes they are too quick. In 2003 an American lawyer who had worked for the Liberian government published a book describing President Charles Taylor as "a complex and fascinating individual, a man of supreme confidence, with an impressive grasp of world events." Four years later an international tribunal indicted Taylor for war crimes and crimes against humanity.

Leaders of armed revolutionary groups are a harsh lot. To survive they must be mistrustful, conspiratorial, and willing to countenance murder and other acts of violence. Those who succeed in seizing power are expected to abandon these habits and adopt opposite ones. Few manage the transition.

By stabilizing Rwanda and giving it hope for the future, President Kagame has already achieved more than many thought possible. Ahead lie even more complex challenges. Whether Kagame can master them, especially given his chronic impatience, barely suppressed anger, and impulsive scorn for critics, will determine his legacy.

"Kagame has been a good person for Rwanda up to now," a Rwandan who has known and worked with him for years told me. "I give him the benefit of the doubt—up to now—if this is a transition to something more sustainable. But if this is what he wants to sustain, it's dangerous. The qualities Rwanda is looking for in a leader in terms of healing, managing power responsibly, sharing power, and building institutions—I don't see these qualities in Kagame. So far he's been okay, but I fear he's building something dangerous."

Acutely aware of Africa's failure to produce many good models for leadership or national transformation, President Kagame has cast his eyes on the "Asian tigers" instead. He wants to achieve what they achieved in the second half of the twentieth century: pull a nation from poverty to prosperity in the space of a generation. It is a brash rebellion against history, geography, and expectation.

Maybe we don't do it just the way Singapore or Malaysia or South Korea did it. But if those people made it—people with whom we had the same level of economic development some few decades back—why can't we do it? Why should we be known for being poor or for killing each other? Has God cursed us? Is it what we deserve? Can't we do things differently? Is there something wrong with us, compared to others who are developed?

Rwanda is a regally beautiful patch of earth, verdant and fertile, long known as the "land of a thousand hills." It is also permeated with tension and inchoate fears. The government, afraid that murderous passions could reemerge and set off another apocalypse, restricts political freedom. Powerful forces in the outside world, including human rights groups, portray President Kagame as a repressive brute. Even some Rwandans, long accustomed to the idea that life never changes, resent the demands he is making of them.

We have to work on the minds of our people. We have to take them to a level where people respect work and work hard, which has not been the case in the past. You have to push and push. I hear whispers of criticism, complaints that people are being pushed too hard. I have no sympathy with that. People have to be pushed hard, until it hurts. I push myself, many days until I almost drop dead.

There is nothing to be complacent about. We are poor, and being poor is bad. If being pushed hurts, it cannot hurt as much as poverty, as much as being hungry and sick. I make no apologies about pushing people hard. I wish I had even more energy than I have to push them. It hurts them, but they come up in the end as winners. There is a cultural attitude that says you must let people be as they are. I wouldn't even call it a liberal attitude. Even a liberal attitude has to be understood in context.

You can't say that people must not be touched or must never be told to do things. I push people to work—what's the problem with that? A lot of people are content to be lazy because they know that in the end, someone will come and feed them. But we should be able to feed ourselves and even feed others.

Although news of Rwanda's leap toward development is spreading, few understand how such a seemingly insignificant country has suddenly come to play such a promising role in the world. Even more puzzling is the question of how Paul Kagame, who grew up in a refugee camp, has limited formal education, and came to office with little experience in anything other than war, emerged to conceive and oversee this grand project. Who is he? Where did he find the visionary passion that drives him? What propelled him to power and then into such a unique position on the world stage? How did he come to believe that miserable little Rwanda has within it such enormous hidden power? Is there really a chance that he can fulfill his dream and turn his country into a gem of Africa?

I found answers to these questions in the story of this remote country and, most revealingly, in Kagame's own story. Both are dramatic and turbulent. They encompass exile, privation, betrayal, defiance, rebellion, sacrifice, war, and apocalyptic violence. Together they explain how such an audaciously radical message has emerged from such an improbable place.

One day while wandering around Rwanda, I met a provincial governor and asked him what he and the country's new regime hope to accomplish. I expected a long exposition, but his reply was curt and concise.

"We want to be first," he told me. "We will be very happy to teach all of Africa."

Is this possible? Can something epochal be achieved in Rwanda, something that could inspire and even transform the wider world? How can President Kagame hope to accomplish what so many well-meaning leaders of developing countries have tried and failed to achieve? The answers to these questions, taken together, compose one of the most intriguing stories unfolding anywhere on earth.

There may have been a time when superpowers alone were able to guarantee global stability, but that era is over. In the century ahead, peace will be possible only if the gaping chasm between rich and poor is narrowed. The question of how to accomplish this is vital to the world's future security.

So many books, articles, and papers have been written in answer to this question that if placed end to end, they might circle the globe. Much scarcer, however, are leaders who have translated development theory into practice and sought to adapt grand ideas to the turbulent, unforgiving world. This is what Kagame has set out to do. He and his comrades are embarked on a course that is at least as full of risk as it is full of promise. History suggests they will fail. If they succeed, they can change the world.

I remember looking out onto the next hill. We could see people burning the houses there. They were killing people. My mother was so desperate. She didn't want to leave this place.

They started shouting and making a lot of noise, saying that we were escaping and that they had to hurry, to come and get us before we could leave. I remember, apart from the burning houses, people running down that hill toward us.

You Can't Just Pretend Nothing Happened

E VERYTHING IMPORTANT IN RWANDA happens on a hill, so it was logical for Paul Kagame's mother to take him out onto a hillside to be murdered. She had spotted an armed mob advancing toward her house, and it took her only a few moments to realize that the family could not escape. With great dignity, she shepherded her two small sons and three daughters outside to face death in the open air.

"Instead of being killed in the house," she told them, "I would rather it be out in the open."

The gang was barely a mile from its prey when an astonishingly unexpected sound echoed from the nearby dirt road. An automobile was approaching. King Mutara III Rudahigwa owned one of the few in that area, and it had come on a lifesaving mission. The queen, who was a cousin of Kagame's mother, had learned of the day's spreading violence, guessed that the Kagame family would be in danger, and sent the royal chauffeur to rescue them. When the attackers saw him approach, they charged ahead ever faster, hoping to reach and kill their victims before he could arrive. They were closing in as the chauffeur screeched to a halt, pulled the intended victims into his car, and sped away.

This "practice genocide," the first in Rwandan history, had been launched three days earlier, on November 3, 1959. "In the morning the grim, blood-curdling cries began about 9 AM," wrote an American missionary who found himself in the midst of it. "Suddenly down the hill and across the site came pouring a motley host of hundreds of men and boys, shrieking and dancing, waving knives and spears." It was a mob like this one that attacked Kagame's home in the heartland district of Tambwe on November 6.

After plucking Paul Kagame from imminent death, together with his mother, brother, and sisters, the terrified chauffeur drove them to safety at the royal palace, a European-style residence overlooking the nearby town of Nyanza. The raid they survived set the rest of Rwandan history in motion. From it grew decades of impoverished exile, a far-reaching conspiracy that ranks among the most audacious plots in the annals of covert action, an insurgent army that deposed a dictatorship, and a new order determined to rebuild a shattered nation.

The family stayed at the palace for eight weeks, until the killing spree ended and Kagame's mother, Asteria, decided it was safe to take her children home. Six months later, after another spree erupted, she brought them back to the palace. This time she found its grounds packed with refugees. As soon as she could, she spirited her children to the sparsely populated northeast of the country, near the border with Uganda, where she had relatives. There she was reunited with her husband, Deogratias, who had been away at the time their home was attacked. The father quickly concluded that even this remote corner of the country was unsafe and took his family into Uganda. All they carried with them were a few bags stuffed with children's clothes.

Death squads that rampaged through the countryside during 1959 and 1960 were the vanguard of a new political movement that asserted "Hutu emancipation." One of its tactics was to terrorize the old Tutsi aristocracy, to which the Kagame family belonged. Both the Belgian colonial authorities and their Rwandan clients supported this bloody campaign. The police did not intervene to stop it. Marauders killed openly and with absolute impunity. After each attack, more Tutsi fled their homeland.

Tens of thousands sought refuge in Uganda, and there they were caught up in a swirl of human misery. After they crossed the border, Ugandan officials rounded them up, packed them onto trucks, took them to remote regions, and dumped them. Every week or two after that, a relief truck came by with rations of beans and flour. For the rest of their sustenance, the refugees were left to their own devices. They began by planting whatever seeds they could find and building crude huts from mud, grass, and branches. Many were uprooted after a year without explanation and brought to another place where they had to start over. Kagame's parents found relatives in Rwanda who agreed to raise two of their daughters—both later made their way to Europe—but their two other daughters and both of their sons remained with them in destitution. They spent much of their childhood searching for firewood and water.

At the refugee camp where the family first landed, in the southwestern Uganda district of Ankole, Paul met another Rwandan boy named Fred Rwigyema, whose parents had also fled the first wave of killings. They became fast friends and remained so after their families were moved to Toro district, farther north. So rarely were they apart that many who met them thought they were brothers.

Paul and Fred explored the strange new world of their camps with the wide eyes of children. One of their favorite things to do was to sit at the feet of an older refugee who had thrilling war stories and wild dreams about reclaiming Rwanda. This man was a veteran of the *inyenzi* raids, a series of cross-border attacks on Rwandan government posts that Tutsi refugees launched in the early 1960s. The army easily repulsed these attacks and in response unleashed murderous repression against Tutsi civilians. Paul and Fred, however, never tired of hearing stories about this mini-insurgency. On Saturdays, with sticks wrapped in banana leaves to stand in for guns, they played at being *inyenzi* fighters.

They were already rehearsing the war to come. The spark of an idea was passing from one generation to another.

Some thought the friendship between Paul and Fred was perfectly balanced, but to others it seemed just the opposite because
the two were different in so many ways. Paul was highly intelligent
but sullen and withdrawn, liable to explode and fight at any moment. He rarely smiled and projected such an air of seriousness that
even older people curbed their rowdiness and rough language
when he entered a room. Fred, by contrast, was exuberant and
charismatic. His ready grin and outgoing manner won him many
friends. He was handsome, suave, and seductive, unlike his thin,
gangly friend. Girls flocked around him and boys wanted to be
like him.

The children of Rwandan refugees attended outdoor schools
that their parents organized amid the squalor of their camps. Paul
proved an eager pupil, and after finishing the equivalent of third
grade, he was accepted into the well-regarded Rwengoro Primary
School. It was a ten-mile walk from his camp, but he seized the
chance. He applied himself single-mindedly to his studies and was
so successful that in his final year of primary school, he won the
highest grades of any student in the district. This was no easy feat.
There were many Rwandan students there, and nearly every one
had been sent to school with the same challenge: study hard, because your generation must find a way to end our exile.

*You're a child when these things happen, but you grow up in an
environment that affects you in such a fundamental way. There is a lot
of thinking, and raising questions in your mind. As you grow, you discuss the whole history with your parents and friends and others. Later
you come to comprehend that with the terrible life you're living, you
are actually somebody with very little, if anything. Things are difficult
because of that. You come to ask why. . . . You hear this history, you see
that the life you are living is so terrible, and you ask: Why did this happen to us? It starts shaping something, maybe more so when you're very
young.*

Propelled by his excellent grades, Kagame won a place to study
at the Ntare School, one of the best secondary schools in Uganda.

Soon after arriving, he surprised everyone by falling into surly indifference. He became distracted and lost his academic concentration. After his early burst of achievement, he had stopped to consider his station in life, and what he saw pained him.

Then, as he was brooding ever more deeply about the injustices that had been visited upon him, the person he most revered began collapsing under the weight of their shared tragedy.

Kagame's mother drew on deep reserves of inner strength to absorb the shocks of exile and loss. She put away memories of privilege and devoted herself to farm labor, toiling alongside other refugees to feed her children. Her husband proved less resilient. He was a hereditary noble who had been a subchief, a confidant of the king, and the owner of many cattle. The blow fate had dealt him proved unbearable.

"If I dig, I will die," he told his wife. "If I don't dig, I will also die. So let me die."

Over the next few years, this broken man fell from melancholy into despair. He spent the little money he found on cigarettes. Finally he faded from life behind a curtain of smoke.

Paul was fifteen when his father died, and the loss deepened his unfocused anger. He let his grades slip and became a troublemaker in school. At first he rallied his Rwandan schoolmates to fight back against Ugandan kids who taunted and insulted them. Then he went further, actively picking fights with the locals. Whenever the headmaster sent him home, his mother punished him without bothering to ask his version of events. She presumed he was guilty, and he always was.

"He was a measured person," one of his school friends later recalled. "He didn't react quickly. He wasn't quick to get involved or embroiled. He would stand aside and assess the situation. He was always intent on listening. But he was also a fighter. We always had someone insulting us, and he wouldn't stand for that. I remember vividly the time when some Ugandans were calling us names and assaulting us. We were living in quarters with forty kids in each one, and he organized ours to fight against them. They were bigger than he was, but he was always saying, 'We can't give in to these guys. We can't let these guys call us whatever they want. We can't be submissive.' He was into this thing of surviving. Life was very difficult. We all knew that if you wanted something, you would have to fight for it. No one would give it to you."

In 1976, when Paul was midway through secondary school, he suffered another loss when his closest friend suddenly disappeared. Both young men had become restless as they searched for ways to channel their angry energy, and both were increasingly aware of the revolutionary currents surging through East Africa. Paul suspected that Fred had embraced some kind of clandestine mission, perhaps in opposition to Uganda's despotic leader, Idi Amin. His disappearance increased Paul's sense of isolation. It also led him to begin wondering whether the wider world might have a place in it for him as well.

Without the steadying influence of Fred's friendship, Paul became more disruptive than ever. Finally he was suspended from school. He found a place at the Old Kampala Secondary School, but there he remained hostile and aggressive, ready to fight whenever he heard an anti-Rwandan remark. In the end he managed to graduate, but without distinction.

I started feeling, in my thinking and whole being, very rebellious. I wanted to rebel against everything in life. I felt some kind of undefined anger. There was something I wanted to overcome, but I didn't know what it was.

You were always reminded, in one way or another, that you didn't belong there, that you were not supposed to be there. You have no place that you can call yours. You have no right to speak, so you keep quiet. Everything reminds you that you're not where you belong. It had almost become normal, but nothing anyone would get used to.

After his lackluster years at secondary school, this troubled young man brooded for a time but then began to regain his energy. He resolved to take advantage of whatever Uganda had to offer him. All of his efforts to integrate himself into Ugandan society, however, failed painfully.

The rebuffs he suffered helped shape one of his most fundamental beliefs: that it is folly to rely on the help of others.

In the months after he graduated from the Old Kampala Secondary School in 1976, Kagame realized that mediocre grades left a poor refugee with few prospects. He decided to return to school and repeat his final year, concentrating fully this time. That would cost money. He had none and decided to approach a well-to-do relative, "a kind of aunt" who lived in Kampala, for help.

She dismissed me. I left her office in anger. My revolt was against depending on anyone else to help me do something. It was anger inside of anger.

Not long after that disappointment, Paul learned that another relative of his in Uganda had become influential in selecting African students for scholarships to study in Switzerland. He visited the man and asked to apply, but nothing came of it. Part of the reason, by his own account, was his reluctance to plead his case.

He sent three other people to study there. It was not because they had better academic credentials, but he related better to them. Maybe if I had insisted and continued begging, he would have done it. It's part of me—I don't like begging or insisting.

The third opportunity that attracted this young man came literally out of the air. In 1977 East African Airlines placed an announcement in Ugandan newspapers that caught his eye. The airline needed new pilots and was offering to train ten qualified young men at its famous flight school in the Ugandan town of Soroti. Kagame had been fascinated by aviation since childhood, and he jumped at the chance. He took the entrance exam along with more than a hundred others, and when the results were posted, he was thrilled to see his name among the top ten. Flushed with excitement and believing that he had finally found a path toward normal life, he strode into the school director's office, announced that he was one of the successful applicants, and declared himself ready to enroll. The director looked up. Immediately he could tell that the young man in front of him was no Ugandan but a refugee from Rwanda.

"You?" he cried out incredulously. "Get out of here, you Rwandan!"

Paul Kagame was hardly the only child of Rwandan refugees who faced slights like these. Waves of pogroms drove more than three hundred thousand Tutsi to flee Rwanda between 1959 and 1964. Most landed nearby, in Uganda, Kenya, Burundi, Tanzania, and the Congo. Others made their way to Europe or North America. Many among them, especially the young, never accepted the sentence of eternal exile that Rwanda's new masters had imposed upon them. They lived without a country and from their ordeal drew a deep sense of purpose. With an almost mystic focus, they came to believe fate and history had assigned them a transcendent task: to find their way back to a homeland many of them barely remembered, but all idealized.

One child of Rwandan refugees who went on to a career in medicine and diplomacy, Richard Sezibera, later concluded that the experience of exile and discrimination had a strongly positive aspect. "It can do either of two things," he said. "It can crush you or strengthen your sense of self-worth. For many of us, it reaffirmed our sense of self-worth. Somehow it spurred us to do more."

Some of these young exiles wanted to visit the country for which they were preparing to sacrifice so much. Paul Kagame, who had been away since the age of two and remembered nothing other than his brush with death there, was among them. Like other refugees, he had no way to obtain a passport, since Rwanda no longer recognized him and Uganda would not grant him citizenship. He managed, however, to persuade a Ugandan official to issue him a "travel document," and with it, late in 1977, he crossed into his homeland.

At the border crossing, the twenty-year-old Kagame hired a taxi and took it to Kigali, the Rwandan capital. One of his relatives, "a kind of uncle," had been part of a celebrated group of young leftists who accepted an offer to study in Czechoslovakia, only to find after graduating that the government had decided not to allow the Tutsi among them to return home. All returned together anyway, setting off a tumultuous confrontation after which several of them, including Kagame's uncle, were imprisoned for more than a year. He became the young man's first friend inside Rwanda. The two of them spent many hours talking about the worldwide clash of ideas, their country's situation, and what was to be done.

Kagame had entered the country legally, but his travel document said nothing about his Rwandan origin, and he was afraid of trouble if the police stopped him in Kigali. Only after dark did he dare venture onto the streets. Once out, he walked endlessly, slowly absorbing the reality of a city that had until then existed for him only in dreams and stories. He relied on the shadows and his instincts to keep him safe.

On one of his forays, Kagame discovered that the bar at a mid-size hotel called the Kiyovu attracted a clientele of politicians, civil servants, and police officers who liked to gather after work for beer and conversation. He became a regular. His routine was to slip in as unobtrusively as possible, sit at a table by himself, speak to no one, and nurse one orange soda after another. He seemed to be lost in his own world, but actually he was listening intently to conversations around him. What he overheard was mostly gossip and news of the political rialto: who loses and who wins, who's in, who's out. It fascinated him.

Kagame stayed in Rwanda for six weeks. A year later he returned for a second trip, this time traveling through the countryside. He watched, listened, and assimilated a torrent of impressions. These experiences shaped him in two important ways. First, they were his introduction to the "homeland" he had never known. From his observations he drew valuable insights into Rwandan life, especially a renewed sense of outrage at the country's apartheid-style political system. Perhaps even more important, Kagame's missions to Rwanda, which were essentially those of a self-employed spy, whetted his interest in the culture of intelligence gathering. He was already devouring James Bond novels and Nick Carter detective stories, and like many restless idealists of his generation he was captivated by the revolutionary image of Che Guevara. In Rwanda, he assigned himself a classic intelligence mission: to make sense of a complex situation by analyzing many scattered clues. Without realizing it, he was moving into the world of subversion and covert action.

Kagame's visits to Rwanda sharpened the conundrum that defined his life and the lives of most Rwandan refugees. Two warring realities tormented them. Exile in hostile countries was intolerable, but return home was impossible. What, then, should they and their people do? This question obsessed the rising generation of exiles. It was the labyrinth that imprisoned them: can't stay, but can't go home.

Around 1977 or '78, I began wondering what it was that could be done. I started talking about it with friends. I wasn't agreeing with many things. We were many who talked about this, but I had contempt for some of them. They were only talking and not translating it into something that was doable. It was an exercise that seemed to be an end in itself: talk, lament, talk about when to meet next, but not about how all this could culminate into some action.

As Kagame was wrestling with the question of what he and his generation could do to bring their people back home, he heard a startling piece of news. His childhood friend, Fred Rwigyema, had surfaced in the Ugandan town of Fort Portal and was looking for him. Paul quickly made his way there and found Fred with a dramatic story to tell. He had left home after being recruited by followers of Yoweri Museveni, then a Ugandan rebel determined to overthrow Idi Amin's bizarre tyranny. For more than a year, he and other rebels had trained at a semisecret base in Tanzania. Now the rebels, supported by a large force of Tanzanian soldiers, were launching their invasion. Fred was part of the force. He had left Uganda as an aimless and impoverished refugee and returned as an ambitious, self-confident soldier. This was a reunion that would change the course of Rwandan history.

There were emotions that are not easily expressed. I don't know how exactly to explain it, but it was very warm. It was something unique. It was something that had not been expected by either of us. Maybe he thought he'd find me dead. Maybe I also thought I would never see him again. So it was some kind of very exciting reunion. We spent most of the time together, talking of all sorts of things, even sleeping in the same room. There was a lot to talk about.

The military training and experience that Fred Rwigyema had accumulated opened a new path for Rwandan exiles. He was the first of his generation to turn himself into a soldier. Paul Kagame and others quickly followed.

It was in this period, without the world noticing, that Rwandan exiles began learning how to fight.

Rwanda's government remained stable during these years, counting as always on unconditional support from its colonial patrons in Belgium and France. No one except a few utopian exiles imagined it could be deposed by force. The Europeans who designed this regime, however, had planted within it the seeds of its own destruction. They imagined Rwanda as a colonial success story. In fact, they had set in motion forces that would propel it beyond the edges of imaginable horror.

Stories were very important. Not recent stories, but ones that would go back far into history. I was very interested in them. They also cultivated in one's mind that we are a people worth and deserving what we had. It attracted you and created some attachment to your own identity. Also, it would constantly remind you that although in this situation you were nothing, stateless, nobody, you had a history. You had a culture. You had a nation. There was that constant reminder. Maybe we didn't have to fall asleep or die. That became a driving force.

2

Elegant Golden-Red
Beauties

T HE FIRST KING OF RWANDA, GIHANGA, was the son of a deity known as the Root of Man. Early historians placed his rule around the tenth century. Modern ones doubt that either he or any of his celebrated descendants, the heroes of epic tales that have been passed down through many generations, ever existed. Mists like those that shroud Rwandan hills during the rainy season also obscure its early history.

Scholars agree, however, that by the eighteenth century Rwandans had developed one of the most highly organized societies in Africa. It evolved into an elaborate system of shared obligations, with a hierarchy of nobles, chiefs, and subchiefs to connect the ruler and the ruled. The symbol of national power was the *kalinga*, a royal drum that passed from one king to the next. From it hung the testicles of defeated enemies.

Although Rwandan warriors fought nearby tribes and conquered their territories, they did not stray far from their homeland on the edge of the Great Rift Valley. They found safety in being landlocked. Arab and Asian merchants who reached other parts of East Africa never reached Rwanda. Hails of arrows and spears greeted early visitors from Europe and other parts of Africa. Even slave hunters failed in their efforts to penetrate Rwanda, and there is no record of Rwandans participating in the slave trade in any way. Isolation is a theme that runs through Rwandan history. From the precolonial era until very recently, Rwanda has been largely cut off from and unaffected by developments in the rest of Africa and the world beyond.

The most perplexing question running through Rwandan history concerns the origin of the Hutu and Tutsi, and the dynamics of their relationship. There is not even agreement on how to describe them: as races, castes, ethnicities, tribes, or simply groups. What is certain is that for centuries they lived side by side, spoke the same language, obeyed the same laws, learned the same myths, and followed the same religion.

Ethnographers believe that as part of a swirling pattern of migration in Africa during the fourteenth and fifteenth centuries, groups of Tutsi found their way to Rwanda from somewhere to the north. They reshaped the society they found, partly through peaceful means and partly by conquering Hutu principalities, and their leaders became *mwami*, kings of Rwanda. Tutsi constituted the governing class, tended to be taller than Hutu, and raised cattle rather than tilling the soil. Little else of substance, though, separated the two groups. It was even possible for people to move from one to the other. If a Hutu became an owner of many cattle, he also became a Tutsi; a Tutsi family that turned to farming would eventually become Hutu. Intermarriage was accepted and communal conflict was all but nonexistent.

All of this changed radically after Europeans seized control of Rwanda. Its colonization began late, another legacy of its isolation. The first European to reach Rwanda, a German explorer, did not arrive until 1892. Two years later, the first to come on an official mission, a German count named Gustav Adolf von Götzen, made his way to Nyanza to visit the semidivine *mwami*. He shocked the assembled nobles by shaking his host's hand. They found this a terrifying breach of custom and feared that it foreshadowed some strange eruption to their state.

They were right.

No one in Rwanda knew that the Berlin Conference of 1884–1885 had awarded Germany control over the territory of Ruanda-Urundi, which today forms the "twin" nations of Rwanda and Burundi. It became part of German East Africa, of which Von Götzen was later named governor. Like the Europeans who came after him, he was deeply impressed by the kingdom's efficiency and its high level of organization. He allied himself with the monarchy and even helped it conquer remaining Hutu principalities in northern Rwanda. Von Götzen was the first, but lamentably not the last, European who saw advantage in pitting Rwanda's two groups against each other.

By losing World War I, Germany also lost its African colonies. In 1916, even before the war ended, the Allies assigned Ruanda-Urundi to Belgium, which was already ruling the neighboring Congo and brutally exploiting its vast natural wealth. Unlike in the Congo, however, where it ruled directly, Belgium held Ruanda-Urundi as a "trust territory." That meant its rule was subject to oversight from the League of Nations and, later, the United Nations. Neither organization provided much, so the Belgians governed largely as they pleased.

In Europe, the early decades of the twentieth century were marked by an obsession with the idea of race. Generalized prejudices of past generations hardened into firm ones that claimed a solid base in science. Many Europeans came to believe that human races were entirely distinct from one another, and that these distinctions led to a natural hierarchy, with some races born to rule and others to be ruled. This conviction justified their seizure of foreign colonies. In Rwanda, it led the Belgians to a series of reckless misjudgments that would culminate in genocide.

The first of these misjudgments was about power rather than race. The two groups in Rwanda had, over a period of centuries, developed a successful society based on a complex web of rights and responsibilities. Tutsi constituted the ruling class, but for most of its existence, that class ruled with the consent of the governed. Roles in society were distributed according to an age-old system of balances. Some kings managed these balances better than others, but for most of Rwanda's precolonial history, people lived side by side without rancor.

Belgians saw none of this when they arrived to take control of Rwanda. The idea of a monarchy living in harmony with ordinary people, of a hierarchical society built on consent, was foreign to them. They looked at Rwanda through a European lens and immediately concluded that its monarchy was a close replica of European feudalism. As far as they could tell, the *mwami* was a commanding overlord, his court and chiefs composed the nobility, and the Hutu, who made up 85 percent of the population, were serfs. That suited them, because it meant they could rule through an existing monarchy that they mistakenly believed to be a dictatorship. With their encouragement, it became one.

Belgian colonizers chose this course through what seemed to them a logical chain of reasoning. There was already a government in Rwanda; it was run by people the Belgians believed to be naturally superior; and many of these people were willing to accept Belgian rule. Why, then, not embrace them as allies?

Even more tragic than the Belgians' misreading of the Rwandan ruling system was the effect of their racism. Immediately after arriving in Rwanda, they observed what they considered a unique racial circumstance. They found the Tutsi so clever and sophisticated that they did not fit into European stereotypes of Africans. To resolve this contradiction, they concluded that the Tutsi were not real Africans at all but members of another race, probably of Caucasian origin, who had migrated to Rwanda. This was called the "Hamitic" thesis, because several of the first Europeans who visited Rwanda believed that the Tutsi were descended from the biblical tribe of Ham, whose father, Noah, set a curse upon him that, according to later tradition, turned his skin black. Other Europeans later theorized that the Tutsi had come from Egypt, Anatolia, India, Tibet, Melanesia, Atlantis, or the Garden of Eden. One Catholic priest—most scholars and schoolteachers in Rwanda during this period were priests from Belgium—described the Tutsi as "elegant golden-red beauties" blessed with "beautiful Greek profiles side by side with Semitic and even Jewish features."

Others found them a "superior race" of people who were "meant to reign," who possessed "a refinement of feelings which is rare among primitive peoples," and who had "an absolutely distinct origin from the negroes."

The Hutu, by contrast, were seen as "less intelligent, more simple, more spontaneous, more trusting . . . extroverts who like to laugh and lead a simple life."

Europeans ruled Rwanda based on these twin misconceptions: that the Tutsi monarchy was absolute, and that this was good because nature had made the Tutsi superior. They encouraged the monarchy to become harsher and to rule by command rather than consensus. Whenever they wanted to impose a hardship on the population, such as taxation or forced labor, they did it through their Tutsi clients. The Tutsi reveled in the power the Belgians gave them. Some came to believe that they really were superior. Many Hutu chafed under their impositions and began resenting the monarchy in ways they had not before.

Slightly more than a decade after taking control of Rwanda, the Belgian authorities decided to carry their racial principles to the logical extreme. Using finely marked rulers and calipers, they measured the height of foreheads, width of noses, length of ears, and other features they believed would allow them to place every Rwandan in a racial category. Those who did not fit were rated by another standard: any family with more than ten cows was deemed Tutsi, and any with fewer was Hutu. In 1933, using these standards, the Belgians issued each Rwandan an identity card classifying him or her as Hutu or Tutsi (a very small number belong to a third group, the Twa). With these cards, they codified into law their belief that Hutu and Tutsi were distinct races and that race was in fact the principal difference between them. The racial designation on the cards, called *ubokwo*, would later consign hundreds of thousands of Tutsi to death.

The Belgians officially described Rwanda as having "two main racial groups." In reality, though, the identity they assigned to Hutu had nothing to do with race. It was a purely political one: that of subject. This system, in the words of one historian, had the effect of "inflating the Tutsi cultural ego inordinately, and crushing Hutu feelings until they coalesced into an aggressively resentful inferiority complex."

No aspect of Belgian racial policy proved more poisonous than the idea that one group in Rwanda was indigenous while the other came from somewhere else—and that this supposed fact must shape all of Rwandan life. It was a novel idea to the Tutsi, but after seeing how seriously the Belgians took it, many embraced it.

No one encouraged them to do so more fervently than Catholic priests.

From the first days of European colonialism in Rwanda, the Catholic Church decisively shaped social and political life. The first missionary priests arrived in 1898, and especially after the Belgians took over, the colonial and clerical establishments worked as one. They shared a common view of Africa and Africans and were committed to the same goals. Belgian priests—many of them from the Society of Missionaries of Our Lady of Africa, known as the Pères Blancs, or White Fathers—had a pervasive influence and played crucial roles at every stage of modern Rwandan history.

Education was a central part of the Catholic mission in Rwanda, since it was through education that a new class favorable to the colonial idea could be trained. In 1930, one of the first Catholics to arrive in Rwanda, Bishop Léon Classé, who had been in the country for more than a quarter century, signed an agreement with the colonial regime that assigned the Catholic Church exclusive control over Rwanda's educational system. Most schools were reserved for well-born Tutsi, and the Belgian government paid the church a fee for every student it enrolled. These schools became increasingly popular as people realized that the only way for a Rwandan to enter the colonial elite was to attend one. This almost always meant converting from their traditional belief in the deity Imana to Christianity. Within months after the 1930 agreement, one priest was able to rejoice that there had been "a massive enrollment in the Catholic army."

The *mwami*, Yuhi V Musinga, refused to enlist in this army. He clung to his traditional faith and would not exchange his royal robes for Western-style clothes. Worst of all, he insisted on exercising authority, even if that meant challenging Belgian power. The Belgians reacted by deposing him in 1931 and replacing him with one of his sons, chosen by Bishop Classé, who ruled as Mutara III Rudahigwa. To emphasize the break, they did not permit traditional rituals at Rudahigwa's coronation. Over the years that followed, he proved a faithful friend of the Belgians, doing their bidding while showing his embrace of Europe by dressing in Western clothes, learning to drive a car, and pledging to live monogamously. Later he even followed the example of the Spanish dictator Francisco Franco by consecrating his country to Christ. Some Rwandans called him *umwami w'abazungu*, the "white man's king."

"Catholicism, after Mutara III Rudahigwa, became not only linked with the highest echelons of the state but completely enmeshed in Rwandan society from top to bottom," the historian Gérard Prunier has written. "It was a legitimizing factor, a banner, a source of profit, a way of becoming educated, a club, a matrimonial agency and even at times a religion."

Colonial administrators came and went, but Catholic priests spent decades in Rwanda. They learned the native language, Kinyarwanda, and came to know more about the country than any other outsiders. Belgian governors relied heavily on their advice. Much of it centered on how to deal with what the White Fathers saw as Rwanda's two separate and unequal races.

As educators and as the principal theoreticians of Belgian colonialism in Rwanda, priests were chiefly responsible for propounding and spreading the racial theories that twisted so many Rwandan minds during the twentieth century. It was they who first came up with the "Hamitic" thesis, which painted the Tutsi as innately superior aliens. In 1933 they promoted and organized the census that produced the infamous identity cards placing every Rwandan into a racial category. So it was logical that the church would also be at the center of the radical shift in colonial policy that reshaped Rwanda in the 1950s.

Most Belgian priests in Rwanda during the first decades of colonial rule were conservative, upper-class Walloons who believed that the ideal form of colonialism was one that used a local elite to control the masses. Gradually they gave way to a new generation of younger clerics. Many were Flemish, meaning that they had humble backgrounds, came from a group that considered itself victimized and even oppressed by other Belgians, and sympathized with socialism. They were idealists who had been repelled by the church's collaboration with Nazism during World War II and fervently wished to place the church on the side of the poor and excluded. Like their predecessors, they viewed Rwanda through a European prism. They saw a powerless Hutu mass ruled by a callous Tutsi aristocracy. This offended their sense of justice, and they set out to change it. Schools and seminaries in Rwanda, which had for years been used to reinforce the system of Tutsi dominance, suddenly began to transmit new ideas. Among them was rule by the *rubanda nyamwinshi*, or "sociological majority." This had an instant appeal to the emerging Hutu counter-elite, whose members had little prospect of finding jobs in either the civil service or the private economy, no matter how well educated they were.

As these new ideas were reshaping the clergy in Rwanda, the nature of Belgian rule also changed. The winds of nationalism were blowing across Africa. As militants in many countries began agitating for independence, colonial powers searched for schemes that would allow them to maintain control of their former colonies in the postindependence era. The UN Trusteeship Council published a series of reports urging Belgium to allow Rwandans a greater voice in their government and ultimately grant them independence. Belgian officials, influenced by their close allies in the Catholic clergy, concluded that they could manipulate a new "democratic" system to their advantage. To do so they would have to ally themselves with the Hutu, who composed the *rubanda nyamwinshi* and were therefore likely to run independent Rwanda. This meant dropping their longtime Tutsi allies, which they did with remarkable alacrity.

Global politics also played a role in Belgium's decision to switch sides in Rwanda. Marxist ideas were spreading through Africa, and Western powers feared the emergence of a postcolonial "Red Belt" of hostile regimes stretching across the heart of the continent from Ghana to Zanzibar. Rwanda's notoriously conservative educated class, the Tutsi, had been exposed to these ideas and was seen as ideologically unreliable. The small core of educated Hutu, which dreamed of revolutionary change, was closer to the Catholic Church and seemed more reliable.

Suddenly determined to promote Hutu hegemony, the Belgians began allowing voters to elect members of local and regional councils. In most places, Hutu candidates won. This whetted the appetite of Hutu intellectuals. In 1957 nine of them, several associated with a powerful Swiss-born bishop, André Perraudin, published a fiery appeal that would resonate through the next phase of Rwandan history. Known as the Hutu Manifesto, it called on Hutu to rise up against "the political monopoly that is held by one race, the Tutsi," which it said condemned them "to remain forever underlings." The signers and their supporters, by one account, "derived a burning sense of grievance from the monopoly exercised by the Tutsi caste over all sectors of the administration and the economy; to break the hold of this monopoly became a central objective of Hutu intellectuals on the eve of the revolution."

A Catholic press in northern Rwanda printed copies of the Hutu Manifesto, and they were distributed in churches across the country. That lent an air of righteousness to the manifesto's central idea: that Rwanda was a Hutu country and should be ruled by Hutu. It spread quickly, and soon many Hutu came to sense that their hour of redemption was at hand. Emotions were reaching a fever pitch when, in October of 1959, Bishop Perraudin's private secretary, Gregoire Kayibanda, announced that he was forming a new political party, the Movement for Hutu Liberation, known as PARMEHUTU. Its platform called not for improved conditions or better treatment for Hutu, but for a completely new system under which Hutu would rule and Tutsi would have to obey. Kayibanda, a seminary graduate who had edited Catholic newspapers and headed a Catholic group called the Legion of Mary, shot to national prominence.

Belgian policy during this period, which was to manage a transition to independence under Hutu rule, found a surprisingly resolute opponent in King Mutara III Rudahigwa. He insisted that he would not support any independence formula that did not guarantee the safety of all Rwandans. Belgian officials invited him to neighboring Burundi to discuss their differences. He arrived on July 25, 1959, and after taking a few bites of the lunch his hosts had prepared for him, he fell ill. He was brought to a Belgian doctor but quickly died. This was a period when Belgians and their friends were assassinating enemies in various parts of Africa. Many Rwandans quickly concluded that the *mwami*'s death was another Belgian crime. Whatever the truth, his passing removed the most visible opponent of Belgian policy and the Hutu militancy it encouraged.

With tensions this high, it took only a small spark to set off a social explosion. On November 1, a Tutsi gang attacked and beat a PARMEHUTU activist. Hutu militants responded with a wave of anti-Tutsi pogroms, including the one in Tambwe that almost cost young Paul Kagame his life. This was the first outbreak of organized violence between Hutu and Tutsi in Rwanda's modern history.

The attacks continued for several months. Belgian authorities, who had decided it was time to change sides and support the idea of Hutu power, did nothing to stop them. On the contrary, they began systematically replacing Tutsi chiefs with Hutu militants, many from PARMEHUTU. In an astonishingly short time, Tutsi went from being the ruling elite, blessed by colonial power, to being hunted and terrorized in the land they had dominated for centuries.

To formalize this radical shift in power, the Belgians called local elections for June of 1960. The UN Trusteeship Council protested, urging a period of "reconciliation" before voting, and the main Tutsi party refused to participate, but the Belgians went ahead anyway. Hutu radicals took 70 percent of the vote and with it control of Rwanda's political process. They quickly began using it to promote their racist ideology.

The decisive episode in the decolonization of Rwanda was the "coup of Gitarama" on January 28, 1961. Very early that morning, mayors and town councilors across the country began boarding trucks headed to the south-central town of Gitarama, home of Gregoire Kayibanda, the PARMEHUTU leader. By afternoon more than three thousand had convened there. So had twenty-five thousand spectators, many of whom sensed that something historic was about to happen. Several PARMEHUTU leaders gave passionate speeches. Then, to general acclamation, they proclaimed the monarchy dead, declared a republic, and chose Kayibanda to lead it.

Formal independence was the next step, and Belgium granted it on July 1, 1962. Kayibanda became Rwanda's first president. He called this a "social revolution," but in fact it marked nothing more or less than the replacement of one Rwandan elite by another.

"The developments of these last eighteen months have brought about the racial dictatorship of one party," the UN Trusteeship Council warned in a chillingly prescient report. "An oppressive system has been replaced by another one. . . . It is quite possible that someday we will witness violent reactions against the Tutsi."

Many African countries were "granted" independence under conditions that guaranteed failure. They faced the impossible task of developing themselves without educated elites, functioning economies, or stable societies. This was fine for the former colonizers, because it guaranteed that new regimes, while officially independent, would have to continue relying on their former masters. It set much of Africa, however, on a course to disaster. No country was more firmly set on this course than Rwanda.

Around 1960 Rwandan history began to split in two. The visible part unfolded within the country, but over the next three decades, another Rwanda took shape outside. The regime in Kigali presumed that Tutsi who streamed out during the years around independence, and those who followed after later pogroms, would fade into a scattered diaspora and slowly forget their homeland. In fact, the opposite happened. Rwandan exiles and their children never adjusted to their status as refugees and never forgot the country they had been forced to leave.

This split, which led to the emergence of a second, ghost-image Rwanda abroad, also divided the Tutsi themselves. Many who remained in Rwanda accommodated themselves to the new reality. They accepted the restrictions imposed on them and lived as unobtrusively as they could. When they heard news of Tutsi being massacred, they were grateful they had not been among the victims.

The hundreds of thousands of Tutsi who fled their homeland after 1959 developed a very different consciousness. They were not only eager to return, but outraged at the way Rwandan leaders repressed their brethren at home. Exile intensified their attachment to Rwanda rather than weakening it. In places as far separated as Uganda, Belgium, Quebec, and California, they formed cultural groups, published newspapers and magazines, and passed their traditions on to their children. Always they returned to the question of how they might finally return home.

One reason nobody in Rwanda ever imagined that these exiles would try to force their way back to their homeland was that their first efforts had failed so miserably. These were the *inyenzi* raids of 1961–1966, in which bands of armed exiles based in Uganda, Burundi, Tanzania, and the Congo infiltrated back into Rwanda to fight the regime. There were about ten of these raids in all, most of them targeting police stations and government offices. They were too sporadic and uncoordinated to pose a serious threat, but President Kayibanda used them to justify waves of anti-Tutsi repression. During two raids in February and March of 1962, for example, *inyenzi* fighters killed three policemen, two government officials, and one civilian. The day after the second raid, Rwandan troops and militia gangs launched a bloody reprisal campaign.

"Between one thousand and two thousand Tutsi men, women and children were massacred and buried on the spot," according to one account, "their huts burned and pillaged and their property divided among the Hutu population."

Rampages like these took as many as twenty thousand lives during the early 1960s. They also led President Kayibanda to reshape Rwandan political life in a typically brutal way. After an *inyenzi* raid at the end of 1963, he decided to kill all of the country's remaining Tutsi leaders. He drew up a list of twenty-seven and had them arrested, brought to the prison at Ruhengeri, and executed. All were moderates who had agreed to participate in a political system designed by and for Hutu. By killing them, the government eliminated any hope that they could have a calming effect on their brethren or serve as a bridge to exiles.

From that moment, the only place Rwandan Tutsi could practice politics was outside their country.

Besides failing militarily and setting off savage reprisals against civilians, the raids of the 1960s had another effect. They provided a name that many Hutu applied to Tutsi rebels, and then to all Tutsi: *inyenzi*. It means "cockroach." No one is certain where the name came from. The rebels themselves may have coined it, to symbolize their nocturnal habits and their conviction that no amount of effort would eliminate them. Later their enemies began to use it, arguing that it was appropriate because the rebels, like cockroaches, were filthy invaders who defiled clean places. Three decades later, during the 1994 genocide, many killers used this word to describe their victims. In Rwanda, as elsewhere, leaders understood that to turn ordinary people into murderers, it is first vital to convince them that their victims are not human beings but animals.

Beyond Rwanda's borders, the anti-Tutsi reprisal campaign stirred ripples of protest. Bertrand Russell published an article in *Le Monde* asserting that it constituted a "holocaust" on a scale "not seen since the extermination of the Jews." Vatican Radio reported that "the most terrible systematic genocide is taking place in the heart of Africa." With those exceptions, however, the world press gave the killings almost no coverage. No foreign government protested. In the minds of many Tutsi exiles, this apathy reinforced a lesson their flight from Rwanda had already taught them: that they were alone and friendless, and that whatever they wished to accomplish, they would have to accomplish without help.

In the first years after they fled, most Tutsi clung to the hope that their exile would be short and they would soon return home. Many planted only three-month crops. But the failure of the *inyenzi* campaign, along with the Rwandan government's murderous response and the world's absolute lack of interest in their plight, slowly forced them to realize that there would be no return. By the 1970s, nearly half of all Rwandan Tutsi, more than six hundred thousand people, were living in what began to seem like permanent exile.

Falling suddenly from stable prosperity to subsistence farming was a great shock to these refugees. Slowly, however, some began to build lives in the countries where they had landed. In some of them, notably Uganda and the Congo, there were already substantial populations of Banyarwanda—a category that embraces all Rwandans—and related groups. They helped their newly arrived cousins adapt to life in exile.

Rwandan refugees in East and Central Africa proved resilient and industrious. Younger ones thirsted for education, but they faced systematic discrimination. Children who wished to enter secondary school, for example, had to score far higher on entrance exams than local children. Instilled with a desperate drive to succeed so they could one day help resolve the crisis of exile, many achieved these high scores. They graduated, often with honors, and went on to success in business and the professions.

These Tutsi exiles, scattered across Africa, Europe, North America, and even Australia, may be the only group that has been regularly compared to both Jews and Palestinians. Like Jews, they prized education and seemed to succeed wherever they landed, despite the odds against them. Like Palestinians, they were condemned to eternal exile by a regime that hated and feared them.

"Most refugees in Uganda, even the most prosperous and seemingly well-integrated, are overwhelmed by feelings of rootlessness and loss," an American researcher wrote after visiting their camps. "They say they long to be in Rwanda, and speak with misery about how they have had to disguise their origins in order to survive reasonably. . . . The trials of Uganda have caused many refugees to romanticize Rwanda, a country most know little about."

Rwandans traditionally think of neighboring Burundi, which has a similar population mix, as their sister country, and events there often resonate in Rwanda. This happened most violently in 1973, when the Tutsi-dominated army in Burundi launched a

campaign of massacres in which as many as two hundred thousand
Hutu were slaughtered. In response, Hutu in Rwanda turned on
their Tutsi neighbors. Waves of Tutsi were fired from their jobs,
the few Tutsi university students were forced to quit school, and
some Hutu leaders began calling for a "final solution." Gangs of
Hutu responded by killing several hundred Tutsi. Some even killed
rich Hutu, or those who were on the other side of the country's
intensifying north-south divide. This disturbed government leaders, and after several weeks of upheaval, they began issuing statements warning that killings must be kept within "reasonable
limits" and denouncing groups that were "trying to cause anarchy."
These warnings had no effect. For the first time since independence more than a decade earlier, President Kayibanda was losing
control of his country.

On July 5, 1973, the army commander, General Juvénal Habyarimana, seized power in a bloodless coup and proclaimed Rwanda's
"second republic." He ordered many officials of the old regime
killed, some after long periods of torture, but hesitated to send his
predecessor to the same fate. Habyarimana was a product of cults
that were powerful in his native northern region and relied heavily
on the advice of soothsayers and shamans. When it came time to
kill the man he overthrew, he was seized by fear that if he spilled
the ex-president's blood, spirits would plague him. Instead he chose
to surround Kayibanda's home with soldiers and starve him and his
wife to death in captivity. The deposed president and former first
lady spent their last days desperately eating pages of the books in
their library and pieces of foam from sofa cushions. By the time
they breathed their last, Habyarimana had consolidated his control
and become the country's new dictator.

Habyarimana played a role that was familiar in postcolonial
Africa. At home, he portrayed himself as "father of the nation,"
showed a certain charisma, and won considerable popular support.
Despite a limp, the result of an injury he suffered while a cadet, he
would sometimes break into dance at local celebrations. He affected a bouffant hairdo that he apparently thought would make
him seem youthful and dashing. On matters of substance, his

regime followed the same two central precepts that had guided his predecessor. The first was sectarianism. During his presidency he killed fewer Tutsi than Kayibanda had, but he believed Rwanda was a Hutu country and that Tutsi refugees must never be allowed to return. Second was fealty to his European patrons. When in Belgium, he stayed as a guest of the royal family. In France he was even more welcome.

France's relationship with Rwanda dated back to the days immediately following independence, when President Charles de Gaulle signed a cooperation agreement with the Kayibanda regime. It became steadily closer during the Pompidou, Giscard d'Estaing, and Mitterrand eras. Rwanda became a pillar of the Francophonie, which groups the world's French-speaking nations, and French leaders came to consider Habyarimana one of their most faithful allies. He had been educated by a French-speaking religious order, and when visiting Paris he charmed his hosts by reciting passages of French poetry. They esteemed him as a valued courtier who willingly accepted his place in the postcolonial system and promised to defend him from any threat.

At home, Habyarimana built his support on clans and families from the northern provinces of Ruhengeri and Gisenyi, which the Tutsi had only managed to subdue with German help at the beginning of the twentieth century. He ruled through a tight group of relatives and childhood comrades called an *akazu*, literally meaning "little house." Its central figures were his wife, Agathe, who later showed herself to be the true radical in the family, and her three equally militant brothers. Their "second republic" was in all essential aspects a new, northern-accented version of the sectarian dictatorship they deposed.

Members of the *akazu* formed what one human rights report called "a special circle . . . to ensure their continued hold on power." An American living in Rwanda wrote that "anyone who appeared a threat to them was quietly arrested, often tortured and sometimes killed." The *akazu*'s guiding force, Madame Habyarimana, became the most feared person in Rwanda. Descended from a deposed Hutu chief, she burned with anti-Tutsi anger. Wherever she appeared—often wearing an arresting snakeskin dress with gold jewelry and horn-rimmed sunglasses—people cowered and did her bidding.

Two years after taking power, President Habyarimana decreed that henceforth Rwanda would be a one-party state ruled by his Revolutionary National Development Movement, known by the French acronym MRND. Later he went even further by proclaiming that all citizens of Rwanda, including infants, were automatically MRND members and thus bound by party rules. In 1978 he promulgated a constitution, convened a presidential election, ran as the only candidate, and was resoundingly elected. With this mandate, he went on to build one of the world's most tightly disciplined tyrannies. Rwandans wore badges bearing his image, and on Tuesday mornings people in every school and workplace were required to gather for sessions called *animation*, at which they listened to his latest messages and sang his praises.

Habyarimana's takeover, and the fact that it changed nothing, had an important effect on Rwandan exiles. It forced them to realize more directly than ever that if they did not want to live out their lives as refugees, they would have to take matters into their own hands. Political upheaval in Uganda gave them their opening.

By this time there were more than eighty thousand Tutsi refugees in Uganda. They suffered systematic discrimination under the regime of Milton Obote and fared only slightly better under Idi Amin, the colorfully murderous tyrant who overthrew him. Then, in 1979, a force of Ugandan exiles supported and led by the Tanzanian army invaded Uganda. After several weeks of fighting, this force succeeded in overthrowing Amin and chasing him out of the country. Among the Rwandans in its ranks was the young Fred Rwigyema.

Tanzanian leaders were eager to shore up Uganda's new government, and at the end of 1979 they offered to give sixty Ugandan soldiers a six-month course in military intelligence. Paul Kagame, then a twenty-two-year-old army recruit, arranged to be put on the list, and the group that went to Tanzania was made up of fifty-nine Ugandans and one Rwandan. For six months they studied techniques of espionage, surveillance, deception, and information gathering. Kagame, who until then had been a self-trained amateur in this business, emerged as a professionally trained intelligence agent.

The new Ugandan regime did not hold together long. Yoweri Museveni, who was its minister of defense, feuded bitterly with the interim leader, Milton Obote. They broke completely after a dubious election in 1980 from which Obote reemerged as president. Having lost their political confrontation, Museveni decided to try to win power on the battlefield.

Like many African rebels of his generation, Museveni sympathized with Marxism and was a convinced pan-Africanist. In the 1960s he had made his way to Tanzania, partly because the South African revolutionary movement was based there and partly because he wanted a firsthand view of President Julius Nyerere's new "African socialism." He enrolled at the University of Dar es Salaam, a cauldron of ideology that attracted idealistic radicals from across the continent. There he fell under the influence of the charismatic leftist scholar Walter Rodney, author of the anticolonialist classic *How Europe Underdeveloped Africa*; was electrified by the American militant Stokely Carmichael, who made a series of speeches at the university; met revolutionaries from Mozambique and arranged to visit "liberated areas" in their country; and wrote a thesis on Frantz Fanon, the Algerian rebel whose impassioned tracts had influenced revolutionaries around the world. For many Rwandan refugees, Museveni was to become a combination of hero, protector, and role model.

Museveni had already helped overthrow one Ugandan leader, Idi Amin. Pushed out of the new regime and ablaze with ambition and revolutionary zeal, he was convinced he could overthrow another. At the beginning of 1981, he began organizing a nucleus of revolutionaries. Into it he recruited forty comrades. Thirty-eight were Ugandan. The other two were Rwandani Fred Rwigyema and Paul Kagame. They called themselves the National Resistance Army and pledged to fight unto death against the Obote regime.

All the Ugandans in this vanguard were fighting for a single cause: to replace a detested regime with one of their own. The two

Rwandans who joined them, Fred Rwigyema and Paul Kagame, shared that goal. Both admired Museveni and, as one historian put it, "shared with him the same left-leaning nationalist views, distrust of the West, hatred of dictatorship and belief in the redemptive powers of 'popular warfare,' then the stock-in-trade of young 'progressive' Third World politicians." They also, however, had a separate agenda of their own.

The first item on that agenda was to ease pressure on Rwandan refugees in Uganda. President Obote was relentlessly hostile toward them. He accused them of abusing Ugandan hospitality, blamed them for many of the country's problems, dismissed those who held civil service jobs, and urged private employers not to hire them. That gave Rwandans a special reason to wish for his overthrow.

Ending discrimination against refugees was not all that Fred and Paul hoped to achieve by joining Museveni's rebellion. Both had concluded that the only way Tutsi would ever return to Rwanda was by force of arms. Both knew that guerrilla movements rarely succeed without at least tacit support from a friendly regime in a nearby country. If Rwandans helped Museveni take power in Uganda, they reasoned, he would become the ally they needed.

The last and perhaps most important reason that these two men joined the National Resistance Army was to gain battlefield experience. By taking to the bush in Uganda and pledging to stay there until victory or death, Fred and Paul were exposing themselves to great danger and many hardships. They were also preparing for the next war, the one they hoped would take them and their people home.

It was for us a very important formative stage. For me and many others, it was a good education. It followed what we went through as refugees, when conditions were bad, but that was a blessing in disguise. It was an example. It showed us we had to live like that if we wanted to win. We saw the difficulties that characterized the struggle we were to face. It was very important, certainly. The lesson was that if you have to wait for a long time, then you do it.

3

THAT'S WHY I SURVIVED

DARKNESS, ALWAYS A FRIEND of guerrilla armies, was settling over the Ugandan town of Kabamba as a band of fighters prepared their attack. They had two goals. First, they desperately needed weapons and hoped to loot a rich armory at the Kabamba Military Police Academy. Second, with this attack they would announce their existence to the world. The shots they fired here would be the first in a long rebellion destined to reshape not only the history of Uganda, but that of neighboring Rwanda as well.

The commander of the grandly named National Resistance Army, Yoweri Museveni, had planned this attack personally and in great secrecy. Defeat, he knew, would probably mean not only his death but that of his incipient movement as well. At his side were twenty-seven armed men and fourteen others without weapons. All were Ugandan except two sons of the Rwandan exodus: Fred Rwigyema and Paul Kagame.

Soon after midnight on February 6, 1981, at a clandestine camp not far from town, these few guerrillas packed into an open truck and headed for Kabamba. They knew its armory was guarded by both Ugandan troops and allied units from Tanzania, and in the hope of fooling sentries, their driver was dressed in a Tanzanian army uniform. The plan was for him to bluff his way onto the

42

academy's grounds, but it failed. Sentries sensed something amiss, and after they challenged the driver, shooting broke out. Guerrillas stormed in through a curtain of gunfire. They might have been massacred, but several soldiers inside were secret Museveni collaborators and protected them. The armory, most of which was underground, turned out to be strongly fortified. Guerrillas reached its outer warehouse but could penetrate no farther. Finally Museveni gave the order to retreat. His men grabbed what they could find and carry—a couple dozen of automatic rifles, several crates of ammunition, some rocket-propelled grenades, and a handful of radios—quickly packed it onto army trucks, and sped away.

The next night, these guerrillas attacked a nearby police station and captured a store of small arms. For the next eight weeks they were constantly on the offensive, hitting police and army posts. Government forces chased them without success. Then, having dramatically announced their presence, the guerrillas melted into the bush. By the time they reemerged several months later, they had stocked their arsenal, absorbed hundreds of new recruits, and built a broad network of clandestine collaborators.

Central Uganda is a good place to wage guerrilla war. Its heartland, known as the Luwero Triangle, comprises three thousand square miles of savannah and tropical forests. Enough people live there to provide a social base for rebels, but there are also vast empty areas where fighters can move and hide. Farmers in northern parts of the triangle tend cattle, while those in the south raise vanilla and upland rice.

This was Paul Kagame's home for five years.

The way the National Resistance Army fought made a deep impression on Kagame. It decisively shaped his idea of what a guerrilla force should be and do. The lessons he learned during the bush war in Uganda proved invaluable to him when he began to forge, and later emerged to lead, the force that would liberate his homeland.

Like other guerrilla leaders who emerged in Africa, Asia, and Latin America during this period, Yoweri Museveni was committed to waging a "prolonged people's war" rather than trying to seize power in a quick coup. He embraced the Maoist principle that no rebellion can succeed without support from local people. That meant he had to politicize them, and to do that, he needed politicized fighters. He shaped his National Resistance Army (NRA) around the principle that a motivated soldier is worth far more than one who does not fully understand and embrace his mission. Every unit had a political commissar, and every soldier attended classes in which African history and politics were taught from a revolutionary perspective.

This strategy had proved successful from China and Vietnam to Cuba and Nicaragua. Kagame absorbed it during the bush war in Uganda. It guided him when, years later, he set out to build a guerrilla force of his own.

"The NRA was a different kind of rebel army from many that had been seen on the African continent since the beginning of the post-colonial period," the Scottish scholar and activist Colin Waugh has written. "Museveni sought to avoid creating an army of one group which would struggle to win power and reassert its dominance over another, thereby restarting the cycle of resentment and counter-resistance. Neither was his movement a front for the takeover by a neocolonial despot, intended to create a client state and serve foreign masters in exchange for personal gain. . . . [It] sought to create an inclusive, national political community in contrast to the privatized partisan states of Obote and Amin. In areas under [its] control, local chiefs were replaced with resistance councils, which explicitly canvassed and promoted the participation of formerly excluded ethnic groups, women and youth."

In this war, as in any other, soldiers needed to be not just fighters but also specialists in one discipline or another. Kagame had no trouble choosing his specialty. For a long time he had been attracted to intelligence work. Later he would insist that he developed this interest only "because the situation demanded it," but it also suited his personality. He was by nature quiet and introspective but also curious, observant, analytical, and conspiratorial. It did not take long for him to become one of Museveni's close protégés and senior intelligence officers.

I used to walk long distances. Sometimes I was sent up to two hundred kilometers away, either in search of contacts or places the guerrilla group could move to in the bush. I would study the territory, see if there was enough water, if there was terrain to hide, if it was likely that people would support us. I would go and spend days, weeks, and months alone or sometimes with a couple of other people. . . .

There were many, many incidents. In one situation, we had a task force very far away from our main base, about three hundred kilometers away. Over time, we learned that these units had developed problems internally, as well as with the enemy. I was sent to find out what was going on and to reorganize them. . . .

Another time we had to go through some villages, and we were caught there when the morning broke before we reached our hiding place. We met some people, and they started shouting. They knew we were not from there. We had to arrest these people and threaten them that if they continued making noise, we would kill them. We had to walk with them for more than two hours. When we got to a place where there was good cover, we told them they could go back.

Most of the recruits who streamed into rebel camps after the spectacular Kabamba raid were Ugandans, but some Rwandan refugees also enlisted. More joined after President Obote began a fierce campaign against refugees in 1982, sending troops and militia units to charge through their settlements and destroy their homes.

"There were killings, rapes and maimings," the U.S. Committee for Refugees reported. "Persecution drove many young [Rwandans] into the NRA, the insurgent force led by Museveni."

By the time it had been in the field for a year, the National Resistance Army had expanded to four thousand troops but still faced great handicaps. It remained desperately short of weaponry—it had just four hundred rifles—and its fighters never had enough to eat. Troops moved for days on only the nourishment provided from stalks of sugarcane or pieces of cassava. Weak from fatigue, they were often barely able to fight.

Conditions in the bush never improved much. Nonetheless the guerrillas' morale remained remarkably high, their area of operation steadily expanded, and new recruits continued to join them. These successes were due largely to Museveni's inspirational leadership and his skillful application of classic guerrilla principles. Every one of his men was expected to be able to explain in detail why he was fighting. A written code of conduct governed all of them. Officers were consulted about command decisions, including those about promotion. This strategy led the Ugandan rebels ever closer to victory. It also deeply impressed fighters of Rwandan origin, who were in the bush to learn as well as fight.

Most of them, according to the U.S. Committee for Refugees, were "aware of an imprecisely defined, long-term plan of some exiles to invade Rwanda."

No Rwandan-born fighter learned more or observed more carefully than Kagame. He proved to be a hardy guerrilla. The tribulations of his youth made it easy for him to survive for extended periods without food. He followed orders, accepted discipline, and survived all manner of trials. Despite being involved in many firefights, he was never injured. At the height of a government offensive in 1983, however, malaria almost killed him.

The doctor, who was also Museveni's doctor, was a good friend of mine. He put me in his tent to observe me. He told me he had not a single tablet to treat malaria, and said, "Why don't I see if the commander, Museveni, has a tablet?" I heard him talking to other officers, expressing serious concern about my health and telling them that this would be a very bad case if they didn't get some way to treat me. He went to tell Museveni I was really in danger. He talked of sending people into government-held areas to find more drugs, which was dangerous because there was an offensive going on. After several minutes he came back rejoicing because he had managed to find four tablets. He said that maybe it was enough to save the situation.

I was vomiting everything I took in, even water. That's when I learned about Stemetil, which is a drug to suppress vomiting. He went and found one or two tablets in a bag or something. Then, over a period, I took the four malaria tablets. Maybe it was not enough, but maybe because of a will to survive and having no alternative, that's why I survived.

Over the next couple of years, Museveni's rebel force grew steadily in size and strength. The government became desperate to crush it. Army units staged repeated sweeps through areas where local farmers supported the rebels. Their campaign was savage even by the standard of African civil wars. Ugandan soldiers turned the Luwero Triangle into a vast killing field, slaughtering peasants by the tens of thousands. Rather than hurt the rebels, these tactics drove many more people into their ranks. Finally, after five grueling years in the bush, they won their victory. By the time they captured Kampala on January 26, 1986, they had a force of four-teen thousand fighters.

About five hundred of these fighters were Rwandan. They of course joined in the victory celebration, but they also had some-thing else on their minds. Whetted by their success, they were ea-ger to wage a second revolutionary war inside their own country. Many of them, including Kagame, had joined the Ugandan rebel-lion as inexperienced recruits and emerged as hardened fighters.

None of the Rwandans in this triumphant army could have failed to grasp the implications of their victory. This bloody trial of sharp war taught them that under the right conditions, even in the face of overwhelming odds, a politicized guerrilla army in Africa could overthrow an entrenched regime. It also gave them the skills to wage such a campaign. As soon as the euphoria of victory wore off, Kagame began concentrating his mind on the question of how he and his comrades could win another war, this time in Rwanda.

"He came out of the bush more convinced than ever that we could make this happen, that we could go into Rwanda and win," one of his friends remembered. "He was also more determined than ever to go back, because even in the bush, where Rwandan soldiers played such a big role in Museveni's army, they were still treated as refugees, always made to feel inadequate, always watching while preferences went to Ugandans. So that experience intensified both his desire to come back and his belief that it was really possible."

While Kagame and his Rwandan comrades were fighting in the Ugandan bush during the early 1980s, their cousins in refugee camps were building a network of social and cultural groups. This gave the Rwandan diaspora both an armed wing and an organized civilian base. Over the next few years, they fused into a united revolutionary movement.

The first step in this evolution was the founding in 1979 of a group called the Rwandan Refugee Welfare Foundation, which sought to disguise its political aims by posing as a charity. After just a year, its leaders decided it should shed its philanthropic identity, change its name, and become more explicitly militant. It became the Rwandan Alliance for National Unity, or RANU, and declared that it would struggle for the right of refugees to return home. Many of its older members were conservative, poorly educated monarchists, but its leaders were from a new generation. They had grown up in refugee camps, absorbed the ideology of anti-imperialism, and been inspired by the revolutionary examples of Fidel Castro, Che Guevara, and the Vietnamese leaders Ho Chi Minh and Vo Nguyen Giap.

After the Ugandan bush war ended in 1986, life became a bit easier for Rwandan refugees. They felt new possibilities opening before them. Visionaries among them wanted to use their success in Uganda to take their own struggle to a new level. How could they do this? To answer that question, RANU turned to one of its wisest and most respected members, Tito Rutaremara, a revolutionary theoretician who had been living in Paris for more than a decade.

Tito, as everyone called him, was older than many other RANU leaders, old enough to have been in secondary school when he fled Rwanda in 1960. He spent several years teaching at refugee camps in Uganda, then went to France to study and was trapped there when both Rwanda and Uganda refused to issue him a passport. He earned a doctorate in geography and land use planning and also, as befitted a third world exile in Paris during the 1970s, joined the Communist Party and supported revolutionary movements around the world. Other RANU leaders considered him a kind of guru and arranged for the new Ugandan government to issue him a passport. He flew from France to Uganda in 1987. Soon after he arrived, RANU leaders asked him to head a task force charged with developing a new, more militant strategy for their cause.

"There was a desire to go back, and to do it on our own because no one was ready to help you, but there was no one to organize you," Tito remembered. "All during the 1960s and '70s, there was this vague idea to go back, but no strategy, no leaders. . . . Young intellectuals began discussing: 'How? If we go back while there's still a dictatorship, that's no good.' We decided we'd have to fight the dictatorship. Fighting to go back was the only way. If you negotiate with the dictatorship and then go back, they would put you in prison or worse. 'No, we have to remove the dictatorship in Rwanda. Only through that can we have peace. It will serve nothing to go back while a dictatorship is in power that is ethnic and anti-Tutsi.'"

Tito began the work of organizing the scattered Rwandan diaspora into a cohesive political force. In June of 1987 he opened a clandestine school in Uganda dedicated to training what he called "political cadres who could understand society." It was a classic application of the Maoist principle that an educated army committed to a cause has an innate advantage over a nonpolitical enemy.

"We would bring in university kids, train them, and send them out to mobilize," he said. "The idea was to go and teach them, and if you do it well and they understand the message, they'll help you go further. We'd have thirty people in a room, on the floor. . . . We told them, 'We have to liberate our country, but we have no means. The means is ourselves. We have a message for people. If you give the message correctly, some will help you go further.' Then later we would ask them, 'We gave you the message in theory, so how did it work in practice?' They took the message out and then, in October, came back to tell us."

For six months, these "political cadres" fanned out through Rwandan refugee communities in Burundi, Tanzania, Kenya, Uganda, and the former Congo, now renamed Zaire. When they returned, they reported that although many older Rwandans feared an armed campaign would be crushed like the *inyenzi* raids of the 1960s, the rising generation was ready to fight. That was what RANU leaders had hoped to hear.

One reason organizers found such broad support was that RANU leaders had abandoned their Marxist rhetoric and social radicalism. They realized that if they wanted to unite all Rwandan refugees, they had to proclaim an inclusive agenda and welcome into their ranks anyone, regardless of ideology, who shared their wish to return home. By embracing a program that nearly every Rwandan refugee could support, RANU became steadily larger and stronger. In December of 1987 it held a semiclandestine convention in Kampala. Delegates decided to rename their movement once again. They became the Rwandan Patriotic Front (RPF) and proudly proclaimed themselves *inkotanyi*—brave warriors who fight relentlessly until victory. Their declaration committed the RPF to democracy, national unity, and above all "an end to the state-induced creation of refugees."

The RPF immediately plunged into active organizing. Its militants set up chapters across Africa, Europe, and North America. In August of 1988, they met in Washington and vowed not to rest until they had won their "right to return." Within a remarkably short time, Rwandan exiles had built the nucleus of a revolutionary movement.

This success, however, was only the public face of the RPF campaign. It also had another face, covert and far more ambitious.

Scores of Rwandan fighters had emerged as field commanders during the five-year bush war in Uganda. Most prominent among them was Fred Rwigyema, who led the rebel column operating closest to Kampala and then became the chief military planner for the entire rebel force. His closest friend, Paul Kagame, was a senior intelligence officer. After the rebels won their victory in 1986, both men entered the new Ugandan army. Rwigyema rose quickly to become a major general and army chief of staff. Kagame was given command of sixty-seven intelligence officers whom the government was sending to Cuba for training. There he learned new techniques and sharpened his understanding of guerrilla theory.

It was useful. Cuba, in its wars with the U.S. and connection to Russia, was quite advanced in matters of intelligence. There was also political education. The struggle is about what? How do you sustain it? That was something that was always present. . . . When you wage armed struggle, fighters have to combine that role with politics. The two are fused into one thing.

After Kagame returned from Cuba in mid-1987, he and "Commander Fred" began to plot more methodically. Together they conceived one of the boldest and largest-scale covert operations ever to spring from the conspiratorial mind. There were already about fifteen hundred Rwandans in the Ugandan army; Fred and Paul would quietly encourage more to enlist. Then, using their command positions and influence, they would discreetly guide the careers of these soldiers, steering as many as possible to training courses and field commands.

They built their guerrilla army in a way no revolutionary group ever had: within the national army of another country.

Under other circumstances, the RPF might have chosen to recruit a small core of fighters, take to the field, and slowly accumulate strength. That was the strategy Museveni had used successfully in Uganda. But because Rwanda is so small and densely populated, there is no place where guerrillas can hide, move, and build a fighting force. This fact, together with the access Rwandans suddenly had to the Ugandan army, led RPF leaders to conceive their audacious plan. They launched a brilliantly successful covert operation that involved thousands of people and stretched over five years. It brought many young Rwandans into the Ugandan army, where they received rigorous training and saw much combat while suppressing antigovernment insurgencies. They were an army within an army, ready to throw off their disguise at a moment's notice.

We planned quietly and very effectively. [Rwandan recruits] understood in broad terms. Many might have had the idea that we were up to something. They had trust in us. They had a sense that we were developing something. Fred and I made lists of people. We encouraged them to take command positions. Others found ways into different positions on their own, without being prompted. There were a couple of thousand of them. We saw each one as a future fighter in our force.

Even at this late date, President Habyarimana might have headed off the looming war. To do so, however, he would have had to reverse the policy of exclusion that had defined Rwanda since independence. Instead, he reaffirmed it. In 1987 he visited Uganda to attend a military ceremony, and while he was there, President Museveni urged him to allow Rwandan refugees to return. He refused.

"Rwanda is full," he insisted, "like a glass of water that is filled up to the very top."

Refugees repeatedly asked Habyarimana to lift the ban on their return. A typical appeal, poignant but also implicitly threatening, came from a group that had landed in Senegal. "In an interview accorded to the weekly *Jeune Afrique*," they wrote in a public appeal, "you reaffirmed your willingness to condemn more than a million Rwandan refugees to perpetual exile, using as your sole argument the pretension that the country is too small. These men, women and children have stagnated for thirty years in refugee camps and in the shanty towns of nearby nations. . . . Mr. President, it is true that you were not born a refugee like some among us, but what guarantees you will not become one tomorrow? Might that not make you understand the fate to which you have so lightly condemned Rwandan refugees?"

Habyarimana never took these exiles as a serious threat, but he was disturbed by the number of Rwandans who were emerging as commanders in the Ugandan army. He complained to President Museveni. At the same time, Museveni was dealing with rising complaints from Ugandans, including some of his own supporters, who also bridled at the growing role Rwandans were playing in their country. In 1989 he succumbed to these pressures, dismissing Fred Rwigyema as army chief of staff and relieving Kagame of his post as acting director of military intelligence. Both stayed on active duty and retained much of their influence, but the demotions were a sign that their project was in danger. That heightened their sense of urgency.

They were suspicious—very, actually, by 1988 and '89. They started realizing we were up to something. This issue surfaced in various ways. People complained in Kampala about Rwandans being so senior in the Ugandan army. Even outside the army, prominent Rwandans were seen as being there because of us. There was a lot of discussion and debate. It helped to galvanize Rwandans, and it also helped in the process of mobilizing. Because we were under pressure, we began saying, "This is an opportunity we can't afford to lose. If we lose this, the project of liberating our country is probably lost forever."

Watching from Kigali, President Habyarimana believed he had won an important victory by forcing the removal of these two officers from their army posts in Uganda. He was especially pleased at having struck a blow against Fred Rwigyema, who had become the region's most prominent and powerful Rwandan exile. Time soon proved, however, that the result of Fred's demotion was exactly the opposite of what Habyarimana had hoped. Instead of separating Fred from power, it relieved him of many time-consuming duties and made him available for a new job: commander of the rebel army that the Rwandan Patriotic Front was secretly building.

"Up to then, the legendary 'Commander Fred' had remained sympathetic to the Front but aloof," one historian has written. "His shabby treatment at the hands of the president after years of faithful service embittered him, and he decided to throw his lot with the RPF. Given his charisma, his military experience and his connections, he was an invaluable recruit for the plotters."

Fred, who assumed the title of RPF chairman, was only one of many Rwandan exiles who were now ready to risk everything in an all-out push to return home. Although most did not know it, their incipient army had reached critical mass. There were three thousand Rwandans in the Ugandan army, many of them combat veterans. Their leaders were ready to strike. All that remained was to decide when and how.

After Fred's demotion at the end of 1989, events began moving quickly for these impatient rebels. The political situation within Rwanda was steadily deteriorating. A collapse in world prices for coffee, Rwanda's main export crop, devastated the economy. Clans fought one another, criminals tied to the government became increasingly brazen, and food shortages led to near famine in several parts of the country. Police opened fire on a crowd of students who rallied at the National University in Butare to demand more freedom, killing several of them.

In the face of this mounting crisis, President Habyarimana sought advice from his friend and chief patron, President François Mitterrand of France. Mitterrand suggested that he allow some opening in Rwanda's one-party political system. That meant a reversal of one of Habyarimana's most cherished principles, but he understood the depth of the crisis and announced that he was now, after seventeen years in power, willing to consider legalizing new parties. His increasingly militant critics, sensing his weakness, demanded more. Thirty intellectuals signed a manifesto demanding a quick transition to full democracy. More remarkably, several prominent Rwandans who had been close to the regime slipped out of the country and made their way to Uganda to meet with RPF leaders. They brought a tantalizing and thrilling message. Rwanda's government, they reported, was weaker than ever and might collapse if some force could deal it a sharp blow.

Desperate to retake the political offensive, President Habyarimana announced in mid-1990 that he was ready to allow at least a few Rwandan refugees to return home. This was a deft move. It made Habyarimana seem less like a dictator and more like a wise leader open to compromise. By his schedule, the first refugees were to return that November. RPF leaders decided that since their entire movement was based on the demand that refugees be allowed to return, they should not allow him to go through with this charade. It would muddy what had until then been a very clear cause. That argued for an attack before November.

The guerrilla force that the RPF had spent five years secretly building inside the Ugandan army was now ready to unmask itself. By 1990, the chief of military training in Uganda, the commander of the military police, the head of the army medical service, and several key brigade and battalion commanders were secret RPF militants. They and the Rwandans under their command understood that their role was to pretend to be good Ugandan soldiers until their leaders ordered them to desert and proclaim their true loyalty.

A few, however, could not wait. They had no idea of how methodically their leaders were secretly preparing for the coming war and suspected that some had become so accustomed to the good life in Uganda that they were losing their focus on the great cause. At the end of 1989, several dozen of these hotheads staged their own mini-invasion of Rwanda.

They went into Rwanda with guns. That created problems for us because it almost exposed us, both in Rwanda and Uganda. We actually had to mount an operation to bring them back. We told them that if they did not come back, we would declare them our enemies and fight them. We had to work against time and consider the fallout of this experience.

This unauthorized attack reflected more than just impatience. It also reminded RPF leaders that not everyone in the movement wanted to follow their orders. An alternative leadership, positioning itself as more militant than the established group—and asserting that Fred Rwigyema was not suited to be RPF commander

because he was not educated or articulate enough—emerged
and began raising money. Its key figures were two of the highest-
ranking and most popular Rwandan-born officers in the Ugandan
army, Dr. Peter Bayingana, who was chief of the army medical
service, and Major Chris Bunyenyezi. They traveled among
refugee communities and presented themselves as the true RPF
leaders.

"The two camp rivalries became so feverish that each camp contemplated an invasion to enhance its position at its rival's expense,"
one Ugandan historian has written. "Their rush to forestall any
possible military initiative by the other competitor made the camps
realize that further delays would erode [RPF] strength and expose
some of its military strategies to the government in Kigali."

Other factors also pushed RPF leaders to decide they should invade sooner rather than later. The Rwandan regime, alerted by the
mini-invasion and by an intense RPF fund-raising campaign in
nearby countries, realized that another attack might be imminent
and began strengthening its army. At the same time, the regime
was facing serious internal challenges, including factional power
struggles, pressure from newly legalized opposition parties, the de-
fection of several prominent figures to the RPF, and intensifying
poverty brought on in part by a devastating "structural adjustment"
program imposed by the International Monetary Fund and the
World Bank.

All of this came at a time when criticism of Rwandan influence
within the Ugandan army was reaching a peak. Much of it was
aimed at President Museveni. His enemies went so far as to accuse
him of being Rwandan himself. This was not true, but he did come
from an ethnic group closely related to the Banyarwanda, and one
of his grandmothers was said to have been a Tutsi from Rwanda.
He tried to placate his critics, but even demoting Fred Rwigyema
and other powerful Rwandan officers in his army did not satisfy
them. Some demanded that he cashier every Rwandan-born soldier. This would have been disastrous for the RPF, and the threat
of it pushed RPF leaders to act quickly.

The confluence of these factors, according to the Ugandan historian Ogenga Otunnu, "sent an unequivocal message" to RPF leaders. He described it as a stark warning: "Mobilize and invade while you still have access to [the] military, economic and political resources of Uganda. . . . Invade while you still stand a good chance of destabilizing the government, or remain in Uganda and disintegrate into oblivion."

Sometimes when I'm with my wife and children, I tell them stories about my life and childhood. . . .

They are very inquisitive kids. They ask pointed questions sometimes. Once my daughter asked, "How did you meet Mommy?" I told her, "I was fighting a war in Uganda, but I wanted to have a family. I was under pressure to have a family because most likely I was going to be involved in another war, and I was not going to venture into a situation like this without having a family." She said, "So you wanted to go to war and leave your family behind?" I said yes, and she said, "Daddy, you are very mean! You wanted to have a family and leave it behind!" I told her, "No. I wanted to have both."

4

A Glass of Milk

P LANNING A REVOLUTIONARY WAR was not all that preoccupied Paul Kagame during the tense year of 1989. He
had remained single, focused intensely on the clandestine
project that obsessed him, while most of his Rwandan friends
married and began raising families. After a time he found himself the only bachelor among them. They rarely missed a chance to
tell him that it was time for him to marry. Slowly he came to agree.

Following Rwandan tradition, Kagame asked relatives to help
him find a suitable wife. One had a suggestion. She knew a poised
and educated young Rwandan woman, Jeannette Nyiramongi,
who had been born in exile in Burundi after her father, a Tutsi
subchief, had fled his homeland. From his spies in Kenya, where
this eligible lady had taken a job, Kagame learned enough about
her to intrigue him. He decided to take a trip to Nairobi, even
though it would not be without risk. Kenya and Uganda were on
bad terms, and the appearance of a senior Ugandan intelligence
officer in the Kenyan capital would be grounds for suspicion or
worse. Certainly no one would believe that he had come to court
a woman.

This was, however, one of the few times in Kagame's life when
he was doing no more than he seemed to be doing.

In Nairobi, Kagame enlisted the help of a friend who knew the woman in question. They decided to drop in on her at work and offer one of the hoariest clichés in the history of courtship, the excuse that they were "just passing by." Years later Kagame was still able to say with evident conviction that Jeannette "didn't know what was going on." In fact, a relative had told her why he was in Kenya, so she understood exactly what he was after.

As a child and teenager, Jeannette had belonged to cultural groups in which older people taught younger ones Rwandan songs, dances, and traditions. Like many people of her generation in Africa and beyond, she developed a diffuse, idealistic socialism and an admiration for romantic rebels like Che Guevara and Martin Luther King. Two years before meeting Kagame, she had made her first and only trip to Rwanda. It left a terrible impression on her. She considered Rwanda her homeland, but on one of her first strolls through Kigali, accompanied by her father and brother, both of whom are tall and have distinctive Tutsi features, they were accosted by a man who shouted at them, "How dare you live in this Hutu country?" That experience, and her realization of how submissively Tutsi were expected to behave in Rwanda, led her to vow never to return.

Like many Rwandan refugees, Jeannette included RPF leaders in her panoply of heroes. Kagame, whose name had for years been whispered from ear to exile Rwandan ear, was among them. Now he had come to court her. Sensing his innate shyness and utter inexperience with women, she casually mentioned that it was lunchtime and invited him and his friend for a snack at her apartment.

"No, I'm in a hurry," Kagame lied.

"Well," she persisted, "if you can't have lunch, how about just a glass of milk?"

That invitation would not excite every man, but it has special resonance among Tutsi. Their culture is heavily cattle-oriented, and they have developed a taste for milk that may be unmatched in the world. Jeannette guessed that she might tempt Kagame out of his awkwardness by offering him some, and she was right. They became one of many Rwandan couples whose romance developed over glasses of milk.

Kagame narrowly escaped arrest in Nairobi and left in a hurry. He told Jeannette by telephone that he could not return and persuaded her to visit him in Uganda. She agreed, and during her visit he spied some marks of love in her. They were married on June 10, 1989.

Around the time of his wedding, Kagame began hearing reports that President Museveni was planning to send him out of the country, probably to Nigeria, for an extended period of military training. Then his closest friend and co-conspirator, Fred Rwigyema, learned that he was about to be sent to the United States for similar training. The evening after Fred heard this news, the two men met at Kagame's house.

"This has meaning," Kagame told him. "You're going to a course in the U.S. I'm going to Nigeria. Another officer or two might be sent to Russia. This is not an accident."

The two talked for a while, and Kagame finally told his friend, "Fred, you can't go. This has to continue. As leader of the RPF, you cannot allow this."

They agreed that at this crucial moment, with their clandestine guerrilla force about to unveil itself and start fighting, it would be catastrophic for Fred to leave. He was indispensable. No other RPF leader had nearly as much charisma, and none commanded nearly as much loyalty from the men who were about to plunge into war. Neither he nor his friend, however, could come up with a ruse clever enough to fool President Museveni. The best excuse they could think of was hardly convincing.

"Why not tell Museveni that you have been through so much, the struggle, the work here, Tanzania, that you've never had time to organize yourself and your family?" Kagame asked. "You should tell the president that your future does not lie in the army of Uganda because of this special problem of identity, that you want to work on a different future, that even if you integrate, ultimately you want to leave the army. Just insist, even if it's not convenient to Museveni. Remain stuck to the idea that you really need a break."

The next day, Fred visited President Museveni and made this plea. Not surprisingly, Museveni rejected it out of hand and

became, in Kagame's words, "very, very furious." Fred finally persuaded him to consider the idea overnight. The next morning, he
called to say that he had softened his view and would allow Fred to
remain in Uganda. On that same day, however, he sent his army
commander to visit Kagame.

"I have a message from the president," the commander told
Kagame. "You need to go for the course that was prepared for
Fred."

Ugandan leaders, suspicious of what the Rwandans were planning and facing heavy pressure at home, had decided they could
no longer allow both of these officers to remain on active duty.
Kagame realized that one of them would have to go. Since Fred
could not, he would have to. He told the army commander he
would accept the assignment and then drove directly to Fred's
house.

"If you think I should say no, okay," he told Fred. "But I didn't
do it because that would result in big problems for us and our
project."

Fred agreed. "If you find an excuse not to go, that would
confirm any suspicion they have," he reasoned. "It would handicap our movement and our people." That night, Kagame told
his new bride that they would spend the next part of their lives
in a place very different from any they had known before: the
U.S. Army Command and Staff College at Fort Leavenworth,
Kansas.

The staff college offers one of the world's most sought-after
courses in the art of military command. Students come from the
top ranks of the world's armies, and once at Fort Leavenworth,
they study everything from field tactics to human rights law. Most
are selected with the assumption that they will go on to play important roles in their home countries. Kagame's class had officers from
Latin America, Asia, and several African countries, as well as from
the United States. When he arrived, he found that all his papers
were still in Fred's name. He had to explain that President Museveni
had changed his mind at the last moment and sent someone else
instead.

For a man who had grown up in an African refugee camp, spent years in the bush, and gone on to become a military intelligence officer in Uganda, Fort Leavenworth and the Middle America landscape that surrounds it were strange new territories. By his own account, though, Kagame made the transition without difficulty. A turbulent life had given him much experience in adapting to new situations.

Kagame's assignment in the United States did not in any way weaken his obsession with returning to Rwanda. In fact, although it took him away at an important moment, it was also a chance for him to learn skills that he knew would prove valuable in the war to come. Within a few weeks after arriving in Kansas, he had found an apartment, begun his course work, and arranged for his wife to join him. Almost every day he spoke with Fred by telephone. From opposite sides of the globe, the two of them orchestrated the final phase of their plot.

Finally they made the decision for which countless Rwandan refugees had spent decades waiting. They chose the date of their invasion, when they would throw themselves into the do-or-die combat that would determine, probably forever, whether they and their people would be able to return home. The date they selected was just days away: October 1, 1990.

We had agreed that when the war started, I would come back. There was nothing very particular about the first day of October, but there were a lot of rumors around, some of them true. Increasingly, the government of Uganda was getting jittery about the level of preparations. They were getting suspicious. They had mounted intelligence against us, so there was that pressure: We should do this sooner rather than later. . . .

There were mixed signals from Habyarimana about letting people come back. We didn't think he was going to do it in any case. He kept saying Rwanda was too small, and asking countries where refugees were to allow them to stay. We would be allowed to visit, but not stay. The leaders there were a bit stupid. They could have resolved the problem by saying, "All refugees are free to come back." But when you say they can't, that increases the desire to come back. They were foolish, not astute enough to say, "Okay, come back." Probably people would have had less desire to go back. When you say they can't come, people say, "It's not up to you to decide people's choices and futures."

As soon as the date of the invasion was fixed, Kagame went to his American commander and told him he was quitting the staff college to return home. The commander and other officers at Fort Leavenworth were astonished. Competition for places at the staff college is intense, and it is highly unusual for a student to leave before the yearlong course is over. Officers closely questioned Kagame, asking him over and over whether he was sure he wanted to turn his back on such a unique opportunity.

Soon after this long interrogation began, Kagame realized that his American hosts had no idea of his background. They did not know that he was Rwandan, that he had been a refugee, or that Rwandan refugees were eager to return home. Patiently he explained all of this, and slowly the Americans came to understand that they could not dissuade him. One finally asked whether there was anything they could do for him. He replied that he would dearly like to take with him a set of the textbooks he was using, which among them covered almost every aspect of military science. No one objected. Those books, Kagame later said, "were very useful during our war."

Rather than rushing away immediately so he could help lead the invasion, Kagame took several days to sort out his affairs in Kansas. Methodically, as is his wont, he arranged to pay his rent and other debts, close his telephone account, and return everything he had that belonged to the staff college. He was completing this work when, five thousand miles away, the Rwandan revolutionary army burst from its secrecy and launched its war.

The choice of October 1 as the invasion date was not entirely random. That week, the United Nations was holding a World Summit for Children in New York. The presidents of both Uganda and Rwanda were attending, which meant there would likely be confusion in both countries when the invasion was launched, rather than a quick and coordinated response. In addition, October 9 is Independence Day in Uganda. That gave army commanders who were part of the Rwandan plot a perfect excuse to move large numbers of troops around the country. The most important of these commanders, then responsible for all forces in northern Uganda, was General Fred Rwigyema. He reported only to President Museveni, and since Museveni was in New York, no one questioned him when he assembled two thousand soldiers—all of Rwandan origin—and ordered them to proceed southward, dressed in battle gear and fully armed.

These soldiers had been waiting for months, and in many cases much longer, for this day. A few senior officers among them knew precisely what was happening. The others understood that they were in the Ugandan army only as a ruse, awaiting a call from their leaders to desert. Most guessed that their sudden move toward the Rwandan border meant that the long-awaited moment had finally come.

Beginning on September 30, trucks packed with soldiers began rolling into Ankole district in southwest Uganda. At outposts near the Rwandan border, they unloaded crates of recoilless rifles, machine guns, mortars, rocket launchers, and even several Soviet-made light automatic cannons, all of which they had taken from armories in Uganda. They packed these onto their trucks and jeeps—also appropriated from the Ugandan army—and then, surging with enthusiasm that at some moments bordered on delirium, ripped the Ugandan insignias off their uniforms. With that act, they declared their true identity. They were no longer soldiers in a national army, but revolutionary guerrillas fighting for power in a country all of them loved passionately, but few of them knew.

At ten o'clock on the morning of October 1, the first of two thousand *inkotanyi*, along with eight hundred civilian supporters who were to work as medics, scouts, and messengers, surged across a rude bridge into the Rwandan border town of Kagitumba. They quickly overran the lightly guarded customs post, took up positions along the border, and then began to push into Rwanda. They captured a regional capital, Gabiro, and celebrated their victory at an open-air party where the main refreshment was looted pink champagne. As news of their insurgency spread, volunteers from all parts of Rwanda arrived to join them. A few were Hutu. Some were not even Rwandan but simply revolutionaries who wanted to help defeat an African dictatorship.

During those first days of war, information from the battlefront streamed back to RPF leaders in Uganda and then on to Kagame in the United States. He understood as well as anyone how crucial these first few days would be. Never, though, did he imagine the catastrophe that was about to strike the rebel force.

I realized from the information I was getting—there was something strange. I wasn't hearing of Fred. Things didn't sound to me like they were going quite well. Something came to my mind. So around the fifth or the seventh, I asked someone in Kampala, "Have you talked to Fred or heard from him directly?" I was suspicious. I had some intuition. Something told me things were wrong. I was feeling a sense of chaos. I told him, "I want you to go to the field, cross over into Rwanda, and tell Fred I want to talk to him directly. If he can't talk to me directly on the phone, I want you to come back and tell me you saw him."

He was taken aback by the sense of urgency in the instructions I was giving him. He asked me, "Is there any other message?" I said, "No, just find him." So he went. After twenty-four hours I started calling his house. His wife kept telling me he was not yet back. Finally, I found him in a town near the border. I said, "Did you find Fred?" I was really feeling something very strange. He said, "Sir, no. I'm very—no sir, I did not find him."

"Why?" He was quiet on the line. He kept quiet. Was he fighting back tears? "Why?"

"No sir. I mean—he's no more."

"What do you mean? Do you mean he's dead?"

"Yes, sir."

"Dead?"

"Yes, sir."

"Who killed him?" The fellow took a long time. It was difficult to explain. "Are you sure?"

"I'm sure."

Then I connected—that this was why I had not been able to speak with him. And while I was asking this question, my wife came in. My wife saw me changed. She asked, "What happened?" I said, "There's nothing."

I kept this from my wife up to the time we separated. I never told her, for many reasons. Fred's death could have had a more negative impact had it been known right away by everyone. The fact that it was kept quiet helped save the situation. Also, it was good for my wife not to know, because she would have thought, I'm sure he's going to follow him now. She'd say, "He's going to take over for someone who was just killed so unexpectedly." There were no tears, but it was grinding me all over inside. I felt an immediate sense of urgency.

For an army to lose its commander on the second day of a war is always devastating. In this case, it proved so stunning that many soldiers believed the war was lost. Fred had for years been the guiding star in the Rwandan exile firmament, the only figure most refugees knew, admired, and were ready to follow without question. Other RPF officers tried to hide news of his death, but when it leaked out, hundreds of *inkotanyi* deserted and fled back into Uganda. Even many who remained were devastated by what had happened. The dream that had nourished them since childhood seemed suddenly dead, their hopes of returning to Rwanda dashed forever. Few had any idea that in faraway Kansas, Paul Kagame had resolved to find his way to the battlefront and recover his friend's fallen torch.

This would be no simple trip. The stakes were enormous, perhaps as high as the fate of a nation and a people. Kagame knew that powerful forces would try to prevent him from reaching his shattered army, though he could not be certain what they would do or even who they were.

The moment Kagame left Kansas, he became the central figure in a cat-and-mouse game that would be played out across three continents. It pitted one man—albeit a veteran intelligence agent who was highly motivated, well trained, richly experienced, and full of native cunning—against the security agencies of Rwanda and, in all probability, several other countries as well. All of this weighed on his mind as he boarded a plane in St. Louis and headed to New York on the first leg of his fateful voyage.

When I saw the confusion and the disarray, I said, "My God, what is this thing I have come to inherit and take over? What is it?" There was nothing in its right place, not a single thing. Casualties were lying in the road, so many in such a short time. Even the commanders in charge—one senior one, when he saw me, he just broke down in tears. I asked how he was doing. He was crying like a child, telling me he was glad I was back. I asked him, "How are things here?" He said, "There's nothing here! Everyone is dead!"

5

DEVASTATION

SOME PASSENGERS ON THE FLIGHT Paul Kagame took to
New York on October 8, 1990, were thinking of nothing
weightier than their upcoming business meetings or the
Broadway shows they would soon be enjoying. Kagame was more
deeply preoccupied. He spent the flight lost in thought, imagining
what sort of traps his enemies might have set to prevent him from
reaching Rwanda and how he might escape them. His wife, who
sat beside him, understood that he was on his way to war, but not
even she realized how urgent and dangerous his mission was.

Jeannette had become pregnant during the couple's stay in
Kansas. Kagame wanted to leave her in good hands before setting
off to fight and decided to send her to Belgium, where one of his
sisters lived. That meant he would somehow have to obtain Belgian
visas for the two of them.

A friend of Kagame's was serving as Ugandan ambassador to
the United Nations. Kagame sought him out and asked whether
he could use his diplomatic contacts to secure two Belgian visas.
The ambassador knew that Kagame was a top leader of the
Rwandan Patriotic Front, and that the RPF had just launched a
war. He found it difficult to believe that at such a crucial moment,
Kagame would be thinking only of assuring his wife a comfort-
able pregnancy.

"What are you guys up to?" he asked suspiciously.

"I don't know," Kagame blithely replied. "I'm just here accompanying my wife, taking her to Belgium." That elicited a laugh.

"Are you sure you're coming back?"

"Yes, they have enough fighters to launch the invasion. I'll finish my course and then go back."

This weak lie was the best Kagame could conjure. His friend was diplomatic enough not to press further. He called a Belgian colleague, and in short order the couple had their visas.

Groups of Rwandan exiles in several parts of the world had been raising money for the RPF, and one of the most effective, based in England, had assembled the tidy sum of $80,000. With troops now in the field, that money was urgently needed. Kagame decided he would stop in London, pick up the cash, and personally carry it to the front.

At a travel agency in New York, Kagame bought a ticket to London and Brussels for his wife, and one for himself on the same flight to London and then through to Entebbe, the main airport in Uganda. They left the next afternoon, arrived at Heathrow early the following morning, and spent their first day resting and planning. The next day, Kagame excused himself, met his Rwandan contact, and picked up a valise stuffed with $80,000 in cash. He used a bit of it to buy medicine and other supplies and brought the rest back to his hotel. His wife was waiting.

That night, we decided that she was to proceed to Belgium and I would continue to Rwanda through Uganda. We went to the airport, and I went to separate from my wife. I was going to go from London to Entebbe, using the ticket I had. But as I was checking in for the flight, something came to my mind. It was foolish to go the way that was expected of me. . . .

As I inquired, I realized that there was another flight—people were boarding—going to Addis. So, quickly I helped my wife to her flight for Belgium. I told her, "You'll be fine. Go to Belgium. We'll meet when we meet again. Keep in touch, but for now, bye-bye."

The moment was very emotional. When I bade her farewell and came back to the terminal building, we realized that when she had entered the plane, she had left behind her handbag, her jacket, her passport, and everything. I had to rush back. Fortunately, everything was where we had left it. Neither of us knew what would happen or when we would meet again, she was pregnant, she was going to stay on her own—that was reflected in the fact that she forgot everything she had. Otherwise she would have been very careful to keep it with her.

This was not a good time for anyone to be passing through Addis Ababa. For several years, the Ethiopian dictator Haile Mariam Mengistu had been slaughtering his opponents in a campaign he called "White Terror." Now, with rebels closing in on the capital, his regime was on the brink of collapse. Panicky soldiers raged through the streets settling old scores. Elite units were posted at the airport, assigned to prevent enemies of the state from fleeing.

Kagame made his way into the city without incident and stayed for a couple of days at the home of a friend who worked for the Organization of African Unity. Then, on Sunday morning, October 14, he headed back to the airport. His friend had arranged for a sympathetic diplomat to escort him through security checkpoints, but when he arrived at the airport, the diplomat was nowhere to be found. Kagame could not delay his departure and decided to try to make his own way through.

At the main checkpoint, guards were searching every bag and frisking passengers they found suspicious. Kagame took his place in line. How, he urgently asked himself, could he pass through without either losing his money or being identified and arrested? He slipped $1,000 into his shirt pocket to use as a bribe if that became necessary, but was still nervous. When he reached the front of the line, he felt unprepared, stepped out, and took a place back at the end. Upon reaching the front a second time, he stepped out again. Then he retreated to a washroom to collect his wits.

I went back in line. People were moving in. Something happened, and just like that, in a split second, I decided to take a chance with very high risk. As a person in front of me entered, someone came running up to the man doing the check-in. The man stepped out. The two of them talked. They kept talking. So what I did, with my briefcase in my hand, I walked past this space of about two meters between the X-ray machines. I decided to walk between the machines and the room where people were being searched. I was waiting for someone to call me and say, "Where are you going? Come back!" If someone followed me, I was going to use the money and say, "How about making a deal?" But the two of them were in a very intense discussion. I made it through and got to the place where passengers were waiting for my flight.

While I was there, I saw a pastor putting on his collar. He was talking to the lady next to him, in the Ugandan language. He said they had been sitting there too long, and then he said, "Haven't they found that person they were looking for?" So I was curious. I asked the pastor why we were waiting so long, what was happening. He told me that fellows from Ethiopian Airlines were running around and that the flight was being delayed. When he asked why, one of those fellows said they were looking for somebody dangerous.

I thought that maybe it was me they were looking for, but I didn't say anything. I sat there for about twenty minutes, and then saw some Ethiopian Airlines officials coming off the plane. They said it was now time for boarding. The pastor asked if everything was okay. They said yes, everything was okay. We started going down into the tarmac.

Before you boarded, you had to identify your luggage. After you identified it, they would put it on a trolley, drive it over, and put it into the airplane compartment. Curiously, as I was looking around for my bag, I couldn't find it. I took my time and looked around. Other people were picking out their bags. I kept searching.

Immediately I realized that in my bag, there were books from the college, army uniforms, compasses, pocket knives—the kind of things you need when you're in the field. I saw a man there supervising. He had picked out my suitcase and put it between his legs. He had documents in his left hand and a walkie-talkie in his right hand. He was talking to some people. So I quickly thought, Should I ask him why, what's wrong with my luggage?

The man was standing between the luggage and the plane. He was quite busy, talking into his walkie-talkie. I decided to go behind him, and I gently picked my bag from between his legs and put it on the trolley. Maybe he didn't realize it. He kept standing with his legs apart as if something was still there. While I was sitting on the plane, I watched that man for a long time. Another man came, and they walked away. He seemed to have forgotten that there was something he was supposed to be watching. I think what made it easier for me was all the confusion in Addis.

With these brazen maneuvers, Kagame escaped from a police force that would certainly have arrested him and perhaps either killed him or turned him over to his enemies in Rwanda. He later learned that other agents had also been waiting for him in at least two other cities.

In Brussels, immigration officers had detained his wife as she left her plane and taken her to an interrogation room.

"Are you alone?" the officers asked her.

"Yes."

"But you were supposed to come with someone else."

"Yes, but I'm alone."

The officers cross-examined Jeannette Kagame for nearly two hours, returning always to the question of where her husband had gone. She could not utter what she did not know, and finally they allowed her to leave. Ethiopian and Belgian security officers, however, were not the only ones on alert that day.

Before leaving London, Kagame had called an RPF supporter in Kenya and asked her to meet him at the Nairobi airport, where he thought he might be landing. There was no time to call again after he changed his plans, so she went to the airport as they had arranged. There she asked an immigration officer she knew to escort Kagame from his plane. After all the passengers had disembarked, the officer came to her with information he had until then kept to himself.

"The person you asked me to pick up and help through was not on the plane," he said. "It's just as well, because we were alerted to be careful with this person. We were instructed that if he came here, he was to be detained and questioned."

Someone had clearly passed on information about Kagame in the hope of keeping him from reaching Rwanda. Could it have been the Ugandan ambassador in New York? The Belgian visa clerk? A Rwandan agent who spotted him in London? He had reasons to doubt all these possibilities. That left only one apparent answer: the Americans he had left behind at Fort Leavenworth.

We were being tracked at least since we left London. I'm not sure if I was being followed right from the college. Maybe it was the intelligence system in the U.S.—they might have alerted someone. . . .

Maybe something I had said at Fort Leavenworth had raised suspicion. It's far-fetched, but I can't think of any other explanation. I never got to know what happened or why it happened.

Having eluded police at airports in London, Brussels, Addis Ababa, and Nairobi, Kagame needed to make his way through one more, at his final destination in Uganda. He had called several friends in the Ugandan intelligence service to tell them he was on his way and ask for help in passing through the Entebbe airport. When his plane landed, he was relieved to see one of them waiting on the tarmac.

"Give me your briefcase and follow me," the agent whispered to Kagame as he stepped off the plane.

The briefcase was full of cash, but Kagame handed it over as if it contained nothing more than dirty laundry. He followed his friend away from the passenger terminal and toward a complex of customs warehouses. They were halfway there when an airport police officer called out to them.

"What are you doing?" he demanded. "I saw this person come out of the plane."

"Yes, it is very strange, but it's a case we handle like this," Kagame's friend suavely replied, flashing a card that identified him as an intelligence agent. "If you want to be more inquisitive, you know who I am and you can take it up with whoever you want." That averted a confrontation. A few minutes later, Kagame was out of the airport and on his way to a safe house.

I learned from another intelligence agent that as my plane was about to land, a senior security person saw my name on the list of passengers and inquired of his superiors what he should do with me, how he should handle it. The security chief said he had to consult President Museveni. But he was out of the country, in New York. We arranged and went though all of this before the security chief at the airport could receive any feedback about what to do.

The person who picked me up took me to his house, and another friend from intelligence came to see me. It was about 3 p.m. First I needed a bed. I shut out everything and went to sleep. I didn't even want lunch. I also asked how I could get to the border that same night. They organized vehicles, one for me and one for an escort. I woke up around 8 p.m., had a meal, and left toward 11. We drove until morning. It took nearly six hours. This border where the first individual drove me was more or less open to us. It was manned by Ugandans who were helpful in our crossings. We arrived there at five or five-thirty in the morning, and I went across into Rwanda.

It was totally disorganized. The first sight was probably the worst I have ever seen, that and the genocide—things that have made a mark in my life, my mind, things that probably changed my life forever. These two things never go away. I live with them. . . .

Around six-thirty I had breakfast, some tea and biscuits. I looked and saw soldiers injured. I went greeting them. They were all happy to see me. Something had gone terribly wrong, and they needed somebody or something. I asked one of them, "What can I do for you?" He said, "Sir, I know you don't smoke, but can you find a cigarette for me to smoke?" Fortunately, in Kampala I had bought three cartons of cigarettes. I started giving them out.

From that time, I don't know how many hours I spent without sleeping. Everything was in motion. I was almost burning myself out trying to figure out what had to be done and how. I asked for a meeting with my commanders. I called them back from the field, told them to leave their subordinates in charge. The senior ones came back to meet. They were terribly demoralized—even that was an understatement. They were not even thinking. It was devastation.

More than Fred Rwigyema's death led the *inkotanyi* to this paralyzing defeat. They had actually moved steadily forward for several days, but suddenly found themselves under withering artillery fire and deadly air attacks from Gazelle helicopter gunships. They were stunned. None had imagined that the notoriously inept Rwandan army would be able to mount such a fierce counterattack. When it came, at least some guessed the truth. France had come to its client's rescue.

Immediately after arriving home from New York and realizing that rebels were slicing into his country, President Habyarimana had appealed to France for help. To dramatize the urgency of his situation, he went to the extreme of ordering his own army to stage a nighttime attack on Kigali that he could blame on the RPF. The next morning, October 5, there was little damage to be seen, but *Le Monde* reported the attack as real, and the French ambassador was fooled into asserting that there had been "heavy fighting in the capital." By the time Habyarimana reached Jean-Christophe Mitterrand, the president's son and one of his chief advisers on Africa, France had already decided to rescue him.

"We are going to send him a few boys, old man Habyarimana," Mitterrand told a colleague. "We are going to bail him out. In any case, the whole thing will be over in two or three months."

On October 6, French prime minister Michel Rocard announced Operation Noiret—Operation North Wind—under which six hundred elite paratroopers would be rushed to Rwanda. He said they were going "to protect French citizens and nothing more." That was not true, since every French civilian was evacuated within a week and the paratroopers made no move to leave. On the contrary, they deployed close behind government battle lines. According to the flamboyant French mercenary Paul Barril, who arrived with them and quickly went to work for Madame Habyarimana, they found that Rwanda's army had "absolutely no training, no motivation, no special commandos, no special action guys, they're a balloon full of hot air." France took over management of the campaign. French soldiers directed artillery attacks, maintained and flew helicopters, advised Rwandan commanders on field tactics, gave the army a modern radio communication network, manned roadblocks around Kigali, and even helped interrogate prisoners accused of collaborating with the insurgents. This strengthened force repelled the assault and sent *inkotanyi* fleeing in retreat.

"France's official special services blocked in '90 the attack by RPF terrorists and Uganda," Barril told an interviewer years later. "There were heroes on the French side who will never be known, extraordinary stories of guys who took crazy initiatives, who went out and blasted all around them with just a few helicopters and a few guns. There is material for a book on the heroism of the secret services in Rwanda."

To bolster the French force and to symbolize a continuing interest in a former colony, Belgium sent four hundred soldiers of its own. President Mobutu Sese Seko of Zaire dispatched several hundred, but they lived up to their unsavory reputation by turning immediately to pillage. "There was not a house they did not plunder or a woman they did not rape," one *inkotanyi* later recalled. Barely a week after the Zairians arrived, Habyarimana expelled them. They returned home in slow-moving columns, burdened by television sets, furniture, and other booty.

Less than two weeks after launching its war, the RPF army was on the brink of collapse. Its commander, several of its top officers, and scores of its fighters lay dead. Many survivors had deserted. Others were ill with dysentery. Elite military units from European armies were deployed against them. Into this desperate situation stepped Kagame.

Every senior RPF officer knew him, as did many lower-ranking *inkotanyi*. Many had fought alongside him in the Ugandan bush war. They knew him as a clear strategic thinker, a brave fighter, and a strict disciplinarian who demanded obedience and tolerated no excesses. He also had years of experience in guerrilla warfare, a full understanding of military intelligence, and a dense network of contacts in Africa and beyond. Some of his comrades doubted that even he could rescue their scattered and disheartened army, but there was no one else.

"It was the logical choice because of the force of his personality," recalled his friend and comrade Richard Sezibera, who was a medical officer in the invading army. "Some people are just natural choices to lead. It wasn't 'Who do we want?' It was 'When is he coming?'"

Few wanted to say so openly, but in planning this invasion, Fred Rwigyema seemed to have turned his back on a basic principle of guerrilla warfare. Rather than prepare for a prolonged campaign, he had chosen to challenge the Rwandan army head-on in an open savannah and then charge toward Kigali. Perhaps his aggressive self-confidence led him to overestimate the prospects for quick victory. Certainly he did not anticipate the power of France's response to his invasion. Whatever his reasons, he made a lamentable strategic choice.

Kagame's first great challenge was to rebuild his decimated force. The future of the rebel movement, perhaps even its survival, hung on his decisions. After several days of meetings and private reflection, he made an astonishing choice. He would move the entire force, except for a few units that would remain behind as decoys, to the coldest, least populated, and most isolated part of Rwanda: the forbidding Virunga mountain range along the northwestern border with Uganda and Zaire, where densely forested volcanoes soar nearly two miles into the African sky.

"Nobody at that time would have thought of taking the force to Virunga," Richard Sezibera remembered. "It is a place with very high altitude and very far from where we were. We had lost the territory we controlled, so even getting there was difficult. The force was not coherent. It was dispersed. The logical thing was to get the people nearby and reorganize in that area. Most people thought that. But he thought, no, the bigger force would go and regroup in Virunga. He had a plan. He had sent people ahead, to see what was up there. We divided into groups. Some stayed behind as decoys and even staged attacks. We developed tactics that kept the Habyarimana army mobilized in the wrong place while we moved to Virunga. This kind of unconventional thinking continued throughout the war, and it worked."

The idea of going there was to give people a place to hide and rest and give us time to plan. It would also enable us to open another front, to spread the government forces out instead of concentrating them in one place, force them to dilute their effort. . . .

I divided the force into two. Close to four hundred of us moved to Virunga, with the rest staying behind, near the Ugandan border. I told them, "We're taking five groups and leaving one here." The plan was for one group to attract attention while another one was moving under cover. That divides the enemy's attention. We used to do that a lot to protect our forces and also to make the enemy act more on our planning than their own plans. They would tend to attack when they saw us. We were there precisely for that reason, to give another group a chance to reach its objective and carry out operations.

The trek to Virunga stretched over nearly a week. It succeeded partly because Ugandan army officers, evidently acting with President Museveni's knowledge, allowed the *inkotanyi* to move in and out of Ugandan territory. "Our most important support was our relationship with each and every soldier in the Ugandan army," Tito Rutaremara recalled. "We had spent years living together and fighting together. When we needed to slip out of Rwanda, we would always find an army officer who would say, 'Cross here. Pass here.' At the time Museveni was saying he was not helping us, they were letting us pass."

Insurgent fighters who moved into the Virunga range at the end of 1990 were not the first outsiders to establish themselves there. This range is home to the world's last surviving colonies of mountain gorillas, and it was here that the legendary primatologist Dian Fossey spent years observing them. After Fossey's mysterious murder in 1985, other scientists took up her work. They were not happy when a rebel army suddenly appeared in a region they wished to preserve as a pristine habitat.

"The aggressors were not even 'real' Rwandans in our eyes," two of them wrote years later. "They were young men who had grown up entirely in Uganda. They spoke English. Their leaders had names like Fred and Peter; even their organization had an English name. To us, this was a Ugandan invasion of Rwanda. But we lacked the Tutsi perspective."

Once the RPF force arrived in Virunga, it faced new and daunting obstacles. Almost no one lived in these rugged mountains, which meant that there were no farms, herds of cattle, or other sources of food. Nor was there any easy way to find medicine or to evacuate the sick and wounded. Supply operations were exceedingly difficult. Worst of all was the freezing cold. Guerrillas wore light clothing, which is suitable for the rest of Rwanda but pitifully inadequate in frigid mountain air. Frostbite claimed many fingers and toes. On some mornings, sentries assigned to guard camps during the night did not return. Comrades found them frozen to death at their posts, with eyes still open and rifles at the ready.

"Seeing soldiers dying in camp, not in war, was very bad," recalled Joseph Karemera, a physician who served in the insurgent force. "That was what depressed Paul most. Fighting was no problem at all, but the conditions of basic life were so bad. There was no food. We got very thin. But the soldiers—everyone understood the mission. We had told them, 'You'll go for days without eating and you may not even have clothes.' We had mentally prepared our people, and it worked."

In this crucible the RPF licked its wounds and slowly reconstituted itself. As it did so, supporters around the world worked to raise money, buy clothing and other supplies, and send them by porter to fighters at their mountain bases. A newly graduated social worker named Aloisea Inyumba directed this far-flung effort. She had been living in Uganda when Tito Rutaremara and other RPF leaders opened their clandestine school for militants, enrolled immediately, and after finishing the course began teaching others. In

1988 she was appointed RPF's commissioner of finance. Of all the militants who did not actually fight, she may have been the most productive.

The first thing Inyumba did in her new post was to organize fund-raising cells in every country where Rwandan refugees lived. They began by raising money in conventional ways, like staging concerts and asking prosperous exiles to contribute. Then they came up with more original ideas, including many that tapped the energy of poor people. Some groups collected and sold empty bottles. Others repaired shoes or old clothing. Many devoted themselves to making biscuits or pocket-size packs of fried sorghum meal that could be carried to *inkotanyi* who were shivering in Virunga. Almost all of these groups were run by women. They dealt only in cash because of the clandestine nature of their work, but their coded records were scrupulously detailed and there was never a case of embezzlement.

Wherever Inyumba went to raise money, she brought photos and videos of the suffering *inkotanyi*. She always called them "our children" rather than fighters or guerrillas or soldiers. "It's not for an army," she would tell Rwandans who came to hear her pleas in Nairobi or London or Washington. "It's for our children. Our children are on the battlefield, and they need food. We are their parents. Parents always have a duty to take care of their children."

Rwandan exiles came to know Inyumba as a tireless fund-raiser, but RPF militants saw another side of her. She turned out to be almost comically parsimonious. Her constant search for bargains even led her to discover, after the fall of the Berlin Wall, that a factory in East Germany had been stuck with several thousand unneeded army uniforms. She flew to Berlin and negotiated for days until she was able to buy them for a rock-bottom price.

"If you had an order from Fred or from Paul Kagame, you might get some money from her," one *inkotanyi* later recalled. "Otherwise it was practically impossible."

One of Inyumba's most successful fund-raising techniques was to arrange for well-to-do exiles to visit the frigid RPF camp in Virunga. Groups arrived from as far away as the United States and

Canada, reaching the camp by torturous overland routes. After a couple of days there, women would begin removing their jewelry and emptying their purses. Men left cash and whatever extra shoes they were carrying.

"Seeing young people withstanding that kind of condition made people go and sell everything they had," Joseph Karemera remembered.

Despite the hardships, new recruits arrived every day. News of the invasion had electrified Rwandan exiles everywhere. Hundreds quit their jobs, bid farewell to their families, made their way to Virunga, and offered their services unto death. Most needed no prodding, but there was plenty available for those who did. Wives, relatives, and friends shamed some young men into enlisting. Those who stayed home faced withering ridicule.

"What are you doing here?" neighbors would ask him. "Shall we get you a dress?"

This was not a guerrilla force composed of society's castoffs. By one estimate, nearly all had attended primary school, half had graduated from secondary school, and 20 percent were university graduates. Scores were physicians. By early 1991, the RPF force had not only doubled in size, counting nearly five thousand fighters in its ranks, but also emerged as the best-educated guerrilla army in history.

Soldiers in this army had proven the intensity of their motivation by the simple act of making the rugged trek up to Virunga. Once there, they were organized into units, assigned to rigorous training courses, and taught a strict disciplinary code for which the RPF would become famous. The code listed eleven capital offenses, including murder, rape, violent robbery, desertion, and acts "intended to disrupt, destroy, divert or otherwise work to the detriment of the Front." It specified twenty-four other crimes for which sentences including corporal punishment could be meted out, among them drinking alcohol, using drugs, being "idle and disorderly," failing to pay for goods in villages, abandoning wounded comrades, spreading "harmful propaganda," promoting "selfish interests," and having sex with anyone other than a lawful spouse. By all accounts, this code was strictly followed. It helped make the RPF, at least in its early years, one of the most strictly disciplined of the world's rebel armies.

"In the way we fight, in the way we conduct ourselves, we must always be different from those we are fighting against," Kagame told his *inkotanyi* at a "political education" seminar that a comrade captured on videotape.

The force that emerged from these months in Virunga was not only well trained but highly politicized. One of its key sections was the Political Department, which trained selected soldiers as "political commissars." These commissars were assigned to every fighting unit. They had three principal duties. First was to keep their comrades aware of the political situation inside Rwanda and remind them constantly of why they were fighting. Second, they directed all RPF contacts with civilians, seeking to assure that the army did not leave a residue of anger or resentment. Finally, they served as confidants for rank-and-file soldiers, listening to their complaints and making sure that officers did not abuse them.

Belief in the supreme importance of the politicized fighter was only one of the vital lessons Kagame and other RPF commanders had learned during their long years fighting in the Ugandan bush. From that crucible they also came to understand the value of having a devoted leader like Museveni, who coolly directed every aspect of the struggle, shared the trials of his army, and was always ready to listen to even his lowest-ranking subordinates. They learned that guerrillas must be patient and prepare themselves for years of war; that lack of weapons is no obstacle to victory, since guerrillas do much of their work while unarmed and can, over time, capture weapons from the enemy; and that when a government realizes it is facing a serious insurgency, it instinctively turns to repressive measures that alienate people and ultimately strengthen the insurgents. All of these principles guided them as they planned and fought their war.

In the months after their disastrous invasion, protected by the isolation of their new hideout and by the fact that their enemy greatly underestimated their strength and determination, *inkotanyi* slowly rebuilt their force. Their morale rose steadily. Commanders and political commissars never lost a chance to remind their comrades of the tribulations that rebels had faced in Uganda a decade earlier. The rebel force there set off to war with just a few dozen fighters, but after years of persistence it succeeded in overthrowing a powerful and seemingly invincible regime. If such an improbable victory could be won in Uganda, Kagame told his fighters, it should also be possible in Rwanda.

An impression had been created that the RPF had been nearly wiped out or totally defeated or had simply resigned and gone back to Uganda. So we had to deal with this problem for own survival, both image-wise in terms of the RPF and also for the survival of the struggle itself. We wanted to make an impact in a totally different area, showing how the war had actually spread.

Some in our ranks were not so agreeable to going to the peace talks. There were people who said, "No, let's fight to the end, it's a waste of time, these people are telling lies, buying time to build their capacity in a situation where we are getting stronger." To an extent, that was the intention of the government. They were just taking advantage. But if the other side agrees to talk and you don't, that creates problems for you diplomatically. And some of us insisted that if the enemy would use that time to prepare himself, we could do the same. Even though you think that the government is playing games, you have to do what is necessary to see that those games won't succeed.

6

CREATURES FROM ANOTHER WORLD

W HAT BECAME OF RWANDAN REBELS after their commander was killed and their ranks were torn to pieces by rocket and artillery attacks? There were two answers. As far as President Habyarimana and his French advisers could tell, the rebels had been routed. Many had abandoned their units, and those who remained were stunned and leaderless. The "armed return" they had attempted on October 1, 1990, seemed to have failed just as completely as the *inyenzi* raids of a quarter century earlier.

No one in the ruling group realized that the rebel fighters had actually not melted away but had trekked to new hideouts in the Virunga range. There, under the cover of rain clouds and triple-canopy forest, their new commander, Paul Kagame, reorganized and trained them. After three months he decided it was time to send them back to war. As his target he chose Ruhengeri, the main provincial capital in northern Rwanda and a stronghold of Hutu militancy. A successful attack there would send shock waves across Rwanda.

We had three purposes. One was to bring to the world and the government news of our continued existence, not only our existence but also that we had the capability carry out such a significant raid on the forces of Rwanda. The second was in search of weapons, to get weapons, because that was really our main source of supply. Third, there were these political prisoners [in Ruhengeri]. We understood if we had them in our hands, it would also hurt Habyarimana's government politically and create some kind of new dynamic. And of course, that would also result in some significant establishment of ourselves in that particular area, a totally new sector, and that would help us in fighting the war.

At dusk on January 22, 1991, seven hundred *inkotanyi* began creeping down from their mountain hideouts. During the night, guided by local collaborators, they slipped into positions on every side of Ruhengeri. At daybreak they burst from their hiding places. Defenders raced for their weapons, but they had been taken completely by surprise and never recovered.

The first targets to fall were grain warehouses, which were full of maize flour and other products the hungry RPF was eager to seize. Guerrillas also easily captured a government-owned farm and made off with several hundred head of cattle; Kagame wanted milk and meat for his many malnourished comrades. Around police stations and army outposts, though, there was unexpectedly strong resistance, and attackers took heavy casualties. Only later, when fifteen French paratroopers were recommended for medals to recognize their valor at Ruhengeri, did it become clear that this resistance came from French-led units.

A terrible massacre was narrowly averted at the prison that was one of this raid's main targets. Hundreds of inmates were confined there, most of them political prisoners. When fighting broke out, the panicked warden called Kigali to report what was happening. He reached Colonel Elie Sagatwa, a cousin of Madame Habyarimana who was the president's private secretary and a key member of the *akazu*. Colonel Sagatwa gave him a chilling order: kill every inmate. He refused. Several minutes later, Sagatwa called back, repeating the order and adding that it came from the president himself.

The warden still could not bring himself to obey.

As this life-or-death drama was unfolding in the warden's office, *inkotanyi* were fighting their way onto the prison grounds. They broke down gates, smashed through doors, and herded jubilant prisoners out. Kagame had drawn up a list of about two dozen he considered especially valuable, and they were found and placed under guard. Among them was Colonel Théoneste Lizinde, a notorious torturer and former chief of Habyarimana's secret police who had been in jail since attempting a coup eleven years earlier.

By midday the battle for Ruhengeri was over, and the town was fully under rebel control. Disciplined platoons of *inkotanyi* spent the afternoon methodically looting the prison, the bank, police stations, military outposts, and food warehouses and packing their booty onto abandoned jeeps. At dusk they withdrew toward their mountain refuge.

Government reinforcements arrived the next day. They imposed a dusk-to-dawn curfew and fanned out through the surrounding countryside. Over the next few months, RPF fighters attacked them almost every night.

"The rebels remained hidden in the obscurity of the volcanoes, from where they would launch their nightly raids," wrote Rosamond Carr, an American-born farmer who lived in Mugongo, a few miles from Ruhengeri. "One cloudy day in February, a Rwandan military helicopter flew low over Mugongo, spraying gunfire and mortar shells into the fields and forests. . . . I watched from the garden wall, fearful that *inkotanyi* would emerge from the forest at any moment. Many nights, I would go outside and stand near the asparagus beds with my night watchman and the shepherds—each of whom stood valiantly clutching long, wooden spears. In the moonlight and cold night air, we would listen to the sound of gunfire from a military camp six miles away and the thundering of cannons coming from the direction of the volcanoes."

Until the spectacular raid on Ruhengeri, it had been easy for the regime to dismiss this insurgency. President Habyarimana may even have welcomed it, hoping to crush it decisively and use his victory to reunify his unraveling government. The humiliation at Ruhengeri stunned him and his *akazu*. No longer could they believe the rebels had been crushed or lost their will to fight. On the contrary, the RPF had announced its full recovery from the October debacle with an attack that showed its mastery of guerrilla tactics. This was a sharp political, military, and psychological blow to the regime. The army responded in a way that prefigured what was to come: by ordering soldiers and militia squads in Ruhengeri to hunt down local Tutsi and "cut them to pieces." Hundreds were slaughtered. Many of their bodies were later found with smashed craniums and missing limbs.

These weeks marked the real beginning of the war. The regime was forced to recognize that its long refusal to allow the return of Tutsi exiles had not produced the intended result. Instead of melting away, these exiles had built a guerrilla army strong enough to contend for power.

"President Habyarimana always used to say that he was very surprised by the outbreak of war in October 1990," recalled Bonaventure Ubalijoro, a Hutu politician who served for a time as Habyarimana's ambassador in Washington. "But that was not true. Many people had repeatedly pointed out to him that unless he did something about the problem of refugees, there would be a conflict. He always replied that the country was too small. But the size of the country could not make the refugee problem go away."

Over the next few months, government troops repeatedly shelled rebel positions in Virunga and even managed to capture several foothills, but the terrain was too rugged for a frontal assault. The RPF was also on the offensive. It won a key victory by capturing an important border town, Gatuna, and cutting the road from Uganda that runs through it. Soon it was launching attacks across a wide swath of northern Rwanda, fighting French-backed government troops for control of strategic hills. The costliest of these campaigns, stretching over many months and involving repeated infantry assaults and intense artillery duels, was for the highest peak in northeastern Rwanda. This peak has an official name,

Kabongoya, but because it was so heavily bombarded for so long, and because so many men on both sides were killed on its slopes, RPF fighters gave it another. On their short-wave radios they were hearing reports almost every day about the relentless bombardment of Sarajevo, and that was the name they gave to this peak: Sarajevo. It was painfully appropriate.

[Rwandan leaders] realized the war was serious and not something they could wish away or deal with and eliminate completely, as at one point they had thought, after we had disappeared in the eastern part of the country after the war started. They started taking it seriously, mobilizing the population and securing more resources and troops. Their whole strategy was to have enough troops, put them along almost every border, cover as much area as possible, deny us any piece of territory in Rwanda, and achieve the objective of convincing the world that we were actually no problem. . . .

They covered almost every hill, every village, every point that had tactical advantage. . . . With this increasing pressure, there was more need on our part to be more active, to achieve more victories, not only militarily but politically and diplomatically. If we were portrayed as people who didn't exist or were not a major problem, who only survived because of help from external factors like Uganda, that increased our need to be active and fight. So there would be almost no lull in fighting. There were engagements almost every other day.

Many times we would stage simultaneous attacks on different positions as a way of weakening them and not allowing them to consolidate positions in places they were trying to deny to us. Sometimes in a single day we would carry out ten different operations across Virunga and the northeast. They would be organized and sequenced so that by the time they were trying to deal with one, there was something happening somewhere else. This made it very difficult for the government to have stability or freedom to operate. So we were constantly either laying ambushes between their points, if they were moving, or if there were supplies coming from Kigali, we used to waylay them and in many cases kill or even capture their soldiers. There was constant activity. Either they were attacking or we were attacking. It was not one-sided, but it was constant.

As war spread across northern Rwanda, President Habyarimana came under new pressures. Outsiders, including his patrons in France, wanted him to resolve the crisis by proclaiming democratic reforms and striking a deal with the RPF. The president's *akazu*, however, pushed him in the opposite direction. It opposed any accommodation with the insurgents, demanding instead that the regime mobilize all its power to crush the "Tutsi feudalist threat."

The *akazu* had good reason to feel threatened. Hutu politicians had ruled Rwanda since independence and believed they had the right to do so forever since they were the *rubanda nyamwinshi*, the "sociological majority." As the RPF grew stronger during the early 1990s, however, Hutu leaders were forced to confront the terrifying prospect of a return to Tutsi rule. In a series of inflammatory speeches, extremists among them warned that an RPF victory would mean death or enslavement for every Hutu. Rwanda's foreign minister told the diplomatic corps in Kigali that the RPF was attempting nothing less than "a reversal of history," and that its leaders were bent on returning the Hutu to "forced labor and feudal servitude."

Behind these public rants lay a private fear. Members of the *akazu* realized that under a new regime, they would be held to account for crimes that, according to one Hutu politician, included "drug rackets, prostitution, extortion, bribery and murder." Their only choice, they concluded, was to kill or be killed.

Soon after the battle at Ruhengeri, *akazu* members launched a new propaganda campaign aimed at intensifying sectarian hatred. Its themes were simple: Hutu have nothing in common with Tutsi, the two groups are in fact natural enemies, and the conflict between them can only end with one exterminating the other. The country was flooded with broadsides demonizing the Tutsi as "assassins," a "race of vipers," "drinkers of untrue blood" who had "used their power, daughters, and corruption" to oppress the Hutu.

"We will never allow them to fulfill their dreams," one of these broadsides promised.

No public document embodied this message more vividly than the "Hutu Ten Commandments," which first appeared in *Kangura*, an extremist newspaper published by a member of the *akazu*, and was then broadcast repeatedly on hate-mongering radio programs. Perhaps coincidentally, the edition of *Kangura* in which it appeared also carried a full-page photo of President Mitterrand with the caption "A True Friend of Rwanda: It Is in Hard Times That You Know Your Real Friends."

Every Hutu should know that a Tutsi woman, wherever she is, works for the interest of her Tutsi ethnic group. As a result, we shall consider a traitor any Hutu who marries a Tutsi woman, befriends a Tutsi woman, or employs a Tutsi woman as a secretary or a concubine.

Every Hutu should know that our Hutu daughters are more suitable and conscientious in their role as woman, wife, and mother of the family. Are they not beautiful, good secretaries, and more honest?

Hutu women, be vigilant and try to bring your husbands, brothers, and sons back to reason.

Every Hutu should know that every Tutsi is dishonest in business. His only aim is the supremacy of his ethnic group. As a result, any Hutu who does the following is a traitor: makes a partnership with a Tutsi in business; invests his money or government money in a Tutsi enterprise; lends money to a Tutsi or borrows from one; gives favors to Tutsi in business (obtaining import licenses, bank loans, construction sites, public markets, etc.).

All strategic positions—political, administrative, economic, military, and security—should be entrusted only to Hutu.

The education sector (students and teachers) must be majority Hutu.

The Rwandan armed forces should be exclusively Hutu. The experience of the October 1990 war has taught us a lesson. No member of the military shall marry a Tutsi.

The Hutu should stop having mercy on the Tutsi.

The Hutu, wherever they are, must have unity and solidarity and be concerned with the fate of their Hutu brothers. . . .

The Hutu must be firm and vigilant against their common
Tutsi enemy.

The Social Revolution of 1959, the Referendum of 1961 [abolish-
ing the monarchy], and the Hutu ideology must be taught to
every Hutu at every level. Every Hutu must spread this ideology widely. Any Hutu who persecutes his brother Hutu for
having read, spread, and taught this ideology is a traitor.

Sharpening the anti-Tutsi campaign this way was not the only
step Rwandan leaders took in response to the rebel advance. President Habyarimana also ordered a rapid increase in the size of his
army, which had fewer than six thousand soldiers at the time the
RPF invaded. It tripled in size within six months and continued to
grow. New recruits were only lightly trained, and few had anything approaching the political commitment that burned in the
hearts of RPF fighters. Many were not from northern Rwanda and
therefore not emotionally committed to the regime; regional divisions within the army were so strong that soldiers from the north
often refused to rescue wounded comrades who came from other
regions.

For all its weaknesses, though, this army counted on an advantage that had long proven decisive in African wars: military support from France.

During the early 1990s, France sold the Rwandan regime more
than $20 million worth of weaponry and helped it buy five times
that amount from arms dealers in Egypt and South Africa. When
Egyptian financiers hesitated to extend credit to Rwanda, France's
government-owned bank, Crédit Lyonnais, stepped in as guaran-
tor. That allowed Rwanda to buy not just small arms but helicopters, tanks, rockets, and heavy mortars. It turned one of the world's
smallest and poorest countries into the third-largest arms importer
in Africa.

"Africa is the only continent that remains within the reach of
French influence," a French foreign minister, Louis de Guirangaud,
had asserted several years earlier. "It is the only place where she
can still, with three hundred men, change the course of history."

France's interests in Africa are broad and deep, and French governments have traditionally felt free to use all necessary means to assure that cooperative regimes hold power in countries of the Francophonie. They act to defend their own strategic interest. In Rwanda, that interest was of a peculiarly French sort. Rwanda does not have oil, minerals, a seaport, or much else of evident value. President Mitterrand nonetheless saw it as crucial battleground. He realized that an insurgent victory there would shake the foundation of French power in Africa, and he was determined to prevent it at any cost.

"In President Mitterrand's analysis, what was important above all was a global reasoning," a French parliamentary commission later concluded. "He believed, as had his three predecessors, that France had subscribed to a security role, and that if she were unable to send aid in a case as simple as that of helping a country suffering an armed invasion, then this guarantee of security meant nothing."

For more than a century, France has viewed Francophone Africa as its special preserve. Rwanda's educated class was French-speaking, its dominant outside cultural influences came from France, and President Habyarimana was fully submissive to France's will. Most RPF leaders, however, grew up in Uganda, spoke English, and felt no connection to France. Mitterrand instinctively understood what this meant. If the RPF were to take power, it would probably do something that had never been attempted in Africa: pull a French-speaking country out of the Francophonie and bring it into the camp of the dreaded Anglo-Saxons. This prospect deeply alarmed powerful groups within the French elite, which had barely digested the shocks of military defeat in Indochina and Algeria, was horrified by the worldwide march of American popular culture, and had come to believe that, as the French scholar Gérard Prunier has written, "the whole world is a cultural, political and economic battleground between France and the 'Anglo-Saxons.'"

"From that point of view," Prunier wrote, "the invasion of Rwanda on October 1, 1990, by a group of rebels from Uganda was a typical test case—an obvious 'Anglo-Saxon' plot to destabilize one of ours, and one we needed to stop right away if we did not want to see a dangerous spread of the disease. . . . This is how Paris found itself backing an ailing dictatorship in a tiny distant country producing only bananas and a declining coffee crop, without even asking for political reform as a price for its support. This blind commitment was to have catastrophic consequences because, as the situation radicalized, the Rwandan leadership kept believing that *no matter what it did*, French support would always be forthcoming. And it had no valid reason for believing otherwise."

French policy toward Africa has traditionally been shaped not by the foreign ministry, but by a small team in the president's office called the *cellule Africaine*. To head this team, President Mitterrand chose his ambitious but inexperienced son, Jean-Christophe. Before long, Jean-Christophe Mitterrand found a soul mate in Jean-Pierre Habyarimana, son of the Rwandan dictator. They went into a variety of businesses together, reportedly including prostitution, gorilla poaching, and drug and weapons trafficking. By night, according to a *New York Times* correspondent, they could often be seen "carousing together in discos on the Left Bank and in Rwanda at the Kigali Nightclub."

While these two young friends partied and made money, and while their fathers worked to preserve the integrity of Francophone Africa, *inkotanyi* were steadily expanding the amount of territory they controlled. By the end of 1991, they held a swath along the northern border that composed close to 5 percent of the country. It included the region where most Rwandan tea is grown, an idyllic chain of hills where sun shines every day and light breezes carry the scent of eucalyptus through the air. Workers at tea plantations, like most other Rwandans in war zones, fled before the RPF advance. When Kagame arrived at the largest plantation, Mulindi, which is perched above the northern town of Byumba, he found an abandoned complex with two dozen buildings set amid verdant fields. He decided it would make an ideal new headquarters. The inhospitable Virunga range had been a good hideout for a bloodied force that needed time to regroup. Mulindi was more like the capital of a mini-state, and it was from there that Kagame directed the rest of his war.

Kagame's first year as leader of the RPF rebellion was a resounding success. He resurrected a crippled guerrilla force, led it to a series of victories, and even captured a chunk of Rwandan territory. Some of his officers wanted to press on, to fight relentlessly until they had deposed the regime and seized power. Kagame overruled them. He decided it was time for a pause in the war and told his troops they were entering a period devoted to "training and production." Many were assigned to work in fields where the force grew its food. They stayed in fighting trim, but most went months without seeing combat.

The insurgents might have been able to win the war at this early stage, but their leaders would have had great trouble governing because most Rwandans had been conditioned to hate them. Kagame feared that a military victory might set off explosive chaos. The RPF, he told his restless officers, should negotiate with the regime and accept any compromise that gave them a voice in government and secured their central goal: freedom for refugees to return and live safely in their homeland.

Sometimes there was an internal debate within the RPF: how can we govern in concert with killers like these who we oppose so strongly, whose ideology is so different, and who don't see the country the way we see it? My position always was that we have to do it. The will to fight does not diminish or weaken if we agree to talk. We would suffer, in a way, if we didn't agree to talk, because what is the explanation when those you are fighting want to talk and you say we won't? It weakens you diplomatically. This part of the struggle is very important. To be seen to be doing the right thing is as important as fighting.

As it became clear that this war would probably have a political solution, President Habyarimana began portraying himself as a peacemaker open to compromise. In 1991, following France's suggestion, he agreed to legalize opposition parties. Several quickly emerged. Some were genuinely interested in helping their country move toward democracy. Others pushed in the opposite direction.

The most militant of these new parties was the openly racist Coalition pour la Défense de la Republique (CDR). Its organizers were key figures in the *akazu*, including the first lady, so it was intimately tied to President Habyarimana's regime. Yet it claimed to be an opposition party, and its leaders rejected Habyarimana's policy—at least the policy he publicly proclaimed—of seeking an accommodation with the rebels. They embodied, by one account, "the lunatic fringes of radical Hutu extremism." In their newspapers and radio broadcasts, they depicted RPF fighters as bloodthirsty aliens, "creatures from another world, with tails, horns, hooves, pointed ears and red eyes." Most important, they portrayed every Tutsi as an ally of the insurgents and thus a mortal enemy.

"Unaccountable before the law, this small group of individuals transformed racial extremism, oppression and violence into a legitimate means of exercising political authority," wrote John and Carol Berry, two of the few Americans who lived in Rwanda during this period. "The incitement of racial hatred was a deliberate political technique used to rally their supporters and distract attention from the real domestic problems of their country. . . . [They] used two very effective mechanisms to manipulate and mobilize public opinion against the Tutsi: hatred and fear. With the support of members of the Rwandan intellectual elite, Hutu extremists propagated a revisionist history of relations between the Hutu and the Tutsi that was not based on cohabitation and exchange, but rather on segregation and violence."

Hutu extremists assumed that all Tutsi covertly supported the rebel cause. It was a logical assumption. Almost every Tutsi in Rwanda had relatives abroad and therefore some tie to the RPF. All would presumably benefit from an RPF victory, because it would return to them their long-lost rights. Despite all of this, however, many Tutsi in Rwanda actually opposed the insurgency. Rather than welcoming *inkotanyi* as liberators and rushing to rebel-controlled zones, they did the opposite. They fled, along with their Hutu neighbors, to other parts of the country.

A great psychological chasm divided the Tutsi who lived in Rwanda from those who had grown up as refugees. The ones who remained at home found ways to adjust to their unpleasant situation. They bowed their heads, kept their opinions to themselves, and did whatever was necessary to placate their Hutu masters. This kept most of them alive. The 1990 invasion, however, upset the delicate balance they had managed to strike. They feared it would bring a new wave of state terror down upon them.

"You want power?" a Tutsi who lived in Ruhengeri asked one of the *inkotanyi* who raided the town in 1991. "You will get it. But here we will all die. Is it worth it to you?"

Because so many civilians fled at its approach, the RPF found that even after capturing new territory, it ruled over little more than ghost towns. Kagame was shocked to realize that many of the Tutsi he had come to liberate considered him an enemy.

As we saw it, that was a very narrow way of looking at things. It was not in dispute that people were being oppressed. In some way, that tends to draw a line, as if those of us outside were different from those here. Yet some of those opposed to us were also part of us. They were our relatives. There was not a single Rwandan outside who did not have relatives inside. We were a family. Yes, in some cases there was a feeling by some people here that things were better left the way they were. But the way things were was simply unacceptable.

Whatever the justice of this argument, Tutsi civilians bore the brunt of the regime's anger. During the nearly four years the RPF was in the field, the government launched four distinct waves of massacres. The first two came in response to specific RPF actions, the October 1990 invasion and the January 1991 raid on Ruhengeri; the other two were aimed simply at sowing terror. Together these "practice genocides" took three thousand lives, making them the bloodiest in more than a decade.

"In the episodes of violence from 1990 to 1994," Human Rights Watch later concluded, "Habyarimana's supporters perfected some of the tactics they would use during the genocide: how to choose the best sites to launch attacks, how to develop the violence—both in intensity and extent—from small beginnings, how to mobilize people through fear, particularly fear aroused by 'created' events, how to use barriers and bureaucratic regulations to keep a target group restricted to one place, and how to build cooperation between civilian, military and militia leaders to produce the most effective attacks."

As the regime became steadily more radical and violent, solidarity within the Hutu elite began to break down. Prominent figures fled the country, and several went so far as to join the RPF. Each one was embraced as a prize. Together, they lent some credibility to the RPF claim that it was fighting on behalf of all Rwandans, not only Tutsi.

Eager to show this side of itself to the world, the RPF gave highly visible positions to Hutu defectors such as Alex Kanyarengwe, a former army officer who had helped President Habyarimana seize power and served as his interior minister; Seth Sendashonga, a well-connected businessman; and Pasteur Bizimungu, who had been general manager of the state-owned electric company and fled after his cousin, an army officer, was executed for supposed disloyalty. Their presence gave the RPF a broader political base and a more reassuring image. It also brought to the rebel side people who had spent their lives in Rwanda and understood how the country worked—something none of the original RPF leaders could claim.

While these Hutu eminences were joining the "enemy," hardliners in the *akazu* were working methodically to turn their fatal vision into genocidal reality. Some of them organized youth gangs that evolved into militia squads. In several towns, local officials sent these squads to carry out massacres while police officers watched. They told the killers that their work was only a form of *umuganda*, the communal work to which Rwandans had been accustomed for generations.

Here developed the vocabulary of Rwanda's apocalypse, with the killing of adult males called "clearing bush" and that of women and children "pulling out the roots of the bad weeds."

The largest and most violent of the new militias—called *interahamwe*, "those who struggle together"—grew out of the youth wing of President Habyarimana's political party and soon became an instrument of the bloodthirsty CDR. It had squads in every part of the country, many trained by Rwandan or French army officers. Members not only learned paramilitary tactics like arson and grenade throwing, but also, grimly foreshadowing the horror to come, practiced attacking human dummies with long machete-like knives called *pangas*.

As the Rwandan army and its militias grew, so did the rebel force. From across East and Central Africa and even from Europe and North America, young Tutsi made their way to RPF territory and signed up. Two years after the RPF launched its invasion with four thousand *inkotanyi*, it had twelve thousand.

This burgeoning army urgently needed weapons. It stole much of what it used from government units, to the point that "the enemy is our quartermaster" became an RPF maxim. Like other rebel groups, it also bought what it could on the semilegal arms market. Drivers, porters, and couriers brought these supplies to the battlefront through Uganda.

Allowing this supply network to operate freely was just one of many ways the Ugandan government quietly supported the RPF during its years at war. They were natural allies. Senior RPF commanders had fought alongside President Museveni when he was a rebel and served in his army after he took power. Like him, they were products of Anglophone tradition, revolutionary passion, and the utopian ideal of "African socialism." Their cooperation was so evident that Rwandan officials and their patrons in France even suspected that Museveni had helped plan the 1990 invasion. In fact, it had taken him by surprise.

"We were woken up by a call in the middle of the night telling us that the boys had gone over the border," one of his aides later recalled. "The president was quite disturbed. We knew they were up to something, but we did not think they would act so soon. With our presence in an international forum, it was quite embarrassing."

Officials in Uganda, including President Museveni, were of two minds about the Rwandan war. In the months before the invasion, they had suspected that their Rwandan comrades were planning something. Only after it began, however, did they realize how fully Rwandans had penetrated the Ugandan army and used it for their own purposes. This realization infuriated Museveni. He became even angrier when he realized how much weaponry defecting soldiers had stolen from his army.

After their emotions cooled, however, Ugandan leaders began to see how an RPF victory might help them. It would not only rid Uganda of a long-festering refugee crisis but also bring a friendly regime to power in Rwanda. President Museveni never went so far as to support the RPF publicly, but officials in his army and police force, many of whom had close personal ties to RPF commanders, turned a blind eye to its operations inside Uganda. One of their first contributions was allowing Kagame to lead his retreating fighters across Ugandan territory to their new base in Virunga after the debacle of 1990. As the war proceeded, the RPF received much weaponry through Uganda and sent many wounded soldiers for treatment at semisecret clinics there.

This unofficial tie to Uganda was a great asset to the rebel force. So was the guerrillas' high level of motivation and political consciousness. There was, however, another important reason for the rebels' success: Paul Kagame's leadership. He was personally involved in every aspect of RPF operations, from organizing ambushes to dealing with overseas supporters. This crucible shaped qualities of his character that would define him in later life. Officers who worked with him during the war years recall a disciplined, austere, and solitary commander; a self-confident, strong-willed figure with a sometimes overbearing intensity of focus; and an insightful tactician who sought to impose his will through a combination of force and persuasion.

"Kagame, a secretive, sober, intelligent and determined man . . . was a truly impressive leader," the British journalist Linda Melvern wrote. "He lived with his soldiers, shared their privations, and knew that the war against the regime in Rwanda was likely to be protracted." He also insisted on a level of discipline almost unknown among rebel armies in Africa. According to one scholarly survey of these armies, the RPF "was run as an extremely tight ship where soldiers stood at attention, saluted their officers, and strictly obeyed orders."

There was no such discipline in Kigali, where the regime was being shaken by demands for political change. After President Habyarimana named a new one-party cabinet in January of 1992, more than fifty thousand people took to the streets in protest. This was the strongest public challenge his regime had ever faced, and as it grew, he concluded that in order to save himself, he would have to accept the protesters' main demands. In March he announced that he would name opposition figures to his cabinet and negotiate with the RPF.

The new cabinet quickly took office, but Habyarimana proved reluctant to open peace talks. In June several Hutu politicians decided to take the initiative themselves and traveled to Brussels to meet RPF leaders. Government negotiators later joined the talks, which moved first to Paris and then to the dusty Tanzanian town of Arusha. They went better than anyone had expected. On July 14 the RPF agreed to a permanent cease-fire and proclaimed its desire to transform itself from an armed movement into a political party. President Habyarimana, pressed by his French and Belgian friends, reluctantly agreed to discuss a new political system under which he would remain in office but share power with the RPF.

As negotiators talked, optimists on both sides allowed themselves to believe the war was ending.

Progress toward peace, however, further unsettled political life in Rwanda. Opposition figures who had been named to the cabinet demanded more power than the president was willing to give them. They began boycotting cabinet meetings, and then called a series of street protests that drew tens of thousands of people. Soldiers, who had gone unpaid for months and feared they would be cashiered under a new peace accord, broke out of their barracks in several towns and went on violent rampages.

Radicals in the regime responded by urging protesters to direct their rage not at the government but at their Tutsi neighbors. To set an example, they sent militias on a series of terror raids in which hundreds of Tutsi civilians were hacked to death. In public speeches, they gave horrific warnings about the terrors that RPF rule would bring and made vivid threats against the Tutsi.

"We have to wipe out these hoodlums!" Léon Mugesera, a leader of the ruling party, declared in one fiery speech to party members. "The fatal mistake we made in 1959 was to allow them to get out. They belong in Ethiopia, and we are going to find them a shortcut to get there by throwing them into the Nyabarongo River!"

Speeches like this left no doubt what members of the *akazu* and other Hutu radicals were plotting. They proposed, explicitly and quite seriously, to resolve Rwanda's conflict through a "final solution" in which every Tutsi in the country—a total of more than one million people—would be killed or forced to flee. In the first weeks of 1993 they tested their tactics by sending gangs of killers on a rampage through communities in northern Rwanda where Tutsi pastoralists called Bagogwe live. More than one thousand were killed. Survivors made their way to the rebel-held zone, and their stories outraged Kagame. He considered this an egregious breach of the cease-fire and reacted immediately. First he announced that the RPF would pull out of the Arusha talks, which in any case were making only glacial progress. Then he decided to launch a new offensive aimed at reminding the government how much power he could wield on the battlefield.

This was the largest-scale military operation ever mounted in Rwanda. More than eight thousand *inkotanyi*, most of them eager to fight after months of waiting, took part. Shortly after midnight on February 8, 1993, they crept down from hillside redoubts across northern Rwanda, slipped through government lines, and stormed toward the capital.

The whole idea in my mind was not to capture Kigali. My mind was on destroying government forces, capturing weapons, and after that extending the territory, and after achieving that, deciding what to do with it. While I was planning on that and planning for the best- and worst-case scenario, it surprised me how effective the whole thing became. The [government] forces were totally defeated, and our forces were just moving. . . . If we had wanted, we could have taken it—no question about it.

That is not how some outsiders saw it. When RPF units reached positions about fifteen miles from Kigali, they suddenly came under withering artillery fire. President Mitterrand, alarmed by news of the offensive, had rushed four hundred more French soldiers and a cargo plane full of artillery shells to his Rwandan allies. Those shells rained down on RPF fighters as they approached Kigali.

Rebel commanders and their men, frustrated after months of tedium and convinced they could take Kigali even if it meant fighting French soldiers, prepared to charge through the artillery curtain and claim their prize. The order to attack, however, never came. Instead, Kagame stunned his *inkotanyi* by ordering them to stop fighting and retreat out of artillery range.

"We had made our way to the edge of Kigali," the commander of one RPF unit later recalled. "A lot of our people had been killed getting there. Then we got the order to go back. Everyone was shocked. We asked, 'Why can't we go ahead? We're practically in Kigali! Why go back?' [Kagame] told us, 'Capturing Kigali is not an end in itself.' We told him, 'But our soldiers are here! We can actually see what we want, so let's take it!' But he was thinking about the day after. 'We can take it, but what would we do on the next day?' He said to us, 'Why did the RPF start the war? Was it for ourselves, or for Rwanda? If, as the French say, we are fighting for the Tutsi, we can fight, win, and then say we won our right to take over. But our philosophy is that we were thrown out of the country and we want every Rwandan to be able to live here peacefully.' That was his vision, not winner-take-all."

Besides showing once again the military prowess of the RPF, this offensive set off the greatest refugee exodus Rwanda had yet seen. By the time it was over, one million Rwandans—more than 10 percent of the country's population—had fled their homes and were packed into fetid camps in central and southern provinces where, according to the United Nations, "serious malnutrition and disease were prevalent." The burden of coping with this upheaval pushed Rwanda even further toward chaos. It also led nearby countries, and some farther away, to intensify their pressure for a peace settlement.

Much of this pressure was applied to President Museveni, the African leader closest to the RPF. He persuaded Kagame to come to Kampala for talks with diplomats from European countries and the United Nations. All demanded that he withdraw his forces from positions near Kigali and bring them back to their enclave in the north. Kagame replied that he would do so only if government forces agreed not to reoccupy the territory he was abandoning. The assembled dignitaries angrily rejected this demand and insisted that the insurgents must withdraw unconditionally. Kagame refused to budge.

"I mean it," he told them. "I have made a concession that we shall leave this territory ourselves, but government troops can never come back. If that's not the case, if you don't agree with me, I'm actually going to go back and fight again and take *more* territory."

The rebels' commanding military position gave them the power to impose their will. On February 22 they signed an accord under which they agreed to end their offensive and return to their enclave, on condition that a demilitarized zone be established between the enclave and the rest of the country. This recognized insurgent rule over a swath of Rwanda for the first time. Because both sides agreed not to cross the demilitarized zone, though, it also gave the government a guarantee that insurgents would stage no more attacks on Kigali or the country's heartland. This outraged some RPF leaders, including the negotiators Kagame had withdrawn from Arusha a month before.

When I talked to them and told them what we had agreed . . . the whole team was, like, "How?" It was as if I had betrayed the RPF. . . . In fact, I remember [chief negotiator Pasteur] Bizimungu telling me, "If that is the case, you better look for somebody else to lead the negotiations. I'm not going back." . . . He argued that this was unprincipled. I had a rough time with them. The whole of them were against me. I told [them] . . . "Some of you don't even know some of the details. While you are there negotiating, people on the ground are fighting, dying, injured. I'm the one there with them. You don't know that they don't even have enough ammunition. You think they should be fighting all the way to Kigali, but that's not how to fight. Secondly, things in politics or diplomacy, as you should know, are not always black and white. Sometimes there are things in the gray area. It's not always 'yes' or 'no.' There's also 'but.' So you can't just tell me you're not going back."

After having rescued the RPF from disaster, commanded it for three years, and brought it to the brink of triumph, Kagame had accumulated enough authority to give orders to these reluctant negotiators. They returned to the peace talks at Arusha and began designing a government in which bitter enemies would share power. Thirteen months later, on August 4, 1993, as leaders of all four countries that border on Rwanda watched, commanders of the warring armies signed peace accords that many hoped would finally end the three-year-old civil war.

The Arusha accords provided for the establishment of a new "broad-based transitional government," with President Habyarimana remaining in office but governing through a coalition cabinet. The RPF would hold five ministries, including the interior ministry. Its fighters would be integrated into a new army, in which they would make up 40 percent of the fighting force and half of the officer corps. All refugees would be allowed to return. Ethnic designations would be removed from national identity cards. Rebels would remain in their northern zone. After a twenty-two-month transition period, free elections would be held. In the meantime, a "neutral international force" would be asked to keep the peace.

This settlement was highly favorable to the RPF. It not only gave *inkotanyi* key roles in the government and army, but also decreed an end to sectarian rule—and thus to the ruling group's hold on power. President Habyarimana signed the accords, one journalist wrote, "with a heavy heart and no doubt a wife incandescent with rage." The alternative would probably have been an all-out rebel attack in which he stood to lose everything.

"Without the RPF forces effectively holding a trigger to his head, he would not have been forced into the political corner he perceived Arusha to be," the British journalist Andrew Wallis wrote. "The reality was that the French military presence had alone kept Habyarimana from defeat and exile, and that Arusha was now the best hope of keeping him and his Hutu hardliners in power—even if it meant some compromises."

As the Arusha accords were being signed, there were already clear signs that they would never be implemented. All understood that President Habyarimana, as one scholar has written, accepted them "not as a genuine gesture marking the turning over of a new leaf and the beginning of democratization in Rwanda, but as a tactical move designed to buy time, shore up the contradictions of the various factions in the opposition, and look good in the eyes of foreign donors." Habyarimana made this clear a few weeks after the signing ceremony, when he traveled to Uganda for talks with President Museveni but refused to meet RPF leaders who had traveled there to see him. That led them to decide that while they would comply with everything they had agreed to at Arusha, they would do so with great caution and, at the same time, prepare for a return to war.

President Habyarimana's doubts were not the only obstacle to realizing the promise of the Arusha accords. There was another, more fundamental problem: the role of the violently racist CDR, which was run by the president's wife and other members of his radical *akazu*. During the talks at Arusha, the CDR had sought posts in the transitional government. The RPF categorically rejected this idea, and at its insistence, the final accords gave the CDR nothing. This ruthless clique, which had dominated the country for years and still exercised great power, suddenly found itself consigned to oblivion.

It is a political truism that enemies, as Machiavelli wrote, "must be either destroyed or conciliated by benefits." The CDR was the main enemy of Rwandan democracy, but the Arusha accords left it neither destroyed nor conciliated. It would have been absurd for Tutsi rebels to share power with a party dedicated to killing Tutsi. Equally absurd was to expect the CDR to accept a new regime under which there would be Tutsi army officers and cabinet ministers—and under which CDR leaders would likely be arrested and prosecuted for grave crimes. Bringing the CDR into the new government would have doomed that government. Keeping it out had the same effect.

"Between the roots of the conflict and the possibility of its resolution," one diplomat wrote afterward, "lay political elites willing to destroy a society rather than concede their own power."

As soon as the Arusha accords were signed, the CDR issued a defiant manifesto declaring that anyone who supported compromise with the Tutsi rebels was guilty of "high treason" and calling on the army and other "democratic forces" to protest. Militants poured onto the streets of Kigali for what became six days of rioting. Chanting slogans denouncing the "sell-out," they slaughtered three hundred Tutsi. At the height of this rampage, the CDR issued another manifesto with a striking new twist. It blamed the country's crisis not only on the RPF, the Tutsi, and Hutu "traitors," but also on their own leader.

"Mr. Juvénal Habyarimana, President of the Republic, has approved the contents of an agreement obviously detrimental to the interests of the Rwandan people," the CDR declared. "This shows clearly that Mr. Juvénal Habyarimana, President of the Republic, does not care any more about the interests of the Nation and is now defending other interests."

As this confrontation reached a peak, the *akazu* was systematically preparing the "final solution" that was to come. One of its most effective tools was a radio station, Radio-Télévision Libre de Mille Collines (RTLM), that broadcast a steady stream of racist venom and chilling threats. President Habyarimana was among the shareholders, as was nearly every member of his infamous *akazu*. Radio is ubiquitous in Rwanda, and as soon as RTLM made its debut in the summer of 1993, it became a central part of national life. It offered a snappy mix of upbeat music, colorful patter, and bloodcurdling threats against the Tutsi, along with helpful tips on efficient ways to kill with homemade weapons.

"It was the endless and mindless expression of ethnic cleansing on a scale hitherto unknown in Africa and rarely in the world," wrote a Canadian aid worker. "After a while, the endless repetition of lies to an illiterate and poverty-stricken population looking for someone on whom to blame all their woes and with no alternative way of assessing reality becomes truth of a sort, capable of inciting an uncontrollable bloodlust."

While some members of the *akazu* were organizing this hate-radio station, others turned to a project that was its necessary complement. They directed the importation of hundreds of thousands of *pangas* and other "agricultural implements" like hoes, axes, scythes, and knives. The *pangas* alone were enough to arm every third adult male in the country. Most came from China, through deals negotiated by the Rwandan embassy in Paris. None of the companies that imported them had ordered such equipment before.

Most outsiders chose not to notice any of this. In mid-1993 the United States pronounced relations between the two countries "excellent" and insisted that there was "no evidence of any systematic human rights abuses by the military or any other element of the government." Several months later, President Habyarimana even made a friendly visit to Washington. While he was there a Belgian scholar, Filip Reyntjens, asserted at a press conference in Brussels that powerful Rwandans had secretly assembled a "Zero Network" composed of militias and death squads that were being trained to commit mass murder. Reyntjens went so far as to name the Rwandans who were organizing this network. All were members of the *akazu*, among them Madame Habyarimana, her three brothers, and a powerful military commander, Colonel Théoneste Bagosora.

Bagosora, popularly known as "the colonel of death," was among the young officers who directed the first wave of anti-Tutsi massacres from 1959 to 1963. Part of his power came from his close ties to France; he was the first Rwandan to have graduated from the most prestigious French military academy, the Ecole de Guerre, and had commanded the Rwandan garrison at Kanombe, near the Kigali airport, where French troops also lived. People who dealt with him found him crude and thuggish.

"He had a quick and nervous temper," one recalled, "and his face would tremble with anger when he thought he was being thwarted."

For a time, Bagosora was part of the government negotiating team at Arusha. When it became clear that the peace accords would force his regime to share power with the hated Tutsi, and that there would be no role for him or other militants, he stalked out. As he was leaving, an RPF negotiator asked where he was going.

Back to Kigali, he replied—to prepare "the second apocalypse."

I said, "No, we cannot just entrust our security, the security of our people, to the UN and the government forces in Kigali. This is a delicate situation. This is a negotiated settlement. This is a situation where all sides have concerns, and our concern primarily is that of security." So I gave them a proposal. I said we should have a force that comes and takes care of the security of our people who would be coming into Kigali. . . . For me it was a make or break. This was a demand that couldn't be wished away.

WE JUST DIDN'T GET IT

O N A CLOUDLESS JUNE DAY in 1993, very far from Rwanda, a Canadian military commander named Roméo Dallaire watched proudly as one of his units marched across a parade ground in strict formation. He had reason to be pleased. After distinguishing himself at NATO posts in Europe, he had been summoned home, promoted to major general, and given a choice command. Soldiers he trained had served as UN peacekeepers in Kuwait, Cambodia, and most recently Bosnia. As he addressed his men in Quebec that day, his reputation was at a peak.

Moments after Dallaire finished his speech, an aide approached and whispered that there was an urgent call for him on the car phone. He excused himself and hurried away. The caller was his commanding officer, with a question: Was there any reason that Dallaire should not himself be deployed on a peacekeeping mission?

"None whatsoever," Dallaire replied.

The United Nations was considering a mission to Rwanda, the officer said. That was enough to set Dallaire's heart racing. He had dreamed for years of a chance like this.

"Rwanda," he stammered. "That's somewhere in Africa, right?"

The United Nations was at that time planning nothing more than an observer mission to monitor the border between Rwanda and Uganda. Dallaire, who was duly appointed as its commander, would have just eighty-one peacekeepers, all unarmed. He was eager to set out and waited impatiently as diplomats in New York slowly made the necessary arrangements. Then, early in August, he heard startling news. Leaders of Rwanda's warring armies had signed peace accords that called for the quick deployment of a "neutral international force" inside their country.

Dallaire's mission had ballooned in size and scope before he even set foot in Africa.

Although he had never led or even been part of a peacekeeping mission, Dallaire seemed well prepared for this command. He grew up in a military family and had been one of those boys who from early childhood play war games and dream of life in uniform. At forty-six, he had behind him an impressive career that included advanced training at the U.S. Marine Corps Command and Staff College. He had acquired the habit of command and with it a flinty profile shaped by deep-set eyes, a sharp jaw, and a graying, closely clipped moustache.

"Pencil out a front tooth and he could pass for an enforcer on the Quebec Nordiques," one of Dallaire's acquaintances observed. A UN diplomat described him as "cultured but straight-shooting, hardworking, energetic and determined." He was also a reflective, ethical thinker shaped by the humanitarianism that is part of Canada's ethos.

As soon as Dallaire was formally appointed commander of the Rwanda peacekeeping force, he traveled to UN headquarters in New York to meet his new bosses. He quickly found that the Department of Peacekeeping Operations, headed by the Ghanaian diplomat Kofi Annan, was small, underequipped, and poorly run. Friends had warned him, he later wrote, that Annan and his colleagues were "incompetent boobs who kept bankers' hours and disappeared when situations in the field came to a head." Everything he saw in New York confirmed that assessment. No one briefed him or gave him even a single page of written analysis of what was happening in Rwanda. All he was able to glean about the country came from a photocopied encyclopedia entry and a Michelin map.

He never even saw public reports like one issued that summer by Oxfam, which warned that Rwanda "stands at the brink of an uncharted abyss of anarchy and violence, and there are all too many historical, ethnic, economic and political pressures that are likely to push it over the edge."

Annan and other starched-collar diplomats at the United Nations envisioned the Rwanda mission as a classic peacekeeping operation, in which an outside force keeps two hostile parties apart while guiding them toward compromise. They even allowed themselves to presume the mission would be relatively easy, with high prospects for a success that would reestablish the reputation of UN peacekeeping after ongoing failures in Somalia and Bosnia. Dallaire was told repeatedly that the United Nations wanted a "quick success."

"This thing has to be small and inexpensive," General Maurice Baril, the chief military officer in the peacekeeping office, warned him as he prepared for his first inspection tour of Rwanda. "Otherwise it will never get approved by the Security Council."

That warning gave Dallaire his first inkling that he might not be given the tools needed to succeed—and that as a result, his mission might not be so simple after all. He was not yet, however, even close to grasping the intensity of the maelstrom into which he was stepping.

. By this time, the rebel Rwandan Patriotic Force had been in the field for nearly three years. It had shown considerable military power, but because many Rwandans saw it as a hostile invading force, it had never become a popular movement. Its leaders, acutely aware of this fact, were seeking not military victory but a negotiated compromise with the regime. The peace accords they had just signed in Arusha, Tanzania, seemed to embody that compromise.

What Dallaire did not realize was that neither party to the Arusha accords believed they would actually take hold. Both were going through the motions of peacemaking while preparing to renew their war. Even more ominously, a diabolical third force—

large, well organized, fully armed, and sponsored by some of Rwanda's most powerful figures—had shown itself determined to block any political compromise even if that meant drowning the country in blood.

Obscure and almost unseen, this force was surging toward power when Dallaire arrived in Kigali on August 19, 1993, accompanied by an eighteen-member survey team.

Dallaire was encouraged by what he found on that first visit. The dynamic new prime minister, Agathe Umwilingiyimana, a former high school teacher and education minister who when asked about her ethnic background would say only that she was "a Rwandan and a person," fervently supported the accords and wanted peacekeepers deployed as soon as possible. Rwanda's future hung in the balance, Madame Agathe told Dallaire, and it must not lose its chance at democracy "because of a few hard-liners."

The figure Dallaire most wanted to size up was Paul Kagame, the boldly successful rebel commander. He arranged a meeting, and on the appointed morning, he and a handful of aides set out toward Mulindi, "curious to meet the man who turned a ragtag group of guerrilla fighters into a force capable of holding its own against French soldiers in the field." On the way, they stopped at a hellish camp where thousands of displaced people were living in conditions worse than Dallaire had ever seen. Their suffering deeply shocked him. As he felt tears welling in his eyes, the camp's children, wide-eyed and laughing, surrounded him, tugging at his pants and pulling him to join their soccer game.

"I am not being melodramatic when I say that this was the moment when I personally dedicated myself to bringing a UN peacekeeping mission to Rwanda," he later wrote. "Until that point, the exercise had been an interesting challenge and a potential route to a field command."

Dallaire's convoy wound its way northward toward the regional capital of Byumba and turned onto a dirt road that climbs to the old tea plantation. An honor guard of thirty men dressed as traditional Rwandan warriors welcomed the visitors and then began a show. Dressed only in underskirts and wearing long white headdresses symbolizing lions' manes, with bells jangling from their ankles, they leaped, twirled, drummed, and sang until their bodies glistened with sweat.

Afterward, the visitors were escorted to the former overseer's residence, where three senior RPF leaders were waiting. In keeping with the rebels' desire to present their movement as representing all Rwandans, two were Hutu: Alex Kanyarengwe, the RPF chairman, and Pasteur Bizimungu, one of its chief political officers. The third was Kagame. He struck Dallaire as looking "more like a college professor than a rebel army commander" and "easily the most interesting of the three, although he was the most self-contained."

"Almost stereotypically Tutsi, he was incredibly thin and well over six feet tall," Dallaire wrote. "He towered over the gathering with a studious air that didn't quite disguise his hawk-like intensity. Behind his spectacles, his glistening charcoal eyes were penetrating, projecting his mastery of the situation."

Dallaire was just as impressed with Kagame's army, which he reviewed in a tour of the area around Mulindi.

"This was a combat-proven and battle-ready army," he reported. "They had very few vehicles, and while their troops appeared to be fit, well-fed and reasonably well equipped, they were a light infantry army that had to fight and resupply by foot or bicycle. Yet they had won all recent contests because of their superior leadership, discipline and morale. If Kagame was responsible for nurturing this force, he was a truly impressive leader and perhaps deserved the sobriquet that the media had given him: the Napoleon of Africa."

Later Dallaire also had a chance to review the government army. He found it full of "poorly trained recruits who lacked weapons, food, medical supplies and above all leadership and morale." But although his military training gave him the ability to assess armies, he was still too innocent to grasp Rwanda's chilling political realities. Radicals were already planning their campaign of extermination, but when he met them, they assured him they wanted only peace. They could smile, and murder while they smiled.

"I did not understand that I had just met men in Rwanda who would become *genocidaires*," he wrote later. "Were they in fact already betting that white, Western nations had too much on their hands to attempt another foray into black Africa? Were the hardliners playing us, and me, for fools? I think so. I believe they already had concluded that the West did not have the will. . . . They knew us better than we knew ourselves."

After his twelve-day stay in Rwanda, Dallaire concluded that the job the United Nations wanted him to do would require a force of eight thousand peacekeepers. When he presented this estimate to his bosses in New York, they were horrified. Reluctantly he cut his request to 4,500, which he insisted was the bare minimum necessary to do the job. That was still far more than the United Nations was willing to provide. Secretary-General Boutros Boutros-Ghali finally agreed to ask the Security Council to send 2,548 peacekeepers.

Two powerful countries, both permanent members of the Security Council, worked resolutely to narrow both the size and scope of this mission. One was France, which had for years been the dominant power in Rwanda and did not want to share that role with anyone else. The other was the United States. President Bill Clinton was under intense congressional pressure to reduce American contributions to peacekeeping operations, and he responded by taking a tough line on the Rwanda mission. When the Security Council was asked to dispatch 2,548 peacekeepers there, already a drastically scaled-down figure, U.S. ambassador Madeleine Albright suggested that the number be cut to 500. At every point as the Rwanda crisis intensified, she worked diligently to keep the UN peacekeeping force small and weak.

"The Americans never took Rwanda or me seriously," Dallaire later complained.

French and American diplomats working to limit the Rwanda peacekeeping mission had a reliable friend in Secretary-General Boutros-Ghali. He was Paris-educated, believed passionately in France's *mission civilitrice* in Africa, and, by one account, "could see nothing unless it was through a Francophone prism." Among the favors he had done for France while serving as Egypt's deputy foreign minister in the early 1990s was brokering a deal that brought the Rwandan government $6 million in weaponry, including seventy mortars, two thousand land mines, and three million rounds of ammunition. He was especially close to President Mitterrand, whose decisive support had made possible his rise to secretary-general.

On October 3, two days before the Security Council was to vote on Boutros-Ghali's scaled-down Rwanda proposal, stunning news came from Somalia. A U.S. military patrol there, part of a UN-sponsored relief mission, had been torn apart by hostile fire. Two Black Hawk helicopters were shot down, and in the ensuing battle eighteen American soldiers were killed. Two of their bodies were dragged through the streets of Mogadishu as onlookers cheered. It was a deep humiliation for the United States and led the Clinton administration to look more dubiously than ever on the idea of intervening in Rwanda.

Some feared that in the wake of this disaster, the Security Council might reject the idea of a Rwandan peacekeeping force altogether. It did not, but before approving Boutros-Ghali's proposal, diplomats from France, Britain, and the United States greatly limited the force's mandate. The Arusha accords stipulated that the "neutral international force" in Rwanda should be authorized to seize weapons and suppress "armed gangs." The Security Council, however, gave UNAMIR—the United Nations Assistance Mission in Rwanda—a far more limited assignment. Dallaire and his force were to do nothing more than "monitor observance of the ceasefire agreement," "monitor the security situation," and "report on incidents."

"UNAMIR was deployed naively and undernourished, a deadly combination," one American diplomat wrote afterward. "[This was] a gift from member states who hoped for a quick victory and were willing to take shortcuts to get there."

Dallaire sensed none of this as he prepared to take up his assignment. On his last day in New York, he paid a farewell call on his boss, Kofi Annan, and then set out to assume his new command.

Without an inkling of the horror that awaited him, he felt "beside myself with energy, optimism and a sense of purpose."

It was inevitable that events would quickly begin to close in on Dallaire, but he did not expect the first shock to come so soon. On October 21, the day before he arrived to take up his post in Rwanda, President Melchior Ndadaye of neighboring Burundi was overthrown and killed. President Ndadaye was a Hutu who preached reconciliation; his assassins were Tutsi soldiers who immediately launched a murderous anti-Hutu campaign. These events electrified Rwanda. Thousands of Hutu, many brandishing brand-new *pangas*, gathered for a terrifying demonstration in Kigali as Dallaire was arriving. Their leaders shouted that Tutsi were "the enemy," and that the Burundi coup had proved it once again. Then they led the crowd in passionate chants.

"All Hutu are one power!" they cried. "Power! Power! Power!"

Dallaire and his handful of aides moved into the Belgian-owned Hotel des Mille Collines, near the center of Kigali, but soon found themselves "less and less welcome" because "guests on vacation and soldiers on a mission do not mix very well." A couple of weeks later they found permanent space at the city's main stadium and an adjacent hotel built for athletes. The quarters were modest but spacious, the airport was nearby, and the stadium had plenty of room for soldiers, equipment, and vehicles. Most encouraging was the stadium's name, Amahoro, which means "peace" in Kinyarwanda.

On November 17, even though barely more than a hundred peacekeepers had arrived, Dallaire held a formal ceremony to inaugurate his new headquarters. By his own account he enjoyed "the Cecil B. DeMille productions of military life, showcase occasions put on to influence and impress people," and was always looking for ways "to regale, excite and sway a crowd." He intended this ceremony to be a demonstration that UNAMIR had arrived and was a power to be reckoned with.

It also had another purpose. Since arriving in Rwanda, Dallaire had not met President Habyarimana. He hoped this event would draw the president out of his shell, and it did.

Both men looked their parts as they shook hands for the first time at the main gate to the new UNAMIR headquarters. Dallaire wore his Canadian dress uniform with a UN insignia and blue peacekeeper's beret. President Habyarimana was stylish as always, in a dark suit and brilliantly shined black shoes. As flashbulbs popped, he welcomed "soldiers of the United Nations, soldiers of peace, soldiers of hope." He took no questions and quickly departed in his armored Mercedes, but his appearance seemed a promising sign. Dallaire reported that the mood was "celebratory" and the proceedings were punctuated by "much applause, cheers and laughter."

The next morning, Rwandan reality crashed into Dallaire's world. An informant telephoned UNAMIR at dawn to report that people had been massacred during the night on the hills of Ruhengeri. It turned out that just hours after Dallaire had officially opened the UNAMIR mission, death squads attacked in five places and killed more than twenty Tutsi.

This was a ghoulish welcome, a message of defiance from Hutu militants.

"The swiftness, the callous efficiency and the ruthless number of men, women and children murdered principally by machetes and bayonets, was obvious in this well orchestrated operation," Dallaire reported to New York. Two weeks later he reported another massacre in which eighteen bodies were found with "hands cut off, eyes pulled out, skulls crushed in and pregnant women cut open." Over the next few months, he sent many anguished cables like these. Their only effect in New York was to contribute to a spreading sense that he was an excitable type, overly energetic, and not experienced enough to place African violence in its "tribal" context.

Dallaire's force was crippled not only by its exceedingly weak mandate but also by its lack of basic equipment. Peacekeeping soldiers who began arriving in Rwanda—all of them from poor countries except for 450 Belgians—found no food, no place to sleep, and no lumber or barbed wire to shape their rustic campgrounds. They never had enough jeeps, tents, flak jackets, night vision aids, or ammunition. Their radios were store-bought, with no encrypting capacity. Dallaire requested twenty armored personnel carriers from the UN office in Mozambique; five months later, eight arrived, "with no mechanics qualified to operate them, no spare parts, no tools, and operating manuals in Russian." Most UNAMIR officers worked without desks, chairs, or filing cabinets. Fax paper was doled out "as if it were gold." Dallaire later estimated that he and his senior staff spent 70 percent of their time in Rwanda fighting "a petty internal war" with New York over supplies.

"We had next to nothing," he lamented. "For a moment I envied the RPF their organization, energy and resolve."

Even more debilitating than the lack of supplies were two crucial weaknesses in Dallaire's mission. First, his mandate forbade him to develop any intelligence capability. This, he saw immediately, left him "blind and deaf in the field." With no analysts to tell him what was happening in the obscure world of Rwandan politics—or on the battlefield—he was forced to rely on what strangers might or might not tell him.

Dallaire's other great handicap was the United Nations' refusal to allow him to operate a radio station in Kigali, a step he insisted was "critical" to counteracting the venom that spilled from the fanatic RTLM. Six months after arriving, he realized that "the general public still did not know what all the blue berets running around in white vehicles really meant. I cursed [UN bureaucrats] in my heart for not understanding the vital need the mission had for a radio station or for a competent public information office, so that we could build on the desire of the vast majority of Rwandans to reach out with both hands for peace."

At the end of 1993, two military operations dramatically changed the face of the Rwandan conflict. The first was the departure of the more than one thousand French soldiers who had given the regime decisive support since the first of them arrived with *Operation Noiret* three years earlier. The Arusha accords contained a clause requiring that they withdraw, and President Habyarimana gave them a glittering sendoff at the Kigali airport on December 10. A number of them—estimates range from several dozen to more than one hundred—remained quietly behind, but the departure of the main force greatly weakened the regime.

The peace accords also stipulated that the RPF should send sixteen of its leaders to Kigali to take up posts in the transitional government, five as cabinet ministers and eleven as members of Parliament. Arranging their move was one of Dallaire's first challenges. He suggested that they simply drive from Mulindi, but Kagame would have none of it. The idea that RPF leaders would be able to ride safely to Kigali, and then work there without danger, struck him as absurd. If militants were willing to kill people for the simple crime of being Tutsi, he reasoned, they would be even more eager to kill RPF leaders. Dallaire promised that UNAMIR would protect the group, but that did not impress Kagame. Given the impotence the Security Council had imposed on UNAMIR and the ruthless violence for which the *akazu* was known, it would have been dangerously naïve to entrust the safety of any RPF member to UN peacekeepers.

Kagame insisted that he would send his designated cabinet ministers and members of Parliament to Kigali only if he could deploy *inkotanyi* to protect them. This was a brazen suggestion. It meant the government would have to accept the opening of an RPF military base in the capital city. Several foreign diplomats, including the U.S. deputy assistant secretary of state for Central and East Africa, Prudence Bushnell, believed this was too provocative, and came to Mulindi to try to dissuade Kagame. He told them he was open to discussion on questions of how many *inkotanyi* he would send to Kigali, what weapons they would carry, and where they would be based. On the question of whether such a protection force was necessary, though, he would not be moved. If he could not send his own fighters to protect his delegation, he told one group of UN negotiators, "Forget about us coming to Kigali."

Finally, in a deal that Dallaire brokered, it was agreed that six hundred *inkotanyi* would go to Kigali. They and the civilians under their protection would be housed in the Parliament building, one of the largest in the city. Dallaire spent several days arranging the convoy that would take them there. He established a "clean corridor" from Mulindi and on December 28 led a three-mile-long caravan of jeeps, trucks, and buses across government lines and toward the capital.

No one expected the jubilant reception Rwandans gave this caravan. All along the road to Kigali, people turned out to wave and cheer. Some may have been RPF sympathizers, but most were simply grateful because it seemed the war was ending. They were cheering not the RPF but the idea of peace. Crowds near Kigali were so big that the government, in a last-minute adjustment, rerouted the caravan through back streets where it would not be so festively welcomed. The crowds, however, simply shifted to follow it.

"As we moved through the streets, there was only euphoria," Dallaire reported. "The RPF soldiers were cheered and showered with flowers."

As soon as this caravan arrived at the vacant Parliament building, fighters began feverishly fortifying it. Kagame had given them precise instructions and even collapsible shovels that they used to dig a maze of foxholes and bunkers, connected by roofed trenches and defended by machine guns and light mortars. In a matter of days, they transformed the building from an unused office complex to an armed camp with full perimeter defense. The RPF may have been hoping for peace, but its troops were preparing to fight again.

"I had to admire the moxie of Major Paul Kagame, who must have sensed the tactical advantage of such a site and seized the opportunity," Dallaire wrote.

Dallaire was not the only one who sensed that the balance in Kigali was shifting. Extremists who were busy planning genocide also noticed it. The appearance of a large enemy force in the heart of the capital was a sign that the peace accords were taking hold, something they could not abide. Their outrage rose when, a few days after their arrival, several carloads of exuberant RPF fighters drove out of the Parliament building and through city streets.

"The *inyenzi* have invaded the capital!" an announcer cried on RTLM that afternoon.

Militants lashed back a week later by disrupting a ceremony at which the new transitional government was to be sworn in. As dignitaries were arriving, several hundred *interahamwe* militia men suddenly appeared, waving *pangas* and shouting vivid threats. Officers of the elite Presidential Guard, dressed in civilian clothes, directed them as they terrorized moderate politicians and impotent UN peacekeepers. The ceremony had to be canceled.

Dallaire was chilled by "the speed and skill with which the mob had been provoked by the Presidential Guard." It showed him for the first time how well organized the *interahamwe* was, and how closely it worked with the police and army. He began to realize that a shadowy and exceedingly dangerous force was at work below the surface of Rwandan life. As he pondered how to penetrate it, a spectacular opportunity fell into his lap.

Late on the afternoon of January 10, 1994, one of Dallaire's aides, distraught and quivering with emotion, burst into his office and asked to speak with him privately. They stepped onto a balcony, and there the aide delivered an astonishing tale. He had found a high-ranking informant inside the *interahamwe* who wanted to tell all. This was the break Dallaire had dreamed of, and he swung immediately into action.

It turned out that the informer, code-named Jean-Pierre, had been an officer in the Presidential Guard until several months earlier, when he was named chief trainer for the *interahamwe*. Since then he had spent his time training militia gangs in "killing techniques," often at makeshift camps set up on army bases. He said he had helped draw up a plan by which death squads in Kigali could slaughter one thousand people in twenty minutes; had participated in discussions about how to kill Belgian peacekeepers, in the hope that killing a few would lead the Belgian government to withdraw the rest; and knew where the army was hiding four large caches of rifles and grenades that were soon to be distributed to *interahamwe* gangs.

"I was silent, hit by the depth of this information," Dallaire wrote. "It was as if the informant, Jean-Pierre, had opened up the floodgates in the hidden world of the extremist third force, which until this point had been a presence we could sense but couldn't grasp."

The informer offered a straightforward deal. He would reveal all he knew, ranging from the location of arms depots to details about the regime's connection to death squads, in exchange for free transit out of Rwanda and foreign residence permits for himself and his family. It was a small price for such explosive information. That night, Dallaire composed a two-page cable to New York outlining his plan to raid the arms depots, whose existence violated a provision in the peace accords that banned the storage of weapons in Kigali. As he wrote, he felt himself not only at a decisive turning point but "in seventh heaven."

A few hours later, Dallaire was stunned by a return cable from New York. It ordered him to suspend his planned raid on the grounds that it "clearly goes beyond the mandate entrusted to UNAMIR." Even more astonishingly, he was directed to prove his "neutrality" by passing all the informant's claims to President Habyarimana. His mood crashed from ebullience to outrage.

"I was absolutely beside myself with frustration," he wrote. "I had pushed for a potentially high-risk offensive, diametrically opposed to the reigning climate at the UN. No wonder the reaction had been so rapid, deliberate and unequivocally negative. Still, as understandable as the UN decision was, it was unacceptable to me in the field. If we did not react to the reality of the arms caches, the weapons could eventually be used against us and against many innocent Rwandan civilians."

Other informers came forward in the weeks that followed. None offered as much detail as Jean-Pierre had, but all warned that powerful Rwandans were methodically preparing to exterminate the country's Tutsi population. Dallaire reacted by sending a series of cables to New York pleading for permission to conduct "weapons search and seizure operations." He promised to carry them out "with concentrated overwhelming force" and avoid any that presented a "risky scenario." Annan turned down every one of these requests, insisting that the UN force "cannot take an active role" and must limit itself to "a monitoring function." Dallaire was warning that a catastrophe was imminent, but his superiors did not want to listen. He correctly sensed a "total disconnect between me and New York."

If powerful nations had shared what they knew about Rwanda, Dallaire's pleas might have had more weight. In January, while UN officials were studiously ignoring his cables, the Central Intelligence Agency was circulating a report in Washington warning that if the Arusha peace process collapsed, half a million Rwandans might die. The British government was receiving equally chilling assessments from its high commissioner in Uganda. French officials, with their deep ties to the Rwandan regime, were fully aware that some of their friends were planning a murder campaign. None of these governments, however, passed their information to others at the United Nations. Annan also made sure that no ambassadors ever saw the "genocide fax," as Dallaire's cable about Jean-Pierre came to be known.

That cable was, as one American diplomat later wrote, "a starkly written warning sign, a scarlet message of danger to civilians, to the peace process, and to peacekeepers . . . [a] graphic cataloguing of detailed plans for violence and sedition." To the few UN officials who saw it, however, it was inconvenient. It proposed an operation that would make the Rwanda mission more complex and therefore more controversial. So, to the eternal shame of the United Nations, it was buried. Jean-Pierre disappeared soon afterward. His fate has never been learned.

"We were cautious in interpreting our mandate," Annan's deputy at the UN peacekeeping office, Iqbal Riza, explained afterward, "because we did not want a repetition of Somalia."

That suited the big powers, especially the United States. The Clinton administration had been deeply scarred by the Somalia debacle and did not want to be seen as supporting other peacekeeping missions. Assuring that the one in Rwanda did not grow in size or ambition, an American diplomat later wrote, allowed officials in Washington "to point to a concrete instance of their ability to say no." Following President Clinton's lead, they kept themselves in willful ignorance of the looming crisis. Even diplomats at the U.S. embassy in Kigali found it difficult to accept the terrifying warnings they were hearing.

"People tried to tell us and tried to explain to us, or help us understand, but we just—maybe we just didn't get it," one of them later reflected. "It was just very hard to conceive of something so awful actually being meticulously planned and carried out."

The first months of 1994, in the words of a UN report, "saw increasingly violent demonstrations, roadblocks, assassinations of political leaders, and assaults on and murders of civilians." Some killings were provocatively carried out in full view of UN troops. This was a way of testing the peacekeepers. Before launching the genocide, militia leaders wanted to see whether UNAMIR would really stand quietly by while they killed people.

"I myself saw a group of those *interahamwe* grab a couple of young women in front of the [Parliament] building," recalled one of the six hundred RPF fighters who were inside. "They started cutting them with machetes. I was standing with some UN soldiers, and I started shouting, 'Look what they are doing! Why don't you stop them?' But they said, 'This is a Rwandan affair. It's Rwandans killing Rwandans. It's not our business.'"

During these months, radio broadcasts became more vividly threatening than ever, with RTLM even calling for the assassination of Madame Agathe, the conciliatory prime minister. Tutsi families in several parts of the country, fearing they would be murdered in their beds at night, began sleeping in schools or churches. Tensions were supposed to be easing during this transition period, but instead they were intensifying.

"Arusha was certainly not working," the Ghanaian deputy commander of the UN force, General Henry Anyidoho, wrote in his memoir. "One could easily smell danger everywhere in Kigali. Hell was certain to break loose. . . . Rwanda found itself sitting on a keg of gunpowder, terrified that someone would light the fuse."

Rebel leaders became restive as they watched all of this from their redoubt along the northern border. Their numbers had increased steadily during 1993, but not all of the new recruits were as strictly disciplined as veteran *inkotanyi*. Some began slipping out of their prescribed zone, raiding villages for food and supplies. Kagame sensed that his force was losing its edge. At the end of January, with his patience running out, he asked to meet

Dallaire. The UN commander flew to Mulindi by helicopter and found his host sitting on the patio of his bungalow.

"He slowly unfolded his long, angular body from one of the chairs as he stood to greet me," Dallaire wrote. "He has incredibly powerful eyes that lock onto your own, probing, searching, testing, and he wastes little time on social niceties. When we sat down, he dived right in. . . . As he spoke of the plight of the refugees, he lost some of his customary reserve and dug deep into his own experience to emphasize or illustrate his points. At times he would get up and walk around restlessly as he described growing up in a refugee camp in Uganda, always the outsider, the minority, tolerated but never really accepted as an equal. He showed flashes of anger as he relived his struggle to maintain a sense of self-worth and dignity against the crushing defeatism of the refugee camps. . . . Near the end of the meeting, he leaned toward me and said with complete conviction, 'If things continue as they are, we are going to face the situation where someone is going to have to emerge as a winner.' In other words, if the impasse was not resolved quickly, Arusha would be swept aside and the RPF would resume the war and battle it out until it achieved victory. . . . I finally rose and, with some regret, explained that my helicopter had no night vision capability and I had to be on my way. It had been amazing to see Kagame with his guard down for a couple of hours, to glimpse the passion that drove this extraordinary man."

Although Dallaire sympathized with Kagame's position, his narrow mandate greatly limited what he could do to stop the country's downward spiral. His force was always on the defensive, able to respond to daily outrages but not to shape the course of events. The peace process was collapsing. Death squads roamed with impunity, terrified civilians flooded the UNAMIR office with requests for protection, and fighters on both sides prepared to resume their war.

On the streets of Kigali and other towns, wild and often drunken young men of the *interahamwe* and other militias were savoring their power. They felt liberated by their discovery that UN peacekeepers were meek and easily intimidated. "Because the extremists now believed that UNAMIR was unwilling or unable to respond to attacks," one diplomat wrote, "they determined that they could adopt a more forceful response. If once restrained by the fear that UNAMIR might meet violence with force, extremists now speculated that the UN would rather retreat than fight, which encouraged them to think more grandly—that is, more violently."

Nothing outraged these extremists more than the fact that six hundred *inkotanyi* were dug in at the Parliament building in the heart of Kigali—and that many people seemed to accept them as brother Rwandans who had as much right to walk the streets as anyone else. The extremists were not at all pleased when Joseph Habineza, a popular athlete who was head of the national volleyball federation, organized a volleyball match at one of the city's main stadiums between a Kigali team and one from the RPF. On the appointed day, January 28, 1994, ten thousand fans turned out for what all understood was far more than a sporting event. The mood in the stadium was buoyant, and at a party afterward in the Parliament building, Habineza proposed a second match for the next day. Both teams agreed, and RPF officers sent a message informing Kagame of their decision. To their great surprise, he vetoed it and ordered his team back to Mulindi. He had received information that *interahamwe* gangs were plotting to attack the match with grenades. Like the master spy he was, he even had sources within the killer militia.

We had a lot of intelligence. We had people who were working for us. Some people, we just used to give them money. Many people needed money here. Some of them had access to good information. Some were even working for the UN. Others were working for the government. These were low-profile, ordinary people, but they happened to have access. We were running effective intelligence, for sure.

The official inauguration of the transitional government was set for February 10, but President Habyarimana announced at the last minute that he was not ready. That led Prime Minister Willy Claes of Belgium to fly to Rwanda and warn him that unless he proceeded, foreign aid to his indigent regime would evaporate. As they met, Kigali was in violent turmoil. Killers stalked the streets, rival gangs fought pitched battles, and militia leaders stepped up their distribution of weapons. Announcers on RTLM reached new peaks of frenzy.

"The grave is only half full!" one cried. "Who will help us fill it?"

On February 20 the firm-willed prime minister, Madame Agathe, tried to lead a peace march through Kigali. Thugs pelted her with stones and only backed off when Belgian peacekeepers guarding her fired volleys into the air. The next day, another gang invaded her office and held her staff hostage for several hours. Soon afterward, an outspoken Hutu moderate named Félicien Gatabazi, who had publicly accused the Presidential Guard of training death squads, was shot dead. People poured into the streets in protest, only to be met by forces loyal to the regime. Thirty-five died in the ensuing riots, among them Martin Bucyana, president of the extremist CDR, who was lynched in apparent revenge. When Dallaire called on Madame Agathe, he found her pacing nervously in her office, "like a weary lion penned up in much too small a cage." With tears flowing from her eyes, she begged for peacekeepers to protect her and her family. Dallaire promised to provide them.

As the Rwandan air filled with what one journalist called "a feeling of impending doom," President Habyarimana agonized over his course. For weeks he swung back and forth, fearing both the effect of complying with the Arusha accords and the effect of rejecting them. He agreed to establish the new transitional government on March 25, but when the time came, his *akazu* would not let him act.

"The president drove in and was in a waiting room," the UN officer overseeing the ceremony reported afterward. "However, a small technical hitch had developed. The president, through the manipulation of certain powers, wanted the CDR party to have a seat in the assembly, an issue that was unacceptable to the RPF because the CDR was a radical party that strengthened the hand of the 'killers.' The ceremony was delayed while negotiations were underway in Parliament House to resolve the impasse. By late afternoon, it was obvious that diplomacy had failed. I had to stand down my troops, to my total disappointment."

A second attempt to install the transitional regime was scheduled for three days later, but it also failed. So did a third attempt on April 2. In the meantime, the government was ordering local officials to raise their levels of readiness and have jeeps, trucks, and other equipment ready for "purposes of national defense." Military officers did their part by sending crates of *pangas* and other "farm implements" to depots around the country.

"The story of the Arusha process is an extraordinary one of a sophisticated process of conflict resolution going drastically wrong," one diplomat later wrote. "The Arusha accords themselves, having failed to resolve adequately the role of the hardliners, actually became one of the proximate causes of the genocide."

What drove so many Rwandans to become murderers during the terrible spring of 1994? Scholars have offered various theories. Some blame the culture of obedience to authority that has long shaped Rwandan life. Others focus on overpopulation, the decline of world coffee prices, or the country's long isolation, which made it easy for uneducated people to believe the monstrous propaganda they heard on the radio. One sees the root of the slaughter in "a colonization process that introduced myths of a superior race." Another finds it in "the longstanding and deeply ingrained racism of Rwandan society," which gave people "the image of the Tutsi as inherently evil and exploitative." In its essence, though, this crisis was political. The ruling elite spent three decades steadfastly refusing to confront the refugee crisis. Now the refugees were back and reaching for power. Powerful Rwandans were determined to stop them at any cost.

Violence intensified as the Arusha process reached its climax. So did the virulence of anti-Tutsi propaganda. Dallaire wrote in a cable to New York that he had an "eerie sense of something possibly coming up."

Then, during the first week in April, people listening to the "killer radio" RTLM began hearing cryptic warnings. On April 3,

Easter Sunday, an announcer twice predicted that a "little something" would happen in the next few days. "You will hear the sound of many bullets, you will hear grenades exploding," he said at one point. Later, addressing the Tutsi, he said Rwandans "hate you in unison and to the bottom of their hearts" and suggested that they begin thinking about "how you are going to escape." Then, in an extraordinary warning that he and other announcers repeated in various ways over the next few days, he added, "Even Habyarimana himself, if the citizens don't want him any more, he couldn't even get to his office. It's impossible."

Half a world away, the Security Council met on April 5 to authorize an extension of the UNAMIR mandate. It was a bad week for peacekeepers. The mission in Somalia was collapsing, and in Bosnia, Serbian troops were storming across UN lines to attack the "safe haven" of Gorazde. No one wanted more bad news, and in his report on Rwanda, Boutros-Ghali did not give any. Instead he wove a reassuring fantasy. He attributed much of the violence in Rwanda to banditry and said the country's leaders were "committed to the peace process." For weeks Dallaire had been sending urgent cables warning that the situation had become explosive—he used the phrase "deteriorating significantly" in no less than seven—but Boutros-Ghali mentioned none of them. Later Boutros-Ghali claimed that if he misled the council, it was only because he had been away from New York for weeks and was not well briefed on what was happening in Rwanda.

"We knew nothing of the true reality," Colin Keating, the New Zealand ambassador who was presiding over the Security Council, asserted afterward.

There was, however, one ambassador on the Security Council who knew Rwanda well. By the luck of the diplomatic draw, one of the countries on the Council that spring was Rwanda itself. This meant that as officials in Kigali planned the genocide, they had a direct line into the UN's inner sanctum. When the United States intervened to block Dallaire's request for a military police force, they found out immediately. They also knew that France, angry at Dallaire for accusing French troops of training the murderous

Presidential Guard and for seizing a planeload of weapons that France had sent to Rwanda in violation of the Arusha accords, was trying to have him relieved of his command. Everything they heard from New York led them to an inescapable conclusion: no matter what they did, the United Nations would not intervene to stop them.

In a perverse speech to the Security Council on April 5, Rwandan ambassador Jean Damasène Bizimana told his colleagues that they need not worry about his country because all parties to the conflict there had pledged "unwavering commitment to the peace process." Despite the horrific crimes that his government was committing at the very moment he spoke, his colleagues accorded him all diplomatic privileges. "Nobody said 'Stop it,'" one UN diplomat later marveled. "Nobody said, 'Your presence disgusts me.' Nobody said, 'Why don't you get out of the room?' There was never a real moment when they dressed him down because if you did, you would be breaking the rules of the club."

Accepting the Rwandan ambassador's mendacity was an easy way out, and that was precisely what the Security Council wanted. Minutes after he spoke, the Council renewed UNAMIR's pitifully weak mandate for another four months.

"Officials at UN headquarters in New York seemed to have no idea of how relentlessly the bloodthirsty *akazu* was planning its extermination campaign," Dallaire wrote later. "They might as well have been occupying separate universes. While Bagosora and his comrades were methodically devising ways to carry out mass murder, the UN was looking for a way to keep its peacekeeping force small and unobtrusive."

The escalating violence and increasingly virulent propaganda campaigns that erupted in Rwanda during these weeks filled some outsiders with dread. Presidents of nearby countries, alarmed by what they saw, decided to invite President Habyarimana to a summit. On April 6 he flew to Dar es Salaam. There, in a conference room at the Kilimanjaro Hotel, the fifty-seven-year-old president held a long meeting with the leaders of Tanzania, Kenya, Uganda, and Burundi. All told him he must comply with the peace accord.

"Now is the time to say no to a Bosnia on our doorstep," President Ali Hassan Mwinyi of Tanzania told him sternly. "Now is the time to ensure that hostilities are not passed on to the children of Rwanda."

This assault left President Habyarimana deeply shaken. After twenty-one years in power, he was running out of options. His only alternative was to return home and try to find his way through the violent hurricane that was sweeping across his country.

He never made it.

I went to pick up the phone and he told us, "We are seeing unusual activity in town. We have just learned that Habyarimana's plane has crashed." I said, "Are you sure?" He said, "It looks like it is the case. There is a lot of activity here. People are moving." I said, "Follow up and put your troops on standby, because most likely this will result in problems."

8

THIS IS A COUP

DUSK WAS FALLING OVER DAR ES SALAAM as a subdued President Juvénal Habyarimana bid his hosts farewell. They had demanded that he embrace a peace agreement he knew was repugnant to violent extremists within his own regime and even to his own family. He had agreed, although according to one account "there was little enthusiasm in his voice." Serious trouble, he knew, would be awaiting him back in Rwanda.

Habyarimana's private jet, a sleek Mystère Falcon, was waiting at the airport. It had been a gift from the French government, a reward for years of faithful service. One of the other guests at that day's summit, President Cyprien Ntaryamira of Burundi, who had no foreign patron rich or grateful enough to give him a plane, asked for a ride home. At the airport, the two presidents agreed with the three-man French crew that the plane would stop first in Rwanda and then fly on to Burundi. The two presidents boarded and sank wearily into the plane's deep leather seats.

Barely an hour later, the plane was descending toward Gregoire Kayibanda International Airport in Kigali, which Habyarimana had named for his predecessor after overthrowing and murdering him. The pilot circled once in the clear darkness and then, at about

8:20, made his final approach. Seconds before he would have landed, someone on the ground fired a surface-to-air missile. Immediately afterward, a second one was fired. Both hit the plane. It exploded in a ball of fire and crashed.

The largest piece of wreckage landed in the garden of one of President Habyarimana's own residences.

On that night, April 6, 1994, thousands of Rwandans were gathered around radios listening to a semifinal match in the Africa Cup of Nations soccer championship. As news of the plane crash spread, many switched to the popular hate-radio station RTLM. Its announcers were angrily reporting that Tutsi rebels had assassinated the nation's beloved leader. One urged citizens to rise up and "avenge the death of our president." Another insisted that all Tutsi must answer for the crime, and that the time had come to "finish them off."

As these messages were spilling into Rwandan homes, gangs of young killers from the *interahamwe* militia moved quickly to set up roadblocks across Kigali. Some were in place by 9:15, less than an hour after the plane crash. Squads of soldiers, many from the Presidential Guard, spread through the city, guided by death lists their superiors had prepared in advance. Copies of these lists were also posted that evening at the RTLM studio. Announcers broadcast the names and addresses of intended victims and urged listeners to find and kill them.

"There was little spontaneity in the whole process, apart from some young street urchins joining in the bloody fun," one historian wrote. "Everything went ahead with the precision of a well-rehearsed drill."

The murder of President Habyarimana is sometimes called the incident that set off the Rwandan genocide. In fact, it was the genocide's first act. It set in motion a sweeping and breathtakingly brutal campaign that had been meticulously planned in advance.

"Don't worry," Colonel Bagosora told the chief civilian at the UN mission in Kigali, the Cameroonian diplomat Jacques-Roger Booh-Booh, minutes after the plane crash. "This is a coup, but everything is under control. We will succeed and save the nation."

No one investigated the crash, not even the French, who would seem to have had reason to do so. They had, after all, lost not only one of their most reliable African allies but also the plane's three French crew members, said to have been secret service agents. Yet over the years that followed, neither France nor anyone else seriously pursued the case. Much evidence was lost or destroyed. The question of who fired the deadly missiles was never convincingly answered. There is no lack of theories. Some implicate French or Belgian agents. Others focus on Paul Kagame and his RPF, and still others on white mercenaries acting on behalf of obscure interests. The most widely accepted theory is that extremist members of the *akazu*, the president's inner circle, were responsible. They could not accept a peace accord that threatened their power and their lives.

Kagame, by his own account, was at his command post in Mulindi watching the Africa Cup of Nations match with a crowd of *inkotanyi* when his aide-de-camp signaled to him. He stepped out, and his aide motioned toward a field telephone. The commander of his battalion in Kigali was calling. He had heard an explosion, and there were rumors that President Habyarimana's plane had been shot down.

I went back and didn't tell my colleagues. Fifteen minutes later, there was another call saying it seemed like it had happened. Some people were already arriving to take refuge with them. They had been told by people from the UN that it was the case. I called the senior commanders, who were also watching the football match, to brief them. I told them, "I see it as having some kind of backlash, or severe effect. We have to have a plan."

I was thinking about our force, thinking of people on the rampage in Kigali. What about our force there and our people who had gone to join the government there? Many people had come to visit us in the north—Belgians, people from the UN—and told us that the government didn't seem to have any intention of having the transitional government established. They had been training not only the army, but various militias that wanted to carry out mass killings of Tutsi or people who were not favorable to the government. That might mean these people might go on a rampage and start killing.

I was not registering at all what scale that might be, to genocide. I suspected that it might go on, that it would endanger a lot of people, but I did not register that it would go to that extent.

Although there remains much doubt about who gave the order to shoot down President Habyarimana's plane, there is none about who directed the horrific events of the days and weeks that followed. The resolute Colonel Bagosora called his comrades to an urgent meeting two hours after the plane crash. To assure that the outside world understood what was happening, he also invited General Dallaire.

Guests arrived to find Bagosora sitting at the center of a large horseshoe-shaped conference table. When they were seated, he made a simple announcement. Military commanders had decided to take control of the country "because of the uncertainty caused by the crash of the president's plane."

"Bagosora looked at me with a straight face and said he didn't want the Arusha process jeopardized," Dallaire wrote in his account of this meeting. "I didn't trust him for a minute . . . I stressed that Rwanda still had a government, headed by Prime Minister Agathe. All matters should now be under her control. Bagosora snapped back that Madame Agathe didn't enjoy the confidence of the Rwandan people and was incapable of governing the nation."

Colonel Bagosora emerged from that late-night meeting as Rwanda's new strongman. His first act was to order the army to reinforce roadblocks around Kigali. Then he set out to consolidate his power.

Minutes after the plane crash, Madame Agathe had called Radio Rwanda and announced that she would arrive at its studio early the next morning to address the nation. Then she called Dallaire. He agreed to send fifteen peacekeepers to guard her through the night and then escort her to the studio.

The peacekeepers, ten Belgians and five Ghanaians, were maneuvering through roadblocks and marauding gangs of drunken youths while Dallaire was in his chilling meeting with Colonel Bagosora. It took them several hours to make the crosstown trip from Amahoro Stadium to Madame Agathe's home. They arrived at dawn and began taking fire immediately. Inside, the prime minister was on the telephone with a foreign radio correspondent when she heard the shooting.

"I have to leave my house now," she said into the phone. "They are coming to kill me and my family. Please tell the world to help us against these murderers."

Madame Agathe and her five children, dressed in pajamas, tried to flee over a wall and seek safety with Joyce Leader, an American diplomat who lived next door. They could not make it over, but managed to climb another wall and jump into an adjacent compound where the UN Development Program had its headquarters. The children hid themselves and were later picked up by a brave UN peacekeeper who spirited them to the Mille Collines Hotel. Madame Agathe was not so lucky. Soldiers of the Presidential Guard surrounded the peacekeepers who had come to protect her and ordered them to surrender their weapons. After radioing back to UNAMIR headquarters, and in accordance with UN protocol, the peacekeepers agreed. They were put aboard a minibus and driven away. Soldiers then smashed into the UN compound. They found Madame Agathe, ordered her to strip, and violated her with a beer bottle.

"We heard her screaming," Joyce Leader recalled. "Suddenly, after the gunfire, the screaming stopped and we heard people cheering."

The murder of Madame Agathe removed the last vestige of legal authority in Rwanda and with it all chance for peace. A few hours later it was announced that Theodore Sindikubwabo, an elderly and infirm politician, was Rwanda's new president. His cabinet did not include a single one of the moderate politicians who had been part of the "transitional government" shaped at Arusha. An RTLM announcer speculated between giggles that the moderates must have "resigned or simply wandered away."

In fact, Presidential Guard units spent much of April 7 finding and killing Hutu "traitors." Organizers of the forthcoming genocide knew that these moderates were the only group that might oppose them and stir the outside world into action. Among those whose deaths they ordered were a former foreign minister who had been the government's chief negotiator at Arusha; the deposed agriculture minister and his chief aide, both of them leaders of an opposition party; the deposed information minister, who had protested the excesses of RTLM and other media outlets controlled by the *akazu*; and a newspaper publisher who had relentlessly denounced the rise of extremist groups.

Once these and about two dozen other Hutu moderates were dead, organizers of the genocide moved on to their real targets, the Tutsi. By midday on April 7, gangs had begun the random slaughter of anyone whose identity card carried the fatal designation "Tutsi."

On that day, Rwanda began its vertiginous descent into hell.

"Rwanda was no frantic explosion of bloodlust, sparked by the anger of a people whose beloved president was shot out of the sky," the Canadian author Hugh McCullum, who in 1994 was working for the All Africa Council of Churches, wrote afterward. "Rather, it was a careful and long-prepared plan to destroy a people. Press reports at the end of 1994 were still talking about a country losing its sanity, but that is too simplistic an analysis. What happened in Rwanda was premeditated murder, a genocide with clear motives, means, and opportunity to carry it out. The plane crash was merely the signal."

Rebel leaders had expected the peace process to collapse at some point, but they never imagined that the government would try to resolve this conflict by killing every Tutsi in the country. Once that became clear, the RPF assumed a new challenge. It was already prepared to fight a war. Now it also had to do whatever it could to stop the slaughter of civilians.

On the afternoon of April 7, less than twenty-four hours after the plane crash, Kagame sent a chillingly simple message to UNAMIR that struck Dallaire as "a straight ultimatum." If the killings did not stop immediately, Kagame said, he would consider the Arusha peace accords dead and order his troops to attack

Kigali. Then, before Dallaire could reply, Kagame sent a second message. He proposed that the RPF join with UNAMIR, and even with units of the Rwandan army, in a campaign against the Presidential Guard, the *interahamwe*, and other death squads.

I told him he should give us access to the weapons and vehicles that the UN was holding, and we would use them for the protection of people. He laughed it off and said it was not possible. Later on I even contemplated capturing them by force, capturing the [armored personnel carriers] and other weapons they had, because we were short of arms and ammunition. But on second thought, in my mind, that would create even more problems, not on the ground but diplomatically.

Kagame's offer—to unite his force with UN peacekeepers in an alliance against the *genocidaires*—confronted Dallaire with a classic political and moral dilemma. By refusing, he set the stage for mass murder. Accepting, however, would have directly violated his orders and probably led to his immediate dismissal.

Military commanders who have spent their lives in disciplined armies normally consider themselves bound by orders. Dallaire's forbade him to make alliances with either side, and he followed them. He played the mediator, assuring Kagame that he was "attempting to stabilize the situation" and warning him that "if the RPF initiates action. . . . this will be deemed to be a serious cease-fire violation."

Dallaire fully understood that this threat was far too puny to deter the rebels under such dire circumstances. Desperate to find a way out, he visited Colonel Bagosora and asked whether there were any conditions under which he would cooperate with the RPF to crush "rogue units" engaged in mass slaughter. It was a predictably bizarre encounter, since both men knew that Bagosora himself was a principal sponsor of those units.

"His face contorted as he tried to maintain his façade of reasonableness," Dallaire wrote. "He told me to pass on his thanks to the RPF for the offer, but he couldn't accept. . . . There was no panic, no sense of urgency animating this man. Bagosora was either the

coldest fish in Africa or he was the ghost of Machiavelli executing a
subversive plan. . . . Out of the blue, Bagosora suddenly volun-
teered that there was something I should think about: it might be
best to get the Belgians out of UNAMIR and out of Rwanda because of the rumors they had shot down the presidential airplane. . . . This was the first time I had ever heard a senior leader
of the Habyarimana government even mention that they did not
want the Belgians here. If the Belgians withdrew, New York would
surely order UNAMIR's departure. . . . A sense of despair suddenly overwhelmed me. The path to war and slaughter was now
open."

The five Ghanaian peacekeepers who had been abducted from
Madame Agathe's home that morning returned to their base at
Amahoro Stadium, but there was no sign of the ten Belgians, and
after hearing Bagosora's words, Dallaire feared for their safety. He
began calling Rwandan officers demanding information. One told
him the peacekeepers were in a Kigali hospital, and he raced there.
He found the wards packed with people lying in pools of blood,
among them many dead and dying. An orderly directed him to a
corner in the darkened courtyard.

"I saw what seemed to be sacks of potatoes to the right of the
morgue door," Dallaire recalled. "It slowly resolved in my vision
into a heap of mangled and bloody white flesh in tattered Belgian
para-commando uniforms."

The ten Belgians had been taken to an army base where they
were shot, stabbed, and beaten to death. Afterward their bodies
were mutilated. It was a crime without parallel in the history of
UN peacekeeping. Those who ordered it had done so, Dallaire
understood, "to secure first a Belgian, then a UN withdrawal. . . .
They knew that Western nations do not have the stomach or the
will to sustain casualties in peace support operations."

Belgium exploded in outrage. Citizens and politicians demanded
that their peacekeepers be brought home. Dallaire knew this would
devastate UNAMIR and that the only way to prevent disaster in
Rwanda was to do precisely the opposite: strengthen the force with
more troops and a tougher mandate. Shortly before midnight, at

the end of a nightmarish day and the beginning of a hideous night, he telephoned UN headquarters in New York.

His boss, Kofi Annan, took the call with two senior aides.

"I went through the failures of the day—the deaths of my soldiers and the moderate political leaders, the systematic killings, the failed political meetings, Kagame's offers and threats, Bagosora's actions, the resumption of hostilities—but they had no suggestions on how to put the evil genie that had been released back in the bottle," he wrote. "I raised the possibility that the moderates might coalesce overnight and give us some opportunity to get things back under control, at least on the military side. This would require me to show support and give them some sense that the international community would provide security. They told me no. . . . I was not to take sides, and it was up to the Rwandans to sort things out for themselves."

Dallaire hung up, "feeling angry, empty, and in a state of moral and ethical conflict." Through his mind raced images of the carnage he had seen on that terrible day. From a nearby room, he heard the strains of music coming from a radio tuned to RTLM. He looked inside and saw Faustin Twagiramungu, a moderate Hutu politician who under the Arusha accords was supposed to become the next prime minister, listing intently. Dallaire asked him the title of the song. Twagiramungu told him it was a popular new one called "I Hate Hutu Who Think That Tutsi Are Not Snakes."

Hundreds of terrified Rwandans had, like Twagiramungu, made their way to the UN compound in search of sanctuary. The sight of them, and the horrifying stories they told, pushed Dallaire to make another effort to calm the breaking storm. He spent much of the next day trying to persuade RPF leaders that they should restrain their troops, maintain what was left of the cease-fire, and try to make a deal with moderates in the new regime. They were incredulous. One of them, Seth Sendashonga, asked Dallaire the obvious question.

"What moderates?" he dryly inquired.

That evening Dallaire stopped at the Mille Collines Hotel, where a throng of Rwandans and expatriates had sought refuge from the madness outside. A gang of *interahamwe* fighters, dressed in baggy, clownlike outfits and waving clubs and pistols, were erecting a roadblock near the gate. When Dallaire demanded an explanation, they told him the hotel was full of "traitors." They were allowing people to enter, presumably so they could later be killed together, but prevented any from leaving. Dallaire radioed immediately for a squad of peacekeepers to guard the hotel and then rebuked the militia men.

"I told them the hotel was under UN protection," he reported afterward. "They laughed at me."

We had a very long discussion, almost to the point of arguing. I said, "I can't understand that people are being killed, the UN can't do anything about it, and you don't want us to do anything about it. Go back, make your own assessment, get back to me, and tell me that you're in control of the situation. Tell me first that the people in the Parliament building are not in danger and that our people in the general population are not in danger. Once you tell me that is the case, there will be no need for us to do anything. But if in a very short time you can't convince me, we will have no alternative but to do something."

9

MADAM, THEY'RE KILLING MY PEOPLE

I N THE FIRST TWENTY-FOUR HOURS after President Habyarimana's plane crashed on April 6, 1994, army and *interahamwe*
units slaughtered six thousand Rwandans, among them almost every opposition figure in the country. Three days later, the
death toll had reached twenty thousand. Then the serious killing
began.

At first, many Rwandans were murdered at roadblocks. The
procedure was straightforward. People in every passing car were
made to show their identity cards. Those who were listed as Tutsi
were removed and shot or hacked to death, often on the spot. Militia men at these roadblocks, many of them drunk on banana beer,
kept their clubs and *pangas* wet with fresh blood.

It did not take long for Tutsi families to realize that venturing
onto the streets could cost them their lives. Some tried barricading
themselves into their homes, but nearly all were ultimately found
and slaughtered. Others, especially those living in the countryside,
fled into marshes, thickets, and forests. Since Rwanda is so small
and densely populated, however, there are few truly remote places,
so militia gangs were able to track and kill most who tried to
hide in the bush.

"While the Presidential Guard shot and killed, the *interahamwe* used machetes, clubs with sharp nails, grenades, knives, spears, and any deadly weapon to kill those they considered their opponents," General Anyidoho, the UNAMIR deputy commander, wrote in his account of the genocide. "It was mayhem. They ran amok and behaved as if they were possessed by some abominable evil spirit. They went about destroying lives cruelly and gleefully, without a twitch of conscience or trace of human feeling. People became numb with the shock of war. Death no longer meant anything to them. The militias went on the rampage and massacred in the hundreds and killed in the thousands. Mutilated human bodies, the charred shapes of dogs and cows, littered the streets as the ravenous dogs dragged dead bodies from one side of the road to the other, until the flesh peeled from the bones. The sight of carnage and the wanton destruction so dazed our senses and confounded our thinking that in order to stand firm and continue our operation, we had to pretend the peril was not present."

Rebel commanders, safe in their "liberated territory" along the northern border, watched this explosion of violence with mounting alarm. A cease-fire was supposed to be in effect, but with the country suddenly in a paroxysm of state-sponsored killing, the idea of respecting it seemed ludicrous. Kagame became steadily more agitated as he took radio calls from lieutenants in various parts of the country.

Our people in Kigali gathered intelligence very efficiently through the UN and their Rwandan contacts. There was also the scale at which people were coming into their position at the Parliament building. They had stories. Some even provided names: so-and-so was taken away or killed, even leaders of the government. People were rushing from their villages saying, "They're killing people!" Information rolled up very swiftly.

In those two days I was in touch with Dallaire. I told him, "I'm continuing to get disturbing news." He would try to paint a picture that this was a situation that was going to be handled. I had a long conversation with him. I said, "What are you going to do about it? What are you going to do? We know that Agathe is dead. . . . The information you have, we have. Things seem to be getting out of control. What are you going to do?"

He said he would try to talk to Bagosora and others. He said, "It would be helpful if we could work out something between you and them." I said, "What can we work out with them? They are killing! They're on a rampage!" He said, "Give me time, don't do anything." I told him, "For us, what should hold us back? Should we stay here and hope that negotiation would work? Habyarimana is no more, and the government is killing people. A totally new dynamic has come in. Naturally for us, we can never fold our hands and just see the country burning. We have our people there. Unless you convince me that you are in control of the situation, the only option left for us is to fight again." . . .

I could see the problem wasn't registering enough with him, that this was more than a serious problem, that we would have to do all within our power. He even suggested, funnily enough, that I go with him to Kigali to talk with his people. I said, "How can I go to Kigali?" He even said we could go in two helicopters, so they wouldn't know which one I was traveling in. I said that they could easily shoot down both. I just dismissed him. I said, "It is ridiculous for you even to be suggesting that I go to Kigali."

[That evening] I told him there was no alternative, and that in the morning we would be moving our forces, principally to reinforce our position at the Parliament building and then to spread out and see what we could do, to fight it out in Kigali.

Before he could launch what would be the final campaign of this war, Kagame had to deal with an unusual problem. His three-year-old son, Ivan, had been visiting him at Mulindi and was there when President Habyarimana's plane was shot down. With the rebels suddenly about to go back to war, this was no place for a child, and Kagame ordered a couple of inkotanyi to take him to Kampala, where his mother was waiting anxiously. After giving that order, he traveled to a staging area where his fighters were assembling, closeted himself with his top commanders, and began drawing up his plan of battle. A few hours later, an aide interrupted to tell him that Ivan was in a fit of anger, crying uncontrollably and insisting that he would not leave Mulindi until he could see his father one last time. Kagame adjourned his command meeting and then, although it was two o'clock in the morning, called a driver and set off toward Mulindi. He arrived shortly before dawn, ate breakfast and spent the rest of the morning with Ivan, sent him on his way, and was back with his troops by midafternoon.

To solidify his hold on northern Rwanda and open a path to the capital, Kagame decided to send a column of several hundred *inkotanyi* to attack the northern town of Byumba, which lies in foothills below Mulindi. His battle plan was a variation of the "baited trap" tactic he had used with repeated success during three years of war. Rebel fighters took up positions on three sides of Byumba and attacked government positions with artillery and small-arms fire. The defenders, who had a larger and better-equipped force and were guided by French advisers, replied with intense barrages of their own, but only after the rebels had retreated back into surrounding banana groves. When the counter-attack ended, the *inkotanyi* surged back, this time with a full-scale infantry charge. That forced defenders to fall back through the only route the rebels had left open. Other rebel units were lying in ambush there and cut the government force to pieces as it tried to escape.

After taking Byumba and leaving a small force there, this column turned south toward Kigali. Fighters had no jeeps or helicopters and so moved on foot. For nearly a week, almost without a break, hundreds of *inkotanyi* trekked and fought their way through enemy territory, carrying weapons and heavy packs up and down one hill after another. They were singing as they departed and were singing when they arrived to reinforce their six hundred comrades at the Parliament building. General Anyidoho found their march a testament to the "stubborn stamina" of fighters who "had trained on the hills so well that they were always strong and battle-ready."

Dallaire was even more impressed. He had already come to admire the rebels' high levels of morale and discipline and believed their greatest advantage was that they "were fighting for a cause they believed in, whereas the [government] soldiers were killing for the sake of killing, not knowing or caring why." After hearing of the successful march these "tough, young and dedicated" rebels had carried out, he went further. The power they had shown left him with "no doubt" the RPF would win the war.

It also led him to conclude that Kagame was "possibly one of the greatest practitioners of maneuver warfare in modern military history."

While the singing column of rebels was jogging from Byumba to Kigali, two other columns were approaching from different directions. One moved along the western border with Tanzania and then turned sharply eastward. Another came from the opposite direction, through Ruhengeri, fighting as it advanced. By the evening of April 12, all three had arrived at the outskirts of Kigali.

As rebel fighters closed in on the capital, militia leaders were opening caches of hidden weapons and distributing pistols, grenades, and *pangas* to their men. The government issued a statement exhorting all citizens to "fight the common enemy." Urged on by radio broadcasters, people in the streets began chanting a familiar threat: *Umwanzi wacu ni umwe! Turamuzi, ni umututsi!* It means, "Our enemy is one! We know him, he is the Tutsi!"

World leaders leaped into action as soon as violence burst over Rwanda following the fateful plane crash. Their action, however, was not aimed at stopping either the fighting or the mass murder. It was to evacuate expatriates. A French plane full of commandos landed on April 9, followed closely by units from Belgium and other European countries. These soldiers swept through the country, gathering up their terrified nationals. American diplomats did the same, rounding up U.S. citizens and packing them onto buses. Within a few days, thirty-nine hundred people of twenty-two nationalities had been evacuated from Rwanda. All embassies except the Chinese closed indefinitely.

At places like the Mille Collines Hotel, many expatriates tried to bring Rwandan friends or coworkers with them onto rescue trucks. Each time, the Rwandans were pushed away. Most were killed soon afterward, sometimes within sight of departing whites. These scenes were heart-rending but also heavily laden with symbolism. They grimly foreshadowed the world's response to this exploding crisis.

Except for these unpleasant episodes, the evacuations went smoothly. Militia gangs were under orders not to obstruct them. Foreigners who were being whisked out of the country, after all, might otherwise have become witnesses. The *genocidaires* knew that their departure would make the killing easier.

"I saw how aggressively the French were pushing black Rwandans seeking asylum out of the way," Dallaire wrote after watching one evacuation. "A sense of shame overcame me. The whites, who had made their money in Rwanda and who had hired so many Rwandans to be their servants and laborers, were now abandoning them. . . . The swift evacuation of foreign nationals was the signal for the *genocidaires* to move toward the apocalypse. That night, I didn't sleep at all for guilt."

One small group of Rwandans did manage to escape. The French made room on their evacuation planes for key members of the *akazu*, including the director of the RTLM hate-radio station and twelve members of the assassinated president's family. Most prominent among them was the elegantly vituperative Madame Habyarimana, who had done as much as anyone to bring her country to this moment. When she landed in Paris, an official delegation was waiting to greet her with bouquets of flowers. Soon afterward the French government gave her a check for the equivalent of $40,000, designated as "urgent assistance for Rwandan refugees."

The sight of planes from Europe arriving empty while UNAMIR was so desperately short of supplies, and then departing full of white people, drove Dallaire to distraction. His messages to New York became increasingly angry. Time and again, he insisted that weakening or dismantling UNAMIR would lead to disaster and begged that it be strengthened instead.

Dallaire's force was pitifully small. It had never reached its authorized strength of 2,548, and its only fully equipped unit, made up of 450 Belgians, was preparing to depart. That left Dallaire with an "excellent" 800-man contingent from Ghana; 40 Tunisian military police who "never shirked their duty and always displayed the highest standards of courage"; and 1,100 "nearly useless" Bangladeshis. Even this modest force might have stopped the killing if it had been allowed to try. Its mandate, however, forbade that. Militia leaders knew that the peacekeepers were under orders not to interfere with murder. Some even seemed to enjoy doing their "cutting" while peacekeepers were watching. These scenes turned UNAMIR into a haunting symbol of impotence.

Late on the night of April 12, an aide to Boutros-Ghali called Dallaire to give him the news he was dreading. Belgium had decided to withdraw its peacekeepers from Rwanda. The aide, breaking off the conversation several times to confer with someone else in the room—Dallaire believed it was Boutros-Ghali himself—gently suggested that this might be a good time to shut down UNAMIR altogether. He asked Dallaire to "consider future options" and then hung up.

Torn by a welter of emotions, Dallaire climbed slowly up to the roof of his headquarters and spent several minutes watching tracer bullets streak across the sky.

Dallaire never managed to persuade his superiors in New York that the violence in Rwanda was state-sponsored terror. They insisted on the entirely mistaken view that it was the result of clashes between two armies. By that logic, the RPF was the guilty party since its fighters had broken the cease-fire by seizing Byumba and assaulting Kigali.

Despite a barrage of international pressure, Kagame refused to call off his offensive. The Tutsi were facing genocide, and his fighters were the only force capable of preventing their total extermination, so he naturally found the idea of a cease-fire absurd. When Prudence Bushnell called from Washington to urge him to stop fighting, he replied simply, "Madam, they're killing my people." Then he sent a cable to the Security Council that was the first document to give this murder campaign its true name.

"A crime of genocide has been committed against the Rwandan people in the presence of a UN international force, and the international community has stood by and only watched," it said. "Efforts have been mobilized to rescue foreign nationals from the horrifying events in Rwanda, but there has been no concrete action on the part of the international community to protect innocent Rwandan children, women, and men who have been crying for help."

Over the next few days, Dallaire fell into what he later described as "a sort of trance." His Belgian peacekeepers were packing up and his superiors in New York were suggesting that he begin closing his mission. Yet just outside his headquarters, bulldozers were methodically digging pits and pushing piles of bodies into them. This dissonance left him "beside myself with anger."

"As Canadian soldiers fought tooth and nail against the Germans [in World War I], King Léopold III of Belgium and his ruthless lackeys kept millions of black Africans in Rwanda and all of the Great Lakes region of central Africa under subjugation, raping these countries of their natural resources," he raged. "And here I was, in the heart of one of the Belgian king's former colonies, watching Belgian troops abandon us in the midst of one of the worst slaughters of the century because they had lost some of their professional soldiers to soldierly duties."

The mood in New York could not have been more different. Diplomats at the Security Council saw Rwanda as a backward land plagued by vaguely understood "ethnic conflicts" and "age-old hatreds." Caught in their stiff paradigm, they insisted that UN peacekeepers must above all, and in all circumstances, remain neutral. The alternative—cooperating with a rebel army to stop a genocide—was beyond their imagination.

"The Rwandan Patriotic Front (RPF) was the only force that had a chance to stop the genocide," wrote Michael Barnett, a professor at the University of Wisconsin who spent 1994 working at the American mission to the United Nations. "The Council refused to recognize this truth because doing so would lend diplomatic support to one of the two combatants, thereby departing from its sacrosanct position of neutrality."

Events in Rwanda during mid-April presented the Security Council with a stark choice. Dallaire wanted several thousand new peacekeepers to help him protect terrorized civilians, especially throngs that had flooded into Amahoro Stadium and other UN compounds. French, British, and American diplomats in New York wanted just the opposite: a quick withdrawal. Boutros-Ghali was traveling in Europe, and nothing symbolized his lack of interest more vividly than his refusal to return to New York as this crisis exploded.

On April 21, the Council met to make its decision. After perfunctory debate, it approved an ignoble document called Resolution 912. It was a veritable lexicon of diplomatic mendacity. First it proclaimed that the United Nations was "shocked," "appalled," and "deeply concerned" by the bloodshed in Rwanda and was determined "to remain actively seized of the matter." Then came the blow. All peacekeepers were to be pulled out of Rwanda, except for 270 whose main job would be to observe the slaughter.

The vote was unanimous, with even the three Security Council states that favored forceful intervention—Nigeria, New Zealand, and the Czech Republic—agreeing to emasculate the peacekeeping force rather than face the alterative of eliminating it altogether. The result might have been different if Annan or Boutros-Ghali had shown Security Council members copies of Dallaire's cables. They made it unmistakably clear that what was happening in Rwanda was, as Michael Barnett later wrote, "a very well planned, deliberate, and conducted campaign of terror initiated principally by the Presidential Guard." The message Boutros-Ghali sent to the Security Council before its vote, however, said something very different: that the violence in Rwanda was "indiscriminate" and the product of "chaos."

"Boutros-Ghali possessed information that illuminated the nature of the crimes," Barnett wrote. "He had an obligation to transmit that information to the Security Council, but failed to do so."

This vote stunned UNAMIR officers in Kigali. The first to hear it, by telephone from New York, was General Anyidoho, the barrel-chested deputy force commander from Ghana. He erupted in anger, screaming at the official on the other end of the line that the decision was outrageous and demanding that the Security Council reverse it. After hanging up, he fell into a chair, "while confusion and desperation engulfed my mind." Dallaire, who was out of the office, was equally devastated when he returned to the bad news.

"Henry," he said after his rage had passed, "we have failed."

Dallaire later said that if he had been allowed to bring the five thousand Canadian soldiers he commanded in Quebec with him to Rwanda, "there wouldn't have been a genocide." Peacekeeping operations, however, do not work that way. The effect of the Security Council vote, as Dallaire immediately understood, was that "suffering, mutilation, rape and murder" would now proceed "with the help of the member nations of the only supposedly impartial world body."

"Ultimately, led by the United States, France and the United Kingdom, this world body aided and abetted genocide in Rwanda," he concluded. "No amount of its cash and aid will ever wash its hands clean of Rwandan blood."

General Anyidoho, one of Africa's most respected military commanders, at first refused to accept what the Security Council had done. Only slowly did he force himself to grasp that it had indeed voted to reduce UNAMIR to almost nothing. Then he made a decision that violated both the resolution passed in New York and the laws of Ghana. He told Dallaire—and his superiors back home—that the remaining 356 Ghanaian peacekeepers would stay with UNAMIR, regardless of what anyone said. Dallaire gratefully accepted. His Bangladeshi troops had left along with the Belgians, so this was his force for the rest of the war: the Ghanaians, 40 steadfast Tunisians, and several dozen observers and staff officers, for a grand total of 456 peacekeepers.

"We had a job to do, and we could not simply run away," General Anyidoho explained later. "The figure of 456 that we kept in Rwanda throughout the war was illegal. It cannot be seen in any Security Council resolutions. We simply held on to it stubbornly, since we could not do otherwise. It was a command decision."

Over the weeks that followed, two historic campaigns unfolded in Rwanda. In one of them, armies fought for control of the country. While their war raged, government soldiers directed militia gangs on killing sprees that took thousands of lives each day. These campaigns were separate but intimately related.

"The more the *inkotanyi* pushed into the country, the more we would massacre their Tutsi brothers on their farms to deter them and halt the advance," Joseph-Désiré Bitero, who led a death squad during the genocide, explained afterward. "That was how we saw the situation."

Dallaire and others later criticized Kagame for moving his forces too slowly. They suggested that if he had struck Kigali more quickly and with all his power, he might have won the war sooner and thereby saved many lives. Kagame has replied that given conditions on the ground, especially his own lack of vehicles and other supplies, he could not possibly have moved any faster.

We had weaknesses that we did not create ourselves, that were created by circumstances, by the UN or whatever. Even for the troops we had, we did not have sufficient weapons. This was created by the kind of sanctions they had put on us. The UN had deployed troops along the border with Uganda to make it difficult for us to get weapons across.

Second, Dallaire himself knows how hard he worked to prevent us from moving from our base. I had long debates with him. But we had already decided to move. . . . We had to move on foot to reinforce troops at Parliament building, and then continued to send forces to take positions around Kigali. But this movement happened under constant, daily fighting and attacks. Every force we sent had to come fighting, all the way up to Kigali. Third, the government actually had so many troops in Kigali. Some of these forces would come moving back to Kigali as they fought us. I think we were outnumbered by four or five times. We didn't have enough weapons or troops. . . .

The situation was so fluid that we had to spread out. We had different objectives to tackle at the same time, and we were confronting very seasoned and committed fighters. The challenge was a much bigger force. We moved as fast as we could, and as fast as any force could have done. I'd bet no other force could have done it as fast as we did it. We

were carrying weapons on our shoulders, we had no vehicles, and we
were fighting all the way.

With nearly every foreigner gone from Rwanda and the UN
force reduced to almost nothing, the killers set out to complete
their job. They did so with terrifying efficiency, determined to continue until not a single Tutsi was left alive. Huge regions of the
country became charnel houses. In the western district of Kibuye,
the Tutsi population was reduced from 252,000 to just 8,000. In
nearby Bushiru, it fell from 70,000 to 2,000. Mutilated bodies piled
up faster than they could be buried. They lay along roads and outside homes, decomposing in the sun as engorged dogs and rats fed
on them.

"Whole families are exterminated," the International Committee of the Red Cross, which normally takes great pains to preserve
its neutrality, declared in the most powerfully worded statement it
had ever issued. "Babies, children, old people and women are massacred in the most atrocious conditions, often cut with a machete
or a knife or blown apart by grenades or burned or buried alive.
The cruelty knows no limits."

Radio fueled this frenzy with ceaseless calls to complete the
genocide. "Kill Tutsi in their homes, their parents and their children—and don't forget the unborn fetuses!" an RTLM announcer
urged his listeners in one broadcast. Another warned that if Tutsi
rebels were allowed to win, they would not only kill all Hutu but
eat them, favoring "certain organs such as the heart, liver, and
stomach."

These broadcasts became such an integral part of the murder
campaign that Dallaire asked his superiors in New York to silence
RTLM, either by bombing its transmitter or jamming its transmis-
sions. Lacking the resources to do either, UN officials passed
his request on to Washington. The Americans found reasons to
refuse. First the cost of an airborne jamming operation, estimated
at $8,500 per hour, was deemed excessive. Second and even more
maddening, lawyers at the Pentagon concluded that any act to
silence RTLM might violate Rwanda's sovereign right to control

radio broadcasts within its borders. These concerns were held to outweigh the fact that by mid-May, when Dallaire made his plea, more than eight thousand Rwandans were being killed every day, incited and directed by radio broadcasts horribly stuffed with the epithets of war.

As the killings continued, Tutsi in every part of Rwanda tried frantically to find hiding places. Tens of thousands fled to churches, but many clergymen did not protect them. One of the most shocking aspects of the Rwandan genocide was how eagerly the clergy supported it and how many of the bloodiest massacres were committed inside churches.

At the time of the genocide, about two-thirds of Rwandans were Catholic. Many bishops were close to the regime. Archbishop Vincent Nsengiyumva of Kigali had been the chairman of the central committee of President Habyarimana's political party for more than a decade and often wore a medallion bearing the president's portrait on his cassock while saying Mass. A few days after the genocide began, he and other Catholic bishops issued a statement supporting "the new government" and urging Rwandans to "respond favorably" to its program.

"By not issuing a prompt, firm condemnation of the killing campaign," Human Rights Watch later concluded, "church officials left the way clear for officials, politicians, and propagandists to assert that the slaughter actually met with God's favor."

Some Rwandan priests, nuns, and lay religious workers saved lives, often at the cost of their own, but a remarkable number cooperated with the killers. Some turned away Tutsi families seeking refuge. Others gave refuge but then summoned militia gangs to kill those they were sheltering. In the western town of Nyange, Reverend Athanse Seromba's church was packed with two thousand refugees when a gang of *interahamwe* killers appeared on April 12; he showed them how to break in and after they had finished throwing grenades into the huddled crowd encouraged them to finish off survivors. At a church complex in the south-central town of Nyamata, ten thousand people were slaughtered; a visitor who arrived soon afterward reported that "blood and body parts were everywhere" and that the roof "looked like a sieve" because of holes made by fragmentation grenades. In nearby Ntarama, militia men drilled through the wall of a church where several thousand people were hiding and threw grenades in; no one escaped.

Atrocities like these defiled churches across Rwanda and drove some RPF soldiers to extremes. Nowhere did they strike back more brutally than at the country's oldest cathedral, in the central town of Kabgayi. Early in June, an RPF squad found an enormous pile of bodies there and went berserk, killing Archbishop Nsengiyumva, who was said to have drawn up lists of Tutsi priests for the *interahamwe* to murder, and thirteen other priests and bishops. It was one of the worst RPF atrocities of that period, reflecting what Dallaire called "a total breakdown of military control."

"The rebel troops had been traveling for weeks and encountering everywhere the effects of the Hutu scorched-earth policy, and they were well aware that the church was very intimate with the Habyarimana family and members of the former government," he wrote. "Quite simply, they killed the princes of the church out of vengeance, their discipline frayed to the breaking point by the atrocities they'd witnessed."

Thousands of desperate Tutsi converged at school compounds, but most fared no better than those who had chosen churches. In one especially grotesque case, more than two thousand survived for several weeks at the École Technique Officielle, a Catholic school near Kigali that was guarded by UNAMIR soldiers. Then one day, the soldiers were ordered by their Belgian commander to withdraw. As they packed their gear, bloodthirsty *interahamwe* killers drew near, waving their weapons in anticipation. The refugees' last act was to beg departing peacekeepers to shoot them so they could be spared the agony of being hacked to death. The peacekeepers refused. Moments after the last truckload of them departed, the *interahamwe* stormed the camp and killed everyone inside.

"Where is your UNAMIR?" the killers tauntingly asked their victims as they hacked away. "They've abandoned you, haven't they?"

At one church in Kigali, Sainte Famille, which was packed with refugees, militia gangs showed up every few days, killed a few people, and then left. One day the army fired mortar rounds into the churchyard, killing thirteen people and leaving the grounds littered with body parts. No one knew when the killers would end their attrition campaign and storm the church, as they had done elsewhere. Then, one night in mid-June, a company of *inkotanyi* staged a daring rescue mission. They slipped through enemy lines under cover of darkness, made their way to the church, rounded up all six hundred people inside, and led them to safety. They had to fight their way back through government lines, but they managed to do it.

"The mission began as a clandestine operation," Dallaire reported with evident admiration, "and ended as a fully supported running battle with carefully planned artillery support—and, by the standards of any military force, ranks as a first-class rescue."

A far larger number of refugees, more than twelve thousand, were huddled inside Amahoro Stadium. They were under UN protection, but all knew that this protection was only symbolic and that killers could storm in at any moment. One day soon after the rescue mission at Sainte Famille, the RPF sent a quiet message into the stadium advising people there to be ready to move. That night, squads of *inkotanyi* mysteriously appeared. They warned the refugees, many of them sick, hungry, and dehydrated, that they must maintain absolute silence. All did. Over a period of several hours, they moved in a ghostly mass through the outskirts of Kigali toward a zone under rebel control. There was not so much as a baby's cry. All made it to safety.

One of the most extraordinary dramas of the hundred-day genocide unfolded inside the Mille Collines Hotel. In peaceful times this had been a relaxing place, attracting a mix of tourists, expatriates, and well-to-do Rwandans who came to sit by the pool with their friends and families. When the killing began, about twelve hundred people, including many prominent personalities, flooded in and packed every room to overflowing. Outside, drunken gangs of *interahamwe* militia men kept a threatening vigil. Only a small

UNAMIR force kept them at bay. No one knew when they might be given the order for which they were waiting, the one that would propel them through the hotel gate to kill everyone inside.

Dallaire repeatedly demanded that government commanders allow him to extract the Mille Collines refugees, and finally, after the siege had been underway for three weeks, they agreed. He decided to start by bringing seventy of the best-known refugees to a rebel-controlled zone outside Kigali. Pandemonium broke out at the hotel when UNAMIR trucks arrived. The selected passengers were packed inside as others wailed in lament. Soon after the convoy left the hotel, it was surrounded by gangs of militia men who had been alerted by broadcasts on RTLM. Passengers were pulled out and beaten. Four hours later, after many frantic radio calls, the gangs withdrew. The convoy sped back to the hotel, its mission aborted but all passengers still alive.

Pressure on the Mille Collines refugees never eased. Dallaire saw them as "live bait being toyed with by a wild animal, at constant risk of being killed and eaten." He went to bed every night fearing that he would wake up to news that all had been slaughtered.

The government had cut off telephone service to the Mille Collines, but no one on the outside realized that it had a separate fax line. Huddled refugees spent their days sending faxes to anyone and everyone they knew in the outside world, desperately appealing for help. These messages produced a stream of calls to Rwandan leaders insisting that the refugees' safety be respected.

"There was so much concern for the lives of those who were in that hotel," General Anyidoho wrote afterward. "They were mainly Tutsi, the elite of Rwandan society. They were very well-known internationally, and UNAMIR received faxes, telephone calls, and personal messages every day regarding their safety."

Other factors also helped the Mille Collines refugees survive. General Anyidoho gave much credit to the force of "brave Tunisians" who manned the hotel's front gate and calmed the *interahamwe* at several points when they seemed ready to launch their assault. The hotel's resourceful manager, Paul Rusesabagina, who took over after his Belgian bosses fled, did his part by appealing to army commanders who, amazingly, continued to show up to drink at the hotel. The combination of these factors—heavy international pressure, a force of highly effective UNAMIR guards at the gate, and Rusesabagina's skillful mix of bribery and persuasion—produced a miracle. Not a single person who hid in the Mille Collines was killed, making it a monument unique in the history of the Rwandan genocide.

Outside the hotel gates, slaughter continued without pause. Killers fell into a routine, as if they were doing their traditional *umuganda* without caring that this time, instead of clearing brush or repairing roads, they were taking human lives. This was not a campaign of secret killing like the one Nazis carried out in hidden camps. Murderers did not have the antiseptic distance that allows bomber pilots and missile controllers to kill without seeing their victims suffer and die. Soldiers and *interahamwe* militia men "cut" people they had known for years, neighbors with whom they had dined just weeks earlier and with whom they had shared work, play, and comradeship. Doctors killed their patients. Husbands killed their wives. Teachers killed their students. A dean at the National University in Butare killed five professors.

"It's a war against the Tutsi because they want to take power, and we Hutu are more numerous," Robert Kajuga, commander of the *interahamwe*, told a British journalist as the killing reached a peak. "Most Tutsi support the RPF, so they fight and they kill. We have to defend our country. The government authorizes us. We go in behind the army. We watch them and learn."

Never in modern history had so many people been killed so quickly. If one million people were slaughtered in the hundred-day spree—the government later put the death toll at 1,074,017—that means there were 10,000 murders on an average day, 400 per hour, more than 6 each minute. Some victims spent their last moments on the telephone pleading desperately with Dallaire to rescue them.

He was the only person they could call for help, but he had none to offer.

"It was terrifying and surreal to be talking to someone, sometimes someone you knew, listening to them pleading for help, and being able to do nothing but reassure them that help was on the way—and then to hear screams, shots, and the silence of a dead line," he wrote. "You'd hang up in shock, then the phone would ring again and the whole sequence would be repeated."

Weapons that fueled this campaign flowed steadily into Rwanda. Most came from France. "These arms shipments were either going directly from a French para-statal and being shipped by a French company, or were being subcontracted by a series of French middlemen and front companies," the British journalist Christian Jennings wrote after an exhaustive investigation. "All were going to a regime that had left such legacies as the mountain of corpses in the church at Ntarama. The [army] and the *interahamwe* were being resupplied."

A handful of brave foreign journalists remained in Rwanda as the slaughter proceeded, but editors back home buried many of their stories. They believed the same lie that had swayed the Security Council: that what was happening in Rwanda was a spasm of "ethnic conflict," not a government-sponsored extermination campaign. That allowed them to relegate reports from Rwanda to the back pages and concentrate on covering stories with greater public appeal. In the United States, these included the murder case against former football star O. J. Simpson, the saga of figure skater Tonya Harding, and the suicide of rock musician Kurt Cobain.

The limited space that most of the world's media devotes to Africa was taken up during those days by reports about the inauguration on May 10 of Nelson Mandela as the new president of South Africa. That story was inspirational; news from Rwanda would be a litany of horror. More than twenty-five hundred journalists from around the world covered Mandela's inauguration. During the week they were in South Africa, killers in Rwanda were dumping five thousand bodies into the Akagera River each day.

A rabble that Gérard Prunier described as "a *lumpenproletariat* of street boys, rag-pickers, car-washers and the homeless unemployed" carried out the Rwandan genocide. One Rwandan witness described them as "bizarrely dressed in combat fatigues covered with strange symbols painted in the red, green and black of the

Rwandan flag, and carrying machetes or carved replicas of Kalashnikov rifles. . . . [They] looked and acted like clowns, but they were as deadly as devils." Left behind by society and with nothing to lose by joining the frenzy, this underclass saw the murder campaign as a rare chance to kill and steal with official sanction.

"This social aspect of the killing has often been overlooked," Prunier wrote. "For these people, the genocide was the best thing that could have happened to them. They had the blessings of a form of authority to take revenge on socially powerful people, as long as these were on the wrong side of the political fence. They could steal, they could kill with minimum justification, they could rape, and they could get drunk for free. This was wonderful. The political aims pursued by the masters of this dark carnival were quite beyond their scope. They just went along, knowing it would not last."

The clearest clues about the killers' motivation come from the killers themselves. A decade after the genocide, the French journalist Jean Hatzfeld conducted long interviews with several of them in their prison cells. Their words are chilling but illuminating.

Pio: The first person, I finished him off in a rush, not thinking anything of it, even though he was a neighbor, quite close on my hill. In truth, it came to me only afterward: I had taken the life of a neighbor. I mean, at the fatal instant I did not see in him what he had been before. I struck someone who was no longer either close or strange to me, who wasn't exactly ordinary any more—I'm saying, like the people you meet every day. His features were indeed similar to those of the person I knew, but nothing firmly reminded me that I had lived beside him for a long time.

Adalbert: The radios exaggerated to get us all fired up. Cockroaches, snakes—it was the radios that taught us those words. The evil-mindedness of the radios was too well calculated for us to oppose it.

Pancrace: Rule number one was to kill. There was no rule number two. . . . When you receive a new order, you hesitate but you obey, or else you're taking a risk. When you have been prepared the right way by the radios and the official advice, you obey more easily, even if the order is to kill your neighbors. The mission of a good organizer is to stifle your hesitation when he gives you instructions. For example, when he shows you that the act will be total, and will have no consequences for anyone left alive, you obey more easily.

Élie: I think the idea of genocide germinated in 1959, when we killed lots of Tutsi without being punished, and we never repressed it after that. . . . We told ourselves that Tutsi were in the way, but this idea was not always in our thoughts. We talked about it, we forgot about it, we waited. We heard no protests about our murders. As with farm work, we waited for the right season. The death of our president was the signal for the final chaos. But as with a harvest, the seed was planted before.

Joseph-Désiré: You will never see the source of the genocide. It is buried too deep in grudges, under an accumulation of misunderstandings that we were the last to inherit. We came of age at the worst moment in Rwanda's history. We were taught to obey absolutely, raised in hatred, stuffed with slogans. We are an unfortunate generation.

For them it was "These Tutsi are coming back and taking over!"

Some of them had never seen us, and they did not expect us to be human beings. They thought we were some subhuman beings.

It was hard for anyone in Rwanda to hear that the Tutsi could come again and join the army, join the police, or even join government. They were used to having a government without a single Tutsi. . . . It was something completely alien to them.

Some people, even today, have still not understood it. They have not in their minds accepted what has happened. In their minds, they are still trying to understand.

10

WHAT A FARCE

A S GENOCIDE PROCEEDED and bodies piled high in Rwanda, world leaders and their representatives at the United Nations seemed blithely ignorant of the unfolding horror. Their ignorance, though, was a matter of choice.

"Everybody knew, every day, live, what was happening in this country," Philippe Galliard, who ran Red Cross operations in Rwanda during the genocide, said afterward. "They cannot tell me that they didn't know. They were told every day what was happening there. Don't come back and tell me, 'Sorry, we didn't know.' No. No. Everyone knew."

During April, May, and June of 1994, reports from UNAMIR commanders, from refugees who managed to escape Rwanda, and from aid agencies—later confirmed by satellite photos—left no doubt that the regime was waging a gigantic campaign of mass murder. The Vatican, which has a comparatively modest intelligence network, was denouncing "genocide" in Rwanda even before the end of April. Press reports from the scene of the horror were available to anyone who wished to read them, like one in *Le Nouvel Observateur* that described the killings as "not an ethnic war between hostile tribes, but an organized and systematic extermination of those opposed to the government, which is armed and supported by France." Those with the power to intervene had to ignore much evidence as they pretended this murder campaign was not happening.

Officials at the United Nations—and in Washington, Brussels, London, and other capitals where leaders studiously ignored the Rwandan genocide—have given all manner of explanations for their failure to act. Some have gone so far as to apologize. There remains, however, a deep puzzlement about how so much of the world was so eager to turn away from such a great tragedy that might have been prevented with only a modest application of force.

"The fact of willful indifference continues to amaze," Michael Barnett wrote in his study of how the world reacted to this crisis. "The Rwandan genocide is not only about the evil that is possible. It is also about the complacency exhibited by those who have the responsibility to confront that evil."

Among these were Americans, who like to think of themselves as defenders of the oppressed. During the entire three-month period when genocide was underway in Rwanda, President Clinton not only failed to act but never even convened a high-level meeting to discuss Rwanda. On June 6 he flew to Normandy to attend a solemn ceremony commemorating the fiftieth anniversary of D-Day. In his speech he paid moving tribute to soldiers who died there to keep others "from tyranny's reach."

"If we should ever falter," he said, facing a granite memorial to the fallen, "we need only remember you."

As Clinton was delivering this evidently heartfelt message in Normandy, his aides at home were under orders not to call the Rwandan genocide by its name. Much was at stake, since recognizing that genocide was underway would have given the United States a moral obligation—and, under the 1948 Genocide Convention, a legal right—to intervene. When confronted with evidence, Clinton's aides argued that there had been "acts of genocide," but not genocide itself. It was as easy as lying.

"As a responsible government, you don't go around hollering 'genocide,'" the American ambassador to Rwanda, David Rawson, reasoned from his temporary office in Washington after the number of Rwandans killed had passed half a million. "You say that acts of genocide may have occurred, and they need to be investigated."

On June 10, the day after Rawson made that statement, his formulation reached its Orwellian peak at a State Department press briefing. A spokeswoman, Christine Shelly, drew the assignment of defending it to a group of incredulous reporters. Her exchange with one of them, Alan Elsner of Reuters, became an instant classic in the history of doublespeak.

> Elsner: How would you describe the events taking place in Rwanda?
>
> Shelly: Based on evidence we have seen from observations on the ground, we have every reason to believe that acts of genocide have been committed in Rwanda.
>
> Elsner: What's the difference between "acts of genocide" and genocide?
>
> Shelly: As you know, there is a legal definition of this. There has been a lot of discussion about how the definition applies under the definition of genocide contained in the 1948 convention. If you're looking at that for your determination about genocide, clearly not all of the killings that have taken place in Rwanda are killings to which you might apply that label. . . .
>
> Elsner: How many acts of genocide does it take to make genocide?
>
> Shelly: Alan, that's just not a question I'm prepared to answer.
>
> Elsner: Well, is it true that you have specific guidance not to use the word "genocide" in isolation, but always to preface it with these words "acts of"?
>
> Shelly: I have guidance which, which, to which I—which I try to use as best I can. I'm not—I have—there are formulations that we are using that we are trying to be consistent in our use of. I don't have an absolute categorical prescription against something, but I have definitions. I have phraseology which has been carefully examined and arrived at as best we can apply to exactly the situation and the actions which have taken place.

As the United States and other world powers were doing all they could to turn away from this crisis, rebel fighters inside Rwanda advanced steadily. They captured new territory and issued a call for

recruits that swelled their force to more than twenty thousand fighters, many of them boys fleeing from rampaging death squads. By
the beginning of June, more than half of this force was fighting
around Kigali.

After three and a half years in the field, the Rwandan Patriotic
Front was approaching final victory.

French leaders were horrified by this prospect. To them, the
idea of "losing" Rwanda was not just anathema but incomprehen-
sible. Not since France's humiliations in Indochina and Algeria had
they faced the prospect of such a complete defeat. "Considerable
political and geo-strategic interests are hidden behind the Rwandan
heap of corpses," warned a confidential memo that circulated
among senior French officials. "The region cannot be left in the
hands of an English-speaking strongman completely aligned to
American views and interests."

Determined to prevent this outcome, President Mitterrand sent
a steady stream of supplies to the Rwandan army. In mid-June he
dispatched two forty-ton planeloads of weaponry, including thousands of the fragmentation grenades that *interahamwe* killers liked
to throw into huddled crowd of refugees. In the end, though, no
amount of armaments could stop an attacking enemy with the advantages the RPF enjoyed.

"The force was very cohesive and disciplined," General Anyidoho, the deputy UNAMIR commander, wrote in one report. "They
received no salaries, but had a vision and purpose for going into
guerrilla warfare. . . . The RPF soldier was alert, day and night.
He lived a life of deprivation but remained steadfast to his cause.
He received no pay, wore any type of clothes and footwear, but his
determination to have a home and a country spurred him on to
success."

While hoping for a reversal on the battlefield, France also pressed
its case diplomatically. At the United Nations and in world capitals,
French diplomats argued that Rwanda needed a cease-fire to prevent the "Khmer Noir" from storming to power. This was another
effort to portray the violence in Rwanda as what Foreign Minister
Alain Juppé called "tribal war." By then, however, much of the

world had realized that this was untrue, so France's call for a cease-fire produced no result. A Czech diplomat at the United Nations compared it to "wanting Hitler to reach a ceasefire with the Jews."

On May 17 the Security Council, eager to seem more concerned about Rwanda than it really was, passed a resolution authorizing the expansion of UNAMIR to fifty-five hundred troops, but no new troops were actually raised. On June 8, the council authorized a six-month extension of the mission's toothless mandate. There was a surreal quality to these votes. They were scenes in an anti-septic, stylized drama that unfolded without any relation to what was actually happening in Rwanda.

"What a farce," Dallaire fumed. "I couldn't help but feel that we were a sort of diversion, even sacrificial lambs, that permitted statesmen to say that the world was doing something to stop the killing. In fact we were nothing more than a camouflage."

By mid-June the RPF had captured the central town of Gitarama and was besieging Ruhengeri in the north. Fighting around Kigali became so intense that the interim government fled; it established itself in Gisenyi, located conveniently on the Zairian border. Huge masses of Hutu—two million, by one count—were on the roads, fleeing the advance of rebels they believed wanted to kill them as punishment for the genocide.

Rwanda's army, despite all the weaponry and field support France provided, proved unable to turn the tide of battle. French efforts to organize world pressure for a cease-fire also failed. President Mitterrand, however, felt the weight of Francophone history on his shoulders and was still determined to prevent an RPF victory. On June 14 he announced to his cabinet that he had made a momentous decision: he would order the French army to Rwanda.

Although its official mission would be to "stop genocide," all understood that this deployment was a last-ditch effort to save a besieged client regime.

Three days later, with Mitterrand's decision still secret, the French activist Bernard Kouchner, a founder of Doctors Without Borders, arrived in Kigali to see General Dallaire. When the two men met, Kouchner said he had come as Mitterrand's envoy. He began with a ritual lament of the world's shameful failure to help Rwanda, to which Dallaire nodded a weary assent.

"Then he floored me," Dallaire wrote later. "The French government, he said, had decided that in the interests of humanity, it was prepared to lead a French and Franco-African coalition force into Rwanda to stop the genocide and deliver humanitarian aid. They would come in under a [robust] UN mandate and set up a safe haven in the west of the country where people fleeing the conflict could find refuge. He asked me for support. Without a pause, I said *Non!*—and I began to swear at the great humanitarian using every French Canadian oath in my vocabulary. He tried to calm me with reasons that probably sounded high-minded to him but, considering the track record of the French in Rwanda, struck me as deeply hypocritical. Surely the French knew that it was their allies who were the architects of the slaughter. . . . I could not believe the effrontery of the French. As far as I was concerned, they were using a humanitarian cloak to intervene in Rwanda, thus enabling the [government] to hold on to a sliver of the country and retain a slice of legitimacy in the face of certain defeat. . . . That night, French media reported France's plan to deploy troops in Rwanda, news that was soon picked up by RTLM and other local stations and broadcast to the nation. The defending forces in Kigali went mad with joy at the prospect of imminent rescue by the French. Their renewed hope and confidence had the side effect of reviving their hunt for genocide survivors, which put in further jeopardy those who had remained in refuges in the few churches and public buildings that had been left untouched. The *genocidaires* believed the French were coming to save them, and that they now had carte blanche to finish their gruesome work."

Diplomats and world leaders, increasingly embarrassed as news of the slaughter in Rwanda spread, were eager to be seen as responding. When France offered to send a "humanitarian mission," they embraced the idea. On June 22 the Security Council voted unanimously—but with five abstentions—to approve a sixty-day French mission. In Rwanda, radio announcers reported jubilantly that French soldiers were coming to save the nation from the dreaded *inkotanyi*. French flags went up on many buildings in Kigali. People ran ecstatically through the streets, shouting, *"Vive la France!"*

The next day, French troops began arriving at airstrips in eastern Zaire and crossing into adjacent areas of Rwanda. Their force was formidable: nearly three thousand soldiers, most of them members of elite marine, paratroop, special operations, and Foreign Legion units, along with five hundred support staff. With them they brought a fleet of helicopters, four fighter-bombers, one hundred armored vehicles, and a battery of 120mm machine guns. Kagame reluctantly agreed to accept their presence, but under two conditions: that all of them stay within their self-proclaimed "Turquoise Zone" along the western border with Zaire and Burundi, and that all withdraw after their sixty-day mandate expired. The French agreed. They wanted to make the Turquoise Zone, which covered about one-fifth of the country, a protected area for the besieged regime—and perhaps turn it into a platform from which the regime could storm back to power.

"The French," one European reporter wrote, "were met as liberators. They were heroes to the Hutu. The welcome party was outrageous, because it was clear that these European soldiers were saving the killers from all the demons that their violence and murder against the Tutsi had stored within their psyches. Freshly made *tricolores* waved from every hand. Men chanted and danced with their machetes and bottles of beer. The crime had been committed, and now it was being absolved; they would be safe."

Over the next several weeks, one and a half million people flooded into the Turquoise Zone. Most were Hutu who had actively or passively participated in the genocide. Many came with their weapons, which the French allowed them to keep. Among them were not just thousands who had joined in "cutting" campaigns, but also some of the genocide's chief organizers. Announcers from the RTLM hate-radio station even turned up with their transmitter, so the station was able to continue broadcasting as if nothing had happened. Dallaire was outraged. Nonetheless he obeyed an order to brief General Jean-Claude Lafourcade, commander of the arriving French force.

"While I was talking about the ongoing genocide, his staff were raising points about the loyalty France owed to old friends," Dallaire reported. "They refused to accept the reality of the genocide and the fact that the extremist leaders, the perpetrators, and some of their old colleagues were the same people. They showed overt signs of wanting to fight the RPF."

In the weeks after the Turquoise Zone was established, French diplomats in New York tried but failed to win Security Council permission to expand its size. Then they lobbied for permission to occupy it beyond the authorized sixty days. That effort also failed. Nor did French intervention intimidate the RPF, which was proceeding methodically toward victory. On July 4, after government forces withdrew from Kigali, the first rebel patrols entered.

France insisted that the Turquoise Zone was serving a humanitarian purpose. By various estimates, between ten and seventeen thousand Tutsi lives were saved there, although these may have been balanced by the number killed after they were drawn from hiding places to French patrols, which then departed and left them exposed. France's claim that the Turquoise Zone was created to save innocent lives, though, was only for public consumption. It was above all a safe haven for the defeated regime and its army.

Dallaire was unable to block the establishment of the Turquoise Zone and unable to prevent the collapsing regime from finding refuge there. As it became clear that the RPF would soon win the war, he turned his attention to the catastrophe he saw ahead. Leaders of the old regime were preparing to cross from the Turquoise Zone into Zaire, taking their army, militias, and more than a million Hutu civilians with them. Dallaire realized that if this happened, "extremists likely would be running the camps in no time, preparing for revenge."

"If such a scenario came to pass," he warned, "it would not only guarantee instability in Rwanda for years to come but destabilize the entire region."

When Dallaire learned that a senior State Department official, Brian Atwood, an undersecretary in charge of foreign aid, was passing through Nairobi, he flew there. They met in a conference room at the Nairobi airport. Dallaire began by unrolling a large tactical map. He used it to explain that huge numbers of Hutu, including many perpetrators of the genocide, had fled into the Turquoise Zone and were about to cross into Zaire, where they would regroup and prepare to fight again. This, he warned Atwood, would produce "a cataclysmic regional problem," and the only way to stop it was to deliver large amounts of food and other aid to Rwanda so people there would have reason to stay. Only the United States, Dallaire insisted, had the capacity to find and quickly deliver this aid. Atwood said he would do what he could, but Dallaire understood from his tone that it would be nothing. His frustration boiled over the next day, when UN officials sent him a cable asking precisely what supplies he would like to have.

"Tell them to send me food, fuel, medical supplies, and water for two million people, and we will work out the details of distributing it!" he barked at an aide. Later he was told that officials reading his pleas to New York dismissed them because they thought he was seeing the situation in a "simplistic fashion."

While the defeated regime was settling into its new home in Zaire, a Pakistani diplomat, Shaharyar Khan, arrived in Kigali to take over as chief of the UN political office. Dallaire took him on a tour of the city, and what he saw stunned him.

"There were corpses and skeletons lying about, picked bare by dogs and vultures," he reported. "The scene was macabre, surrealistic and utterly gruesome. Worse was to follow. We went to the [Red Cross] hospital, where hundreds of bodies lay piled up in the garden. Everywhere there were corpses, mutilated children, dying women. There was blood all over the floors, and the terrible stench of rotting flesh. . . . I did not throw up, I did not even cry. I was too shocked. I was silent. My colleagues who had lived through the massacres were hardened. They had seen worse, much worse."

On July 18, with no enemy left to fight, the RPF declared a unilateral cease-fire. After nearly four years in the field, it had taken over a country that was shattered morally, politically, socially, and economically. This was an improbable victory, and it brought far more than simply a change of power. It stopped a genocide in progress.

With the war over, the spirits of some UNAMIR peacekeepers began to break. Every day, every hour, they had been forced to face unfathomably brutal proof of their impotence and failure. The scale of the carnage they saw around them, the ever-present smell of decomposing bodies, the sight of animals feeding on human flesh, the madness of the killers they saw every day, and above all their inability to stop the slaughter drove some of them beyond the breaking point. General Dallaire's military assistant, Brent Beardsley, who was UNAMIR's specialist in rescue missions and had often found the people he came to rescue already dead, collapsed into paralytic delirium and had to be sent home. The second-ranking official in the UN political office, Mamadou Kane, went berserk at UNAMIR headquarters and had to be physically restrained until he could be evacuated. Finally, inevitably, it was Dallaire's turn.

"I would just sneak away and then drive around, thinking all manner of black thoughts that I wouldn't permit myself to say to anyone for fear of the effect on the morale of my troops," he later wrote about his mood at the end of July. "Without my marking the moment, death had become a desired option. I hoped I would hit a mine or run into an ambush and just end it all. I think some part of me wanted to join the legions of the dead, who I felt I had failed."

In an effort to remind himself that life could sometimes triumph over death—a proposition that contradicted everything he saw around him—Dallaire had bought himself a small family of goats. He let them roam freely inside Amahoro Stadium, took time to feed them, and sometimes even allowed himself to smile as he watched them play. One day a Ghanaian soldier rushed into his office to say that a pack of wild dogs was attacking the goats. He erupted in outrage, grabbed his service revolver, ran into the stadium, and began firing wildly at the dogs. By the time his clip was empty, he had not hit any of them. He returned to find Shaharyar Khan and several dozen of his soldiers staring silently at him.

"They said nothing," he wrote later, "but the message was clear: 'The general is losing it.' . . . The next morning I told Khan I had to leave. He was sorry but also not surprised. The guilt I felt was incalculable."

When we took over, there was nothing we could with certainty rely on. Even we ourselves—we had inherited a situation, but what capacity did we have, in an organized way, systematically, in order of priorities, with the means we had, to deliver anything? Absolutely nothing. Even some of our cadres handling issues like those—it was their first time. People have had to build their capacity over these years. You would put somebody there and say, "What do you think we should do about this?" And they would just tell you, "I don't know." It was a very serious, chaotic situation.

What I was trying to do was at least create some sense of sanity. We had to start from somewhere.

SOMETHING REALLY FILLS UP IN YOUR MIND

A S WAR AND GENOCIDE ENGULFED RWANDA during the spring of 1994, Paul Kagame was in constant motion. He designed the three-pronged assault on Kigali and then spent his days either in radio conference with his officers or shuttling among fighting units. Every night he adjusted his battle plan according to the outcome of that day's combat. From a temporary headquarters, he would summon a group of officers, review the course of the war in their sector, send them back to their men with fresh orders, and then move on.

Kagame directed his army's final assault from a makeshift camp within sight of Kigali. On July 4 he awoke there to news that during the night, government forces had withdrawn from the city. Cautiously, he ordered several platoons to move toward downtown. They reported that although there were still some pockets of resistance, the bulk of the army was indeed gone and government offices were empty. A couple of days later, after the city was secure, Kagame set out with a company of soldiers to see for himself. He found a scene to harrow up the soul. Kigali was ghostly and abandoned, its streets littered with debris and human remains.

It was the worst thing I had ever seen or experienced. More important and more challenging was knowing that we still have to deal with this. We had defeated the murderers, we had taken over, but now we had an equal or bigger challenge. Where do we start? How do we bring back some sense of life? What do we do about the effects created by so many dead? Something really fills up in your mind, like filling a glass until it starts overflowing.

Everyone who made it to Kigali in July of 1994, including every RPF soldier, was shocked first by the piles of decomposing corpses. In the city, on the outskirts, and in most of the surrounding countryside, bodies lay in ravines, in half-dug graves, and heaped atop each other inside churches. Many were mutilated. Some had been exposed to the elements so long that they were nothing more than bleached bones. Others still had enough flesh on them to attract dogs, rats, and vultures. The literal stench of death, a putrid and nauseating cloud from which there was no escape, hung heavily over corpses, deserted streets, and stunned *inkotanyi.*

The murder of so many people in such a short time, under such horrific circumstances, was and remains too overwhelming a reality for most Rwandans to grasp. Searching for its meaning, many have entered remote realms of the human soul and felt themselves collapsing under the weight of pain, loss, and desperation. During that summer of 1994, though, most Rwandans were still too dazed to reflect on anything. Even RPF commanders felt disoriented, unable to comprehend what had happened. It was too far beyond the scope of human imagination.

This devastation counted Rwanda itself among its victims. More than 10 percent of the population had been murdered in the space of a hundred days. At least another 30 percent had fled or was fleeing. There was no government or security force. Even if any institutions had remained, there would have been no one to run them. Nor was there any cash; leaders of the old regime had fled with every cent in the treasury, a sum reported to have included $100 million in gold from the national bank. Others had stripped offices of everything they could carry, from furniture and computers to windows, door frames, and electric switches. Even Kigali's fleet of green-and-white municipal buses, recently donated by Japan, was gone.

Beyond the impenetrable tragedy of mass murder, beyond the looting that had left Rwanda with no foundation on which to build a new state, lay another, more ghostly challenge. It was buried within the broken hearts and spirits of survivors. They moved, walked, and spoke, but few were truly alive. To call them traumatized would be to trivialize their anguish. People knew them as *bapfuye bahagazi*, the "walking dead."

Rwanda was in a state of extreme shock, crippled to the point of catatonia. The rotting human remains that lay impiously scattered about the countryside, like debris after a great storm, and the haunted souls of those still breathing were apt symbols of this shattered nation. After four years of war that culminated in mass murder, the RPF had inherited a wasteland.

At this moment the "international community," which had so resolutely ignored the genocide, finally awoke to Rwanda's tragedy. It did so in a deeply perverse way. Instead of reaching out to the survivors of genocide, it embraced the perpetrators.

In mid-July a great mass of Hutu, organized by their mayors and convinced that the new regime was bent on killing or enslaving them, surged out of Rwanda. Many were *genocidaires*, but because they were now suffering refugees—and because television cameras recorded their suffering—the world saw them as victims. It was an easy mistake for uninformed outsiders to make. Their reasoning was simple: there had been a tragedy in Rwanda, and in its wake, huge numbers of refugees had poured out of the country. It seemed logical to presume that the refugees were survivors of the genocide.

The truth was exactly opposite.

"The first time most of the world got a real glimpse of the massive human suffering that occurred in Rwanda in 1994 was through the media coverage of the refugee camps," an Anglican priest, John Rucyahana, wrote later. "Very few people understood that the real tragedy of Rwanda was a million dead Tutsi—there had been no television coverage of that. In modern society, if a catastrophe isn't shown on television news, it doesn't exist. The world felt sorry for the huddled masses in the camps, but no one told them that the same men who helped to engineer the torturous deaths of a million men, women and children were running the camps."

Most of the defeated *genocidaires* and their families headed for Zaire, just as General Dallaire had predicted. They overran the border town of Goma, a placid resort on Lake Kivu, and in a matter of hours turned it into one of the most awful places on earth. One who was there reported "a human torrent of incredible proportions." Another called it "the exodus of a nation."

"It was a staggering sight of unrelieved horror," a Canadian relief worker wrote. "Overnight the pleasant resort town of about 150,000 on the shores of a lovely lake became an indescribably filthy, sick city of eight hundred thousand or more desperately poor people stretched out to the edges of the lake as far as one could see through the stench and smoke."

No one knows the exact number of Hutu who fled Rwanda in the summer of 1994, but the United Nations High Commission for Refugees later described this as the largest dislocation of a population its aid workers had ever witnessed. Within a few days after it began, there were seven hundred thousand refugees in Goma and another four hundred thousand at other camps in Zaire. More than half a million more flooded into Tanzania. Another quarter million chose Burundi. These are all countries that have difficulty caring for their own people, and they were immediately overwhelmed. Lack of hygiene and clean water in refugee camps made the spread of epidemic disease inevitable. By the end of July, three thousand people were dying of cholera every day in the wretched camps around Goma. These were, by one account, "the largest refugee camps in history for such a short time from one nation. . . . [they] quickly became another version of hell."

Among the refugees were tens of thousands of fighters from the defeated government army, the Forces Armées Rwandaises, now known as the ex-FAR, and from the *interahamwe* and other militias. Many had fled into the Turquoise Zone fully armed, and when it came time for them to cross into Zaire, they took their weapons with them. They had been defeated on the field of battle but were still a fully equipped fighting force—and eager to reclaim Rwanda.

"On the 17th of July," according to one account, "twenty thousand [ex-FAR] soldiers arrived in Goma as intact fighting units. Their leaders said they had run out of ammunition to fight the RPF, but they in any case retained much of their hardware. Their equipment included sixty-two armored cars with either cannon or machine guns mounted, over 250 mortars, twelve howitzers, thirty-five air defense weapons, fifty anti-tank guns and six helicopters, some of which were armed as gunships. Once regrouped with the militias, in September 1994 it was estimated that the total forces available around Goma from the losing side in the Rwandan civil war numbered between 34,000 and 37,000 fighting men. . . . For the hard core of defeated Hutu leaders and their murderous militia cohorts, the determination to finish off a bloody mission which had begun in April 1994 remained undiminished."

Aid workers who descended into Goma quickly realized that a fully equipped army was thriving inside the refugee camps. This presented them with a dilemma. Humanitarian practice forbade them to aid fighters, but if they did not cooperate with ex-FAR and *interahamwe* commanders who controlled the camps, they would not be allowed in. They responded by striking a tacit deal with the commanders that allowed an urgent relief mission to proceed. It also set the stage for another war.

The UN High Commission for Refuges and other aid agencies agreed to feed, clothe, and shelter tens of thousands of exiled soldiers at camps in Goma and elsewhere; hired scores of them as translators, drivers, and warehouse workers; and even, according to *New York Times* correspondent Howard French, allowed them to ship weapons on relief flights. "Foreign staffers from UNHCR and the World Food Program winced as they acknowledged. . . . that crated weapons and ammunition, along with uniforms and other supplies, were making their way into the bellies of the shiny old DC-3s, the aluminum skinned workhorses that were ferrying sacks of food and medicine to the desperate Hutu," French wrote after visiting an airstrip in eastern Zaire. "They insisted this was the price of cooperation from the local authorities."

During the summer of 1994, sympathy for Hutu refugees suffering in the Goma camps seized many hearts around the world. Americans, responding to horrific images they saw on television, pushed President Clinton into action. On July 21 the United States launched a perfectly coordinated three-day airlift that General Dallaire, watching from inside Rwanda, called "massive and magnificent." Waves of American planes landed at Goma and disgorged four thousand fully equipped soldiers. They spread out through the camps, feverishly building shelters, digging latrines, and distributing relief supplies worth nearly half a billion dollars. This was a focused military deployment on a scale that could have stopped the genocide. Only now, however, did the world discover the plight of Rwandans— and it discovered not the victims but the defeated *genocidaires*.

"Yesterday the genocide of the Tutsi by the Hutu militia, today the genocide of the Hutu refugees by cholera?" mused Alain Destexhe, secretary general of Doctors Without Borders. "This comparison, which one can see widely used in the press, puts on the same plane things that have nothing to do with each other. Through this confusion the original, singular and exemplary nature of the genocide is denied, and the guilt of the perpetrators becomes diluted in the general misery."

Leaders of the new regime in Kigali were naturally outraged by this injustice, but it reinforced one of their fundamental beliefs: that the outside world, especially when it speaks through aid agencies and human rights groups, is ignorant, misguided, often malicious, and utterly lacking in moral authority. The world had been silent when their parents were chased from Rwanda beginning in 1959. It had abandoned them during decades of exile. While genocide raged, it turned away. Seeing it now open its heart and purse to *genocidaires* reinforced the scorn that Kagame and his comrades felt for—they spat out the phrase with venomous sarcasm—the "international community."

"Must we get cholera to be helped?" wondered one frustrated RPF leader in Kigali.

The teeming chaos of sprawling refugee camps had its surreal counterpart in an empty Rwanda. Half of the Rwandans who had been alive three months earlier were either dead or in flight. Whole regions were left without a single inhabitant.

One of the few Western journalists who traveled through Rwanda in the weeks after the genocide, Fergal Keane of the BBC, found it eerie to the point of desolation. "Nothing moved or breathed anywhere that we could see," he reported. "With nobody to cultivate the fields, the weeds and wild grasses were sweeping across the countryside. . . . Only the breeze rising occasionally to flatten the rampant grass and the steady growl of our diesel engines interrupted the silence. It was as if a giant Hoover had been directed down from the heavens and sucked away everything that moved."

Amid this spectral emptiness, the new regime in Kigali struggled for its bearings. Its first decisions were about how to govern the country. Kagame, as commander of the victorious army, had the power to name himself president. He knew instinctively, though, that after decades of relentless propaganda, Rwandan Hutu were not ready to accept a Tutsi, an *inyenzi,* as their leader. Instead the RPF decided to form a government along the lines of the one agreed to at Arusha. Each political party was given the posts assigned to it in the Arusha accords, although the former governing party was excluded. The new president was one of the most prominent Hutu in the RPF, Pasteur Bizimungu, a former accounting professor who had served the old regime for years before defecting. Another Hutu, Faustin Twagiramungu, who was not an RPF member, became prime minister. Most cabinet ministers were also Hutu.

Kagame, then thirty-six years old, became an army general, minister of defense, and vice president.

"That was very necessary after all the tension and the genocide," said Joseph Karemera, who became minister of health in the new government. "We knew we were unpopular. They thought we were going to kill them. So we said, 'Let's do the reverse to win their confidence.' Some of us had difficulty believing this. Paul was saying, 'Bring them in.' We'd say that these were very bad people. He said, 'Bring them in and teach them to be good.' Some of us were annoyed. All of us had relatives killed. It was difficult to think that way at that time. But he knew how to convince us."

On July 19 several hundred people gathered inside a heavily guarded salon in the bullet-scarred Parliament building to watch this "broad-based government of national unity" take office. It was a somber ceremony, without a trace of the euphoria that normally accompanies a revolutionary victory. When it was over, newly named ministers began trying to orient themselves. Most had no staff, no offices, no equipment, no vehicles, and no money. Several set up shop outdoors and held their first meetings under trees. The challenge their new regime faced was daunting beyond imagination.

Security was paramount. Establishing some semblance of order and some basic structures of administration was very important. There were cries of "What should we do about the victims, people affected by the genocide directly?" There were also cries of "What do we do with these killers?" They caused the genocide, yet these were the ones we had to work with, to integrate. We had to try to make the survivors, the victims, live together with the perpetrators in such a confused way, even before you [were] able to identify who was responsible for what—who is a victim, who is not, to what extent, who is responsible for what happened, to what extent—and really finding you had nowhere to start from. You had to create it. . . . Constantly, every day, I was involved in meetings. I would hardly sleep. Out of twenty-four hours, I was probably having three or four hours of sleep. It is work, it is moving, it is meeting, it is fighting—fighting everybody, even fighting my own people.

French troops withdrew from the Turquoise Zone in mid-August, but as they did, another threat to Rwanda's new regime was taking shape. The defeated army, settled into camps in Zaire, was receiving planeloads of weaponry from Bulgaria, Israel, South Africa, and the Seychelles. RTLM was back on the air from a studio near Goma. Rwanda's war was not yet over.

"Former soldiers and militia men have total control of the camps," a team of UN investigators reported at the end of 1994. "It now looks as if these elements are preparing an armed invasion of Rwanda."

The job of repelling this threat fell to Kagame. It was a quick turn of fate, transforming him almost overnight from an insurgent to a counterinsurgent. By some measures his position was strong. The power of a state lay behind him, and his army was potent and combat-hardened. Against these advantages, however, lay a harsh reality. Most people in Rwanda, even after the mass exodus, were Hutu and hated the new regime. They would welcome the ex-FAR and *interahamwe* as liberators. That gave commanders in the Zaire camps good reason to hope they might be able to retake power in Kigali.

"They are said to be recruiting thousands of teenagers from the refugee camps and bringing the regular and professional militias back into fighting trim, ready to wage guerrilla and conventional war to force the Kigali government into a power-sharing arrangement with the extremists, something Vice President Paul Kagame has vowed will never happen, even if it means another war," one visitor to Goma reported. "New recruits are being whipped into shape to invade Rwanda and 'finish' their job."

Kagame's new regime asked the United Nations to disarm these camps or at least move them away from the Rwandan border, as required by humanitarian practice, but to no avail. Ambassador Madeleine Albright of the United States, who at President Clinton's behest had worked assiduously to assure that the United Nations did not intervene in Rwanda during the genocide, was also the key figure in assuring that it took no steps to assert control of refugee camps in Zaire. She blocked a Security Council effort to establish a special police force to patrol the camps, arguing that its "objectives, rules of engagement and precise costs" were unclear and that the few UN soldiers in the area should function "within existing resources." That meant there was no force able to challenge the authority that ex-FAR and *interahamwe* commanders exercised over the camps. Several aid groups withdrew in protest.

"It is now ethically impossible for us to continue abetting the perpetrators of the Rwandan genocide," Doctors Without Borders declared in a statement as it withdrew.

As the new regime confronted this growing threat from the army it had just defeated, it also had to deal with an angry and resentful population. It did not always do so gently. Some RPF soldiers who returned to their hills and found their families massacred sought out and killed those whom they believed were responsible. Others attacked anyone they thought had supported the genocide in any way.

During the last three months of the war, as the genocide raged, nearly ten thousand recruits had joined the RPF. In the weeks after the war ended, another ten thousand enlisted. Most were quite unlike the tightly disciplined *inkotanyi*. Many were teenagers whose families had just been killed and who were burning with homicidal rage.

"There was not time to do proper screening," one officer lamented as reports of revenge killings multiplied. "We needed a force, and some of those recruited were thieves and criminals. Those people have been responsible for much of our trouble today."

The new government reluctantly accepted evidence that some of its soldiers had committed revenge killings, but insisted that instead of being blamed for tolerating them, it should be praised for keeping them to a minimum. "Most of our soldiers are highly disciplined," Seth Sendashonga, the new interior minister, told an American reporter. "Many of them are young men who went home and saw their mothers and fathers were killed. You must appreciate that the discipline you are seeing here is phenomenal."

Every Tutsi family in Rwanda had been torn horrifically apart. Wounds were deep and fresh, emotions were volatile, and the country was in chaos. This was not an environment conducive to forgiveness or reconciliation.

Everybody was saying, "These are the people who did it." That was the kind of outcry there was in '94 and '95. We had to put our foot down. . . . If we had been weak, we could easily have had another genocide. The anger was out there with some of these young people who had lost their parents, their relatives, and with arms, and having fought and defeated these genocidal forces, feeling there has to be justice. Yet justice couldn't be delivered so easily or so fast. And therefore there was an argument to carry out justice by themselves—and we having to stand in between and say, "Wait a minute. Let's create some sanity and some sense of order from which you can start building." It was such a task.

Not everyone is convinced that Kagame did all he could to prevent revenge killings. Some believe he grossly understated the number of victims and allowed perpetrators to go unpunished. They doubt that attacks like one near the southern town of Kibeho, where soldiers fired into surging crowds and killed as many as two thousand displaced Hutu in April of 1995, could have been launched without official sanction.

"It was never RPF policy, but there was a certain tolerance," a member of that era's RPF leadership later recalled. "It was kept to a certain level, but there were serious abuses."

Kagame replied to these charges by insisting that the number of atrocities was greatly exaggerated, and that all offending soldiers had been arrested, tried, and punished. Evidence suggests that many were indeed brought before military tribunals. Their trials, however, were conducted quietly and out of public view, apparently because the RPF did not want details of killings by its militants to be made public. When an American diplomat asked for information about the case of one arrested officer, he was summoned to the defense ministry and curtly told that such information was "a matter internal to our military" and that his inquiry was "an intrusion on our national sovereignty."

Justice may have been done in the wake of many crimes committed by RPF soldiers, but it was not seen to be done. Because the government gave Rwandans little information about military trials, many who witnessed or knew of crimes by soldiers never learned whether anyone was punished for them. Conducting these trials in semisecrecy may have helped protect reputations, but it also led some Rwandans to conclude that the government tolerated or even encouraged mass killings by its soldiers. The American military attaché in Kigali, Colonel Richard Orth, reported that RPF leaders seemed "reluctant to chastise and hold accountable selected senior officers who had endured hardships as guerrilla fighters and fought well during the civil war." Kagame, though, swore he had done everything humanly possible to control his soldiers.

I was following soldiers so that they didn't get involved in excesses, because many of them were really aggrieved and would have done anything. I had my own escort killing people. Later on he killed himself. We had many officers doing that. They knew that if they did that and we got hold of them, they would be punished. But some of them were so aggrieved and angry that they would kill people and then kill themselves. You can imagine also such a case being blamed on me, but what could I do? If someone is even willing to take his own life after satisfying his anger, what can I do to prevent that? It gets reported or interpreted as if there was a conspiracy or a plan to kill people. The way it is brought up, it is as if we were there fighting people and trying to kill. There is a big difference between someone who is angry and ready to do the wrong things out of that anger, which is justified in a sense, and a killing that is politically motivated. There is a huge world of difference.

As reports of revenge killings continued reaching Kigali, however, the government's Hutu ministers became alarmed. "When these start to accumulate, we can no longer view them as isolated," the increasingly outspoken interior minister, Seth Sendashonga, told a British journalist at the beginning of 1995. A few months later his close political ally, Prime Minister Twagiramungu, went even further, denouncing the government of which he was the titular head for allowing "bandits" to take control of the country.

"We cannot go on lying to the international community and Rwandan people, saying these are only isolated incidents," he told a radio interviewer. "People have been killed and the government's instructions have been ignored. We cannot accept the existence of two governments in this country."

Kagame took this attitude as defiance, and it provoked the first crisis in the new regime. Rival factions emerged. On the surface, they were arguing over the specific question of how to investigate charges against RPF soldiers. This confrontation, however, was about far more than military conduct. It was a duel for power.

The new regime embraced two circles of authority. On the surface it was dominated by Hutu, which sent the world a reassuring message that this had not been a Tutsi revolution after all. Although most cabinet ministers were Hutu, however, all of the important ones were assigned RPF militants as deputies. Kagame and his inner core of ex-refugees from Uganda never wavered in their conviction that by deposing the old regime, they had earned the right to shape Rwanda's future.

That did not sit well with Sendashonga, who had a hard-charging personality and was once described by General Dallaire as "extremely self-confident, ambitious and aggressive." His work as interior minister took him to every part of the country, and during his trips he made a point of showing solidarity with local Hutu, asking about abuses committed by soldiers, and building a network of supporters. All understood that he was tacitly challenging Kagame's authority. Kagame never took kindly to such challenges. In mid-1995 he forced Sendashonga and Prime Minister Twagiramungu out of the cabinet, along with three other ministers.

Rwanda's official news agency denounced the departed ministers as "Hutu supremacists" who had shown "unprecedented levels of arrogance." The American ambassador in Kigali, Robert Gribbin, reported that most Rwandans believed they were ousted "because they dared push for a greater role for Hutu—that is, more democracy—in the system." All understood that Kagame was behind their removal, and that he was sending a clear message: I rule.

As the regime narrowed its political base by dumping prominent Hutu ministers, insurgents based in Zaire intensified their campaign of cross-border raids. By the end of 1995 they were attacking every night. Sometimes they stormed into Tutsi homes and massacred people in their beds. They assassinated mayors and other local officials. In some towns they seized schools, forced students to separate according to their group identity, and then slaughtered the Tutsi. When students refused to separate, as happened at several schools, insurgents killed them all.

"Buses would be stopped at roadblocks, emptied of their passengers at gunpoint, then Hutu separated from Tutsi," one correspondent wrote. "The Tutsi would be shot or hacked to death. . . . Operating with supply lines back in Zaire, the ex-FAR and *interahamwe* were able to mount sustained attacks in the northwest with forces of as many as a thousand men, in some cases managing to take on the RPF in set-piece battles before melting back into the civilian population. The RPF, frustrated at the continued ability of their enemy to mount attacks and then disappear, increasingly resorted to revenge against civilians."

At the end of 1995 human rights monitors estimated that the Rwandan government was arresting seven hundred people each month, and that soldiers were killing five to ten civilians each day. Army patrols struck fiercely against people they believed were harboring insurgents or were insurgents themselves. In the border village of Kanama, for example, an RPF officer was killed in mid-September; his unit stormed through the village soon afterward, and UN monitors later counted more than one hundred bodies.

"The army can only halfway guarantee security by day, and not at all at night," one diplomat in Kigali reported. "If they can't catch the intruders, they catch the sympathizers in the population instead."

One reason Hutu civilians welcomed the insurgents so warmly was that many had participated in the genocide and feared that if the new regime stayed in power, they would someday be arrested and punished. They had good reason to fear it. Survivors were crying for retribution, and the RPF was responding by arresting huge numbers of suspected *genocidaires*. Rwandan prisons had been built to house a total of 10,000 inmates, but by the beginning of 1996 they held 70,000. Ultimately the number reached 130,000. In some prisons, inmates were so tightly packed that there was no space for them to sit or lie down. At one point ten were dying every day from disease, hunger, gangrene, and suffocation.

These conditions forced the government to recognize that no traditional justice system could deal with the crimes committed by *genocidaires*. As many as two million people are believed to have participated in the murder campaign. Even if Rwanda had a functioning legal system—and it had nothing of the kind, since nearly all of the country's lawyers, prosecutors, and judges had either fled or been killed—it would have been impossible to try all of these suspects within a reasonable period. The country's prisons could never hold more than a small fraction of them. Perhaps most important, these criminals were also citizens—mostly able-bodied males—whose labor was desperately needed in a prostrate nation where, after genocide and mass exodus, 70 percent of the adult population was female.

Late in 1995, the government convened a series of conferences at which legal experts and human rights advocates from more than a dozen countries, along with their Rwandan hosts, tried to come up with a solution to this dilemma. Slowly the outline of a new and highly unorthodox legal system took shape. For the relatively small number of people who had organized and directed the genocide, there would be conventional trials. The rest, those accused of taking up grenades and *pangas* to kill their neighbors or encouraging others to do so, would be tried before community-based courts in the places where the crimes were committed. Courts like these, called *gacaca*, which translates roughly as "justice on the grass," had existed in Rwanda for centuries but only to adjudicate minor crimes like trespassing or petty theft. Now they would be reconstituted across the country. The government hoped they would administer justice and also contribute to the urgent process of reconciliation.

As Rwanda was pondering how to prosecute *genocidaires*, so was the United Nations. While the killing was under way, the United Nations had not been able to move itself to act, but once the genocide ended, diplomats quickly concluded that the new regime in

Kigali was not up to the task of bringing killers to justice. In November of 1994 the Security Council voted to create an International Criminal Tribunal for Rwanda, to be based in Arusha, Tanzania. Rwandan leaders, instinctively scornful of the United Nations in any case, took this as an insult.

"This tribunal was created essentially to appease the conscience of the international community, which has failed to live up to its convention on genocide," said Charles Murigande, chairman of the Presidential Commission on Accountability for the Genocide. "It wants to look as if it is doing something, which is often worse than doing nothing at all."

The international tribunal was painfully slow to begin work, had great trouble locating and capturing suspects, and spent more than $1 billion to try the less than seventy it managed to arrest. Defendants enjoyed private cells, television, and three meals a day. They also had free access to the world's finest medical care, meaning that rapists among them who had infected Rwanda women with HIV during the genocide were given expensive antiretroviral drugs, while their victims, mired in Rwanda's poverty, wasted away and died with little or no care. Some survivors called to testify before the tribunal were mercilessly cross-examined by defense lawyers and made to describe their rapes in such explicit detail that many felt they were being violated a second time. As a result, others refused to make the trip.

Trials of those who conceived and directed the genocide, among them Colonel Bagosora, who was apprehended in Cameroon, dragged on for years.

As the process of accounting for genocide began, many of the chief criminals were at camps in Zaire, busily plotting their return to Rwanda. Kagame continued to plead with the UNHCR and other relief groups to stop sending aid to these camps. He made the same appeal to every dignitary who visited Kigali. On July 4, 1996, at a ceremony marking the second anniversary of the RPF victory, he repeated it to an audience at Amahoro Stadium that included the Kigali diplomatic corps.

"We must find a solution to the problem, by fair means or foul," he warned. "There will be casualties."

We had the problem of these genocidal forces out there threatening to come back, and you had the international community feeding them in the camps. What camps were they? There were armored personnel carriers, tanks, anti-aircraft weapons—in the camps! But they called them refugee camps.

12

RWANDA DOESN'T MATTER

THE OUTSIDE WORLD had never shown much interest in Rwanda, and by nature Vice President Kagame was disposed to scorn its platitudes. Nonetheless he understood that before ordering the invasion of a neighboring country aimed at crushing an enemy army that had regrouped there, he should try to explain himself to powerful foreigners. He set off on a tour of world capitals. At each stop, he warned whoever would listen that tens of thousands of *genocidaires* were drilling in Zaire and preparing to invade Rwanda so they could retake power and complete their extermination campaign. In Washington he met with Secretary of Defense William Perry. One American official later wrote that Kagame's presentation was unfocused and "replete with circumlocutions," but Kagame remembers it differently.

I told him that we had a huge problem on our hands—people wanting to come back and attack our country—and asked if there was anything he could do to convince the UN or someone to take care of the situation. Otherwise it would be on our own shoulders to do it. I not only told Perry and people in the State Department, I also went to the UN. I wasn't mincing my words over it. Not only did I give this message in meetings, I also gave it to journalists. There was no ambiguity in what I said: if the international community cannot do it, then we will.

This attitude did not surprise outsiders who had come to know Kagame. One of them, Lieutenant Colonel Thomas Odom, an American officer posted at the U.S. embassy in Kigali, described him as having "an iron will well-tempered by the ruthlessness necessary to fight and win a war of rebellion." Odom and other Americans in Kigali, however, were never able to persuade their superiors in Washington that Kagame was deadly serious when he threatened to attack Zaire if no one else cleaned up the camps there.

Western powers had been dealing with the spectacularly corrupt Zairian dictator, Mobutu Sese Seko, for more than thirty years and had made him the most powerful man in Africa. When ex-FAR and *interahamwe* fighters sought to enter Zaire with their weapons after their defeat in Rwanda, he welcomed them. Once they were there, he embraced them as allies. Attacking their camps would be a direct challenge to his entrenched regime. It seemed absurd to think that tiny Rwanda, which had never figured in African geopolitics and was still recovering from a devastating civil war, would seriously contemplate it.

Zaire, now the Democratic Republic of the Congo, is ninety-four times larger than Rwanda, as big as all of Western Europe or the United States east of the Mississippi. It is also incomparably richer. Mobutu had immensely powerful friends in the West, not just government leaders but also directors of corporations who had made fortunes by exploiting the Congo's rich resources. Like many African leaders, though, he had never built a strong army because he feared it might turn against him. Instead he kept his military fragmented, weak, and—as it had shown during its brief appearance in Rwanda following the 1990 invasion—partial to rape and pillage. The core of Rwanda's army, by contrast, was made up of tough, ready-for-anything *inkotanyi* who had defeated a powerful enemy just a couple of years earlier.

Kagame believed they could defeat another one.

He had reason to be confident. International sympathy for Rwanda was high in the wake of the genocide. The end of the Cold War had made Mobutu less valuable to his longtime allies in Europe and the United States. Many in Africa were tired of his long tyranny. Perhaps most important, the area around Goma had a large population of Tutsi who had emigrated from Rwanda in several waves beginning early in the twentieth century. Mobutu oppressed them, and they were eager to join any movement opposed to his rule.

Soon after Kagame returned empty-handed from his visit to Washington and New York, he decided the time had come to strike. He conceived a military campaign aimed at destroying paramilitary camps in Zaire and scattering or killing the genocidal soldiers based there. It also had two other goals. The first, which he considered vital to Rwanda's future, was to repatriate the hundreds of thousands of Hutu who had been living as refugees in eastern Zaire for more than two years. Humanitarian groups disapprove of "forced repatriation," but Kagame blamed those groups for creating this crisis and cared little for their opinions. In fact, he had accomplished a successful "forced repatriation" the year before, working with officials in Burundi as they closed border camps and pushed fifty thousand Hutu refugees back into Rwanda. Now he planned a military campaign aimed at bringing home more than a million.

His final goal in this campaign was the most ambitious of all: to overthrow Mobutu. Unless he achieved this, he concluded, Zairian territory would always be available to enemies of the RPF. Dozens of attempts to depose Mobutu over the years had failed, but Kagame, self-assured as always, had no doubt his could succeed. The outlandish idea that he could invade Zaire, defeat the large insurgent army entrenched there, force huge numbers of Rwandan refugees to return home, and then topple one of the world's most durable tyrants seemed to him not outlandish at all.

"Kagame is not expected to stand idly by waiting for hostilities to break out," one prescient correspondent reported from Kigali in mid-1996. "He has [been] quoted in radio interviews about the possibility of taking pre-emptive action by invading eastern Zaire to 'neutralize' the former regime. The political consequences of such an action would be extremely serious."

Although Kagame fully understood those consequences, he had concluded he must attack. One of his central beliefs, rising at times to the level of obsession, is that security is the essential prerequisite to national development. He warned repeatedly, in public and in conversations with world leaders, that he would not rest while an enemy army just across Rwanda's borders threatened its stability and prevented refugees from returning home.

We said to them, "Solve this problem for us. We have had genocide. Here is a situation that is going to repeat. We are going to see genocide taken to its completion. Help us." There was nowhere I didn't go—to the U.S., Europe, the UN. I was appealing, literally begging. The intention was to come back and finish what they called an unfortunately failed genocide. Not a single person, country, or institution stood up against this with us—not a single one! The way they looked at things was: Rwanda doesn't matter, what matters is the Congo [then Zaire]. Rwanda doesn't constitute part of their material interest. Senior people in Europe and the United States have stood up and said that. . . .

It really became Rwanda against the world. No one really came to our side and said, "We understand your problem, stay put and we'll address it." Nobody stood up, except for a few people telling us we didn't count for anything. Why should they send troops to die there? If they can't do that, why expect us to remain silent? So we took on what we took on.

An invasion of Zaire was "what we took on." Kagame had concluded that his only choice was whether to strike first or wait for his enemies to attack. It was an easy decision.

Although this invasion may be understood in various ways, its central cause was the emergence of an exile army in refugee camps along Rwanda's borders. "The larger responsibility lay with France and with the UN," the Ugandan-born scholar Mahmood Mamdani concluded. "Through Operation Turquoise, France had gone out of its way to create a protective corridor to save those politically responsible for the genocide in Rwanda. The UN had watched the unfolding of the genocide in Rwanda without so much as lifting a finger. In similar fashion, they watched with complacency as refugee camps were established in the vicinity of international borders, and then they were turned into camps to arm and train refugees."

Under other circumstances Kagame might have ordered a direct cross-border invasion. Zaire, however, was already in turmoil, so all he had to do was ally himself with local rebels who had their own reasons for wanting to overthrow Mobutu. They were striking at a propitious moment. Mobutu's refusal to embrace the new Western agenda of political reform had turned his longtime patrons against him. In 1990 all three of them—France, Belgium, and the United States—suspended bilateral aid to his regime. A year later the World Bank and the International Monetary Fund announced that they would no longer lend him money. These outside pressures heightened discontent that had spread steadily during two decades of uninterrupted economic decline. Public order began breaking down. Warlords and rebel factions emerged in several parts of the country.

Late in the summer of 1996, Kagame offered his services to a coalition of these disaffected factions. He made a secret alliance with a Congolese rebel leader, Laurent Kabila, that suited both their needs. Their plan was simple. Rwanda would send a powerful army into Zaire to fight alongside rebel units. This army would disguise its true origin; Rwanda would not admit its involvement, and all would pretend that the rebel force was purely Zairian. It would attack the camps, defeat the ex-FAR and *interahamwe* forces based there, push refugees back into Rwanda, and then press on to Kinshasa, the Zairian capital, to depose President Mobutu and install Kabila in his place.

This last aspect of the plan was especially ambitious. No decent roads connect eastern Zaire to Kinshasa, only roundabout paths that traverse a dense expanse of jungle bigger than Texas. This has given eastern provinces a form of lawless autonomy from which African warlords and European corporations have reaped enormous profits. It also poses a nearly insurmountable barrier to any force seeking to attack Kinshasa from the east. Kagame's faith in his *inkotanyi*, though, was so complete that he believed they could cross it.

This prospect thrilled Kabila. He had been seeking power for more than three decades and in the 1960s had even attracted Che Guevara to fight at his side. Guevara left in disgust a couple of months later, concluding that "Kabila and his cohorts [were] more interested in women and whiskey than politics," but Kabila soldiered on. For years he supported a large private army by smuggling gold, ivory, and guns. In the West he was known mainly for a 1975 incident in which his forces kidnapped two Stanford University students from a chimpanzee research center in Zaire and held them until a large ransom was paid. From time to time he turned up preaching third-world revolution in places like Libya and China, but he had never been strong enough to threaten Mobutu's regime. One American report described him as a "feisty authoritarian" who was "thick mentally," "overly impressed with himself," and desperate for a "chance to realize his ambitions." Suddenly, thanks to Kagame, he had one.

For Rwanda, this alliance also held great promise. If its campaign succeeded, Rwanda's enemies would be destroyed, refugees would be brought back home, and there would be a new regime in Kinshasa—one that Rwanda had helped place in power and that would presumably respond to Rwanda's wishes.

The war began in October of 1996 with a series of assaults on camps around Goma. Defenders retreated behind thick clusters of refugees who were quickly rounded up to serve as human shields. That might have saved them on some days, but not on this one. Rwandan forces and their Zairian allies simply attacked the human shields and, when they were dead or had fled, swooped down on their enemies. Thousands of innocent refugees were killed this way. So were thousands of ex-FAR and *interahamwe* fighters.

As the fighting raged, Kagame steadfastly insisted that his troops were not involved. The American ambassador, Robert

Gribbin, was among those who suspected the truth, especially after he began receiving reports of "Tutsi-looking troops" in Zaire. "I flagged such reports to Vice President Kagame," Gribbin wrote later. "He acknowledged having heard rumors as well, but denied that troops under his command were participating."

Defenders who survived the first assaults on their camps retreated to a fortified base at Mugunga, ten miles deeper inside Zaire, to make a last stand. Attackers stormed it on November 13, sending their enemies fleeing into the bush in three directions. Then they formed lines behind the camp and began pushing refugees out, toward Rwanda. Many were tired of life as refugees and seemed willing to leave. Others were herded back with the rest, whether they wanted to return or not.

Two days later, Major Orth, the American military attaché, telephoned Ambassador Gribbin from the border and told him simply, "They're coming."

"Who?" Gribbin asked.

"All of them."

For as far as Orth could see, a great torrent of refugees was streaming back toward Rwanda. They quickly overwhelmed border checkpoints. After a short time Rwandan officials even gave up trying to search them for weapons. Like a single living organism, this huge mass of people left the squalor of refugee life and trudged toward an uncertain future at home.

"What occurred in the coming weeks in and around Mugunga stunned the world and baffled the aid community," one relief worker wrote afterward.

> The bulk of the refugees, over half a million people, were by now no longer trapped. . . . Their kidnappers had fled, and in the space of around forty-eight hours, the vast majority of them simply took their belongings and walked back to Rwanda, in silence and often with trepidation, but in reasonable conditions of security and humanity. . . . Without assistance, other than the provision of some trucks and buses which waited at the other side of the border for the injured and infirm, an estimated 550,000 refugees did for themselves in a few days what the UN had been unable to

do for them in over two years. . . . Some weeks later the Tanzanian government began a concerted effort to close its camps too, and return the masses of Rwandan Hutu in the northwest of their country back to their homeland. In this way, in a matter of days of decisive action, they too were ridding their country of the festering sore which their neighbor's fugitive population and its accompanying security and political and environmental complications had by now become. Thus a tumultuous chapter in the story of Rwanda's post-genocide era came to an end.

During those weeks in the autumn of 1996, more than a million people returned to Rwanda along the same roads they had used to flee two and a half years earlier. At one point, twelve thousand were entering every hour. Once home, they posed an overwhelming challenge. Nearly all had been hearing vicious anti-Tutsi propaganda all their lives. Most had participated at least indirectly in the genocide. There were no jobs for them. Many of their homes and farms had been taken over by Tutsi squatters. Bringing them home was a dangerous gamble. Kagame had concluded, though, that as long as these refugees were at camps in other countries, Rwanda would not be stable. Their return was a great victory for the fledgling regime and a turning point in Rwanda's modern history.

Many problems were not resolved, but for us, the most important problem was resolved. There were millions of refugees in the Congo [then Zaire], and hundreds of thousands of former soldiers and militia members, armed and supplied by Mobutu, and through Mobutu by others. Waiting for that force to come and overwhelm us here would have been not only foolhardy but outright foolish and a risk to our well-being.

It was a huge problem that was solved. We repatriated two and a half million refugees in broad daylight. . . . Second, we disarmed the army that had settled in those camps. If we had not done that, I don't know where we would be today.

Attacks on these camps did more than scatter Kagame's enemies and bring refugees home. They were the starting point for one of the most remarkable military campaigns in modern African history. For the next four months, led by Lieutenant Colonel James Kabarebe, a battle-toughened veteran of the Rwandan civil war, the anti-Mobutu force hacked its way through dense jungle. It slogged over a distance that measures a thousand miles as a hardy crow would fly, and far more by foot. Finally, after facing plagues that included intense heat, swarms of insects, lack of food, and dauntingly hostile terrain—and after fighting several fierce battles in which Mobutu's troops were led by Serbian and Romanian mercenaries—it burst through on the other side and struck Kinshasa.

Weak Zairian defenses crumbled, and the once-mighty Mobutu, who had withstood every imaginable threat during more than thirty extravagant years on the world stage, was forced to flee. His French friends arranged for him to be given asylum in Morocco. On May 17, 1997, the day after he departed, rebels stormed into Kinshasa and proclaimed their new regime. Kabila became president, fulfilling a lifelong dream.

The most bizarre discovery the *inkotanyi* made in Kinshasa was one that solved the mystery of what had happened to President Habyarimana's body after he perished in the 1994 plane crash. It turned out that Mobutu had obtained the body—no one ever discovered how—and enshrined it at a private mausoleum in Kinshasa. One of his last acts before fleeing was to order it cremated.

The world was so stunned by Mobutu's fall that in many places, a later piece of news was overlooked. During the entire campaign in Zaire, despite mounting evidence, Rwandan leaders had stuck to their story: they were merely bystanders, and no Rwandan troops were involved. Once Mobutu was gone and the new regime was safely in power, there was no need to maintain that fiction. Kagame finally admitted that his troops had been involved all along.

"There are not many people who thought that Mobutu was very weak," he told the *Washington Post*. "They thought of Mobutu as a big monster who couldn't be defeated, with his big hat and his big stick. They thought, 'Little Rwanda and big Zaire.' Only when we started did they look at the map and see the possibilities."

Rwandan soldiers who fought in Zaire, which Kabila renamed Democratic Republic of the Congo, had shown themselves to be astonishingly tough and disciplined. After they installed Kabila in power, he promoted their commander, Colonel Kabarebe, to general and named him army chief of staff. Before long, perhaps inevitably, people in the Congo began complaining about the fact that their national army was being commanded by a foreigner, and that so many foreigners were among its top commanders. Some also bridled under the influence that Rwandan businessmen came to exercise in resource-rich eastern provinces.

"We were not able to manage our victory," one former RPF leader concluded afterward. "We tried to micromanage, and that caused trouble."

The spectacularly rich region known today as the eastern Congo was once ruled by vassals of the Rwandan *mwami*. In 1881 one *mwami*, Kigeri V. Rwabuguri, was killed in battle while trying to consolidate his power there. This history has given some Rwandans a quiet sense that they have special rights in the region. It has also made many Congolese highly sensitive to anything they see as an attempt by Rwandans—especially Tutsi—to dominate them. Soon after Kabila seized power with Rwanda's decisive help, they began to complain that Rwandans were reveling too fully in their victory. Before long, Kabila himself came to agree.

Less than a year after Kabila took power, he was giving speeches denouncing Tutsi influence in his country. When scattered ex-FAR and *interahamwe* forces began regrouping at their old border camps, he did nothing to stop them. Nor did he act when groups of these fighters began launching cross-border raids into Rwanda. In one of those raids, at the end of 1997, insurgents stormed a prison and freed five hundred genocide suspects. General Kabarebe, who owed his first allegiance to Rwanda, tried to launch a crackdown on the camps, but Kabila held him back.

Kabila had switched sides. He would not have come to power without help from Rwanda, but after a remarkably short time in office he turned against his patrons and embraced their sworn enemies. The 1996 invasion turned out not to have been as successful as it seemed at first. Rwanda had installed a leader in Kinshasa who turned out to be faithless—or independent-minded, depending on one's point of view. It had also failed to destroy the ex-FAR and the *interahamwe*. In fact, they had returned to the border region with unexpected power. From there they launched a new military campaign.

During late 1996 and early 1997, more than thirty thousand insurgents infiltrated into Rwanda. Many came disguised as refugees. They returned not to resume peaceful lives but to fight.

"There were a lot of strong, well-fed men among those refugees," recalled Major Orth, who watched them return. "I'm a soldier, and I could tell those men were soldiers. And they were confident. I looked into their eyes, and their eyes were saying, 'We are not defeated.'"

Part of the problem that we inherited, that people fell prey to, was leaders who thought leadership meant just sitting there and being adored, not even respected, and having privileges. We had arguments in the cabinet, quarrels, people claiming, "As ministers, we must have this." Literally quarrels! I would ask them, "You are claiming this, where do you get it from? First you have to create what you want to claim. You cannot claim vehicles, money, upkeep, allowances—you can't claim it because you have nowhere to grow it from. Secondly, there are other priorities. If that money was there, if there was somewhere to grow that money from, it should go for other things, not what you are talking about."

And in this cabinet, me or maybe another one or two people would be totally isolated. And I would go to the extent of explaining. I would say, "Some of us stayed there in the trenches, in the cold, in the night, without eating. We didn't come here to start claiming that we should be paid back what we lost, or that we need more than others, therefore we should be given more. Even today we are saying we should have less!"

Paul Kagame was not yet two years old when he and his family narrowly escaped murder at the hands of a Rwandan death squad. The family fled to Uganda, where Paul grew up destitute in refugee camps. For a time he was an outstanding student (below, seated second from right with classmates at Ntare School), but then he grew rebellious, let his grades slip, and became consumed by "undefined anger."

Kagame's first commander and role model was the Ugandan revolutionary Yoweri Museveni, who seized power in 1986 and has ruled Uganda ever since.

Before setting off to overthrow the Rwandan government, Kagame took time to marry.

The Rwandan civil war raged from 1990 to 1994 and culminated in a hundred-day genocide that took as many as a million lives.

General Roméo Dallaire, shown here with Kagame at Kagame's wartime headquarters in Mulindi, commanded UN peacekeepers in Rwanda. He begged for enough troops and support to stop the killing, but the United Nations turned him down.

Kagame is the world's only head of state to have received military training in both Cuba (above) and the United States (below, with classmates at the Army Command and General Staff College at Fort Leavenworth, Kansas).

This cartoon, published by the extremist newspaper *Kangura* in 1993, shows Paul Kagame leading his army to power over a field of bones and coffins. He is saying, "The cockroach fighters are coming!! We will force you to live with us!!"

President Kagame shocked some of his supporters when he chose a genocide suspect, Boniface Rucagu, as governor of a restive northern province. Together they managed to calm passions in the country's most explosive region.

Bishop John Rucyahana, Rwanda's most prominent clergyman, speaks the languages of evangelical Christianity, African redemption, and self-reliance.

The success of Solange Katarebe's restaurant reflects the emergence of a new, young Rwandan middle class.

Gerard Sina has built a series of businesses that are pulling an entire mini-region out of poverty—and making him rich.

Drocella Kruger is one of many Rwandans who returned from abroad to work in projects that serve survivors of the genocide.

The rebirth of Rwanda's capital, Kigali, reflects the country's progress.

Kagame was elected president of Rwanda in 2003 with a reported 95 percent of the vote. In politics as in sports, "There is always the urge to win, no doubt about it."

13

THE TRICKY PART

ONE MORNING IN THE SUMMER of 1997, people in the
northern Rwandan town of Ruhengeri awoke to find
that during the night, insurgents or their supporters had
littered the streets with leaflets headlined "Notice to the Tutsi of
This Town." In a few stark sentences, this broadside crystallized
the essence of the spreading insurgency.

"You Tutsi, we have always told you to leave this town because
it is not yours," it said. "We have already warned you three times.
This is the last warning. There will be no more. If you have nowhere to go, take a rope and hang yourselves."

Insurgents who infiltrated the northern regions of Ruhengeri
and Gisenyi quickly became a formidable force. They moved freely
over much of northwest Rwanda and controlled main roads at
night. At the height of their power they deployed battalion-size
units of three to five hundred fighters to engage the army in fierce
combat.

Rwanda's future hung on the outcome of this war. The insurgents vowed that if they won, they would resume the genocide.
Even without winning, they were strong enough to keep the
country in violent turmoil. President Kagame realized that his
government would never be secure, and he would never have a
chance to try reshaping Rwanda, unless he decisively crushed this

insurgency. That is what he set out to do. Like the insurgents, he obeyed no rules but his own and used harsh tactics that brought suffering and death to many innocent Rwandans.

In an exhaustive study of this insurgency, the London-based group African Rights listed its key characteristics:

- The insurgency was . . . a full-scale military operation, intended to challenge the government of Rwanda either by toppling it or by forcing it into negotiations.
- [Insurgents] were mostly ex-FAR soldiers, militia men, and former refugees recruited from camps in Zaire. They are united by fear of the RPF. . . . Many of them are *genocidaires* who have good reason to avoid returning home.
- The insurgents have made it clear that they intend to wipe out the small Tutsi population in the northwest. They aim to complete the genocide.
- The insurgents have also killed Hutu hostile to their agenda.
- The backbone of the insurgency are the local people. . . . They act as informants, messengers, and as reinforcements during large-scale attacks. They give shelter to infiltrators and are also being used as human shields for infiltrators fleeing the army. . . . There are high penalties for those who refuse to collaborate.
- The RPF . . . also stands accused of murdering civilians. Infiltrators have confirmed support among local people. . . . Their strategy of hiding amongst civilians and using them as human shields is responsible for the highest number of casualties in this war. But there are also cases of RPF soldiers killing those suspected of working with the insurgents.

The Congo's open support for these insurgents—many of them actually wore Congolese army uniforms—led to a final break between President Kabila and his Rwandan ex-allies. In July of 1998, Kabila fired his Rwandan-born chief of staff, General Kabarebe; cashiered all the Rwandan-born troops in his army; and ordered them out of the Congo. They left immediately. Five days later, to Kabila's shock, they returned in a blaze of artillery and cannon fire. Rwanda had invaded the Congo for a second time. Kagame was paying a soldier's debt, and this time he did not try to hide his involvement.

We had pulled all of our forces back, but we said the same thing: "If we continue to have incursions from the Congo, we will go back— and it doesn't matter what they accuse us of. Remove this problem and we stop. But you are not eliminating the problem."

Soldiers were coming back into Rwanda and killing people. The Congo government was directly abetting this and perpetuating this situation. For some reason, it turned and began supporting the same forces Mobutu had been backing. So it was for the same reason that we fought Kabila.

For a time, Rwanda's second invasion of the Congo went well. Rwandan troops and their Ugandan allies—Kagame had planned this operation with Uganda's President Museveni, his old friend and comrade—seized border areas and pressed toward Kinshasa. Soon, however, they ran into unexpected obstacles. Congolese did not welcome or support them as they had during the anti-Mobutu invasion two years earlier. Three African countries ruled by Kabila's old comrades from anticolonial campaigns— Angola, Zimbabwe, and Namibia—sent troops to help defend his regime, along with heavy weaponry, including fighter planes that cut up advancing columns. Western countries that had quietly accepted Rwanda's first invasion reacted more sharply to the second. Most unexpectedly, allied Rwandan and Ugandan forces turned against each other and fought battles around the prized Congolese city of Kisangani, once known as Stanleyville. They were fighting for control over Kisangani's rich gold and diamond mines.

This conflict was part of a far larger rivalry for control over the immense natural wealth of the eastern Congo, an African "great game" that has been under way for more than a century. Nothing that happens there is unrelated to this rivalry. Why did the deposed Hutu army choose to regroup in the eastern

Congo? Why did Rwandans invade their sanctuary? Why did Kabila ally himself with the Rwandans and then turn against them? Why did Ugandan troops join Rwandans to launch a second invasion? Why did they then fight each other? Strategic questions like these cannot be answered without considering the fortunes that are to be made by looting the eastern Congo's vast resources.

Rwandan leaders never admitted that they used their occupation of the eastern Congo during the late 1990s to make money. According to UN reports, however, the Rwandan army mined large amounts of gold, diamonds, and coltan, the "gray gold" that is a vital component of cell phones. The reports also recounted episodes in which Rwandan soldiers surrounded banks and stole all the cash inside, and one in which an entire sugar refinery was dismantled and moved to Rwanda.

Kagame protested his innocence, but if Rwandans did not grab some of the eastern Congo's wealth while occupying it, they were unique among that region's many occupiers.

While Rwandan forces were bogged down in the Congo, the insurgency inside Rwanda intensified. The insurgent force was large, well equipped, commanded by professional officers, and welcomed by the local population. Kagame was determined to destroy it at any cost. Many civilians die in wars waged under these conditions. The one that raged in northwest Rwanda during the late 1990s was no exception.

"The *interahamwe* hid out in the volcanoes or blended into the general population during the daytime, emerging at night to continue their genocidal campaign against ethnic Tutsi," wrote an American woman who lived there. "At 1:00 AM on August 21 [1996], *interahamwe* attacked the refugee camp at Mudende, killing one hundred and twenty Tutsi and wounding many more. . . . Retaliation was swift. Within hours, Tutsi civilians began killing Hutu civilians at random, looting and setting fire to their homes. . . . On October 8, 1997, more than a thousand *interahamwe* attacked Gisenyi and nearly captured the airport in a seven-hour battle. Many were killed. . . . [During 1998] Gisenyi became the target of repeated terrorist attacks. Massacres of Tutsi refugees, followed by retaliation killings of Hutu civilians, occurred daily. . . . The hospital was overflowing with burn and amputee victims. Dozens of funerals were held each day."

Kagame's army waged this war with harsh counterinsurgency tactics. Soldiers saw every civilian as a potential enemy, and in threatening situations they shot first. When they were attacked, they often returned in force to conduct murderous revenge sweeps. They herded tens of thousands of people into guarded camps and turned large areas into free-fire zones. Bodies of some victims are said to have been burned or buried in mass graves.

Justice of a more formal sort was meted out to twenty-two *genocidaires* whom Rwandan courts had convicted of grave crimes and sentenced to death. On April 25, 1998, they were brought to stadiums in different parts of the country, fitted with black hoods, tied to stakes, and publicly shot. "Painful medicine was necessary to heal our sick society, an example to all that the days of impunity are over and everyone must answer for his crimes," a columnist wrote in the government newspaper.

Over the next few days, hundreds of imprisoned *genocidaires*, suddenly fearing that they too might be shot, gave full confessions and appealed for mercy. Many outsiders, however, were repelled by the executions. There were no more, and Rwanda later abolished its death penalty.

Some Rwandans in exile denounced the RPF for its severe rule, but most of them were *genocidaires* or apologists for the old regime, so their complaints did not count for much. There was one sterling exception. Seth Sendashonga, the former interior minister, had moved to Kenya and emerged as a potent anti-Kagame figure. Leaders of the insurgent force embraced him.

"He was very intelligent, he had opposed Habyarimana, he was not involved in the genocide, and he was strong inside the country," Tito Rutaremara recalled years later. "Those people were always looking for a clean leader, and he was clean."

The insurgents had their unofficial command center in Kenya, and Kagame ran an active intelligence network there. In 1996 one prominent Hutu exile, the former secret police chief Théoneste Lizinde—who had joined the RPF after its raiders freed him from Ruhengeri prison in 1991, became an RPF deputy in Parliament, then broke with the regime and fled—was assassinated in Nairobi. Soon afterward, a gunman opened fire on Sendashonga's car, wounding him in the shoulder. Police arrested the assailant at the scene. He turned out to be a diplomat attached to the Rwandan embassy.

"I told him he was too close, it was too dangerous," one of Sendashonga's friends said later. "He told me, 'If you want to catch a lion, you have to be close to the lion's den.'"

The lion Sendashonga wanted to catch, of course, was Kagame. He was well placed to do it. His untainted background, intimate knowledge of the regime, and wide-ranging international connections, together with the support he had inside Rwanda, made him a uniquely credible figure. From his base in Nairobi, he gave a stream of impassioned interviews warning that a "second genocide" was taking shape in Rwanda. In one of them, he charged that the regime had killed sixty thousand Hutu civilians and had embarked on a campaign "to systematically eliminate all those who had even a semblance of leadership in the population."

"General Kagame was the invisible hand that planned and executed what was going on in Rwanda," Sendashonga asserted. "These were not slip-ups born out of anger, as I believed at the beginning. There was a master plan. . . . If the international community doesn't watch out, it's going to wake up one of these days and realize that the genocide of revenge has been consummated."

On the evening of May 10, 1998, as Sendashonga was being driven through a neighborhood on the outskirts of Nairobi, a gunman opened fire on his car. He was killed instantly, along with his driver. Nairobi is a corrupt place where anyone with a hundred dollars can arrange an assassination, and Sendashonga had many enemies. Suspicion, however, fell first on Kagame. He denied having ordered the killing, but there was every reason he might have. Sendashonga posed a political and military threat to Kagame's regime. It was not in his nature to abide such threats.

There was an odd anomaly in Kagame's position at this point. He was the most powerful figure in Rwanda but not the president. The same was true of his position in the RPF; he was its undisputed leader but officially only its vice chairman. He could not take the presidency without provoking a conflict, but things were different in the RPF. In 1998 he arranged to have himself elected its chairman. That gave him added authority as he waged his counterinsurgency campaign.

Some of the tactics Kagame used in this campaign would undoubtedly qualify as gross human rights violations. He justified them all with his conviction that only by crushing this threat could he bring Rwandans the security that he believed was their most basic right. As a lifelong student of guerrilla principles, however, he understood that imposing his will by force would give him no more than a temporary victory. Only by bringing the famously militant northern Hutu to support his government would he be able to claim true success. Even while the insurgency raged, he ruminated about how to do it.

It's one thing to fight a war purely militarily. You can have overwhelming force and defeat the attackers. But here there is a huge component that is political. . . . When it comes to the hearts and minds of people you have to win over to be part of your campaign, that's where the tricky part comes. So it was serious, especially because we had not even had time to sensitize and mobilize the people of this country. They still had fresh wounds, either way—those associated with those who committed genocide and those insurgents who had their relatives here, who are telling them, "We are trying to fight people who tomorrow are going hold you responsible for genocide." You are really supposed to feel sympathetic. So to try to drive a wedge in between these forces, the insurgents, and their people on the ground was a very, very hard task.

One tactic Kagame used to great effect during the late 1990s was the recruitment of Hutu soldiers who had been part of the defeated Forces Armées Rwandaises. About four thousand of them eventually joined the new Rwandan army, called the Rwandan Defense Forces. Many were deployed near their homes in northern provinces, where people had once seen the army as a Tutsi occupation force. Their presence helped calm Hutu fears. Kagame, though, wanted to make a grander, more dramatic gesture. He chose to do it in Ruhengeri.

Many who lived in Ruhengeri had been *genocidaires*. Nearly all supported the insurgency. Thousands of families had relatives in prison. The army's brutal tactics had intensified people's anger at the regime. To win them over, Kagame decided he needed a local partner, a civilian he could install as provincial governor. This person would have the daunting task of persuading northern Hutu to embrace a regime they detested.

The most popular politician in Ruhengeri during pregenocide days was an effusive, glad-handing populist named Boniface Rucagu. As a young man Rucagu had supported the Kayibanda dictatorship, and after the 1973 coup he joined the "second republic." He won a seat in Parliament, built a political base in Ruhengeri, and for more than a decade was a pillar of the regime. During the 1990–1994 civil war, the RPF considered him an important enough enemy to burn his house down. When the war ended, survivors charged that he had been a *genocidaire*. He was arrested and imprisoned.

Several months later, Rucagu was released. This outraged his accusers. They managed to have him rearrested, but he was again released. By his own count, he was arrested and released six times. In 1997, after the sixth time, Kagame made him an irresistible offer. Instead of going back to jail and ultimately facing trial for his actions during the genocide, he could become governor of Ruhengeri.

Kagame arranged for President Bizimungu to make this extraordinary appointment, but the normally compliant Parliament, which had to approve it, exploded in protest. Many deputies vowed never to vote for Rucagu. No political goal, they insisted, was worth the moral price of tainting Rwanda's government with so odious a figure. Their government had come to power by ending a genocide and represented antigenocide ideology more purely than any in the world; how could it name an accused *genocidaire* to a key government job?

The future and not the past, Kagame replied, should guide government policy. His reasoning was simple: Rwanda could not develop unless it was secure; it would not be secure until people in Ruhengeri changed their minds about the regime; no one from the RPF could make them do that; Rucagu, however, might. It was a powerful argument for Kagame and others who believe that security is the most fundamental of social needs, but it did not change many minds. Even some of Kagame's longtime comrades thought he was making an unethical compromise with evil. In the end, though, he managed to push the nomination through Parliament.

Rucagu became not only a highly effective governor but also a vigorous campaigner for reconciliation. He plastered roads, public buildings, and classrooms with signs exhorting, "Pull Genocide Ideology Up by Its Roots!" As the insurgency wound down at the end of the decade and peace began returning to the north, Kagame felt vindicated.

Even some of my allies were incensed to see him made governor, but I was convinced that this was a good way to turn things around—and it worked. Sometimes you use people who are ready to change, regardless of their background. Through that, you change those who have not changed. . . . The whole idea is to remove that image of a movement with commanders and leaders people don't know, to straddle the divide between the leaders and the led. . . .

I'm telling these critics, some of whom are my colleagues, that by seemingly not prosecuting one individual who committed crimes, who maybe could have killed people, I am saving many more lives. That is priority number one. If I did what they recommended, the only thing that would come out of it would be that we would lose more people. If I can stop this by using—let's even say—a criminal and, therefore stop the devastation wreaked by the insurgency, I think I'm doing something positive. . . .

The moral aspect of the thing comes later. People first must be safe. The moral dilemma is always part of the equation, but you don't look just at that. If that's your only factor in decision making, you don't move forward with what you might otherwise achieve. . . .

Rucagu is born of that area, and Rucagu had influence under Habyarimana's regime in that area—although he had enemies as well, he had conflicts with the Habyarimana group. But he had his own strong base there. So irrespective of what they were accusing him of, unless I had been totally convinced of the gravity of it, I wanted to build on what he had in the area and use him to try to influence people there. And the strategy worked very well. I have no regrets about it. . . . It contributed a lot to dealing with the insurgency.

A combination of harsh counterinsurgency tactics and skillful political maneuvers, especially the integration of ex-FAR soldiers into the army and the naming of Boniface Rucagu as governor of Ruhengeri, ultimately brought victory to the government side. By the beginning of 2000, a measure of calm had returned to Rwanda. "The government apparently is winning its fight," an American officer reported. "[Insurgents] still have the capacity to use terror, but it is doubtful that violence can coerce large portions of the population to again support the Hutu extremist genocidal insurgency."

Victory was more elusive across the border in the Congo, where Rwandan troops were feuding with their allies and failing to make military progress. Foreign donors began pressuring Rwanda to withdraw its troops. With the insurgency inside Rwanda under control, Kagame was increasingly willing to do so.

On January 16, 2001, President Kabila was assassinated in Kinshasa. His twenty-nine-year-old son, Joseph, succeeded him, and to many people's surprise turned out to be a skillful conciliator. Rwandan troops remained in the Congo for a while longer, but finally withdrew after signing a peace accord in 2002. Under the accord, President Joseph Kabila pledged to disarm all Hutu fighters who remained on Congolese soil. That did not bring full peace to the region, since some fighters refused to be disarmed, regrouped in the Congolese hinterland, and continued to attack targets inside

Rwanda. The war that tore Rwanda apart in the late 1990s, though, was over.

The cruelest legacy of this war was the humanitarian catastrophe it helped provoke in the Congo. Beginning in the mid-1990s political, ethnic, and regional conflicts multiplied there. Over the next decade, no fewer than seven African countries sent soldiers to fight on behalf of one Congolese faction or another. Huge populations were forced from their homes. Epidemics devastated entire regions. Wars and plagues took an unfathomable toll, as many as three million lives or more.

If the Rwandan invasion of 1998 was among the factors that provoked this holocaust, ultimate responsibility lies with those who allowed the defeated forces of Rwanda's genocidal regime to regroup in the Congo (then Zaire). France was their chief patron. French intercession with the Mobutu regime made it possible for the defeated army to enter the Congo with all its weaponry. France then encouraged that army to believe it could fight its way back to power in Kigali.

"The consequence of French policy can hardly be overestimated," the Organization of African Unity concluded in a report on these events. "The escape of *genocidaire* leaders into Zaire led almost inevitably to a new, more complex stage in the Rwandan tragedy, expanding it into a conflict that soon engulfed all of central Africa."

If defeated soldiers who fled Rwanda in 1994 had been disarmed when they crossed into the Congo, or if relief agencies had maintained control of their camps, Rwandan forces would not have invaded. Their two invasions were extensions of Rwanda's civil war onto Congolese soil. They were, as *New York Times* correspondent Howard French reported, a "campaign to empty the refugee camps and thereby prevent a repeat of the 1994 genocide . . . and in this struggle, moral complications presented no more obstacle to the invaders than the feeble military resistance they faced." Kagame never wavered from his insistence that mortal threats to Rwanda made both its invasions of the Congo necessary.

The deaths of Congolese are very unfortunate, but when did that start? Most of it started with the Mobutu regime. Hundreds of thousands of Congolese were dying before we entered, under Mobutu, of disease and poverty, even in that wealthy country. The same people accusing us were mining, taking out gold, diamonds, timber, anything. . . . The Congo majority is the poorest of the poor, but they thought that wasn't killing. They share responsibility for the deaths of those Congolese. . . .

Much as I sympathize with the Congo's situation, my first responsibility is to Rwanda's well-being as a nation. We went into the Congo because of what the Congo constituted in terms of a huge security threat to our existence. That is the starting point.

The end of this devastating insurgency gave Kagame a chance to turn his attention to what he and his comrades had long considered their transcendent historical mission: the transformation of Rwanda. During decades in exile, they had developed outsized ambitions for their unhappy country. They became fervently convinced that Rwanda was not fated to remain mired in poverty and isolation but could triumph over history and soar toward prosperity.

After winning the civil war in 1994, RPF leaders realized they could not govern directly. They were unfamiliar with Rwanda, mistrusted by most of its people, and preoccupied with security threats posed by Hutu insurgents. So instead of installing a government headed by Kagame and his close comrades, as they could have, they handed the reins of state to the handful of Hutu politicians who had defected to their side.

By the end of the 1990s, it was clear that the Hutu-dominated regime did not share the utopian passion that drove many RPF leaders. The regime was plodding and self-absorbed, while Kagame and his comrades, gripped by the extravagant dreams to which exile can give birth, were bursting with revolutionary zeal. It was inevitable that the two groups would ultimately clash—and just as inevitable that Kagame would emerge from their clash as Rwanda's unchallenged leader.

Although Kagame accepted a subsidiary position in the government that emerged after the genocide, it was clear from the beginning that he held ultimate power. President Bizimungu and his cabinet enjoyed considerable autonomy, especially during the years when Kagame was busy fighting insurgents. Still, it was not uncommon for high-level visitors to Rwanda to insist on meeting the vice president, rather than the president or the prime minister. When Kagame visited Washington in 1996, the *Washington Post* called him as "the effective, if unelected, leader of the Rwandan government." This uncomfortable state of affairs naturally led to tensions within the regime. At first Kagame sought to soothe them. That made sense, because the system he had designed—a Hutu superstructure behind which he exercised final authority—served him well. Once the great distraction of war ceased to preoccupy him, though, he found time to assess the government he had installed. He did not like what he saw.

They were doing nothing. Actually, some of these people, including Bizimungu, were just enjoying being leaders, in the wrong interpretation and definition of it. . . .

[In 1997] I had caught malaria, I was down in bed taking medicine. I wasn't feeling well. And while in bed, around ten o'clock in the morning, one of my assistants calls me and says, "The minister of finance is giving one million dollars"—we had got some bit of money—"in cash to the prime minister to go to Europe and buy Mercedes-Benzes for ministers." I got a telephone and called President Bizimungu. I said, "Either you don't know, or you have actually authorized the prime minister to go to Germany to do this. First of all, why give somebody a million dollars cash to move with? Secondly, why do we buy Mercedes-Benzes? Is it imperative? Have ministers failed to work because they don't have Mercedes-Benzes? Is it really one of our priorities today to buy Mercedes-Benzes for our ministers? I know that they might need vehicles, but even then, it could come after other priorities." And I found he had actually consented.

I argued with him. I said, "President, I'm sorry, but I don't agree with this. From a personal point of view, but also from the point of view *of the situation we are trying to handle, I think it is wrong and I think it should not proceed." I pleaded with him, and reluctantly he gave in. To show how reluctant he was, he even pushed it back to me. He said, "Maybe you can tell the minister of finance not to release the money." He wanted to push it back to me. And I did that. The minister of finance said to me, "But the president authorized me to do this." And I said, "I talked to the president. I am not going to accept this. With my conscience, I cannot allow this to happen." Then the prime minister calls me. The man was literally crying on the telephone. Then he tells me something I didn't even know. He said, "Are you even stopping the $100,000 I was going to get for furnishing my house?" I was really caught off guard. Finally, I told him, "Don't cry over the $100,000. Let them give it to you." . . .*

Morally I thought it was wrong, but we had been doing things that were not necessarily right as a way of winning people over. For them to do the right thing, they had to be bought. So it is in this context that I said, "Give him the money." I don't know whether he used the money to buy furniture or whether he used it to go shopping in Brussels. This was the kind of thing I was dealing with.

President Bizimungu had an erratic personality. His ethical standards were flexible. Most important, he did not share the sense of urgency about issues of national development that gripped Kagame and his old comrades. He governed as a caretaker, always taking time to tend to private business deals and cater to his friends' ambitions, and resented having to take direction from the RPF. Kagame, however, insisted that the RPF was Rwanda's ruling power and that everyone in government must carry out its program.

"Bizimungu was difficult to understand," one of Kagame's close comrades, Efraim Kabaija, recalled later. "This was not a person who could go into dialogue. He would rip up papers and shout at you. He had the working methods of the old regime. Politicians in Africa think power and money should go together. He went into business as early as 1994, and not straight business. . . . Kagame used to talk to him privately. Sometimes he would deny what he was doing, but often he would fire back. He would say,

'What's wrong with that? Do you need a president who is poor?'
Kagame was busy with the war half the time. While he was occupied with the war business, Bizimungu was not organizing the
country. It was more about money and political support. . . . Seth
[Sendashonga] was pressing for quick elections so the traditional
parties could take power. He quit the cabinet in 1995, but even
while he was in power, he was trying to organize a base. He had
been in charge of local affairs and used that job for his own purposes, the way people would in a traditional political system. This
doesn't work in the RPF, to try to create your own group or base.
This was old politics. . . . It was a government of schemers. Almost
all of them had been in the old government. They were thinking,
'Elections are coming, where should I go for the best advantage?'"

Soon after taking power, RPF leaders had concluded that
allowing conventional politics to unfold in Rwanda would lead
quickly to renewed ethnic divisions and, quite possibly, another
genocide. Some foreign diplomats agreed. "The government of
Rwanda must be strong to avoid a new catastrophe inside the country," the European Union's first postgenocide representative wrote
soon after arriving in Kigali. "Once the current government can
feel that it is strong and stable, it will be able to allow the Hutu
population to participate in power. It is only a strong government
that can engage in a sincere process of reconciliation."

As years passed and the country settled into peace, some Rwandans and others began wondering how long the government
would insist on being so "strong." They complained that behind
the ban on "genocide ideology" lay an effort to repress political
rivals, demonize all opposition figures as *genocidaires* or "division-
ists," and remain in power indefinitely. Several leading Hutu figures in the government, including President Bizimungu, began
distancing themselves from Kagame. On March 22, 2000, as these
tensions were reaching a peak, Bizimungu and senior RPF leaders
held a long meeting in Kigali. It ended with a series of agreements
that seemed to set the stage for a more harmonious government.
Someone suggested that the group celebrate its success with a
round of drinks at Cadillac, one of Kigali's chic night spots, and

they drove over. Bizimungu left early, but that did not dampen the mood.

"We thought that the issues were all over," Kagame recalled, "and we had calmed down the situation."

The next morning, one of the president's friends called Kagame with the startling news that the president was preparing to resign. An hour later Bizimungu confirmed it by fax. Then, after what by some accounts were several rounds of drinks with a close aide, he drove to Parliament and delivered a long, rambling speech. It cast little light on his decision, but confirmed to some that he was less than an ideal head of state.

No one doubted what would happen next. The RPF held a per-functory meeting and announced that it had decided Vice President Kagame should become the country's new president. Parliament ratified the choice by a vote of eighty-one to three. For six years, Kagame had dominated Rwanda from behind the scenes. After taking the oath of office on April 22, 2000, he had the title to go with his power.

"He always considered the presidency to be his right," one of his aides said. "During his years as vice president and minister of defense, no matter what else he was doing, he never lost sight of that goal."

In the months that followed, more Hutu officials quit the gov-ernment. Prime Minister Pierre Rwigema, who had taken office after his predecessor quit and fled the country, quit and fled him-self. The speaker of Parliament, Joseph Sebarenzi, soon followed. This purge was, an American diplomat later wrote, "a blatant ef-fort to ensure that the RPF remained unchallenged," but one that "made good sense because Kagame had always been the most powerful of Rwanda's leaders, and selecting him as president was a confirmation of reality." Nonetheless it further narrowed the government's base and tarnished Kagame's image.

"The façade of multi-ethnicity crumbled quickly," the Scottish analyst Colin Waugh wrote, "and Kagame increasingly found him-self forced into the stance which he had long sought to avoid: that of an embattled military dictator, maintaining power by force and internal repression, representing the interests of only a minority of the total population which he purported to govern."

In authoritarian countries, the rules of politics dictate that defeated politicians must accept their defeat quietly. Bizimungu refused to do that. A presidential election was scheduled for 2003, and he wanted to run. He had not distinguished himself in office, but he had the asset of Hutu background, and that made him a formidable candidate. Even though the Arusha accords forbade the establishment of new political parties until after the presidential election, Bizimungu began organizing one. He was asserting what he believed were his political rights—and confronting a leader not known for tolerating rivals.

Few were surprised when Bizimungu was arrested. A trial was later convened. The former president was charged with corruption—a charge that was undoubtedly true but that would probably not have been brought against him if he had agreed to retire quietly—and with appealing to Hutu identity, the crime known in Rwanda as "divisionism." This latter charge was based on a statement Bizimungu made to an interviewer from *Jeune Afrique.*

"If the current state of affairs continues, the Hutu will prepare for war and in fifteen or twenty years they will have driven out the Tutsi," he said. "Mechanisms need to be set up so that each community can genuinely participate in government. . . . If the situation does not change, the only possible outcome is violence."

Some may have read those words as a well-intended warning, but prosecutors called them an appeal to rebellion. In any case, there was no doubt how Kagame wanted this trial to end, so the guilty verdict was a foregone conclusion. Bizimungu was sentenced to fifteen years in prison. By moving from his country's presidency to a crowded prison, he shared the fate of other African politicians who presumed to challenge power.

We told him, "Don't push us too far, because you're going to have big problems. Don't do this, because you know it is wrong at this time." He was counting on creating a crisis for us. He thought we would fear, under international pressure, to arrest a former head of state. We sent

people to go and talk to him. We told him he was free to have his own
political party outside the RPF, but that he would have to wait until
things were in order. He became adamant and was arrested. It was not
engineered. We were reacting to things he was doing. But it is as well it
happened. . . . From 1994 to 2000, a lot of time was wasted.

Kagame and his comrades may truly have hoped that the Hutu
politicians they chose to run the country in 1994 would perform
brilliantly. That would have allowed them to continue ruling from
behind the scenes while presenting the image of a broadly representative regime. After a few years, though, both sides tired of this
arrangement. Hutu who held high government posts thought it
only fair that they should have the authority that normally accompanies their positions. When it became clear that the RPF had another idea, many quit and left the country. Others were forced out.
A few were imprisoned on corruption charges. All of this was fine
with Kagame and his comrades. In effect, they had turned to their
erstwhile allies and said, "We gave you a chance to run the country
for us, but you failed. Now we'll do it ourselves."

In a sense it is unfair to compare the achievements of the first six
postgenocide years to the next six. During the first period, Rwanda
was wracked by war, refugee crises, and all manner of upheaval.
That made it almost impossible for the country's leaders to address
the urgent challenges of development. By the time Kagame assumed the presidency in 2000, the country was secure and more or
less at peace. Even with those advantages, most governments in
poor countries fail. Kagame's was determined to press on until
Rwanda was poor no longer.

Six years as vice president had given Kagame a sense of how he
might realize his outlandish dream. Security was, as always, his first
priority. With hatred still bubbling close beneath the surface of national life and at least one foreign power apparently hoping for a
return of the old order, he had no compunction about imposing a
"security state" in which police kept close watch on the population.
Under that umbrella, he set out on his visionary development project. For ideas he turned with special interest to South Korea,

China, Taiwan, Malaysia, Singapore, and Thailand. All had sky-rocketed from poverty to modest prosperity in the space of barely more than a generation—and done it under the leadership of authoritarian visionaries who demanded discipline and had little patience with the niceties of Western-style politics.

Soon after assuming the presidency, Kagame convened an intensive series of meetings aimed at formulating a coherent plan for national development. From these meetings emerged a far-reaching and in some respects utopian program called "Vision 2020." It set a series of lofty goals and gave the government a framework within which it could begin to act. From this blueprint, and from Kagame's own vision, came a straightforward list of priorities.

Since Rwanda has few natural resources and is too small for large-scale agriculture, the new government concluded that it needed to find another niche. It proclaimed a new mission: to make Rwanda the trade and commercial hub of East and Central Africa, a region awash in resources but plagued by poverty, corruption, and paralyzing inefficiency. That would require it to build a modern network of road, rail, air, and Internet connections; improve the education system, especially in science and information technology; promote gender equality; encourage private investment; and oversee all of this with a state that is honest, impartial, and transparent.

The regime's passion quickly produced tangible results. New buildings sprung up in Kigali. Clinics opened in midsized towns. Neighborhoods and streets were cleaned. Businesses began to thrive, and even a few foreign investors turned up. Rwandans began to sense that something extraordinary was happening around them. Foreigners who returned to visit after long absences were impressed and even shocked.

"I returned to Kigali after eight years and I was astounded," said Richard Orth, who had been a military attaché at the American embassy in the mid-1990s. "Not surprised, but astounded. It was everything from seeing the police force acting like real police, driving patrol cars and using traffic tickets, to the banking reforms that have turned that city into the Zurich of Central Africa. All of this stems from Kagame and his vision."

One messy detail remained to be addressed. Kagame had never been elected to the presidency, and until he was, some in the outside world would question his legitimacy. The first step in this process was to write a constitution. Rwanda's new one allowed the president two seven-year terms and made no provision for a vice president. The election was set for August 25, 2003.

When RPF leaders met to choose their candidate, a few grumbled about Kagame's autocratic style. One or two even mumbled that they might prefer someone else. In the end, though, the result was as everyone expected: Kagame would run for a full term.

Who would be so bold as to run against him? The former president, Pasteur Bizimungu, might have been a strong candidate, but he was in jail. Several other possible contenders, including former cabinet ministers, were living outside Rwanda and afraid to return. Those who had stayed in the country concluded that since the purpose of the election was only to ratify Kagame in office, it made no sense to compete. Finally a challenger stepped forward: Faustin Twagiramungu, who had been the first postgenocide prime minister, was dismissed after a year and had been living in Belgium ever since. He was Hutu, had impeccable antigenocide credentials, and was even married to a daughter of Gregoire Kayibanda, Rwanda's first president.

"The Rwandan people have been disappointed by the RPF," Twagiramungu declared as he began his campaign. "They were promised a democracy which has been turned into a dictatorship. . . . Newspapers are being closed, journalists are put in jail, people are forced to adopt the words of the president. It is intolerable. Today people are tired of Kagame, not only in Rwanda but throughout the region."

Soon after Twagiramungu began making speeches like this, Parliament voted to ban his political party. He stayed in the presidential race, but the press gave his campaign little coverage. His supporters were harassed and intimidated. Several of them, including Leonard Hitimana, a prominent member of Parliament, and Augustin Cyiza, an army colonel and former vice president of the Supreme Court, disappeared and were never seen again. Kagame began lacing some of his speeches with promises to "wound" those who opposed him and "relieve them of their duties so they can go away." At some point he evidently decided that he needed not simply to win this election but to win it overwhelmingly. The final result showed him with 95 percent of the vote.

Most Rwandans were grateful to Kagame for having brought them peace, security, and a measure of hope for the future. He might well have won a fully free election. But fear that he would not, or that a strong opposition campaign might weaken his ability to govern, or that it would reopen genocidal passions, led the government to stage a decidedly imbalanced one.

All sorts of conclusions came up. Number one was that there was no strong opposition. My answer to that was, "My duty is to create an atmosphere where an opposition can develop, but if one doesn't develop, it's not my fault." Then there was the issue of the result, which was about 95 percent in favor of the RPF. Some people questioned this high margin. But for me, I don't see why, unless someone can show that it wasn't possible or that it didn't happen. . . . The country was really at a turning point. The scars of the genocide were no longer so fresh. Changes were taking place. People were eager for whatever guarantees there could be for peace and security. They wanted security first of all. Even people who didn't know the RPF program in detail saw us as the party that would guarantee that.

Kagame had used his political and military power to rid himself of domestic opponents and then won an election some found dubious. Few Rwandans protested. Most are miserably poor agro-pastoralists whose hopes are concentrated on essentials like security, work, and food. Many find the idea of competitive politics terrifying. Their only experience of it was during the final period of the Habyarimana dictatorship, and it brought catastrophe. Few are eager to try again.

At midday on September 12, 2003, before an animated crowd at Amahoro Stadium in Kigali—the same stadium where thousands of terrified Tutsi had sought refuge when the genocide erupted—

Kagame was sworn in as Rwanda's elected president. For years the RPF had felt alone, besieged, threatened by murderous enemies, and compelled to impose harsh measures. By the time Kagame was inaugurated, much had changed. Armies of the ex-FAR and *interahamwe* had been defeated. Refugees had returned home. The process of reconciliation had begun. Life was returning to Rwanda and with it even sparks of hope. Many in Amahoro Stadium that sunny day dared to believe a new era was dawning.

"When you read about wartime leaders, there is always some element of dictatorship or authoritarianism—and this president has been a war president throughout," one of Kagame's longtime comrades, Emmanuel Ndahiro, mused when asked why the regime insisted on controlling politics and public life so closely during its first decade in power. "There was so much pressure on us. Things seemed to be hanging by a thread. But some time around 2002 or 2003, President Kagame made an assessment that we were into a new phase. The international community was putting real pressure on the Congo, for the first time, to stop working with our enemies. We were able to begin focusing our resources on other things. You could sense President Kagame breathing a sigh of relief. He had gotten to a point where he felt the situation was stable. From a strategic point of view, we had space. It's something the president never felt he had before."

Kagame and his comrades set to work with abandon. If the list of obstacles before them was endless, so was their enthusiasm. They had already brought Rwanda from chaos and devastation to peace and stability, in itself an astonishing achievement. Pulling the country out of poverty would be even more difficult, but the challenge thrilled and energized them. The third great task before them was more diffuse. Somehow they had to manage a transition to fuller democracy, to a system that would allow all to participate without reopening wounds that could lead to another catastrophe.

"Rwanda's key dilemma," the East African sage Mahmood Mamdani observed, "is how to build a democracy that can incorporate a guilty majority alongside an aggrieved and fearful minority in a single political community."

Over the years that followed, Kagame led his country on an epic march. He set in motion what he hoped would be a transformation as radical as any in the history of postcolonial Africa. His methods were unorthodox, his drive unflagging, and his array of foreign friends unmatched. People searching for new ideas about how to save the world began traveling to Rwanda, eager to see for themselves what was happening there. I was one of them.

In the people here, there is something that I cannot reconcile with. It's people taking their time when they should be moving fast, people tolerating mediocrity when things could be done better. I feel they are not bothered, not feeling the pressure of wanting to be far ahead of where we are. That runs my whole system.

14

WHEN YOU'RE NOT SERIOUS, YOU CAN'T BE CORRECT

THE LOVELIEST BREAKFAST SPOT IN KIGALI is the open-air terrace atop the Mille Collines Hotel. Terrified refugees cowered there during the 1994 genocide, but now breezes are sweet and the buffet features sliced papaya and flaky croissants imported from Belgium. On one of my first mornings in Rwanda, I sat on that terrace with an American who has spent much of his life in troubled places and moved to Rwanda because he wanted to watch President Kagame's audacious experiment unfold. I asked him what he had concluded so far.

"Let me tell you something," he replied reflectively as our waiter poured African coffee from a shiny pot. "These are serious people."

I heard that word many times in Rwanda. There is no higher compliment than to call a Rwandan serious. The most devastating epithet is "not serious."

One other word kept cropping up when Rwandans told me what they expect of themselves and others: "correct." A good Rwandan must always be serious and correct. It is a stern ethos, born of both tradition and the crucible of modern Rwanda.

"In Africa, many people are not serious, and when you're not serious, you can't be correct," Tito Rutaremara told me. "Being serious means making plans and putting them into effect. We came from poor families. We struggled for years. If we were not serious and correct, we would not be where we are."

Some students of modern Rwanda call it "the Prussia of Africa." Discipline, especially self-discipline, is expected of every citizen. Everything should not only work but work well. Streets are to be clean, appointments are to be kept, regulations are to be followed, and deadlines are to be met. Shops must display tax certificates. Drivers who play car radios too loudly are fined. Those who park illegally are ticketed. People without shoes are not allowed to shop at markets. Livestock may not be kept within city limits. Houses built without permits are summarily bulldozed. Vagrants are arrested.

Hardly a week goes by in Rwanda without a crackdown on some business or public agency where proper standards are not upheld. Usually these are decreed with little or no discussion beforehand. When President Kagame concluded, for example, that Rwandans were using too many plastic bags and that the bags were causing an array of environmental problems, he banned them by decree and sent the police to enforce his dictate. When he decided that the traditional Rwandan method of making bricks was producing too much smoke and consuming too much wood, he outlawed it, sharply increasing the price of bricks. The ramshackle kiosks that had long been part of life in Rwandan towns offended his sense of order, so he ordered them shut even though they provided sustenance for many poor families.

While I was in Rwanda, a health inspector in Ruhengeri closed half a dozen restaurants because they did not "maintain hygiene and cleanliness." Around the same time, an even more ambitious inspector in another district closed forty-seven restaurants and cafés; he had found some with dirty furniture, others lacking clean dish towels, and several with overcrowded dining rooms. Then the education ministry ordered two Kigali schools shut in the middle of their terms because they were not offering clean water or sanitary toilets. In the university town of Butare, thirty people were arrested for being "idle and disorderly." They were poor and looking for work, but the police chief saw them only as potential troublemakers.

"We shall continue arresting them until they stay in their homes and villages instead of coming here in town to cause disorder and insecurity," he warned.

This style repels some Western governments and human rights groups. Their censure does not bother Kagame. On the contrary, he and his comrades seem to revel in defying the outside world.

"They present everything in an authoritarian way," the unofficial dean of the Kigali diplomatic corps, a wise European who has spent decades in Africa, told me one afternoon.

> They just announce what they've decided, and everyone has to do it. The international community likes discussion and consultation. This is not their style. So there is a problem of perception in the international community. In the old days, they saw this as a fine place, a land of milk and honey. Habyarimana, like Mobutu, knew exactly how to please the Europeans, and the West shut its eyes to what was happening here. There was a kind of complicity. This was a period when Cubans were in Angola, Burundi was a little bit "red," the Central African Republic was a problem, and Kenya and Uganda were also becoming hard to manage. So in Rwanda, the perception became "Yes, they kill each other a bit, but it's Africa, and in any case the fire is not reaching our houses." Now we've got this new group that doesn't care what the international community says. They just decide what they want and do it. I have to tell you that people on the outside are not happy. They're saying, "Who is this little Negro to tell us what's good for a country?" And the Rwandans respond by thinking, "These people abandoned us in 1994 and ran away with their people. So why should we listen to what they say?"

Nowhere is the Rwandan regime's determination to break with pernicious tradition clearer than in its campaign against official corruption. More than four thousand public officials are required to file net worth statements each year, and Tito Rutaremara, who is Rwanda's "ombudsman," combs through them searching for suspicious increases in wealth. Anyone caught with a hand in the public till, or found to be using a government post for financial gain, can expect no mercy. Even cabinet ministers and longtime friends of the president have fallen into disgrace and worse for failing to meet the regime's rigid ethical standards. Some protest that they were only doing what has long been tolerated in Rwanda and elsewhere, but judges do not heed those pleas. Nor are the guilty quietly rehabilitated after the storm passes, as happens in nearby countries. They can never return to public life, because they are considered guilty of something even worse than dishonesty. They have shown themselves to be not serious and not correct.

Corruption, of course, still exists in Rwanda. It ranges from large-scale, like the president of a state-owned bank who gave his friends millions of dollars in unsecured loans, to petty, like a police officer who accepted the equivalent of two dollars to free a young European he had caught buying marijuana outside a nightclub. All understand, however, that these are risky things to do. Streets in Kigali are hung with posters exhorting, "Corruption Is the Enemy of Development" and "He Who Practices Corruption Destroys His Country." They are warnings as well as slogans.

Corruption is something we talked about way back in the old days of our struggle. It is also something that is clearly, very largely, behind the problems African countries face. It is very bad in African or Third World countries, in that it actually involves leaders. It is not just corruption with ordinary people. In some places it has become systemic, part of the system. It is hard to change because it has become a way of life in some places. We don't even need to debate that any more, or the fact that it prevents or works against development. That's a fact. You can't make a difference if you don't fight it. You have to look at things that have high impact. You can't fight corruption from the bottom. You have to fight it from the top.

In seeking to promote this new mentality, Kagame has made effective use of symbols. Among the most striking is the complete absence of his relatives from public life. None has a government job or enjoys special status. One of the president's sisters runs a small dairy business, buying milk from the countryside and distributing it to restaurants and cafés in Kigali. Another operates a modest souvenir stand at the Kigali airport. Lucrative privileges that rain down on relatives of the Big Man in some other African countries are not part of Rwandan life.

Early in 2004 Kagame took aim at another practice that has undermined public confidence in many African governments. At several cabinet meetings, he mentioned that he was unhappy about the amount of government money that officials were spending to buy and maintain their vehicles. Many were plush, high-performance gas-guzzlers imported through Dubai at costs of up to $70,000 apiece. A couple of ministers took Kagame's hint and turned in their vehicles, but the rest chose to ignore it. Nor did they react when he started complaining about their driving habits in public speeches. Finally, in evident frustration, Kagame ordered an operation no one in Africa had ever imagined. He sent police squads to main intersections in Kigali and ordered officers to stop every luxury car they saw, check who was inside, and, if it was a government official, inform him or her that the vehicle was being confiscated. Over the next couple of days, the police seized hundreds of vehicles. They were driven to a large parking lot and then auctioned off to private bidders.

"When I travel to other African countries, the one thing you hear the most, the thing people know and admire most about President Kagame, is this thing about the cars," Gerald Mpyisi, who runs a computer company in Kigali, told me with a proud smile. "It's because this represents a huge change in mentality. In other countries, even the most successful people will do anything to become a minister. It means you can have a big car, a big house. People will bow down before you, and you have a thousand ways to make yourself rich. Here it's just the opposite. It's not just that you have a low salary and no benefits of office. It's that when you work for Paul Kagame, you are working twenty-four hours a day. The ministers absolutely dread those Wednesday-afternoon cabinet meetings. Kagame is so sharp with them. He will look right at a minister and say, 'I am not satisfied. You are not performing well. Either improve or I will find someone else.'"

Not all Rwandans approve of this rigorous, absolutist approach to governing. Some wonder, for example, whether closing a school because toilets are not working—or even, as was the case in Kigali, when feces fill an outdoor latrine—is really best for students. Once in a great while, protests against Kagame's fiats are so strong that he backs down, such as when he threw hundreds of people out of work and inconvenienced thousands by banning motorcycle taxis in Kigali. Drivers and passengers erupted in anger. At first he dismissed their protests, saying he would not "abolish a policy just because someone has said it is a problem [for] him." People did not calm down, though, and finally their protests reached such intensity that Kagame agreed to revoke his order. He did not do it happily.

The overriding idea in all of this is that there has been a lack of a sense of order or playing by the rules or obeying laws. We have existed in an anarchic situation, to the extent that even killing had become normal. If you are angry with someone and have a panga *nearby, you just cut his neck and it's finished. This is the kind of society we developed. The political process was part of it. The relatively rich got away with everything, and the poor had no rights.*

Rwanda is a dumping ground for everything people don't want. If we had coasts or waterways, maybe we would have had ships coming here to dump waste from other countries. Everything bad was found here. So this attitude—I feel strongly about this—may be a way of returning to social values, of making people value a certain order. Perhaps it is the only way to restore some level of dignity and integrity to the people of this country.

It is always dangerous to assess a national character, but many who visit Rwanda come away with similar impressions of its people. They seem restrained and introverted. The embrace with which they greet friends is a cool and distant one. They do not like to gossip, tell stories, or give personal advice. Some outsiders find them opaque.

"Rwandans developed the practice of lying on an individual scale," says a handbook for teachers prepared by the education ministry. "It became a virtue, and anyone who could lie without being discovered was praised as being more intelligent than others."

People in countries near Rwanda have for centuries produced some of the world's most magnificent tribal art. Rwandans do not overflow with that kind of creativity. The seminal African art show of the 1990s, organized by the Royal Academy of Arts in London, contained more than a hundred items from the Congo, among them exquisite figurines and haunting masks like those that transfixed Picasso's generation of modern artists. Rwanda was represented by a handful of baskets. Africa's next great poet, novelist, painter, or singer will probably not come from Rwanda, but that does not bother most Rwandans. They have different ambitions.

Rwandans appreciate their country's low crime rate, clean streets, and civic order. So do outsiders. President Kagame wants development groups and entrepreneurs from other countries to embrace Rwanda. One reason they have done so is that Rwanda is a safe and pleasant place to live. If keeping streets clean and maintaining public order is in part a strategy to impress foreigners and lure them to Rwanda, it's working.

"Rwanda is one of the safest countries in Africa," an American doctor who places medical students in African clinics and hospitals, told me. "Kigali is now a place where I could send my predominantly female students, and they'd be fine."

All of this has led some to grumble. They say the regime is creating a protected bubble in Kigali, a Potemkin village where expatriates can walk safely at night to Thai or Indian restaurants while the wretched realities of Rwandan life remain safely hidden. More than a few Rwandans, including some in Kigali itself, live on the brink of starvation, but pains are taken to assure that visitors do not have to confront their misery. Outsiders marvel, for example, that in Kigali they rarely see street kids scrounging in dumpsters or begging for coins. Not all realize that the police regularly scoop up these kids, hold them in unpleasant detention centers for periods of up to several weeks, and then require them either to return home or sign up for vocational courses run by the Red Cross. Very poor people or people who are barefoot or dressed in rags are a rare sight in Kigali and other Rwandan towns. That is at least in part because the police prevent such people from entering towns.

One reason Rwanda is so peaceful is that the government spies on people. "If we two are talking, no problem," one of my Rwandan friends told me. "If we are three, no problem. But if we are four, one is from intelligence. Everyone thinks there's someone watching. It's not true, because they can't watch everyone. But it has an effect."

My friend finds this level of social control reassuring. Like many Rwandans, he fears what people would do if the regime were less strict. Spying is discreet, but not so discreet that people don't notice it. Everyone understands that it is happening.

"Someone is watching me here, for sure," a hotel manager told me. "I don't know who it is, but without a doubt someone on my staff is reporting to intelligence."

President Kagame's famously demanding style, and especially his impatience with aides who are not both scrupulously honest and brilliantly effective, also has a hidden side. He has fired enough cabinet ministers to make up an entire Rwandan government. More than a few have felt so uncomfortable after breaking with him that they have left Rwanda to live abroad. Some were undoubtedly corrupt or incompetent. Others fell because their ideas, personalities, or ambitions clashed with the president's.

There are taboos in today's Rwanda. The strongest of them prohibits appealing to ethnic identity. Even using the words "Hutu" and "Tutsi" in conversation is frowned upon.

It is permissible to assert that the government oppresses people, but not that it oppresses Hutu. To complain that political power is concentrated in the hands of an elite is acceptable; to say that it is concentrated in the hands of a Tutsi elite is not. This prevents the public spread of ethnic anger that might one day lead to a second genocide. It also chills discussion on a topic of urgent national importance.

Accusing the army of atrocities, or investigating massacres or unexplained disappearances of past years, is another taboo. So is digging into the holdings of Tristar Investments, the RPF's shadowy business empire. Restrictions on free expression, though, have eased steadily since Kagame was elected president in 2003. Every year newspapers become more daring. During my visits, I saw stories with headlines like "RPF Hijacked by Clique"; "Let's Face It, No Political Space in Rwanda"; "Habyarimana's Son Accuses Kagame of Murder"; "Plundering of National Resources Compromises Vision 2020"; and "Kagame Consolidates Dictatorship in the Name of Democracy; Absolute Power Has Corrupted Kagame to the Extent of Believing He Is a Semi-God in a Semi-Paradise."

Yet there are still limits. At the beginning of 2007 the rabidly antigovernment Kinyarwanda newspaper *Umurabyo* published a column asserting that "those who killed Hutu are free" and that "corrupt officials and criminals in the RPF" were covering up murders because "they think the Hutu who perished are not human beings." The columnist called on President Kagame to remove "prostitutes" from his government and named nearly a dozen, among them the army chief of staff and the director of the intelligence service. In previous columns, she had asserted that "Rwandans who disagree with the government's version of past events face big problems," that "those who talk about what happened are hunted down," and that the government was responsible for the abduction of dissidents like Augustin Cyiza, who disappeared shortly before the 2003 presidential election. This proved too much for the authorities. The columnist was arrested, tried, found guilty of spreading "divisionism," and sentenced to one year in prison.

"This is not a democracy," shrugged one of Kagame's admirers, an American who has lived in Rwanda for several years and works closely with the government. "You're not supposed to criticize the president or the executive branch. There's no real free press or multiparty system. The ministry of defense is certainly the strongest institution in the country. That's in part because of very real security concerns and in part because a beneficent dictatorship is what's going to get Rwanda through the postgenocide period and develop."

Mistrust and anger quietly permeate Rwandan life. In every village and on every hill, there are people who have not only been brought up on hatred but have killed to express it. Authoritarian regimes often sow the seeds of their own destruction, but President Kagame and many others believe that in postgenocide Rwanda, only such a government can prevent another cataclysm.

"Most Rwandans understand that if we want to have a peaceful future and develop our country, this reconciliation process is absolutely necessary," one of my Rwandan friends told me. "But when they look inside themselves, inside their own hearts, they may find very different feelings."

That friend, Anastase Shyaka, is director of the Center for Reconciliation Studies, a think tank based at the National University in Butare. He told me it is almost hopeless to try to change the hearts of older Rwandans, since they spent their formative decades being bombarded with messages of hate. As for young people, he is only cautiously optimistic. He believes they are open to the idea of a new Rwanda, but only as long as they see hope and opportunity.

"It doesn't work simply to tell them that their old idea of identity is meaningless," Anastase told me. "What does work is to show them that embracing the new idea is important for economic development, which everyone agrees is the key to our future as a nation."

This was a message I heard time and again from Rwandans who reflect on their country's future. Pulling people out of poverty, they told me, is a wonderful goal in itself. In Rwanda, though, the stakes are especially high. If Rwandan leaders do not impose a radical development project, or if they impose one and it fails, their country could face a tragedy of biblical proportions.

Rwanda's sweeping development plan, Vision 2020, envisions "a credible and efficient state governed by the rule of law," a society that is "politically stable, without discrimination among its sons and daughters," and "a prosperous knowledge-based economy" shaped by "a modern, competitive private sector based on a culture of initiative and creativity." Among its specific targets for 2020 are a 50 percent reduction in the number of Rwandans living in poverty, compared to the number who were poor in 2000; a 50 percent drop in infant mortality over the same period; a leap in the average

Rwandan's annual income from $220 to $900; a sevenfold increase in the number of medical doctors; a 100 percent literate population, up from 48 percent; an increase in the number of people with electricity in their homes from 2 percent to 35 percent and in the number with easy access to clean water from 52 percent to 100 percent; and a host of infrastructure projects ranging from a string of hotels in the countryside to East Africa's most modern airport. All of these goals will be difficult to achieve. Others seem impossible. When Kagame is told this, he replies with palpable irritation, "I do not apologize for having big dreams."

Can those dreams become real? That is the question I sought to answer in months of travel around the new Rwanda. I wanted to discover how a miserable country sets out to become a happy one.

MY BASE IN RWANDA was the Mille Collines Hotel. I chose it because it is near the center of Kigali, the staff is friendly, a lively crowd gathers at the poolside bar, I was able to negotiate a long-term rate, and other housing is hard to find. The real reason, though, struck me the first time I appeared there. At the front gate, a tourist was taking a photo of her companions standing next to the sign that says "Hotel des Mille Collines." Tourists do not pose for pictures in front of other Kigali hotels. This one, albeit under another name, is probably the most famous place in the country. Almost every Westerner who has heard of Rwanda knows *Hotel Rwanda*.

Hollywood first came to Rwanda in the form of Stewart Granger and Deborah Kerr. They arrived to shoot a film version of the nineteenth-century jungle adventure *King Solomon's Mines*. The film, released in 1950, includes a spectacular sequence of traditional dance performed by Watusi, as the Tutsi were then known to Westerners. Outtakes turned up in a series of shorts aimed at enthralling young boys and also in a 1959 sequel called *Watusi: Guardians of King Solomon's Mines*. Several pop groups made songs based on rhythms from the music in these films. In 1962 the Orlons had a hit with "The Wah Watusi," which had a catchy beat and lyrics that pleaded, "I just gotta fall in love with you / Watusi is the dance to do."

This brief cultural fling did little to create an awareness of the Tutsi in the outside world. At the time of the 1994 genocide, Rwanda was still a blank in the minds of almost everyone in the world. America's ignorance was so complete that when news of the genocide broke, staff officers at the Pentagon reacted by asking one another, "Is it Hutu and Tutsi or Tutu and Hutsi?"

Today Rwanda is probably the best-known country in sub-Saharan Africa, with the single exception of South Africa. That did not happen simply because such a heinous crime was committed there in 1994. It is because of the rich lode of poems, stories, films, memoirs, and stage plays that the crime inspired. All are devastating in their portrayal of human brutality. Most are also inspirational. *Hotel Rwanda*, released in 2005, reached more people than all the others combined. It defines what most of the world knows, or thinks it knows, about the Rwandan genocide. Nonetheless it is President Kagame's least favorite movie.

As viewers around the world know, *Hotel Rwanda* tells the story of twelve hundred refugees, nearly all of them Tutsi, who survived the genocide barricaded inside the Mille Collines Hotel. It is an uplifting Hollywood drama, complete with requisite hero: the brave and endlessly resourceful hotel manager who does whatever necessary to protect refugees from menacing army units and *interahamwe* gangs. Best of all, it is based on a true story.

The Kigali premiere of *Hotel Rwanda* was a glittering affair staged at the city's best hotel—not the Mille Collines but the brand-new Intercontinental. Senior government officials attended. Later thousands of people attended an outdoor screening at Amahoro Stadium. In Rwanda and around the world, critics and humanitarians alike praised the film. Their love fest culminated at the end of 2005 with a ceremony in the White

House at which President Bush presented Paul Rusesabagina, the real-life hotel manager, with the Presidential Medal of Freedom.

"By risking his own life, he helped save the lives of more than one thousand fellow Rwandans," the citation said. "He represented the best of the human spirit."

Matters might have rested there if Rusesabagina had not begun using his new platform to criticize Rwanda's government, first indirectly and then with increasing venom. *Hotel Rwanda* gave him moral authority, and he used it to accuse President Kagame of everything from oppressing and killing Hutu to covering up famine. He compared RPF leaders to the old regime's murderous *akazu*, and Kagame to masterminds of the genocide like Colonel Bagosora. His foundation, the Hotel Rwanda Rusesabagina Foundation, became a magnet for anti-Kagame forces around the world.

No one was surprised when Kagame fired back. In a series of speeches and interviews, he scorned Rusesabagina as a "hero made in Hollywood." The official Rwandan daily *New Times* published a stream of articles depicting the film as pure fantasy and ridiculing the claim that Rusesabagina had saved lives. Witnesses testified that dignitaries hiding in the Mille Collines had sent hundreds of faxes to protectors in the outside world, and that these messages, along with a uniquely resolute contingent of UN peacekeepers, kept the refugees safe. The film was wrong, *New Times* asserted, to give any credit to this "rotund kitchen manager" who later came to espouse "genocide ideology as a lasting alternative to unity and reconciliation." Never had Kagame's government launched such a bitter and sustained public campaign against any individual.

Antagonism between the world's two best-known Rwandans undermined a unique chance for national development. If they had found a way to work together, they might have been able to shape world opinion in ways that could have brought new resources to their struggling country. Kagame, however, is not the sort of man who reaches out to critics.

"His DNA rebels against compromise," one of his former aides told me.

He's no celebrity at all. His claim to being a celebrity is false. What is it he did? Most of the things happened by accident. He didn't save people, as he claims, not a single one I know of. . . .

The film did well to highlight the issue of genocide and bring it to people who did not know what happened in Rwanda. But it has nothing to do with the true history of Rwanda. That people were in the Mille Collines is a fact, but what is not a true fact is Rusesabagina's story as a person.

Did the world's most famous hotel manager really save lives, or is he a fraud? Debate over this question has become so politically charged that finding an honest answer is all but impossible. I sought one from Senator Odette Nyiramirimo, who was a refugee inside the Mille Collines in 1994 and went on to become a much-admired figure in the new government. "Many people want me to say Paul is not a hero, so I say, 'Okay, he's not a hero,'" she told me. "But he helped me. Because of him, I'm here."

"I really loved him," she mused after a pause. "Even today, I can't hate him. I love his wife and children very much. He can't be my friend because he's fighting against the government in which I believe and in which I am. He lies about a lot of things, like when he talks about how much money is going to our leaders. He is trying to get the world to have a bad opinion of Kagame and the people working with him. I wonder how it is possible for people to change like that, because when we were together during the genocide, he was so nice."

The only direct flight from Rwanda to Europe lands in Brussels, and once while passing through, I stopped to visit Paul Rusesabagina. He has built a prosperous life there, starting as a taxi driver, building a small fleet, investing in a trucking company in Zambia, and then, since the release of *Hotel Rwanda*, giving speeches around the world. We sat in his sunlit living room, which is dominated by a large, impressively framed photo of him receiving the Medal of

Freedom in Washington. I told him I had just read his memoir, in which he asserts that Rwanda is "in pieces and in danger of exploding again before long," largely because it is "governed by and for the benefit of a small group of elite Tutsi." He smiled and pointed up to the photo.

"On November 9, 2005, I got the Medal of Freedom," he said. "That was the beginning of open war on the part of Paul Kagame. He thought that medal should have been his."

Rusesabagina's memoir is called *An Ordinary Man*. In it he describes himself as "a good natured fellow" and says, "There are very few people with whom I could not sit and enjoy a cognac." I found him solicitous and hospitable. He has the experienced hotel manager's ability to put people at ease. During our conversation he smiled often and never became emotional—even when he told me that Rwanda's government is "a pure and simple dictatorship," compared its army to the genocidal *interahamwe*, and said its leaders tolerate "no opposition, no freedom of speech, no democracy."

"Any opposition leader is taken by the government today as a threat," he told me. "Any Hutu who can be an opposition leader, any Hutu who can plan, any Hutu who can implement a plan, any Hutu who is an intellectual or a businessman—always this is seen as a threat."

In many of the countries Rusesabagina visits, he is honored as a dark-skinned Schindler, a moral man who risked his life to save others in a time of national insanity. I asked whether he had actually saved lives or whether the film exaggerated his role.

"I never claimed to have saved anyone," he replied. "I helped people to survive, and all together, we managed."

It was a deft answer. Over the next few hours, Rusesabagina gave me many more. Slowly I began imagining him as an opposition figure in Rwanda. He has a knack for catchy lines, and his warm, reassuring style contrasts sharply with Kagame's stern, aloof intensity. Because he has a Hutu background, he might win votes from people who believe the Hutu majority has been unfairly marginalized. I asked whether he might one day return to Rwanda and try his hand at politics. He seemed eager but also acutely aware of how difficult it is to challenge an authoritarian regime that equates some forms of dissent with treason.

"People like me have no place in Rwanda," he sighed as he drove me toward the train station at the end of our half-day together. "I talk a little bit too much. I speak my mind. Rwanda is not ready for that, for people who won't keep quiet. But I don't see myself getting old in Belgium, being an old man here, with a small dog as my only friend."

I LOVE RWANDANS, but I don't want there to be too many of them. There are enough already. President Habyarimana might have been exaggerating when he said in the early 1990s that Rwanda was full, but not by much. It was and is one of the world's most densely populated countries. If its population continues to grow at current rates, it is doomed.

For more than a decade after the genocide, few Rwandans wanted to admit this harsh fact. With so many dead, it seemed almost sacrilegious to suggest that overpopulation could ever again become a problem. Yet Rwanda has long had more people than its meager resources and small area can support.

The first Rwandan census, taken in 1911, found that the country had about two million inhabitants. The population grew steadily over the next half-century. By 1969, it was 3.6 million, which may be the limit of what an agricultural country of this size can support with traditional farming techniques. Then the growth rate began rising more sharply. At the time of the 1994 genocide there were nearly seven million Rwandans. In the years that followed, those born far exceeded the number who had been killed. By the end of 2007 the population was approaching ten million.

The average Rwandan woman has six children. At this rate, there will be thirteen million Rwandans in 2020. That will make any substantial social or economic progress impossible. It will deeply destabilize Rwandan life. Some believe it could also lead to another outbreak of mass murder.

"Rwandans in general view the genocide as related to over-population," Dr. Cassing Hammond, a professor of obstetrics and gynecology at Northwestern University Medical School, told me after returning from a research tour. "As we get population back to pregenocide levels—and Rwanda is once again the most densely populated country in Africa—if they don't control population, not only will there be a serious effect on infant and maternal mortality, but they may face another war. This was driven home to me time and time again."

President Kagame was among the Rwandans who closed their eyes to this looming crisis. That allowed cabinet ministers and members of Parliament to do the same. Few of my experiences in Rwanda were as maddening as hearing senior officials blithely insist that Rwanda can hold a limitless number of people as long as they are educated, or that a large population is beneficial because it creates a market for local products.

Those officials were reflecting social beliefs and conventions that are deeply rooted in Rwandan society. They make Jeannette Mukabalisa's job hard. She is a young health promoter who travels among villages in south-central Rwanda trying to persuade women to have fewer children.

"They say we're not Christian," Jeannette lamented when I visited her base in the town of Mayange.

> They say, "You're town people, we're traditional." Children bring these families prestige. For them, children come from God. So it's difficult, very difficult. . . . We have to show them precisely the bad side of having many children. The first example we use is land, which is the main source of most people's income. If you divide your land among many children, the parcels will be too small. Dividing in two, maybe, but if you have ten, what will you do? The second thing we talk about is education: "You're going to have to pay for the education of each child." The same goes for medical care; everyone needs it. And there's food security; if there are many children, there won't be enough to eat. We're working on it. We have good policies and good planners, but not enough resources are being put into implementation. The role of the government is to change traditional beliefs. This is something they have to change.

It was changing even as we spoke. A handful of outspoken women—of whom there is no shortage in Rwanda—were demanding that the government make population control a priority. One of the most dynamic among them, Senator Odette Nyiramilimo, went as far as to introduce a bill in Parliament that would limit families to three children, with harsh punishment for violators.

"It has to be coercive," she told me without hesitation when I visited her office soon after she introduced her bill.

Diplomats and aid administrators quietly explained to Senator Odette that the outside world frowns on coercive population control. Nonetheless she had forced the issue onto the national agenda. When I asked President Kagame about it, I was surprised to find him not only eager to act, but apologetic about his failure to do so sooner.

"We realize we are late on this," he admitted.

In 2007 Rwanda launched a population-control program that will, if it is fully realized, be the most sweeping in African history. Under its provisions, everyone of childbearing age who visits a clinic or hospital for any reason is counseled on birth control and offered a choice of methods. Heath workers give women Jadel, a small silicone pin that is inserted beneath the skin and is effective for up to five years. Sex education classes are being introduced in schools. President Kagame has begun promoting the program, which makes it effectively impossible for anyone to oppose it. Nor is the Catholic Church resisting; it was so shamefully compromised by its collaboration with genocide that it no longer dares to enter public debates.

What led to the government's change of heart? Part of the answer lies in a PowerPoint presentation that the ministry of health made at the government's annual retreat in early 2007. Slides made clear that if Rwanda could achieve "zero population growth," everyone would be more prosperous. Most persuasive was a slide that displayed data from Thailand. It showed that between 1975 and 1990, the fertility rate there dropped by half and average income more than doubled. The headline over this slide proclaimed,

"Thailand Emerged as a Middle-Income Country in a Single Generation!"

For the visionaries who run Rwanda, that was unbearably tantalizing.

Soon after that government retreat, messages exhorting patriotic Rwandans to limit the size of their families began filling the airwaves. President Kagame and other officials led the campaign with speeches across the country. *New Times* published a weekend supplement headlined "Rapid Population Growth, a Constraint on Resources." The front page carried a photo of an idyllic landscape with the caption "This beautiful scenery will diminish if population is not controlled." An editorial said that Rwanda's population "is already big enough" and that "drastic measures" were needed to keep it from growing.

Response to these calls was more positive than anyone had imagined. That created unexpected problems. Heath clinics were overwhelmed, and demand for contraceptive devices, especially Jadel implants, far outstripped supply. Government officials realized that their financial resources did not come close to matching their newfound passion for population control. They began quietly casting about for an "angel" from abroad who would agree to underwrite the entire effort.

Several Americans are discreetly involved in designing Rwanda's population-control program. Some are physicians like Dr. Hammond. Others are aid workers like Laura Hoemeke, who helped assemble the PowerPoint show that dazzled officials at their 2007 retreat, and Josh Ruxin, who runs the highly promising Millennium Village development project, where population control is a top priority.

"If Rwanda wants to be an Asian tiger," Josh told me, "this is where it all starts."

This trauma, the results of these horrible events—we are trying to find some silver lining and build on it. It's very complex. People miss seeing it. It always has to be factored into the things we have to do and expect. The process of healing is proceeding probably better than I expected at the time of the liberation, but it will take a long time.

What is the future? Do we become prisoners of the past and live like that? It happened. We can't undo it, unfortunately. If we could undo it, that would be ideal, but life isn't like that. It's a change you have to make. Otherwise you suffer twice. You suffer in the present and you continue to suffer forever.

15

BREATHLESS WITH FEAR

"V ERY TERRIBLE," my friend Régis sometimes answers when I ask how his sister is doing.

The two of them are among the many Rwandans condemned to bear unbearable burdens. They are the only members of their family who survived the genocide. Régis has somehow managed to regain his balance and imagine a new life for himself. In it, he will have a driver's license, use the Internet, and ultimately become an accountant. Whatever happens, he knows he will have to care for his sister. She is one of many survivors who have not managed to climb out of their emotional abyss.

It is no surprise, and is in fact eminently reasonable, that many Rwandan survivors still inhabit "very terrible" private worlds. Régis's sister, Imaculée, was twelve years old when her life was torn apart. Hers is one of the faces behind stark statistics the United Nations compiled soon after the genocide. They say 99.9 percent of Rwandan children witnessed violence during the spring of 1994. Ninety percent believed they would die. Eighty-seven percent saw dead bodies, 80 percent lost at least one relative, 58 percent saw people being hacked with *pangas*, and 31 percent witnessed rapes or other sexual assaults.

I met a European engineer who lives in Kigali with a Rwandan woman whose family perished in the genocide. She often has nightmares and fits of weeping. When he asks what is wrong, she moans, "*Quatre-vingt-quatorze! Quatre-vingt-quatorze! Toujours quatre-vingt-quatorze!*" It's always 1994.

Rwanda is struggling to create a health-care system that can address its people's urgent physical needs. It has barely begun to confront the mental illness that envelops the country like an oppressive black cloud, unseen but unavoidable. Most victims have no access to counselors or therapists, much less antidepressant drugs or other treatments that are familiar in the developed world. Many struggle alone in a country that faces, as the Harvard Program in Refugee Trauma reported, "a nationwide mental health crisis."

A study published in *World Psychiatry* reported that one-fourth of Rwandans suffer from post-traumatic stress syndrome. In a culture where people have traditionally resolved their personal problems in private, there was not even a name for this disorder. Now that so many people are collapsing under its weight, one has been found. Victims are said to be *ihahamuka*. It means "without lungs" or "breathless with fear."

The extent of this is quite big, and its effects are very long term. People, even with all their smiles and everything, live painfully inside—quite many of them. It's a seriously wounded society that we're managing. That complicates the work we have to do, and I expect that to be the case for a long time. This is what people from outside miss. They expect things to heal all of a sudden. The moment the genocide was over, people started treating Rwanda as if it was just another country. Very few people took this into consideration, yet it is the reality of our situation. We are trying to think of how this tragic situation and its effects can be turned into something of value. It's a big challenge.

In the months after the genocide, Régis and Imaculée, like many Rwandan orphans, were adopted by a sympathetic family. Régis managed to push aside some of the demons that plagued him. Part of the reason, he told me, was that his sister had fallen into a near-catatonic state, and he resolved to spend his life supporting and caring for her. Whenever he has extra pennies—and especially during April, when Rwandans commemorate the genocide with ceremonies and television programs that bring awful memories flooding back—he buys her a trinket, a biscuit, or some other small gift to distract her.

Years of a brother's love have slowly begun to bring Imaculée out of her private hell. During her teenage years she spent much time curled up in bed, sobbing in the darkness and praying for deliverance. Now she sometimes sleeps soundly. She even attends school and, on good days, imagines a happy future for herself.

"I am everything to her: mother, father, sister, brother, friend," Régis told me once. "I tell her, 'It happened, but it will never happen again. Try to be normal. Don't cry. It's finished. Leave it.' I think about her all the time, every day, every minute. One day we will be happy again. That's what I have to believe."

TRIALS OF ACCUSED MURDERERS—the *genocidaires* of 1994—have become part of Rwandan life. One warm morning in 2007 it was Samson Rogira's turn. He was charged with leading an *interahamwe* gang that hacked people to death in his hometown of Ruhongo, a commercial crossroads in central Rwanda. I drove there to watch him meet his fate.

These trials are not like any others. They could not be, because bringing Rwandan *genocidaires* to justice is uniquely challenging. Government investigators have named more than eight hundred thousand suspects. The true number of killers may be twice that or more. Justice cries out for their punishment. Only reconciliation, however, can guarantee Rwanda's long-term stability.

It's a difficult balance to strike, but it must be carried out. As we try to build our country, there is a very evident need to reconcile our people and find ground on which they can live together again in peace and harmony. But there is no way to ignore the responsibility that some people, or many people, have in what has happened, in the genocide. These are two processes that are opposed to each other in a sense, but that must be carried out at the same time—reconciliation on one hand, justice on the other. Because this crime of genocide involves millions of Rwandans, it would be difficult to find a solution that only affects a few individuals. The whole society of Rwanda was, in one way or another, involved and deeply affected.

In the first months after the genocide, the new regime arrested tens of thousands of people whom neighbors identified as killers. One of them was Samson Rogira. By the time he was called for trial, he had been in jail for twelve years.

The cavernous brick community center in Ruhongo, where this trial took place, sits atop a hill only a few miles from the spot where two-year-old Paul Kagame narrowly escaped death in the "practice genocide" of 1959. I was standing in the crowd outside when a pickup truck with the word "Police" stenciled on the door pulled up. Samson Rogira, bright as a chrysanthemum in the loose pink outfit that all Rwandan prisoners wear, sat in back with an armed guard.

Many who watched the prisoner climb down had known him as a child and young man. Some witnessed his crimes. Rather than jeer him, though, they stood silent. He scanned the waiting faces and then, without visible emotion, walked slowly into the hall where he was to be judged.

On days when a trial like this is being held, all local businesses must close. Everyone in town is expected to attend. These are group therapy sessions as much as judicial proceedings. They are cathartic and often excruciating. Nowhere else do Rwandans have a chance to mourn together while confronting those who terrorized them.

Samson Rogira was led inside. The rest of us followed, taking seats on long rows of benches. A couple of minutes later, nine judges—six men and three women—filed in and sat behind a table at the front of the hall. They were all from Ruhongo, chosen by their neighbors and given a few weeks of training. Each wore a sash bearing the colors and emblem of the Rwandan flag and the word *inyangamugay*, meaning "person of integrity." Once they were settled, the chief judge asked all assembled to stand for a minute of silence. I dared not imagine what images might be flashing through other people's minds during that long minute. Instead I reflected on the extraordinary process that was unfolding around me.

Courts like the one that convened to try Simon Rogira are the result of a decade-long process of study, debate, and trial and error. Under the system Rwanda has adopted, defendants are categorized according to their level of alleged guilt. Only those charged with the most serious crimes are tried before regular courts or the International Criminal Tribunal for Rwanda. The rest face judgment at specially constituted local tribunals, called *gacaca*, that are modeled after those used in past eras to adjudicate land and property disputes.

The backdrop was that the whole population should be involved and seen to be buying into the processes of justice and reconciliation. Historically, gacaca *meant people sitting on the grass to discuss and resolve problems. It's part of Rwandan culture. We took this concept and developed it because it would reach people, and they would see themselves in it. It's the way our culture traditionally resolved problems. We have picked it and developed it to deal with present-day problems. . . .*

Conventional systems have not provided a solution for us. They do not come close to giving us a solution. Gacaca, with all its weaknesses—and there are not so many, fewer than in a conventional system if you're dealing with our problems—opens up opportunities for us.

Rwanda's *gacaca* courts are admirable for several reasons. They convene where crimes actually happened. Victims and witnesses are encouraged to speak. Sentences are limited to thirty years, with half to be served on parole. Defendants who make full and sincere confessions are treated mercifully and encouraged to rejoin their communities. Most are released.

These courts do not, however, give defendants rights they would enjoy in other legal systems. They are not entitled to defense lawyers and have no way to collect exculpatory evidence. Prosecutors are also judges. Pressure for self-incrimination is strong. Appeals are rarely successful and sometimes result in increased sentences.

As this system was taking shape, the Belgian government asked a prominent development-aid specialist, Peter Uvin, to examine it and recommend whether Belgium should support it financially. Uvin found that the system "profoundly compromises on principles of justice as defined in internationally agreed-upon human rights or criminal law standards" but that it deserved support anyway. Belgium's government agreed and became an early supporter of *gacaca*.

Uvin wrote in his report that "some compromise simply is unavoidable" because "criminal law standards were not designed to deal with the challenges faced when massive numbers of people— victims and perpetrators of crimes—have to live together again side by side in extremely poor and divided countries." He even suggested that in Rwanda's unique situation,

> the *gacaca* proposal actually respects the spirit of international criminal and human rights law, if not the letter. In other words, the practice of *gacaca* may well be able to respect key conditions of fair trial and due process, but in an original, locally appropriate form, not in the usual Western-style form. For example, while there is no independent legal counsel, one can argue that the play of argument and counter-argument, of witness and counter-witness by the community, basically amounts to the same fair defense, maybe even better than what the formal justice system has until now produced.

In an apt summation, Uvin called the *gacaca* process "simultaneously one of the best, most dangerous, and possibly last chances Rwanda has."

The first trials were held in 2002, and in the years that followed, the government created more than twelve thousand local tribunals, each with its own panel of judges. Then, in mid-2006, with a publicity barrage that included speeches, billboards, radio plays, a television series, and even a song contest—which a prison group won—the intense trial phase began. Fifty thousand defendants were judged in the first four months. Judges set more than two-thirds of them free, either for lack of evidence or after ruling that the years they had already served in prison were sufficient punishment. Thousands more were freed in the months that followed. That lent some credence to suggestions that the *gacaca* system was created not simply to administer justice and promote reconciliation but also as a way to empty prisons without issuing an official amnesty. Yet most outsiders—including officials from Holland, which took over from Belgium as the main foreign backer of the process—pronounced themselves much impressed.

"They are doing this with all good intentions," a Dutch diplomat told me. "It's a very carefully managed process. They stick to the rules, they are always correct, and the whole process is very transparent. There is no side effect they haven't thought of. They are trying to make this work for reconciliation."

When I asked whether the process had a weakness, this diplomat answered immediately. "There is a perception that no one is paying attention to the crimes of the RPF," she said.

Objections to what Amnesty International calls the "extra-judicial" nature of *gacaca* trials are serious, but the special conditions of Rwanda require an unconventional form of justice. The charge that the *gacaca* system is inherently flawed because it judges only suspects in genocide-related crimes—meaning only Hutu—is more fundamental. Why not expand its mandate to include all crimes committed in 1994, so that cases of revenge killing and other RPF abuses could also be judged?

"We didn't want to confuse matters," presidential adviser Richard Sezibera told me when I asked this question. "People say the RPF also committed crimes. Yes, and they require justice, but this is not genocide. Don't judge them with people who committed genocide. Those are different crimes that can be dealt with in different ways."

Not all Rwandans accept that argument. Some believe that crimes committed by the RPF have never been "dealt with" and never will be. If the state cannot give citizens confidence that justice is applied fairly to all Rwandans, *gacaca* trials could slow and even subvert the process of reconciliation they are designed to encourage.

Spectators at Samson Rogira's trial sat back down after their minute of silence, but the chief judge remained standing. No one present had ever attended an event like this, and none knew how it would unfold. Speaking clearly and simply, the chief judge told them.

"Everyone here today has the right speak," he began. "If you wish to speak, raise your hand. We will call first on those who have come from other places, and then on elders. Do not be abusive. Do not threaten. Do not speak for too long—let others have their chance. People giving evidence should not be afraid. No one will be punished in any way for what is said here, as long as it is true. Do not cause a commotion or disturbance. Those who do so will be punished."

The judge then asked the prisoner to present his identity card, which was duly checked, and read out his name, year of birth—1968, meaning that he was in his midtwenties at the time of the genocide—and former occupation, market porter. The judge asked all who wished to give testimony to leave the hall, so they would not be influenced by what others said, and directed them not to speak to one another. Then he asked two questions that the law requires be posed before every *gacaca* trial.

"Do any of the judges feel unable to participate because of a conflict?" he began. None responded.

"Does anyone here know of a conflict that any of these judges may have?" Again there was no response.

With that, the chief judge nodded to the tribunal's secretary. In a loud and unemotional voice, she read the indictment. It charged that Samson Rogira helped direct an *interahamwe* gang that attacked, robbed, and killed people around Ruhongo in April of 1994 and that maintained a roadblock near the center of town at which Tutsi were captured and taken away to be murdered. He was also said to have carried a pistol and hand grenades and to have looted the homes of his victims. The indictment was carefully detailed, full of names and dates, and took nearly half an hour to read. The rapt crowd listened in motionless silence.

After the secretary finished, she produced and read a second document, the defendant's written statement. In it, he admitted to being an *interahamwe* member, carrying weapons, and looting homes. His gang, he further confessed, had killed some people and pulled others from their cars so they could be taken off to be killed elsewhere. He insisted, however, that he had not personally killed anyone.

"Think," the chief judge warned him. "Did you forget anything? If it is shown that you committed crimes you have not confessed, that will be held against you."

This is a fundamental aspect of *gacaca* trials. Defendants who are thought to be telling the full truth are treated more leniently than those found to be lying, even if their crimes were more serious. Confession is considered not simply a purging of the killer's tainted soul but also a sign of his willingness to reconcile with victims. Yet some guilty defendants insist on their innocence, often because they or their families have been threatened by other prisoners who would be implicated by honest testimony.

Samson Rogira faced his former neighbors for five hours. Several asked him pointed questions that he refused to answer, such as who gave him his pistol and how his gang disposed of bodies. Eight testified that he had been a merciless *interahamwe* leader.

"Every time they came looking for me," said a man who survived the genocide by hiding in a hole in a neighbor's yard, "he was one of the hunters."

Frustration grew palpably as hours passed and Samson Rogira refused to acknowledge doing what many in the hall swore they had seen him do. At one point a woman rose in anger and shouted, "He is not telling the truth! He led attacks in this whole area— even in this very building!"

At that last line, some in the crowd winced and bowed their heads. All knew that when the killing began, more than two hundred Tutsi had crowded into this community center, hoping the authorities would protect them. They had fatally misplaced their trust. On Friday morning, April 22, 1994—few in Ruhango will ever forget the date—an *interahamwe* gang stormed the building and killed everyone inside. Their remains are buried in a mass grave a few hundred yards away.

Throughout that long day, all nine judges remained intently focused. Each asked questions. At several points the chief judge gently encouraged witnesses to finish, but he never cut anyone off. When one witness approached the bench, saying she had something private to say, he held up his hand and told her, "This is a public hearing. If you have anything to say, use the microphone."

The prisoner was less engaged. He wiped his face often. For long periods he stared through the open door at hills on which he had played as a boy and where he later wreaked murderous terror. Had he dreamed of this judgment day? Wished for it to come? Dreaded it? Nothing in his demeanor offered a clue. At the end of the afternoon, when given a final chance to sum up his case, he seemed oddly diffident.

"I can say I participated, because I was part of a group that selected people and sent them to be killed, but myself, I never killed," he insisted. That set off an unhappy murmur in the crowd. "I never cut. I would have done it if I had the chance, but my friends did it first. I did wrong. I ask forgiveness from this court, from the victims, and from all Rwandans."

When he was finished, the tribunal's secretary read out her transcript of the proceedings. The prisoner agreed that it was a faithful record and signed it. So did the chief judge. Then, at his signal, the judges rose and filed out to consider their verdict.

Some spectators drifted away, but most remained nearby. Few spoke. Many seemed distracted. I approached several and found none who believed what Samson Rogira had told the court. One of them, a schoolteacher, answered firmly when I asked whether he was satisfied with the trial.

"Only if the sentence is thirty years," he replied.

After deliberating for two hours, the judges emerged and returned to their seats. Spectators also filed back in. When we were settled, the chief judge spoke.

"After considering the charges, examining testimony given by the defendant and others, weighing the circumstances, and discussing every point, we have rejected the defendant's confession as untrue," he announced. "The defendant participated in the killing of Tutsi and played an important role in organizing the killing."

The chief judge then read from laws that fix the punishment for these crimes and from those that vest judicial authority in *gacaca* tribunals. Finally he turned to the defendant and told him, "In accordance with these legal provisions, we sentence you to twenty-five years in prison." Half of that term would be served on parole, meaning that since Samson Rogira had already spent twelve years in jail, he would be free in a matter of months.

The defendant did not react. Neither did anyone in the crowd. Most had long since been wrung dry of emotion. Justice was done, or at least seen to be done, but whatever satisfaction there was in that paled beside the enormity of the horror that was visited on this town.

A few people cast sidelong glances at Samson Rogira as he was led back out to the pickup truck on which he had arrived, but no one said a word. Some must have felt anger or hatred. Others may actually have pitied their former neighbor, an ignorant wretch who, although evidently a perpetrator, was also a victim. The schoolteacher who had hoped for a thirty-year sentence told me he was satisfied.

"It was fair," he reflected. "In the end, does it really accomplish anything? I don't know. I have to think about that."

DEEPLY ROOTED SOCIAL CONFLICTS like the one that devastated Rwanda in 1994 cannot be resolved through trial and punishment alone. A country torn so violently apart can stabilize only if former enemies reconcile. In Rwanda, this means that people must forgive those who slaughtered their families and even live beside them in newfound brotherhood. This is not a rational thing to do. Yet it is happening in Rwanda, on a grander scale than it ever has any-where. As news of this phenomenon has spread, a host of out-siders—anthropologists, sociologists, Christian believers who see behind it the hand of God, legal scholars, filmmakers—have come to Rwanda to investigate. They witness scenes like one I saw at Mbyo, a dusty village in southern Rwanda.

Thickets of low palms shield Mbyo from the rough dirt road. This village is new, built by the government to house a combina-tion of genocide survivors and released *genocidaires*. It consists of about fifty concrete huts, a well, and a patch of farmland suppos-edly big enough to support its residents. The terrifying spirits that possess millions of minds in Rwanda haunt places like this. My friend Deo Gashagaza, a psychology professor and itinerant pastor who has assumed the mission of bringing Rwanda's victims and killers together, has done much work in Mbyo.

For months Deo had been meeting with two people there, first separately and then together. One, Rosaria Bankundiye, lost her husband and four children in 1994, when she was twenty years old; the man who hacked them to death also attacked her and left her for dead, as the long scar across her face testifies. The other is the killer, Xavier Nemeye, who is free after serving nine years in prison. On the day I came to Mbyo, their neighbors had assembled in a shady grove to hear both of them testify. Most were women, brightly colorful in patterned batik dresses. All fell silent when Deo rose to speak.

"Look into the eyes of the person next to you," he began, and then paused so people would do as he asked. "Look, and see that person, and realize that you can never do anything to hurt that person. Whatever you believe, however much you pray, it means nothing if we don't love each other. It is not possible to love God, who you cannot see, if you don't love your neighbors, who you *can* see."

Deo held the people of Mbyo spellbound for several minutes. He exhorted them to leave their rancor behind and devote all their energy to fighting Satan, whose name in Rwanda, he said, is poverty. When he invoked God's presence, many people closed their eyes and turned skyward. Then he called on Rosaria and Xavier.

They came forward haltingly, as if in pain. Finally they settled onto a log, beside one another but not touching. Everyone before them knew their story. Many have similar ones.

Rosaria was small and frail, aged beyond her years and bent by toil. She wore a flowing yellow skirt and a full blouse in a brown-and-yellow batik pattern. After taking a long moment to steel herself, she looked up and began describing how her family was murdered. She spoke softly but clearly. After a few minutes, when she reached the part about maggots infesting her skull wound while she lay beneath a pile of corpses, she broke down.

All of Rosaria's neighbors had wept many times, so this was nothing unusual. They waited quietly and even approvingly, some clutching each other's hands, until she regained her composure and began again. She started by gesturing at the man sitting next to her, although she never looked at him.

"When he killed us, he also destroyed our home and took all our belongings," she stammered, struggling to resist another breakdown. "I lived off help from other people. But thanks to God, we had the blessing to reconcile with those who committed these acts. It is so hard to talk to someone who killed your family. So I thank God that we have had the chance to live together and reconcile."

These words puzzled me. They were undoubtedly sincere, but the emotion they conveyed—the willingness of this woman to forgive the person who had so grievously harmed her—was difficult to fathom. I grappled with it during the long silence that followed Rosaria's testimony. Then Xavier began to speak. He looked sometimes at the congregation and sometimes at his feet, but never at Rosaria.

"Considering what I did, if you asked me to sentence myself, even killing me would not be enough," he said. "I confessed to the people I committed crimes against. God helped me. I found those people I had wronged—God talked to them. So it was quite simple for me to ask forgiveness, and for them to give it to me. I felt very happy and relieved in my heart. I thank the pastors for what they did in making us reconcile. They helped us talk to each other. We had thought that since we were killers, we would be killed. We didn't expect to be forgiven. We were surprised."

I fixed my gaze on Xavier as he spoke, and when he paused for the first time, I looked over to see how Rosaria was reacting. She was gone. The prospect of hearing Xavier tell his story was too much for her, so she had slipped away. An hour later, back at the village, I met her again.

She told me she had seen Xavier at a market near Mbyo soon after his release from prison three years earlier. She felt no emotion "because I was already dead, and nobody dies twice." Later he approached her and asked for forgiveness, but she was too overwhelmed to reply. Soon afterward, Deo arrived in town. He invited people to an outdoor meeting and told them he had come to promote reconciliation. It was the first time people in Mbyo had heard of this concept. They were shocked.

"Very many people were traumatized on that day," Rosaria told me. "They were saying, 'Reconciliation? How did you come up with this idea? Why do you want us to reconcile?' I don't have my children. My family was rich, with cows, goats, and money in the bank, and I will never get that back. But today I don't wish anything bad for that person. He will die the death God planned for him. If someone kills him, it will not be me."

The number of victims and perpetrators who have reconciled this way is the most remarkable fact of modern Rwandan life. Sessions like the one I witnessed in Mbyo challenge the imagination and raise perplexing questions about the human spirit. On the long, bumpy ride back to Kigali, I asked Deo Gashagaza what he has learned from his work.

"Reconciliation is not a philosophy," he replied. "It's a practice."

Deo has spent much of his time since 1994 running a small and chronically underfunded mission called Prison Fellowship. He started by visiting prisons to counsel *genocidaires* about ways to cleanse themselves of hatred. Then he tracked down some of these prisoners' surviving victims. Each time a prisoner was

released, he would work with him and with the person he wid-
owed or orphaned. Finally he would bring them together. His success rate is amazingly high.

"A woman sees the man who raped her and killed her family,
and she reacts with horror," he told me. "She says, 'How can I live
with this killer?' After a month or six weeks, we bring them to the
point of sharing a meal. You start with psychological preparation.
You talk about her history. She will say, 'It is not easy to stay here
with this man who killed my husband and children. How can you
ask me to do that?' I say, 'You're Rwandan. This man is Rwandan. We can't divide the country, with victims on one side and ex-
prisoners on the other. We all share a destiny and a future.' It's
very complicated. Sometimes I spend three months talking to a
victim. They say, 'I can't sleep at night. My terrible memories are
like a film that keeps playing over and over in my head.' You talk.
You share feelings. It's a process of healing. I use different methods.
Some want to hear the word of God. Others can be reached without the Bible. But everyone, whether they are Christian or Muslim
or believers in Imana, shares the concept of God. I say, 'How can
you hate someone who is made in the image of God? It is not good
to create one bad situation out of another. We need to love one another.' I tell them that no one is born bad, but they grow up in
environments that make them bad. I say we have to change our
environment, change our history."

"Reconciliation" is a byword in today's Rwanda. Everyone
is supposed to favor it. Two government agencies, the National
Gacaca Commission and the National Commission for Unity
and Reconciliation—both run by women—are charged with defin-
ing and promoting it. Much of the front-line work, though, is
done by self-appointed healers like Deo.

"When I first went into a prison to speak," he told me once,
"the prisoners told me, 'What you say sounds good, but we don't
know if you are sent by Kagame.' I tell them, 'I want to build
a new Rwanda. We need peace for our future and for our children.
Why do you want to destroy? Why not change? If all Rwandans hate, what will Rwanda be like in the future?' It was not easy

at the start, but after three months, people in prisons all over the country were inviting me. Then one day, four years after we started, I had a problem with my car. Driving on back roads all that time killed my car. I had no way to move around. A man came to me and told me he was wealthy and wanted to give me a car. He was a Hutu. I said to him, 'Do I know you?' He said, 'No, but I know your story. I have heard about you. I want you to continue your work. Give us peace.' It was an important moment for me. It made me think that nothing is impossible, that we can change our destiny."

How have so many Rwandans come to forgive those who trespassed so terribly against them? Most of those I met gave me the same answer: this is what God wants. The process of postgenocide reconciliation in Rwanda has been shaped largely by religious faith, religious imagery, and religious language. That makes sense, because the depth of forgiveness being asked of Rwandans can be understood only in a spiritual context, not a rational one. Rwanda is not a country that drips with religiosity, and its leaders are not ostentatiously religious. Its reconciliation process, though, is shaped largely around New Testament parables and Christian imagery. Reconciliation is Rwanda's supreme political imperative, but religion drives it.

The fact is that religion, in the history of the genocide—before it happened and when it happened—played a key role. But religion, even having played that negative role, is very much alive in our society. . . .

People always follow religion. Some even follow it blindly, not on a rational basis. . . . People take refuge in religion from their sorrows, things they don't have answers for. If that can create a cushion for people and their sorrows, on which they can rest, it's something people can lean on. Even we, as leaders, are ready to encourage that.

Not every survivor in Rwanda, of course, leaps to embrace his or her tormentor after being told it is God's will. Those who are more educated tend to be less susceptible to religious or spiritual appeals. Many find it difficult to transcend their emotions.

Instead of forgiving the killers, they would like to bring all the stored vengeance of heaven down upon them.

Bonaventure Niyibizi, now a bank president, was living in Kigali when the killing began. He and a group of neighbors decided that their best hope was to pack into three cars and smash their way through roadblocks to the Sainte Famille Church, half a mile away. Miraculously, they made it. For two months they hid inside the church complex with several hundred other terrified refugees. While they were there, Bonaventure's mother was hacked to death in her village. Her killers took several days to complete the job, returning periodically to cut their victim some more and taunt her about how little use her "rich son" was to her now. They later served prison terms and were released. Bonaventure finds that unjust.

"To me as a survivor, I think this government is not being fair to me," he said when I asked him about reconciliation. "It has passed a law saying that if a person who participated in genocide confesses, he can go home. My family was killed. My mother was hacked to death and thrown into a river. I know the people who did it. They confessed. According to law, they have been released after serving seven years in prison. On the political side, I understand this. As an individual, I do not understand."

Bonaventure Niyibizi told me a self-evident truth: "On the survivor's side, it is almost beyond human capacity to think of reconciliation." Yet this thought has been planted in the minds of many Rwandans and has flowered with astonishing richness. In a country where everything is supposed to be measured and rational—or "serious" and "correct"—the most important process in the country, the one without which nothing else can succeed, is in its essence deeply mystical.

FOUR YEARS AFTER THE RWANDAN GENOCIDE, one of the eminences who might have tried to prevent it, Kofi Annan, visited the country he had helped consign to hellfire. During 1994 Annan was chief of the United Nations Department of Peacekeeping Operations. In that capacity, he was principally responsible for assuring that the UN Mission to Rwanda remained small and weak, that General Dallaire did not raid arms depots or take other actions he deemed necessary to prevent mass murder, and that diplomats on the Security Council were kept unaware of Dallaire's vivid warnings and frantic pleas for help.

Rwandans eagerly awaited Annan's words. Many hoped he would offer more than simply an apology. They wanted some explanation of why he and others at the United Nations had so resolutely opposed every effort to stop the killing in Rwanda—and perhaps some ideas about how such tragic misjudgments could be avoided in the future.

Dignitaries greeted Annan when he stepped off his plane in Kigali. From the airport he was driven to the Parliament building, its façade still pockmarked with bullet holes. Nearly the entire Rwandan government had assembled there. The foreign minister spoke first. He reminded his comrades of the gravity of this event, which marked the first time survivors would hear from one of the figures whose inaction led to the greatest failure in the history of the United Nations. Then he turned the podium over to Annan.

Annan began with a long set of platitudes about the work of the United Nations. He said he had come on "a mission of healing" and offered "the hope and the prayer that you will overcome." The audience waited patiently through these preliminaries, but when they were finished, so was Annan's speech. He expressed no remorse and refused even to concede that the United Nations had played a dubious role in Rwanda. The closest he came was to say that the Rwandan genocide was "the world's tragedy" and that "the world must deeply regret this failure." No institutions and certainly no individuals were to blame, he seemed to be saying—only "the world."

It was an astonishing performance that, by one account, left the assembled dignitaries "stunned" and "numbed in their incredulity that this opportunity to rebuild relations with their country's

decision makers with a frank statement and formal apology had
been passed over." Several members of Parliament stood up and
called out to Annan, asking that he address the question of his personal responsibility and that of the United Nations. He brushed
them aside, saying he had not come to engage in "polemics."

Later that afternoon, Annan was the guest of honor at a formal
reception hosted by President Bizimungu and Vice President
Kagame. He stepped from his limousine with a smile and a wave
and began making his way methodically through the reception
line. When he reached the last guest, he looked around in confusion and then absorbed a shock of his own. President Bizimungu
and Vice President Kagame were nowhere to be seen. They boy-
cotted their own reception to protest Annan's speech.

*I've stopped thinking about the UN, but I continue to think about
people who would ever need such a thing as the UN. My advice is that
when you have problems, try to sort them out, because the international
community never comes, or if it comes, it comes in the wrong way at the
wrong time. . . .*

*What is the UN? Is there really a UN? In the end, it's the individual
powers that be. If France or America or China or Russia don't want
some things to be done by the UN, they won't be done. Yet all of us are
called members. We falsely believe in the UN as something that is ready
to move, but it doesn't move. We should look more to ourselves.*

Most of the powerful foreigners who helped shape the world's
response to genocide in Rwanda have, like Kofi Annan, offered
quasi-apologies of the "mistakes-were-made" variety. They lament
that "the world," "the international community," or "all of us" did
not behave differently. Yet individuals—not only institutions—
made the Rwandan genocide possible. Most were Rwandans.
At least a dozen foreigners, though, had it in their power either
to help prevent the genocide, help stop it once it began, or at least
force the question onto the world's agenda. In the years since, each
has had to decide how much to apologize for, how much to admit,
how much to remember.

"I was not realizing that there was a real genocide," Boutros Boutros-Ghali said years later when asked why he did not act. "It takes time for us to understand."

Others stained by the Rwanda tragedy have explained themselves with similarly disembodied logic. "We, the international community, should have been more active in the early stages of atrocity in Rwanda in 1994 and called them what they were: genocide," the former American ambassador to the UN, Madeleine Albright, said in a speech to the Organization of African Unity in 1997. A few months later, during a three-hour visit to Rwanda, President Clinton said "people like me" had failed to grasp "the depth and speed with which you were being engulfed by this unimaginable terror." Secretary of State Warren Christopher, who knew so little about Rwanda that his first act upon learning of the crisis was to check its location in an atlas, devoted twenty pages in his memoir to the Bosnia crisis, but the word "Rwanda" does not appear in the index.

Not all outsiders who helped make the Rwandan genocide possible worked in Washington or at UN headquarters in New York. Some blame lies in Britain, where Prime Minister John Major's government worked hand in hand with the United States to cripple the UN peacekeeping mission. Neither Major nor any of his successors have expressed remorse.

Belgium, which has even more to apologize for, has been marginally more forthcoming. "I confirm that the international community as a whole carries a huge and heavy responsibility in the genocide," Prime Minister Guy Verhofstadt told a hushed crowd at the Kigali genocide memorial in 2000. "Here before you, I assume the responsibility of my country, the Belgian political and military authorities. We owe the people of Rwanda a sincere apology, which I now extend."

Nowhere does the cloud of guilt hang more heavily than over France. Others failed or refused to see that genocide was raging in Rwanda. President Mitterrand and his government armed the Hutu regime; sent soldiers to defend it; supported it resolutely as it carried out the genocide; helped many of its leaders escape when the war ended; granted asylum in France to some of the most bloodthirsty among them, including Madame Habyarimana; and then helped the defeated genocidal army launch a brutal insurgency in a vain effort to retake power.

Soon after the genocide, French journalists began publishing books and articles highly critical of the Mitterrand government's role. Outraged human rights activists demanded an official inquiry. In 1998, Doctors Without Borders said it was "high time the French government broke its traditional silence on its shameful role in the genocide." Foreign Minister Alain Juppé replied indignantly that no one could question the "good intentions of our humanitarian intervention of that era" and that he would never consider "investigating an action our country should be proud of." Pressure did not dissipate, however, and finally Parliament formed an investigating committee. It concluded that President Mitterrand sent aid to Rwanda's army despite knowing that it was killing civilians, and that French and Rwandan troops cooperated closely while the genocide was unfolding. Yet France, the investigators asserted, "did not encourage the Rwandan genocide," which "was committed by Rwandans against Rwandans" and which the United Nations could not stop because "the United States did not want to consider an immediate increase in UN forces." That allowed France, like almost every other guilty party, to point the finger of blame elsewhere.

"Bullshit!" Jean-Christophe Mitterrand exclaimed when an interviewer asked him whether his support for the old Rwandan regime ever gave him sleepless nights. "I reject the question in the sense that you have put it to me, in suggesting that I had some kind of responsibility."

A year after the Rwandan genocide, President Jacques Chirac, who succeeded Mitterrand, made an eloquently moving confession. "France, the country of light and the rights of man, land of welcome and refuge, carried out an irreparable act," he admitted. "Abandoning its word, it delivered protected people to their horrors. These dark hours have sullied our history forever and are an insult to our past and our traditions."

Those words could have been the basis for a new relationship between France and Rwanda, but they were not about the Rwandan genocide. President Chirac was describing France's failure to protect Jews during World War II, not its acts in Rwanda. The freedom he felt to acknowledge this damning episode came above all from the passage of time. If fifty years is the amount of time that must pass before proud nations can admit their crimes, French leaders may be expected to speak frankly about Rwanda around the middle of the twenty-first century.

One night in the summer of 2006, as the World Cup soccer tournament was approaching its climax, an argument broke out over dinner at President Kagame's home. One of his sons announced that he was rooting for France because it was the team of Thierry Henry, his favorite player.

"How can you root for France?" his older brother protested. "They were fighting against father!"

Kagame, by his own account, smiled and said nothing. A few days later, he flew to Berlin for the final World Cup game, and there he chatted with President Chirac. "We didn't have any problem," he reported.

Trouble began soon afterward. In October the Rwandan government announced the formation of a commission to study France's role in the genocide. The commission, according to an official statement, would "clarify the roles individuals in the French establishment played" and also consider "whether their activities are criminally indictable."

A few weeks later, France's chief counterterrorism judge, Jean-Louis Bruguière, issued a stunning report charging that Kagame and nine other *inkotanyi* had assassinated President Habyarimana twelve years earlier. Judge Bruguière interviewed only witnesses who believed Kagame guilty and considered no evidence pointing to any other perpetrator. Nonetheless his report had an instant effect. As a head of state, Kagame is immune from prosecution, but the grave charge against him cast a shadow over his reputation. His nine aides—including General James Kabarebe, who had been President Laurent Kabila's chief of staff in the Congo and then gone on to hold the same position in Rwanda—had to curtail their foreign travel for fear of arrest.

France's foreign minister, Philippe Douste-Blazy, insisted that issuing these charges had been "a judicial decision" and "not a political decision by the French government." It was in any case the latest blow in a long-seething confrontation. Since coming to power by overthrowing a French-backed regime, Kagame had worked resolutely to weaken France's position in Africa. He did it in a way no African leader ever had: by taking his country out of the French sphere of influence, changing the language of government from French to English, and applying for membership in the British Commonwealth. When he named a commission to investigate France's role in the genocide, the conflict escalated. After Judge Bruguière charged President Kagame and his comrades with murder, it exploded.

Kagame reacted to the indictments by hiring a high-powered team of defense lawyers based in London. He also encouraged his investigating commission to intensify its search for evidence of French complicity with genocide—especially evidence that might justify criminal charges against present or former French leaders. Then he did something no one had expected. He announced that Rwanda was breaking diplomatic relations with France and closing the French School and the French Cultural Center in Kigali.

Over the next few days the government was ablaze with anti-French passion. The official newspaper, *New Times*, published a flood of articles detailing France's support for the genocidal regime. People were mobilized for street protests and shepherded to stadiums to hear speakers denounce French perfidy. At a rally in Kigali, President Kagame scornfully rejected the right of a French judge "whose name I cannot even pronounce" to judge him.

Breaking diplomatic relations with France was a radical step, but it fit with Kagame's determination not to cede ground in this conflict. Several hundred Rwandan children attended the French School, though, and big crowds enjoyed films and concerts at the

French Cultural Center. When I asked Kagame whether he might have spared them, he shook his head.

All those are one and the same. The issue is deeply political. It is not technical. France, in the wrong it has been doing to us, has used all subtle ways, including the so-called cultural center and the so-called French School. All these were their institutions, run by the embassy and used to create problems here. We really intended to send a message about what they were doing and how they were doing it to inflict damage on our country and our system of government—a message that was clear. We sent away the ambassador not because he was necessarily doing anything wrong. He was an employee. We can't send back the French president or foreign ministry or military establishment or intelligence establishment. The effect of it is in that symbolism.

Of all the principal foreign actors in Rwanda's 1994 tragedy, the only one who tried mightily to prevent it, General Dallaire, has paradoxically also been the only one to accept personal responsibility. Pangs of guilt began tormenting him even before he left Kigali in the summer of 1994. They never subsided.

"I was the commander, my mission failed, and hundreds of thousands of people died," he once explained. "I can't find any solace in statements like 'I did my best.'"

Dallaire tried more than once to take his own life. At one point he lost the use of his right arm—apparently a psychosomatic reaction to his memories of Rwandans being hacked to death by killers wielding *pangas* and clubs. Whenever he saw an article of clothing dropped on the street, he had to fight the urge to check whether a corpse lay beneath it. At the request of the Canadian army, he made a video about post-traumatic stress syndrome.

"I became suicidal because there was no—there was no other solution," he testified haltingly. "I couldn't live with the pain and the sounds and the smell and the sights. I couldn't sleep. I couldn't stand the loudness of silence."

In 2000, after Dallaire refused to stop speaking publicly about Rwanda or testifying at war crimes trials, he was forced out of the army with a medical discharge. A month later he was found drunk and unconscious on a park bench in Quebec. In a letter to the Canadian Broadcasting Corporation, he said he was suffering from a "new generation of peacekeeper injury" caused by "the anger, the rage, and the cold loneliness that separates you from your family, friends, and society's normal daily routine."

Dallaire could have made his warnings about impending genocide public after his superiors in New York chose to ignore them. He could have raided *interahamwe* arms depots without asking permission from New York or ordered peacekeepers to intervene when they saw civilians being murdered. In the first days of the genocide, he could even have joined with the RPF and tried to stop it. Had he done any of these things, he might have saved many lives. Almost certainly, however, he would also have been relieved of his command and sent home to face disgrace and possible court-martial.

Should Dallaire have disobeyed his orders or resigned to protest them? That question has become part of his identity. It has also occurred to President Kagame.

[Dallaire] was quite an intelligent fellow, with some good understanding of the military, although I gather that maybe in the previous period he hadn't been a combat commander as such. He was involved in logistics and things like that. But he had a very sharp and clear grasp of military strategy and tactics and science. So he was as a person, a military person, a good commander and a good officer. For me, it was good to deal with him. He is a person who has substance in his mind.

Now that is to be, on the other hand, put into the context of what he was serving. He served the UN, so he really had to put himself in the suit of the UN, which no doubt had influence on his behavior, in contrast to his personality. And I remember that many times when we met, we argued about what was happening, especially in the first days [after] Habyarimana was killed. We were monitoring and being told by our people that people are fleeing, that they were hearing screams and cries, getting information that people were being killed and so on. So I talked to General Dallaire on the phone, and the first thing he said to me was

*"Please, I plead with you not to make any move." So I told him, "Well,
I really don't have to make any move if there is nothing happening. But
is it logical not to do anything at a time when people are being killed,
and also our people in the parliamentary building are in danger? Should
I just sit here? If you give me assurance that you are in control of the
situation, that you will protect our people in the parliamentary building
and protect the Rwandans, then why should I do anything?" But he was
here urging me not to do anything when he was not able to do anything
himself! I said, "What does this mean? What is the logic? Is it military?
What science is it? What are you telling me? What is it?" So you can
see, this already steps in as a weakness. . . . That showed me that there
was a serious problem with him.*

*There was a point when I even asked him. I said, "You are still
pleading with your headquarters. You can't do anything. Why don't you
use the force that you have at your disposal, and actually we combine
efforts to try to save people?" I said, "In your shoes, I would be able to
breach anything that the UN had put in the way of saving people, and
live with the guilt of having breached UN regulations but saved people,
rather than live with the guilt of having people being killed under my
eyes and just protected my job with the UN and not breach the regulations." I said, "If I were to choose as an officer, as a person, I would
certainly rather be faulted on not obeying the UN, than being faulted
for being there watching people being killed. Ultimately, this is the
choice I would make." People can make their own judgment on that. I
have my own judgment.*

Dallaire stayed away from Rwanda for a decade. In 2004 he accepted an invitation to participate in ceremonies marking the tenth
anniversary of the genocide. He predicted that the trip would be
"like going back to hell," and he was not far wrong. At a conference in Kigali soon after he arrived, Alain Destexhe, a Belgian senator and former secretary general of Doctors Without Borders,
stunned him and many in the audience by charging that Dallaire
"obeyed orders that were criminal, instead of saving the lives of
Tutsi." Dallaire reacted angrily, but later, during a visit to the
National University in Butare, he sounded as if he agreed.

"Standing here," he told an assembly of professors and students, "I say to you that Roméo Dallaire, as force commander, failed the Rwandan people."

Dallaire does not mind sharing blame for that failure with others who embrace it less willingly. He scorns their half-hearted apologies as pathetic efforts "to get rid of the blood on their hands." In particular, he has rejected as "outright lies" President Clinton's claims that he did not realize what was happening in Rwanda.

Dallaire rarely grants interviews, but he does give public speeches. I attended one in Chicago. He spoke broadly about brotherhood, solidarity, and global responsibility, but inevitably also referred to Rwanda. Several times he returned to the essential point: that Rwanda's genocide was not an eruption of tribal violence stemming from ancient hatreds but the work of a few dozen calculating and supremely cynical politicians.

"A bunch of them sat down at a meeting and said, 'How are we going to sort this out once and for all?'" he told the audience. "And one of them simply said, 'Well, wipe them out.' And they developed a plan to slaughter 1.2 million Tutsi. They had plans all the way down to every ten huts in the country."

I had hoped to ask Dallaire a question, but he took none. Evidently there are things he prefers not to discuss in pubic. Alone among the outsiders whose judgments allowed the Rwandan genocide to happen, he is consumed by his failure. He accepts the blame that others maneuver to avoid.

During one of his appearances as a witness at the International Criminal Tribunal for Rwanda, Dallaire described the evacuation missions that foreign armies launched when the genocide broke out. He explained that soldiers rescued their own nationals but left Rwandans to die and called their conduct "inexcusable by any human criteria."

"It seems as though you regret that," his questioner observed.

"You cannot even imagine," Dallaire replied.

Fundamental is the security and stability we had to build in our country. That would be the only base on which to build other things. Security also means reconciliation, justice, putting back other things that hold society together and allow people to live together in peace. From that grows the possibility for social and economic and political development.

In my life, I always ask questions. You won't tell me a thing and I won't find a question to ask you about it. Even in my routine work, reading intelligence reports about events and people, I always find gaps. Why? Who did this? Was there another way of doing it? This has become part of my life.

16

FAMOUS FOR JUST ONE THING

F OR YEARS, THE IDEA OF TOURISM IN RWANDA would have seemed absurd. As peace has taken hold, though, tourists are starting to arrive. Souvenir stands have sprouted in several towns. Hotels are often full. In their lobbies, tour guides shepherd groups of European, American, and Japanese visitors into jeeps and minibuses.

Plenty of moments might be singled out as turning points in Rwanda's climb back to normality. Among the most symbolically important was the appearance in 2001 of the first book-length travel guide to Rwanda, part of the insightful Bradt series published in Britain. According to the foreword, it was published "because the authors wanted to highlight the fact that the Rwandan government has put its tainted past aside, and the country is now a safe and fascinating tourist destination." Five years later a second edition appeared, with a new introduction marveling at how this "truly stunning country" has transformed itself "from a shell-shocked ruin, site of appalling horror, into a vibrant, prosperous, safe and energetic nation."

Some visitors to Rwanda today are politically aware, socially engaged, and eager to visit places like the Millennium Village development project, where activists working with the American economist Jeffrey Sachs are trying to pull an entire region out of poverty. Others want to watch the reconciliation process unfold, perhaps by meeting genocide survivors or attending the trial of an accused *genocidaire*. Many, however, are drawn at least in part by Rwanda's most extraordinary natural wonder. They want to climb a volcano in the Virunga range and see mountain gorillas.

I appreciate wildlife. As for mountain gorillas, only a cold soul would remain unmoved by their majesty. Seeing them in films, though, is enough to satisfy me. Other people want more. Thousands fly to Rwanda every year for the sole purpose of gazing at mountain gorillas. Some later describe these encounters as profound, even life-changing experiences. I was eager to discover everything I could about Rwanda, so I decided to make the trek. Even as I set out, though, I sensed that primate tourism is not for me.

President Kagame may feel the same way. When I asked what it means to him personally that Rwanda is home to most of the twelve hundred mountain gorillas left on earth, he answered with a restraint I took for diffidence like my own.

They're part of our national heritage. Happily, they seem to be valued beyond our borders. So be it. They are also part of our ecological zones and our whole ecosystem. We are lucky to have them as unique beings, sought after to be seen by people around the world. The tourism they bring also has a money aspect. We value all of these backgrounds.

The modern history of Rwanda's mountain gorillas is inextricably linked to the impassioned primatologist Dian Fossey. Her book about them, *Gorillas in the Mist*, and the film in which Sigourney Weaver played her, brought the story of these apes to world attention and made her a celebrity. For much of Fossey's eighteen years in Virunga, though, she was in bitter conflict with the Habyarimana regime. Powerful members of the *akazu* were involved in gorilla poaching, and she fought them relentlessly. She developed intimate relationships with dozens of individual gorillas. At some point she may even have begun considering their lives more intrinsically valuable than those of human beings.

"In pursuit of her singular goal, the protection of the endangered mountain gorilla, Fossey had shot at her enemies, kidnapped their children, whipped them about the genitals, smeared them with ape dung, killed their cattle, burned their property, and even sent them to jail," one biographer has written. "Anyone who dared threaten her gorillas, or even to challenge her methods, set her off, and the force of her malevolence was difficult to imagine."

Some of Fossey's friends were shocked but not surprised when she was murdered by an assailant who broke into her cabin one night at the end of 1985. As she wished, she was buried in a rustic cemetery on Mount Karisimbi where she herself had interred fifteen of her beloved gorillas, most of them victims of traps set by poachers. Some evidence suggested that one of President Habyarimana's brothers-in-law was involved in her murder, but the case was never solved.

In the years after Fossey's death, volunteers streamed into her Karisoke Research Center. They had repeated conflicts with the government. Then, at the end of 1990, the Virunga range was suddenly invaded by several thousand rebel fighters led by Paul Kagame. Army bombardment of their positions became so intense that the research center had to close.

For the next year and a half, two hunted bands, gorillas and guerrillas, lived close together in Virunga. The animals, though, knew enough to stay away from men with guns. Kagame never saw one.

They would run away from us. We used to go to places where they were found. There was a lot of fighting, with shells landing everywhere. We might have been passing without seeing them. They stay under cover in those situations. In our movement, we would never move in what is called an extended line, with people abreast of each other. We always used the single file, with one behind another on one path. Often we could not see even ten meters in any direction. So they may well have been watching us, but we did not see them.

In 1993 the Habyarimana government sent a distressing but not unexpected message to scientists who had worked at the Karisoke Research Center. The center, they reported, had been overrun by *inkotanyi*, and everything inside, from computers to voluminous files, had been stolen or destroyed. Several months later Katie Fawcett, who had been the center's director, received a curious fax forwarded by the American embassy in Kigali. It was from the RPF, and it directly contradicted what the government had told her.

"The fax said they had taken over our center and removed everything inside, but that every item and every scrap of paper had been listed on an inventory and taken to a safe place," Katie told me when I visited her at her base in the Virunga foothills. "Sure enough, when the war ended we got everything back. We have a very, very cooperative relationship with the military now. They've really bent over backward to assure that our work continues. I think their experience of living in Virunga as guerrillas was probably very important in shaping this commitment."

All surviving mountain gorillas live in a compact range where Rwanda, Uganda, and the Congo meet. They live in groups, and scientists in Rwanda have chosen eight groups to be "acclimated," meaning that humans can visit them. Every visitor must buy a permit, and despite the high cost—$400 per person, and steadily rising—there is always a waiting list. Rwandans can have a permit for just $10, but few make the trip. Most have more pressing needs.

On the day I was to go, I rose early from my bed at a guest house in Ruhengeri and drove over a newly paved road to the base camp at nearby Kinigi. There, along with gorilla watchers from more than a dozen countries, I was told that just fifty-six people are allowed to visit gorillas each day. We would travel in clusters of seven, each with a guide assigned to find one of the eight "acclimated" groups. Many of my fellow tourists had been looking forward to this day for months or longer and were gripped by excitement and expectation. These animals have a remarkable hold on the human imagination.

"I always wondered," General Dallaire wrote after the genocide, "if the international community would have done more if eight hundred thousand mountain gorillas were being slaughtered."

Some visitors find their assigned gorilla group easily, but that was not my fate. For three hours my comrades and I pulled ourselves up a mountainside that was not only nearly vertical—or so it seemed to me—but so heavily overgrown that our guide had to hack his way through with a *panga*. I was not the only one who had to stop and gasp for breath in the thin mountain air. Finally we staggered into a small clearing where we found the group we had been seeking: an alpha male, called a silverback, two females, three "subadults," and an infant. Our guide, following strict rules, allowed us to come no closer than ten meters and stay no longer than one hour.

The gorilla is a familiar beast to man, and the ones we found paid us little heed. They glanced up when we arrived, but after concluding that we were simply another band of primates passing through, they returned to their languid routine. They climbed on each other, groomed each other, pulled leaves from trees and slowly masticated them. One even swung from a low branch for us. For a while the clicking of camera shutters was the only sound. Then, as if to certify the authenticity of the experience, thunder began to echo around us. Our allotted time expired just as the clouds above us burst. The trek down, in a driving rainstorm, was marginally less taxing than the way up.

After finally making it back to flat ground, I slogged through a quarter mile of mud to a clearing. My friend Cathy Emmerson, who abandoned life as a real estate agent in Canada and moved to Ruhengeri in a fit of what she calls "the midlife crazies," was waiting in her jeep.

"Wow, you had a long one," she told me with a sympathetic smile as I staggered toward her, drenched and exhausted. "At least now you can say you've done it."

Cathy drove me to the Ruhengeri bus depot, and a couple of hours later I was sprawled across my bed at the Mille Collines. The next morning I awoke with sore muscles and a few scratches. My clothes and shoes reeked. By nightfall, though, I was feeling fine again and quietly pleased that I now had another story to tell, albeit one that placed me in something less than a heroic light.

"You have no idea how rugged Virunga is!" I joked to President Kagame the next time we met.

"We lived there for two years," he replied without a smile.

Mountain gorillas are as close as Rwanda has to a national symbol. An imposing silverback adorns the five-thousand-franc bill. I even bought a small wooden carving of a gorilla and keep it on my desk as a souvenir. But although some outsiders know enough about Rwanda to associate it with gorillas, most make a different connection. The word-association test never fails. Rwanda: genocide.

"It turns out that Angelina plans to give birth in Namibia," a Rwandan newspaper columnist wrote when the film star Angelina Jolie was on one of her African jaunts. "Like me, you must be wondering: why Namibia and not Rwanda, for instance? Let us consider the facts. Namibia is a hopeless banana republic famous mainly for its empty spaces and large Kalahari Desert and backward bushmen, right? On the other hand, Rwanda is a beautiful, evergreen country with flowing hills and valleys, which is known for, mmm . . . er, so sorry to break this to you, but Rwanda is famous for just one thing, genocide. Ouch, that hurt."

Given this fact, it is natural that many visitors ask whether there is a site connected to the 1994 genocide that they can visit. There are many. One reason they exist is to receive outsiders. Painful as it is to stand in places haunted by so many unquiet spirits, it seems almost disrespectful to visit Rwanda without offering some tribute to their memory.

The main genocide memorial is a modern but understated museum in Gisozi, an outlying district of Kigali. The cream-colored building, designed with help from a British foundation, dominates a hillside. Below the entry is a pool in which a flame, traditionally an African symbol for unity in mourning, burns during April, May, and June, the months of the 1994 genocide. A plaque near the door says, "This is about our past and our future, our nightmares and our dreams, our fear and our hope."

Inside, phrases that mark Rwanda's advance toward the abyss leap from wall panels.

"Identity card . . . Hutu Ten Commandments . . . ruling Hutu elite . . . Between 1959 and 1973 over 700,000 Tutsi flee Rwanda. . . . The French government continued to support Habyarimana despite the massacres. . . . Roadblocks went up in Kigali within hours of the plane crash. . . . Ten thousand people were killed in and around the church at Nyamata. . . . Rwanda was dead."

Visitors to this museum are quieter than visitors to any other museum I have ever visited. Even many who know the story it tells are shocked into silence by powerfully evocative photos, documents, and videos, and especially by a display of the crude weapons with which killers did their work. The walls of one room are hung with snapshots of children, each accompanied by a small card. Some record random facts, like ten-year-old David Mugiraneza's last words: "UNAMIR will come for us." All end with the same shock:

Fillette Umwuse
Age: 2
Favorite toy: doll
Favorite food: chips with rice
Best friend: her dad
Behavior: a good girl
Cause of death: smashed against a wall

Like most other visitors, I found walking through these rooms deeply draining. Nowhere in my palette of emotions could I find a response that seemed even remotely adequate. Yet there is another, invisible aspect of the Kigali Memorial Center that takes visitors even further from the knowable world. Beneath a wide terrace outside are eight mass graves that hold the remains of 258,000 human beings. Most were gathered from streets and fields where they lay in 1994. Many were never identified. Their remains lie packed atop one another in underground crypts ten feet high.

Two hundred fifty-eight thousand: I was never able to wrap my mind around that number.

The director of the museum, Freddy Umutanguha, has a story like that of many survivors. An *interahamwe* gang stormed into his house on April 14, 1994, and clubbed his parents and four sisters to death. He and one surviving sister managed to flee. For three months they foraged in the bush, hiding, running, and praying. Most who tried this were hunted down and killed, but Freddy survived with his sister. He returned to school, studied geography, found a job working for an aid group that was mapping genocide sites, and became director of the memorial center when it opened in 2004.

Whenever I felt able, I asked Rwandans whether they think genocide could happen again in their country. Most told me it could. Every time I heard a Rwandan defend the government's authoritarian rule, it was with the same justification. For now and for years to come, they told me, a strong and even repressive regime is necessary to avoid another cataclysm.

"We are in the process of reconciliation, but it's just started," Freddy Umutanguha told me when I visited his office at the genocide museum. "People were taught hatred for thirty years. A generation grew up hearing their mothers and fathers and neighbors preaching hatred. To remove that hatred is a process. It may be impossible until a whole generation has passed away. It could easily take thirty or forty years. What this museum does, what our schools do, what the speeches of our leaders do, is only to offer an alternative. Many young people are still hearing the message of hatred at home. By offering an alternative to that message, all we can hope to do is set off a struggle or a fight within the hearts of our young people. Our goal is that they will finally come home one day and say, 'Dad, you were lying. Hatred is not the answer to our problems.'"

Disorienting as the Kigali museum is, it is a memorial and mass grave rather than a massacre site. For anyone who travels in Rwanda, the sites are impossible to avoid. One Sunday, as I was driving along a dusty road south of Kigali, I found myself in Nyamata, where thousands were killed in a Catholic church. I found the church easily. The gate in front was closed, but a few minutes after I arrived, a young woman appeared, opened it, and escorted me in. Walls of the church were perforated with bullet and shrapnel holes. On one of them hung a banner I had seen at other genocide sites. It carries the lament of an archetypal victim: "If you knew me, and if you really knew yourself, you would not have killed me."

The story of what happened inside this church is no less mind-numbing because similar stories envelop so many other places in Rwanda. When the genocide began, terrified Tutsi from around this region streamed into the church complex at Nyamata. Ten thousand were there when, on April 14—the same day Freddy Umutanguha's family was killed many miles away—a gang of soldiers and *interahamwe* militia men burst in. They followed a pattern that was repeated across Rwanda: a grenade attack followed by a storming of the church, mass rape, long bursts of automatic weapons fire aimed at cringing masses of bodies, and the clubbing and hacking of survivors. A group hiding in the rectory resisted the onslaught, so attackers simply set it afire.

At the rear of the church, hundreds of human skulls are neatly lined up on shelves, like coffee mugs in a pottery store. The floor has been left as it was, littered with bloodstained clothes and bone chips. In a nearby shed are piles of objects that refugees brought with them for what they hoped would be a short stay: plates, shoes, baskets, water jugs, and many crucifixes. No visitor who has been to the museum at Auschwitz could fail to see the connection.

The mind surrenders to scenes like this. In the guest book, visitors from many countries try to give voice to their emotions. None writes more than a few words. The most common phrase is "Never again." Others I saw were: Unbelievable; May their souls rest in peace; This is what hate can do; Speechless; I will never, never understand; No words; God have mercy on us all.

I signed the book, writing only my name, and handed a small donation to the woman who had guided me. Then I asked whether she would tell me her story. She was from Nyamata, she replied softly, looking away from me. Her mother and father were killed in this church, along with all her brothers and sisters. She knows some of the killers. Many were her lifelong neighbors. A few were friends. Most have returned to their homes after serving prison terms. She sees them every day. How does she bear that?

"Living with them is difficult, but we accept it," she said. "What choice do we have? What else can we do?"

In Rwanda there is no escape from places like this. One day while traveling near Lake Kivu, I stopped for lunch in the beach-front town of Kibuye, where boats are for hire and lovely guest houses offer idyllic views of lushly forested islets. On the way into town I passed a church where four thousand people were slaughtered. Farther on, I saw a sign hanging from a fence in front of an open field next to the Kibuye stadium.

"More Than 10,000 People Were Inhumated Here," it says. "Official Ceremony Was Presided Over by His Excellency Pasteur Bizimungu, President of the Republic of Rwanda, April 26, 1995."

Gorilla tourism and genocide tourism: these are thriving growth industries in Rwanda. Much more awaits curious visitors. They can swim in Lake Kivu, hike in the pristine Nyungwe rain forest, or watch elephants, hippos, crocodiles, and a dozen species of antelopes in Akagera National Park. Those pleasures, though, mirror ones that are available in many African countries. I wanted to see what was uniquely Rwandan. Watching a performance of traditional dance, touring the former royal capital at Nyanza, and visiting the National Museum in Butare all qualified, but still left me unsatisfied. No one yet offers an All Rwanda Tour, so I devised my own.

The story of today's Rwanda may be seen as beginning at the border town of Kagitumba, where RPF fighters crossed from Uganda to launch their "armed return" on October 1, 1990. Rwandans told me no one goes there except to cross the border. I was an exception. Because the war began there, I wanted to visit.

I found a veteran of the 1990 crossing who agreed to accompany me to Kagitumba. When we arrived, I could see why it is no tourist attraction. It looks like the sleepy border outpost it is, with an unadorned bridge crossing the shallow Muvumba River that separates

Rwanda from Uganda. For me, though, the scene was vividly evocative. With my companion's help, I was able to visualize hundreds
of *inkotanyi* moving methodically across this bridge and pushing
into their long-lost homeland. A sign reading "Welcome in the
Republic of Rwanda" is the same one that stood there on that day.
It is pockmarked with bullet holes and would be a central artifact
in the Rwanda Historical Museum if such a museum existed.
Barely a mile away is the hillside where General Fred Rwigyema,
commander of the insurgent force, shouted his last words before
falling dead on the second day of the war. "*Mginga amenipiga!*" he
cried. The fool has hit me!

"Fred was a difficult guy," the doctor-turned-*inkotanyi* Joseph
Karemera told me. "He couldn't lead men to fight without being
at the front so he could see what was going on. He was shot by a
guy who was giving cover to retreating forces."

Staring at this hillside, I realized that if Fred Rwigyema had not
been killed on that day, all of Rwanda's subsequent history might
have been different. Paul Kagame might never have become either
the RPF leader or president of Rwanda. The RPF might not even
have won its war. But did "Commander Fred" really die from hostile fire? Some in the RPF, and others outside, have their doubts.
They suspect—although there is no evidence to support their
theory, and witnesses vehemently reject it—that he was killed by a
rival RPF faction led by two officers who were themselves killed in
an ambush a couple of weeks later.

That episode, one former *inkotanyi* told me, "created a lot of
tension in the movement, but it was quickly off the table. Everyone followed the explanation that the organization gave, that they
died in an ambush."

From Kagitumba, my companion and I drove along a rugged,
rock-strewn road that twists through a mountainous region where
warring armies fought intense battles in the early 1990s. At one
point we passed close to the peak known as Sarajevo, on whose
slopes many died in artillery duels and infantry assaults. Finally
we arrived at the second place I wanted to visit: the Mulindi tea
plantation, which served as Kagame's headquarters for much of

the war. The plantation is back in limited operation, but as I had hoped, the underground bunker where Kagame and his officers took cover during artillery attacks remains as it was, complete with plywood walls and a single lightbulb dangling from a ceiling cord. Nearby is a guesthouse with a columned stone veranda. During the war, Kagame received many visitors on that veranda. General Dallaire came several times. I had no trouble imagining the two of them debating beneath the fragrant eucalyptus trees.

Back in Kigali, I sought out places where the events of 1994 unfolded. Some are easy to find, like the hulking yellow Parliament building that six hundred *inkotanyi* turned into a fortress during the last phase of the war, and Amahoro Stadium, where UNAMIR had its headquarters, thousands of fearful refugees hid during the genocide, and General Dallaire kept his family of pet goats. Others can be located only with help from someone local, among them the field into which President Habyarimana's plane crashed, the compound where Prime Minister Agathe Uwilingiyimana was killed the next day, and the spot where Rwandan soldiers murdered ten Belgian peacekeepers several hours later.

I was drawn to these places for the same reason I had, in years past, felt pulled to the church in Germany where Martin Luther proclaimed his break with the Church of Rome, or the room in St. Petersburg where the Russian cabinet was meeting in 1917 when Bolsheviks burst in and seized power. I like standing in places where history was made. The spot I came to enjoy most in Rwanda, however, attracted me for an entirely different reason. It is Nyamirambo, the most exuberantly offbeat neighborhood in a country where being offbeat is not encouraged.

"People who live in Nyamirambo would never live anywhere else," one of my Rwandan friends told me. "But people who don't live there stay away. They think it's a very bad place."

I first ventured into Nyamirambo without understanding where I was going. The man responsible is one of Rwanda's most colorful expatriates, a Belgian architect named André Verbruggen, who has lived in Kigali since the 1980s. By his own account he has not eaten a single meal at home during all those years. That makes him the preeminent authority on dining out in Kigali. He knows every eating establishment, no matter how modest, and has even published a guidebook in which he rates each one.

"Take me to a place where only Rwandans eat," I proposed to André one day. "I want the opposite of the Mille Collines."

"How about a place with no floor, no refrigerator, no menu, no choice, no change given, and no French or English spoken?" he asked.

"Perfect!" I exclaimed.

The next Saturday night, four of us—André, his Rwandan girlfriend, my colleague Shyaka Kanuma, and me—piled into Andre's beaten-up Toyota and drove through the darkened city. It was nine o'clock. Most of Kigali was shutting down, but in Nyamirambo we found the streets full of life. Bars and restaurants were packed. Pulsating African music wafted through open doors and windows. Vendors sat at small grills, selling brochettes and other delicacies to passersby—something I never saw anywhere else in Rwanda. Taxis, which are hard to find in other parts of Kigali at night, cruised slowly with radios blaring; they are wildly painted and have racy names like J-Lo and Air Force One. Every shop was open. Tailors, cobblers, and radio repairmen sat on stools, joking and haggling with customers. Couples embraced. People were animated and exuberant. This is the most un-Rwandan place in Rwanda.

Among the first people to settle in Nyamirambo were Rwanda's few Muslims. They suffered discrimination during the Habyarimana regime and sought safety in numbers. Unwelcome in public schools, clinics, sport clubs, and community centers, they built their own. During the 1970s and 1980s, other Rwandans who felt uncomfortable with mainstream life joined them. Refugees from nearby countries, especially the Congo, were also drawn to Nyamirambo and brought with them new attitudes and habits. It would be an exaggeration to call this neighborhood a center of counterculture, but it has attracted a rich mix of outsiders who revel in one another's company. They have built a mini-society where many of Rwanda's social conventions do not apply.

Less than 10 percent of Rwandans are Muslim, but in Nyamir-ambo they are a visible presence. Their austere moral code, which might on the surface seem to contrast with the neighborhood's live-and-let-live ethos, actually guarantees a certain order within its seeming chaos. There are plenty of bars in Nyamirambo, and bar girls in them, but the crime rate is surprisingly low for such a tight-packed urban quarter. Many merchants operate on an honor system. People leave their cars unlocked.

Most remarkably, Nyamirambo was the only place in Rwanda where large numbers of people refused to kill their neighbors in 1994. Dozens of Tutsi hid in its mosques. There is no known case of any being turned away, nor was anyone given up to be killed after taking refuge.

On the night André took me to Nyamirambo, driving was slow because the main drag was crowded with stylish boulevard-iers. Finally he maneuvered his car onto what passes for a side-walk. He left it there—unlocked—and led us slowly through the crowd. We followed him through an unmarked wooden door into a dark room with a dirt floor and sat down at an unsteady wooden table. When a waiter arrived, André simply held up four fingers. A few minutes later, four cold beers arrived; al-though the place has no refrigerator, the owner has a deal with a friend nearby who does. After a few sips, we ventured to the open kitchen. It comprised a single grill covered with sizzling goat steaks, the only main course available, and a pan for frying potatoes, the only side dish. When our dinners arrived, the goat proved hard to chew, but the atmosphere, shaped by a constantly changing crowd of revelers, more than compensated. On our way out I asked André this restaurant's name. He told me it has two; some people know it as Chez Fofana, others call it Machopo. Its address is also a Nyamirambo classic: on the main street, halfway between the two big mosques.

After dinner we wandered through the teeming streets until midnight. I understood why even many Rwandans who never deign to visit this neighborhood recognize it as integral to the city that is the heart of their country. That explains a famous Swahili war cry that RPF fighters used to shout as they charged into battle. "*Songambere mpaka Nyamijos,*" they would yell at one another—Keep going until we reach Nyamirambo!

After visiting Nyamirambo several times, by day as well as by night, I realized how dangerous it is to romanticize such places. Deep poverty grips most of the people who live there. Pretty girls who laugh with bar patrons are often teenagers hoping to sell their bodies to earn money for food. Here, as in the rest of the country, hope illuminates the future, but the future still seems far away.

Another place in Rwanda I wanted to visit was the house in Tambwe where Paul Kagame spent his first two years, and from which the king's chauffeur rescued him and his family from certain death. I met the district mayor one day and asked whether he could direct me to the house. He shook his head apologetically. Apparently he feared that giving out this information might be seen as a security breach. Only after I arranged for one of Kagame's aides to call him did he relent—and offer to guide me himself.

We made an appointment to meet outside his office the following Sunday morning. From there we drove along the main road and then for several miles over a rough dirt one. The mayor told me that Kagame's house is no longer standing. When families fled Rwanda after anti-Tutsi pogroms, he explained, neighbors normally dismantled their homes and appropriated bricks, doors, beams, and fixtures for themselves.

As we bounced along, the mayor spotted a dignified-looking gentleman with a white beard, dark sport jacket, and walking stick. He pulled over and introduced us. This man, slightly stooped with age but still of regal bearing, told us he had been a member of the royal police in the days before 1959 and had known Kagame's father.

"He had sixty cows," the man told me. "The *mwami* wanted to make him a chief, but he refused."

Struck by an impulse, I asked this formidable gentleman whether he thought the Belgians had poisoned King Mutara III Rudahigwa in 1959. "Absolutely, one hundred percent," he replied without hesitating. "Before the *mwami* went to meet them in

Burundi, he said good-bye to his friends more strongly than he ever had before. He gave away his money. Somehow he sensed they were going to kill them. He preferred that it be in Burundi. He was afraid that if it happened here, his people would become angry and rebel. He didn't want to be responsible for that."

We drove a bit farther, then pulled over and began walking. As we made our way along narrow dirt paths that separate tiny farm plots, laughing children, unaccustomed to visitors, approached us. So did some adults. Several called out to the mayor, and he translated for me.

"They want to know why we're here," he said. "They're amazed when I tell them. No one has ever come looking for this place."

Finally we arrived at a clearing on the edge of a banana grove that neighbors told us was the spot where Kagame's first home had stood. They said they knew this was the place because an orange tree that once dominated the front yard is still there. Later I asked Kagame whether there had been an orange tree in his yard, and he replied, "Yes, I remember it clearly."

No one in the group surrounding us had set eyes on Kagame when he was an infant. Several, though, said that a woman named Thérése Mukankanza, who still lived nearby, had been his nursemaid. We found her rustic cottage, which like others in the area had neither windows nor a floor. She was standing outside, leaning on a staff but resplendent in a vividly colored batik gown. When the mayor told her why we were looking for her, she was first confused, then flustered, and then, I thought, a bit flattered. She invited us in for milk. When I asked whether she had ever sensed that the baby she cared for was destined for great things, she looked at me quizzically and replied, quite logically, "How could I?"

"Paul Kagame was born in a hospital but came home the next day," she told me. "I was there. When the baby's mother was away, I took care of him. I never knew what happened to him until he became vice president. One day I saw his picture in a newspaper, and I knew it was him. Later his mother invited me to visit her in Kigali. It was very special. We took a photo."

If I were a tour guide in Rwanda, I would also bring visitors to a place for which outsiders have searched as passionately as they sought the Holy Grail: the source of the Nile River. Rwandans have long known it is in their country. "Source du Nil" is the most popular brand of bottled water in Rwanda. In my travels I found a café, a hotel, and a gas station that also bear that name. Now it's official.

Few quests in history have obsessed as many explorers over as many centuries as the one aimed at finding the source of the Nile. Their reasoning went like this: Egypt was the great wellspring of civilization; the Nile nurtured Egypt; therefore the source of the Nile must also be, at least symbolically, the source of modern culture and life. Ancient Egyptians, Greeks, Persians, and Romans tried to find it. Their failures became part of classical legend. Artists took to depicting the river as a male god with his head obscured.

During the Victorian Age, when launching expeditions to remote places was all the rage in Britain, flamboyant adventurers like David Livingstone and Richard Burton risked their lives searching for the source of the Nile. In 1858 John Hanning Speke became the first European to see the inland sea he named Lake Victoria. He concluded that one of its inlets, near what is now the Ugandan town of Jinja, was the source of the Nile. Burton rejected this conclusion, setting off an epic row that shook the Royal Geographical Society. To this day, government-issued maps in Uganda carry a legend next to Jinja that says "Source of the Nile."

Doubt about Speke's claim fueled many expeditions over the next century and a half. Some explorers claimed to have found the "true source" in one place or another. Others acknowledged failure, some after concluding that the Nile may have no single source. In 2005 a team from South Africa claimed that the true source was a river in Rwanda that flows into Lake Victoria. A year later three explorers from Britain and New Zealand—a fourth perished on their epic eighty-day, four-thousand-mile voyage—announced that they had not only confirmed that claim but reached the exact spot. It is a "spill" in the heart of Rwanda's dense Nyungwe rain forest, a muddy hole where brackish water bubbles from the ground and trickles toward the Rukarera River, said to be the Nile's most distant tributary. The nineteenth-century German explorer Richard Kandt had placed the source just ten miles away, but he did not have the global-positioning technology available to his modern descendants.

"All of the greatest names failed—until now!" the head of the 2006 expedition, Neil McGrigor, jubilantly announced over a satellite link as he placed a sign reading "Furthest Source of the Nile River" over the hallowed spot. One of history's most tantalizing mysteries had finally been solved—and it placed tiny, long-isolated Rwanda at the very center of the world.

But was the mystery really solved? Uganda's tourism minister angrily rejected the claim and stood firm for Jinja. A specialist at the Nile Basin Initiative, which works with governments to preserve the river, suggested diplomatically that there might be no such thing as a "true source." That provoked an indignant response from Rwanda's environment minister. He insisted that no doubt remained and called on others to "stop misleading the world."

President Kagame held one of his monthly news conferences as this debate was escalating, and he was asked about it. His response was not what some expected. Instead of reveling in Rwanda's new-found glory, he brushed aside the whole controversy. He seemed to consider it silly, nothing more than the latest chapter in a long-running and ultimately meaningless imperial fantasy. When I told him later that I was surprised by his response, he shook his head. Other explorers may one day find another "true source," he said, and no one other than geographers should care.

My feeling was to leave it to international specialists. If you make so much noise about it, it appears that you bought people to write this story the way you wanted it. But these were explorers who studied on their own, did their own research, and used modern technology. We wanted them to be the ones to tell the story. It speaks for itself. We were very happy and proud, but we didn't want to sow opposition, like we were dying to have it and might be bribing people to tell lies. These things can be counterproductive: one day it's here, then it's there. It's better to give it a firm foundation in research than to jump up and claim it.

The rain forest of Nyungwe is dense and largely trackless. Penetrating to its heart is not easy. No one is yet taking visitors to the supposed source of the world's most fabled river. It would be part of my personalized tour, though. This would be the itinerary: gorillas to symbolize Rwanda's place in cosmic evolution, the source of the Nile to represent its colonial history, the spot where Paul Kagame was born as an emotional introduction to its modern troubles, the border crossing at Kagitumba to mark the beginning of the Tutsi "armed return," battlefields and genocide memorials to convey the terrors of the 1990s, and finally a night crawl through Nyamirambo to sample the spice that adds a touch of zest to this serious and correct culture. Together, these places reflect a country desperate to find in its past anything that will help it shape a better future.

I think the West does some injustice to us. They don't want us to be ourselves, to develop into partners, into people who also have sense, values, and a culture to live by. It is another version of the West's economic policies. We can't process our own coffee here, we're supposed to send it to other countries to be processed and then buy it back from them. Even in politics, we are never meant to graduate from being pupils of democracy or governance. We are always people to be brought up, educated, told what to do, to be consumers of ideas and practices that come from the West. There is no point at which you graduate.

17

THE WEB GROWS BIG

ONE NIGHT AT THE CORNELL CLUB in New York City, I attended a dinner at which a dozen "friends of Rwanda" gathered to share their enthusiasm for the country and discuss their plans to help it. There were no philanthropists present, no ex-diplomats, and no one with a long-standing interest in Africa. A couple of the guests were clergymen. Most of the others were business executives, among them a fund manager, a retired banker, and a wine merchant. Americans like these do not often become "friends of Burundi" or "friends of Paraguay." Yet Rwanda has attracted them and, in many cases, turned contented millionaires into passionate antipoverty activists. Few developing countries have reached so deeply into American society, and none can count on such a richly productive network of new friends in the United States. How did this happen?

Each guest at the Cornell Club that night was asked to explain his or her involvement with Rwanda. One of them mentioned that the first Rwandan he met was an Anglican bishop, John Rucyahana. "You all know Bishop John, right?" he asked. Most of the other guests nodded, but a few seemed puzzled.

"Let me put it very simply," he told them. "After you meet Bishop John, you're going to walk away thinking, 'That is one of the most impressive people I have ever met in my life.' Then you're going to look in your wallet, and you'll see that it's empty."

Less than a quarter of Rwandans are Anglican, and Bishop John is not even the country's senior Anglican prelate, but he is by far the country's most active and influential clergyman. He is a force of nature, passionate, driven, outspoken, always in motion. Through an odd theological coincidence—or was it because "God had a plan for me," as he believes?—he crossed paths with a group of wealthy American Christians. They became his fervent admirers, and when he asked them to embrace his struggling country, they agreed. Of all the outsiders who have rallied to Rwanda's cause, no group is as potent as the one Bishop John has forged.

"When the circle grows big, the web grows big, it accommodates all," he told me. "This is not about serving the church or churchgoers. It aims at serving the community of Rwanda, the Rwandan people."

Bishop John is short and heavyset, with a round face, flat nose, and prominent ears. That is the stereotypical Hutu physiognomy. When he meets foreigners who think they know something about Rwanda, he sometimes asks them to guess his background. Those who answer usually say, "Hutu," and he gleefully corrects them. Not only is he Tutsi, he says, but his example shows the foolishness of trying to divide Rwandans into races.

During the turbulent 1950s, as Rwanda's monarchy was dying and the new Hutu state was emerging, John Rucyahana was a schoolboy in Ruhengeri, devouring geometry and dreaming of becoming an engineer. In 1962, when he was sixteen, a wave of anti-Tutsi violence shook Ruhengeri. He fled with his family to the Congo. Later they moved to Uganda and sank into the mass of tempest-tossed Rwandans.

"I lost my dreams and my nation," he reflected one chilly afternoon as we sat in the garden of a guesthouse his diocese runs in Ruhengeri. "I became a stateless refugee. I left this beauty, which was my inheritance. Naturally I responded with anger and despair."

Like many educated young exiles, Rucyahana became a schoolteacher in refugee camps. He came to believe that his mission in life was to help shape a generation that would one day take Rwandan exiles home. "I didn't want my people to become street children," he told me. "They needed to have strong character and excel, because God would use some of them to redeem their country."

In 1972, increasingly drawn to his Christian faith, Rucyahana entered a seminary in Uganda. He graduated, was ordained, became a parish priest, and rose to the rank of archdeacon. Then, at the suggestion of his bishop, he left Uganda to attend Trinity Episcopal Seminary in Pittsburgh. He traveled widely in the United States, preaching and making many friends. After graduating, he returned to Uganda, where his children had been born and where he had even managed to become a citizen. He told me he expected to spend his life running a mission church there, "but when the RPF emerged, I heard something calling me, a voice within myself."

Rucyahana was in Uganda when war and genocide devastated his country. Soon after the fighting ended, he returned to Ruhengeri, and he was living there when the region was ravaged again in the insurgency of the late 1990s. During those years he also spent several periods crisscrossing the United States, rousing congregations like a prophet newly inspired. By the time peace finally settled over northern Rwanda, he had built a network of passionately committed American supporters. Among its most fervent members were dissident Episcopalians who were in rebellion against their leaders in the Anglican hierarchy.

During the 1990s, conservative Episcopalians became disenchanted with their church's liberal positions, especially its support for gay bishops. They looked for support from Anglicans in other countries and found African bishops sympathetic. Several of these bishops went so far as to "adopt" congregations in the United States. Bishop John was among them, agreeing in 1998 to oversee fourteen believers who founded a breakaway congregation in Little Rock, Arkansas. These fourteen, like others around the United States, fell under his spell and began raising money to support his projects. In 2006 one of them, an effervescent businessman named Dabbs Cavin, went so far as to quit his job and

move to Kigali with his family. There he set to work establishing
a micro–finance bank Bishop John helped conceive.

Over lunch with his children beside the Mille Collines pool one
Saturday afternoon, Dabbs told me he is "not the camping-out
type." He had his home appliances shipped from Little Rock to
Kigali, and when he decided there was no school in Rwanda that
met his family's needs, he and a handful of friends founded the
Kigali International Community School. Like many religious believers who have embraced Rwanda, he sees it as a place where
political conditions create an ideal environment for doing God's
work.

"Rwanda is an example of where the church and the country's
political leadership came together to make a difference," Dabbs
told me. "It's the best example I know of in the world today.
Kagame has let the church come in and play a role. They share
the same goals. The time will come when the government will
want to rein in the church, but now the need is so great that the
state needs all the help it can get. When a country gets to be two
hundred years old and everybody has water and schools and
medical care, maybe the agendas diverge. But at this moment in
Rwanda, they're on the same page."

Bishop John appeals to people like Dabbs not simply because he
has a magnetic personality, is a committed Christian, and wants to
help needy people. He is also a born entrepreneur. That is what
Dabbs meant when he joked about losing his money to Bishop
John. Many of the bishop's inspirational homilies end with a sales
pitch, subtle or direct as the occasion requires. He simultaneously
speaks the languages of evangelical Christianity, African redemption, and self-reliance. That combination has stirred hundreds of
American Christians into action on behalf of Rwanda.

One who visits Kigali regularly, Dale Dawson, told me that the
most gifted leader he met during his years as an investment banker
in Arkansas was Sam Walton, the founder of Wal-Mart. Inspired
by Walton's super-entrepreneurial ethos, Dawson set out on a
career of buying, reshaping, and selling companies. By midlife he
was comfortably prosperous. So was his wife, a high-achieving

stockbroker. He told me he was "getting ready to go out and find that next company" when he was struck with the sense that his life had become unfulfilling. While casting about for ways to live a rewarding "second half," he met Bishop John in Little Rock and was struck by an epiphany: he was facing "a man whose leadership skills are equal to Sam Walton's."

"I used to think that a life of Christian service meant being a preacher or missionary," Dale explained. "But John told me, 'You can keep doing exactly what you've been doing all your life, exactly what you're good at, but instead of building companies, you can build schools and development projects.' . . . It got to the point where I just felt that Jesus was looking over my shoulder and saying, 'Dale, I'm trying to make it as clear as possible. This is what I want you to do. This is how I want you to serve.' So that's what I'm doing, and I plan to do it until I drop dead. My mission in life is to build a bridge between the United States and Rwanda, and transform lives at both ends of that bridge."

What does commitment like this produce? Dale Dawson's first major project as a soldier in Bishop John's army was to raise money for a Christian boarding school in Ruhengeri. It opened in 2001 and has been steadily expanding since. Nearly all of the students are orphans. When they arrive, most have never seen a toilet, used a toothbrush, or slept in a bed. Instruction is rigorous, with Christian morality taught alongside academic subjects. Discipline is strict.

This formula quickly bore fruit. In 2005 students at the Sonrise School—not "Sunrise," as I had thought until I saw the sign outside—scored higher on standardized tests than students at any other school in Rwanda. Wealthy families began placing their children there.

Because most of its students come from such miserable backgrounds, Sonrise offers powerful evidence for the transformative power of education. It is also one of the country's most promising development engines. Students are taught that they make up an elite corps, and that after graduating they must work together to transform Rwanda. This school exists because of Bishop John's ability to inspire people like Dale Dawson.

I spent one long afternoon talking with Bishop John, and as shadows lengthened, much of what he said began to sound familiar. He is an impassioned nationalist who scorns the Belgians ("Our nation was dismantled and destroyed by Belgium"), the rest of the developed world ("It waited until the corpses were burned and scattered into latrines to love them"), and Western human rights groups ("caught in the colonial mentality"). The development projects he now oversees, he told me, are possible only because Rwanda is secure, since "I can't build a school in a country where soldiers are coming to attack me and rob me and take the windows off the building." Always he returns to the theme of self-reliance: "No one will do it for us. We have to do it ourselves."

As Bishop John spoke, I was struck by how closely his views parallel those of President Kagame. They do not often work or appear together, but they share essential beliefs, passions, and ambitions. The bishop told me Kagame had given Rwanda "exemplary governance" and thereby "liberated our abilities, our capacities and our energies." Then he went further.

"There is a unique gifting in the person of this president," he said, lapsing into the evangelical vernacular he favors. "He is a curative to the nation, like medicine. He is an intended blessing from God to us. I think he's a divine prescription from God for this nation. He may not see it this way, but that's what I see. This is not an accident. It's not luck. There is a divine plan, and its purpose is for him to heal this nation and make it an example for all of Africa."

The relationship between these two remarkable men is based on what they share: an audacious vision of Rwanda's future; a brisk, businesslike style; and a rigorously goal-oriented agenda that stresses entrepreneurship, private enterprise, and self-reliance. Yet there is one thing they do not share. Christian belief and practice are central to Bishop John's character, but although Kagame is a baptized Catholic, he rarely attends church and makes no show of religiosity. Their alliance ties the country's most prominent clergyman to an apparently nonreligious president. When I suggested to Bishop John that this was odd, he bristled.

"How do you define 'religious'?" he asked. "It is not the uniform of a bishop. Kagame has a concept of life. He may even be more religious than some so-called religious people. It all depends on what you call religion. Maybe he prays in private, I don't know. But he produces the fruits. Some preach in words, but others preach by deeds, by your life. Only when it's necessary do we preach in words."

President Kagame has not concentrated on bringing Christian activists to Rwanda, as has Bishop John, nor does he show much interest in people's religious motivation. What he admires about Bishop John, he told me, is his "very realistic, very pragmatic" approach to his religious mission.

Rucyahana is a very interesting man. He's a family man. He's deeply cultured in our traditions. He's a man of God. He's very entrepreneurial. He does things that create worth for himself, and he extends that to others. He provides for people's basic needs and empowers them to stand up for themselves. Not many people combine these qualities the way he does.

Some Christians who embrace Rwanda have no connection to Bishop John. Many come because they were deeply moved by stories of the genocide or inspired by accounts of reconciliation between survivors and murderers. They return from visits to Rwanda convinced that it is becoming, as *Christian Century* reported, "a global lab for testing new models of Christian forgiveness."

One clergyman whose shock over the genocide led him to focus on Rwanda, Reverend Ian Cron, pastor of Trinity Church in Greenwich, Connecticut, has dispatched more than a hundred parishioners to work on projects in Rwanda. Another, Rick Warren, pastor of the Saddleback megachurch in Lake Forest, California, and author of the inspirational bestseller *The Purpose Driven Life*, concluded after visiting Rwanda that President Kagame is a "wonderful Christian leader" who has brought "a spirit of hope and reconciliation" to his country. Warren is among evangelical leaders who call for a "revolution" in religious practice, a "new vision" in which social action thrives alongside religious belief. He has begun sending volunteers to Rwanda and says he wants to make it "the world's first purpose driven nation."

"I fell in love with the country," Warren told an interviewer. "I say, 'Lord, help me find out what you are blessing and help me get in on it.' I think God is blessing Rwanda."

In 2005 Warren's church celebrated its twenty-fifth anniversary with a giant celebration at Angel Stadium in Anaheim, California. One foreign leader was present: Paul Kagame. "God is going to use you to change the world!" Warren cried out in the midst of his sermon, evidently addressing both the crowd and Kagame. Two years later Kagame was able to say that Warren had "connected us with a lot of people" in ways that were "extremely useful."

I like listening to what Rick Warren tells me. It's about combining three responsibilities that are important to society: the state, business, and religion. Being entrepreneurial—does it prevent you from believing in God or doing things that are godly? Or does it weaken the state and its relation to society? It doesn't stop you from looking in those other two directions.

An inescapable irony shadows this surge of interest in Rwanda by white Christians. The legacy of more than a century of Christian evangelism in Africa is decidedly mixed. Some of the continent's bloodiest crimes unfolded without a peep from missionaries. In several countries missionaries even helped make these crimes possible—as in Rwanda, where Belgian priests oversaw the destruction of traditional culture and then designed the political and social system that produced the 1994 genocide. The sight of missionaries now returning to "help" delights some, but others have their doubts. Among them is a newspaper columnist who criticized the government-run TV station for broadcasting sermons by the American preacher Joyce Meyer.

"Those who publicly proclaim their Christian religiosity are cramming their beliefs down our collective throats," the columnist wrote. "The neo-evangelical movement is slowly but surely spreading its tentacles into every facet of Rwandan society, whether we like it or not."

Thankfully for people like him, many Americans drawn to Rwanda come for reasons unconnected to religion. A remarkable number are corporate executives who see a kindred spirit in Kagame: a hard-driving manager who sets goals, demands results, punishes malfeasance, and even subscribes to the *Harvard Business Review*. On visits to the United States he is unlikely to meet a single member of Congress, but spends hours with executives from companies like Costco, Bechtel, and Google. Their admiration has spilled into the business press, producing articles like one in *Fortune* headlined "Why CEOs Love Rwanda."

African Americans are another part of the growing Rwanda lobby in the United States. Their leaders were as stunned as others by the genocide, but only a decade later did some begin to focus on Rwanda as a possible African success story. Andrew Young visited in 2005 and again in 2006 and after his second trip called Rwanda "a country with important lessons for all of us." The chairman of the Los Angeles–based philanthropy Operation Hope, John Bryant, came back so impressed that he not only launched a project to teach Rwandans "financial literacy" but also bought a plot of land near Ruhengeri and made plans to build a house there. Chicago's leading African American radio announcer, Felicia Middlebrooks, made an hour-long film about her trip and shows it wherever she goes, usually after an introduction in which she pronounces herself "in love with Rwanda." Representative Donald Payne of New Jersey, chairman of the Africa subcommittee of the House Foreign Affairs Committee, has praised President Kagame as "a moral leader" who "has done an outstanding job of moving Rwanda forward." Quincy Jones, responding to an inquiry from *Vanity Fair*, listed President Kagame among his "heroes in real life," along with others including Sidney Poitier and Nelson Mandela.

More than most world leaders, Kagame claims followers from across the political spectrum. Many of the American executives and Christian activists who admire him are conservative Republicans. They admire his pull-yourself-up-by-your-bootstraps ethos, his belief in business-driven development, and his dislike of foreign aid. Yet many leftists, thrilled by what they see as his sharp anti-imperialism, are also drawn to him. One of them, Dennis Roumestan, an Algerian-born activist who has spent decades working on African development projects, told me he admires Kagame for confronting "powerful forces in the world that are still trying to take out of Africa what doesn't belong to them."

"If you pretend to be on the left side of the sphere, if you're really progressive, you should love this project," he said. "It's about development and true independence for Africa. What's happening here is the great hope for Africa in the twenty-first century."

Rwanda has become a uniquely powerful magnet for Americans. It attracts devoted Christians, business executives, and African Americans, along with ideologues who want to promote what some see as a rightist project and others see as leftist. A remarkable number of freelance idealists also feel the pull, ranging from South Boston women who are raising money for a girls' school in Nyamata to Washington State University students who spent a vacation helping to open an Internet café in the blossoming southern town of Kizi. Most first heard of Rwanda in connection with the genocide, were transfixed by what they later learned about the reconciliation process, and then, usually after spending some time in the country, came to admire Kagame. They return from visits to Rwanda full of enthusiasm and eager to engage others.

Impressive as this network is, it has not yet produced great tangible benefits for Rwanda. None of the American companies Kagame so assiduously cultivates has made a major investment. Christian-oriented development campaigns like the one Rick Warren envisions are just beginning. If Rwanda's friends match their admiration with deeds, they can contribute decisively to its future.

IDEALISTS FROM FARAWAY LANDS are not the only people who
have poured into Rwanda in the years since 1994. So have thousands of Tutsi who spent most of their lives as refugees.

Many of these exiles left Rwanda as children. Others were born
abroad and had never even seen their "homeland." All supported
the RPF during its years in the wilderness. Victory, however, gave
them no cause for joy. Eighty percent of Rwandan Tutsi were
killed in the genocide. That left hardly any Tutsi family in the
world without dead relatives. In the face of such horror, it would
have been understandable if many exiles chose to stay away. Instead
they flooded back.

*The diaspora has made a huge contribution in two ways. During the
struggle itself, our people made a valuable contribution in terms of
finance, the money we needed. They also did diplomatic work, explaining what we were doing to different people wherever they had access.
Later on, some returned and directly participated in rebuilding. They
left their jobs and took on other responsibilities to rebuild our nation.
They brought in some kind of new outlook, new ideas, new thinking,
things they learned outside about how to do things differently. There's
no doubt about the impact that made. One significant thing that contributed to the genocide and other things was the inward-looking aspect
of people here. They had nothing to do with the outside world. Returning people diluted that and brought in new influences. That has been a
great contribution to development.*

Some of the thousands of exiles who returned to Rwanda after
1994 joined the government, like Charles Murigande, who gave up
his job as chief of biostatistics at Howard University College of
Medicine, took a series of posts in Kigali, and ultimately became
foreign minister. Others are religious figures like Bishop John
Rucyahana, who returned to help guide Rwanda's moral and spiritual recovery. Most, however, found less public niches. Some
started businesses. Others threw themselves into projects aimed at

helping the overwhelmed survivors of genocide. Wherever I went in Rwanda, I found them.

They constitute the best-educated and most highly motivated diaspora ever to return in such numbers to an African country.

The most elegant of these pioneers is the arrestingly statuesque Solange Katarebe. Heads turn when she enters a room. She is tall and impeccably stylish, with eyes that sparkle even more brightly than the silver bracelets she favors. The essence of her attractiveness, though, is the exuberant self-confidence she exudes. This is a woman who could dazzle New York or Paris. She chose Kigali instead.

"Rwanda is a poor country, but we're on a great track," she bubbled one afternoon when I asked her why she had made such an incongruous choice. "I think we can do anything we want to. We have the tools, we have the drive, and we have the leadership. This is our time!"

Like many Rwandan exiles of her generation, Solange was not born in the country to which she is so passionately attached. She spent her first years in Burundi, where her parents landed in 1959. The family moved several times—her father, who died when she was young, was "a bit of a revolutionary, a bit of a communist, I'm not really sure"—so she had the chance to sample life in several African countries. She settled in Kenya and became a manager for the air freight company DHL. When Rwandan rebels launched their war in 1990, she was approached, like nearly every prosperous Tutsi in the world, by an RPF fund-raiser who asked her to contribute a fixed percent of her income to the cause. She did so willingly, but never developed an interest in politics. By her own account, she "had no concept whatsoever of what Rwanda is."

"We collected coats in Nairobi to send to the boys who were fighting, but that was the extent of it for me," she recalled. "The change came when I started to see reports about the genocide on CNN. That's when I began feeling really—I felt I was one of them, that I could have been hacked to death."

Solange was a star at DHL, and after a six-month course in London she was named to manage its operations in Botswana.

After the RPF won its victory in Rwanda, for reasons she still cannot fully explain, she hesitated to visit. Finally, at the end of 1996, she set foot for the first time in the country she had been brought up to called home.

"I can't even tell you what a powerful impression it made on me," she recalled a decade later, still able to shake her head in wonder at the memory. "I had a picture in my mind, but nothing prepared me for the lushness of the countryside. There was no horizon, only hills. The moment I stepped off that plane, I knew I was home. I met relatives I had never known. One of them was a great-aunt who had made up a list of more than eighty people from her immediate and extended family who had been killed in the genocide. The whole experience gave me a powerful sense of belonging. I cried when it was time for me to go back to Botswana."

There was only a small DHL office in Kigali, and Solange could not find work there. Besides, Rwanda in the late 1990s was a turbulent place, shaken by guerrilla war and harsh counterinsurgency campaigns. By the end of the decade it had returned to a semblance of normality, and Solange found a promising job: director of the national tourism board, known by the acronym ORTPN.

"I only lasted eighteen months," she told me. "I was coming from a great job with an American company, and I was very private-sector oriented. The ORTPN job was very frustrating. I was naïve about what it meant to be a bureaucrat. After I quit, DHL took me back and gave me a job in South Africa. That also turned out to be uncomfortable, but for a different reason. It was a great job, but I was realizing that I could only be happy in Rwanda. So when Doudou called, I was ready."

Solange's brother, Doudou, had worked at several restaurants in Canada and wanted to try opening one in Kigali. Together the brother-and-sister team conceived a lounge with an outdoor terrace that would be decorated like a safari lodge, serve a combination of bar food and African specialties, stay open late, and cater to a clientele of expatriates, foreign visitors, and young Rwandan professionals. They called it Republika.

"We wanted an ambiance more like a kitchen than a bar," she said. "The whole idea was to create a place that would be an extension of our own home—not formal or stuffy, but the kind of place where we would want to hang out with our friends."

The night Republika opened in January of 2004 may be seen as a turning point in Rwanda's modern social history. On that night, it became clear that a new class had emerged in Rwanda, one that was hip, worldly, and boundlessly ambitious. If it is true that a strong middle class is the key to stability in any country, the crowd that night suggested Rwanda was on its way.

"It was shocking how successful it was," Solange recalled. "Doudou and I were totally taken aback. This was a soft opening with no advertising. We had just told a few friends to come by on a Thursday night. The guy at the door was counting guests, and we had over seven hundred. People were ready for a place like Republika. It wasn't just the food or the ambiance or the fact that it's open late. It was about timing. A lot of young people were coming back from college, and they didn't like hanging around at the Mille Collines, sitting with the tourists and paying crazy prices. It was the right time and the right concept."

Solange considers her restaurant more than a business. It is her contribution to building a new nation, her answer to an inner call. Like many other returned exiles, she feels a visceral connection to Rwanda that seems astonishingly strong considering the fact that she grew up in exile and did not even lay eyes on her "homeland" until she was nearly forty years old.

"I don't know if people who lived here through the genocide are attached to Rwanda in the same way," she mused during one of our conversations. "A lot of blood was shed so we could be here. It made sense for those of us who were outside to put our two cents in. I have not regretted this decision for a single minute. I have lived everywhere and I have the chance to live anywhere, but this is the only place that feels right for me."

The cool camaraderie of the crowded Republika bar is a promising symbol of the new Rwanda. Most Rwandans, though, still struggle through every day on hardscrabble hills like the one near

Nyanza where Drocella Krüger has built her Open Hands project. Drocella is making at least as great a contribution to her country's recovery as Solange is, but a very different one. She is the driving force behind a project devoted to educating orphans and teaching new skills to widows.

Finding Drocella's hill is not easy, but once I did, I fell quickly under her spell. She is a small bundle of energy who would be settling into late middle age if "settling" were part of her character. Instead she is ablaze with energy.

Drocella fled Rwanda with her family after an anti-Tutsi pogrom in 1973. She later married a German veterinarian, settled in the German town of Murnau, and then, in 1989, decided to return home. For the next thirteen years she moved freely between Nyanza and Murnau. She spent much of her time helping to run a small AIDS clinic in Nyanza, but in 1994 it collapsed under the weight of war and genocide. Drocella watched the tragedy from Murnau.

"All I was hearing at home was 'Rwanda is dead, forget about it,'" she told me. "I couldn't do that. Then, a couple of months after the genocide, one of the boys I had treated in the clinic wrote me a letter that said, 'You also forgot us.' That letter was like a knife in my soul. I had to do something."

Drocella returned to her devastated homeland in September of 1994. Ten of her fourteen coworkers had been killed. For Drocella, this was, as it would have been for anyone, a deeply traumatic experience.

"I couldn't understand what had happened," she recalled. "I was asking myself, 'Who are we? Is Rwanda a nation of murderers? Do I have anything to do with these people?' I was deeply shocked. People I knew and helped were killing each other. How can a person kill a child? What was inside those people? I had always seen my country as a paradise, and suddenly it had been destroyed by something so evil. I would tell people I'm Rwandan, and they would recoil in horror. I was asking myself so many questions. Then I thought: No, never again. I have to do something to make that 'never again' become real."

Much to Drocella's surprise, her neighbors in Murnau, including the pastor of the local Catholic Church that she, as a nonbeliever, had never attended, came up with tens of thousands of dollars in response to her first appeal. Using their contributions, she bought a plot of land at the end of a rough dirt road near Nyanza and hired a handful of local people to clear it and start building. On the day I visited, children were swarming everywhere. Each one ran to Drocella for a hug.

The Open Hands campus embraces flower gardens, a barn where livestock is kept, a kindergarten with room for sixty children, and a hall where traditional arts like dance, storytelling, and basket weaving are taught. Drocella hires carpenters to build new homes for widows, laborers to till her soybean farm, and women to process the soy into milk, tea, and tofu. Open Hands also pays school fees and buys textbooks for three hundred local kids. Money comes from what Drocella can collect on fund-raising trips in Germany.

"We are teaching morality," she told me as we sat on her porch, looking out over the campus and an idyllic lake beyond. "How do I live with other people? What does 'my neighbor' mean? For a long time there was no moral education in this country. We are fighting against the mentality that created this war. People will say, 'We did it because the government told us to do it.' So we're trying to teach them that each person is an individual with independent free will."

Drocella and I were finishing lunch when a jeep pulled up and a tall, stately woman in a long dress stepped out. When she and Drocella hugged each other, I sensed that they were sharing something more than I could immediately grasp. Our visitor turned out to be Eugénie Musayidire, author of a slim but devastating book of poems about the genocide that won many admirers in Europe. It is an anguished cry from a woman who happened to be safely away from Rwanda when the genocide exploded, but could do nothing to save her mother and other relatives.

Ms. Musayidire now runs a one-woman project that aims at teaching marketable skills to girls. She had come to share with Drocella the good news that she had just persuaded an aid agency

to give her seven used sewing machines. I asked her about the difficulty of returning to the scene of tragedy. She answered with the
same combination of eloquence and pain that moved so many
readers of her book.

"When I first came back to my village, I looked at every person
and wondered: Was it this one? That one? Finally I found out who
it was. He never admitted that he did anything wrong. He just
said, 'It was the government.' I have a huge problem helping people like him, people who committed genocide. I see them working
in my house and I say, 'These are the great murderers, the great
criminals!' And all they say is, 'It wasn't my fault.' It's terrible. It's
awful. But thinking of our country and our future, reconciliation
is the only solution I can imagine."

Visitors to the Open Hands project naturally come away inspired, and so did I. But without knowing it, the sight of so many
widows, orphans, and other devastated souls, the knowledge of
what horrors had befallen them and what demons were tormenting
them and will torment them forever, also had another effect on me.
By the time I visited Open Hands, I had been in Rwanda for several weeks. I had read dozens of books about the genocide and
understood exactly how it unfolded. But for anyone who becomes
deeply engaged with Rwanda, there comes a moment when its
story overwhelms the intellect and the conscious mind. Floods of
grief and pain, sharpened immeasurably by the realization that an
outsider's emotions can never even approach the agony that envel-
oped and still envelops most Rwandans, become a torrent that, at
least momentarily, drowns thought and reason.

It happened to me the morning after I visited Open Hands.
I was sitting in the shade beside the swimming pool at the Mille
Collines, transcribing my notes. Suddenly and without warning,
visions of the children who had surrounded me the day before,
along with nightmarish images of what they and their families had
suffered, began surging through me. When I looked up, trying to
regain my balance, I saw a young European woman in a bikini sitting at the bar, sipping a drink with a paper umbrella in it. That
disoriented me even further. I gasped for breath, began to quake,

felt tongues of flame shooting through my body, and then collapsed in spasms of tears. When I finally came back to my senses, I saw other guests staring at me with evident discomfort.

Can it be, I wondered, that they do not know what makes people cry in Rwanda?

The next day, more or less recovered, I thought to myself: You're really in Rwanda now. Later it dawned on me that if tourists at the Mille Collines are only vaguely aware of the genocide, if they have not come to grips with this country's tragedy, if they think it is a picturesque country like any other, perhaps that is good. It suggests that some rays of normality are penetrating a country where life has for too long been defined by horror and tragedy. Rwanda is not a genocide, any more than Cambodia, Germany, or the United States is a genocide. These are places with genocide in their history, but each has a rich story to tell that far transcends even the most shattering single aspect of its past. One reason Rwandans today have reason to hope for a future radically different from their past is that so many of their long-exiled cousins—people like Solange Katarebe and Drocella Krüger—have returned from far away to the land that broke their hearts, but that they still fervently love.

THE TWO-LANE HIGHWAY that winds northwest from Kigali toward Lake Kivu qualifies as a fine one by African standards. That means it is paved and kept in reasonable repair. It also has a feature rare in Africa and unique in Rwanda: a short stretch of it is illuminated by streetlights. At night you drive through the unbroken dark, always slowly in order to avoid hitting people. Suddenly the road is bathed in light. A couple of miles later, as you are still marveling at this wonder, it is over and you pass back into blackness.

The first time this happened to me, I wondered: Of all the highway stretches in Rwanda, why did the government choose to illuminate this one? Friends gave me a startling answer. The government did not choose this stretch, nor did it erect these streetlights, nor does it pay the electric bill. It is all Gerard Sina's work.

Sina is the living crystallization of tomorrow's Rwanda, the exemplary citizen of the country President Kagame sees in his dreams. As a young man his prospects would have seemed quite dim. His father was a subsistence farmer who could not afford to send him to school. By rights he should have settled into a life like those his ancestors had lived for centuries, tilling a tiny plot of land and struggling to live off whatever potatoes or cassava he could coax from the overtaxed soil. But a spark burned within Gerard Sina. Like Rwanda itself, he had no resources to exploit except those within him. They turned out to be rich.

"By nature I am very creative and innovative," he told me earnestly as we climbed a steep hill in the heart of his rugged domain one morning. "When I was very young, I was already dreaming of ways I could create a job for myself. I dreamed of starting my own business."

Sina was born in 1963, and in his early twenties he went into business as a baker, specializing in wedding cakes. Like almost everyone else in Rwanda, he lost most of what he had in the maelstrom of violence that engulfed the country in 1994. By the end of that year, though, he had already started baking again. Then, inspired both by his own ambitions and those of the new regime, he began to broaden his interests. Now they are as diverse as anyone's in Rwanda.

The reason Sina illuminated a two-mile stretch of highway is that he owns a strip of businesses there. He has a grocery store with its own bakery, a sit-down restaurant, a snack bar that offers take-out service, a motel, and a pair of clean public restrooms. It is the only highway rest stop in Rwanda. Cars, trucks, and buses are always parked out front. This complex, though, is just one jewel in Sina's uniquely Rwandan crown.

Sina has a mantra: add value. Since Rwanda will never be big enough to produce large amounts of anything, he reasons, it should process everything it grows. This dawned on him soon after he tried exporting fruit in the mid-1990s. He found that fruit prices were too low to guarantee a good income, that they fluctuated wildly in response to forces he could not control, and that much of the fruit he tried to sell spoiled quickly and had to be dumped. His solution was to stop exporting raw fruit and begin making and exporting fruit products instead. Now he is one of East Africa's leading producers of juice, jam, preserves, and banana beer. He even sells bottled hot sauce made from Rwandan chili peppers.

"Other countries in Africa aren't doing this," he told me. "They aren't dynamic enough. They are sleeping, but Rwanda is awake."

To make his products, Sina needs great quantities of fruit. He has persuaded two thousand farmers in areas around his processing plant to give up subsistence crops and grow fruit instead. His traveling agronomists teach them how, and at harvest time he buys everything they produce. This project has allowed people in an entire mini-region to make the decisive leap from acute poverty to bearable poverty.

In fields near his highway rest stop, Sina maintains a demonstration farm where Rwandans can learn to grow crops many of them have never heard of. He has brought vanilla seeds from Uganda, apricot saplings from South Africa, and macadamia plants from Kenya. There is an herb garden, the only one of its kind in Rwanda, where he has introduced parsley, basil, thyme, rosemary, and chamomile. Nearly every day, curious farmers from nearby—and, increasingly, from far reaches of the country—come for lessons. They pay nothing and are even told that if they want to try growing any of the crops they see, Sina will buy all they wish to sell.

Near the demonstration farm is a carpentry shop that produces lumber for Sina's various enterprises. There is also a brick factory that, at Sina's direction, employs mainly women. In a livestock compound, pigs, ducks, and chickens thrive on specially designed diets. Beyond are rabbit hutches, beehives, and fish ponds.

Many farmers in this part of north-central Rwanda have been isolated for generations because no roads reach the remote hills where they live. Sina has built rough but serviceable ones to all the areas from which he buys fruit. At the end of one of them is a school he has established for local children. It is free for all, with instruction in English, French, and Swahili, as well as Kinyarwanda.

Wide eyes and bashful smiles greeted me when I appeared at a class being taught under a tree outside Sina's school. At a signal from their teacher, the blue-uniformed students rose, glanced at each other for an anxious second, and then recited together in English, "Good morning, visitor. How are you? We are very happy to see you."

I asked these six- and seven-year-olds about their ambitions. They were extravagant. One wanted to travel the world. Another wanted to be president of Rwanda. The most popular ambition, though, was one I should have expected: to be like Gerard Sina.

Any driver whose car or truck breaks down near Sina's rest stop can stay in his motel for free. He will give a cow or goat to any farmer in the region where he works, with the price to be paid over the following year in milk—which Sina hopes will be the basis of his next big enterprise, a mechanized dairy to produce high-quality yogurt and cheeses. Foreigners interested in African development will soon be able to stay in an "agro-tourism" lodge he is building near his school. He wants to develop his own energy grid, powered by windmills. Spending a few hours with this man is as dizzying an experience as any in Rwanda.

Sina told me he loves journalists because "I learn so much from your questions." When I asked him what he sees in Rwanda's future, he broke into a broad smile.

"Our goal as a country is to escape from underdevelopment by 2020," he said. "I think we will succeed in doing this. The big advantage we have is good leadership. That energizes people and encourages them to work. Bad leadership destroys countries. It takes a rich potential and destroys it. That is the story of Africa. Here, the opposite is happening. People see that if they work hard, they can improve their lives. Every country was underdeveloped at one time. Here in Rwanda, our problem is that we are underdeveloped not just economically, but also in our minds. We have to change this. Education is the way, because when people are educated they become filled with ideas that can pull a country up. I have dreams. I like President Kagame because he encourages me to realize them."

Sina has never asked the government for a penny, even to illuminate a public highway, build roads the country needs, or pay teachers at his school. Once when he was attending a business conference in Kigali, President Kagame, who was giving the keynote address, picked him out of the crowd and praised his work. That thrilled him and spurred him on.

He has some of these enthusiasms that are present in people who are not schooled to a high level. But he's so modern, so entrepreneurial, and so productive in his own way. He wants to work. He wants to be innovative. He wants to do things. I think that's very important. We need more people like that, rather than some advanced graduates who come back and start quarreling, who look for jobs but can't find them and can't create them. He is a very interesting person to me. He has the kind of attitude that our people should develop. He's a hardworking fellow. You can see that he wants results. He wants to make money. He's also a good example. People like him. They like the idea that a person from such a background can be very productive. So many people don't realize they have that potential within them. I would like to encourage people not to lose hope in themselves. If this man can do it, why can't they do it?

Sina is doing so many things and has so many ideas that some find it difficult to decide what is most remarkable about him. I have my own answer. What impresses me the most about Sina, after the obvious fact of his endless enthusiasm, is that he has almost no formal education. His parents were poor people from the Hutu mass who left him no tangible inheritance. Despite these handicaps, he has become a front-line commander in Rwanda's war on underdevelopment. He believes fate has given him a historic chance, and he is making the most of it.

"I vaguely knew of him as a guy who made cakes and passionfruit juice," James Kimonyo, a Rwandan diplomat who became ambassador to the United States in 2007, told me when I asked him about Sina. "After a while I started seeing his products in foreign countries. Then I'd hear people say things like, 'Gerard Sina just won a medal in Geneva.' Slowly I understood the scale of what he has accomplished. It makes me wonder: what would he have been able to do if he had gone to school?"

I don't give too much time to some of these criticisms. They are misplaced, out of context, made by people who are used to dealing with ordinary situations. Ours is not an ordinary situation. It has built into me some sort of contempt for people who don't see the situation as it actually is, who don't see the depth and breadth of what we are facing. People are trying to give us lessons who know nothing. They are trying to set an example when they are no example. They want to be emulated when they do not deserve to be emulated.

For me, human rights is about everything. Even languishing in poverty as a result of colonization and other situations of the past violated human rights. If you solve that, you resolve the human rights issue. People in the West shy away from that and don't even want to talk about it. They run away from the significant blame that would be put on their shoulders. This is not just one person here or there. This is the killing of societies or nations we're talking about.

18

WE ASPIRE TO BE LIKE OTHERS

O NE MORNING I WAS AWAKENED EARLY by a great commotion below my first-floor window at the Mille Collines Hotel. I looked out and saw a crowd of distraught people pressing around a man who was dressed in a Canadian army uniform and wore the blue beret of a UN peacekeeper. Desperation was etched on their faces as they shouted at him in various languages.

"This hotel is under the protection of the United Nations!" the officer barked. "There's no danger!"

I walked quickly downstairs, and as I passed the officer, I saw the name on his uniform: Dallaire. A few steps away, just outside the hotel gate, crude roadblocks made of logs and wrecked cars had suddenly appeared. Crazed-looking young men with bulging eyes clustered around them, waving clubs and *pangas*. They eyed the gate menacingly, looking ready and eager to kill.

These figures were all actors in a film that was being made of General Dallaire's harrowing memoir, *Shake Hands with the Devil: The Failure of Humanity in Rwanda*. Even though I knew I was witnessing a re-creation of events that had unfolded more than a decade earlier, the scene was a powerful reminder of how far

Rwanda has come since the enormous horror that was visited upon it. This triumph is largely Paul Kagame's work. Will it prove to be his greatest achievement, or can he go on to even more improbable successes?

"Work is first," Kagame told me when I asked him how he spends his time. "Family is second. Reading is third. Fourth is sports. Fifth is visiting with friends and relatives."

One afternoon I shared a couple of beers with a former *inkotanyi* who has held high positions in Rwanda's government. He told me that living in the frigid volcanoes of the Virunga range, fighting for years, and then helping to revive prostrate Rwanda were "bigger challenges than you can possibly imagine." Those were nothing, though, compared to what this senior RPF figure considers the highest-pressure assignment of his life: being Paul Kagame's doubles partner in tennis.

"If you miss a shot," he said, "you think he wants to kill you!"

That is not true, Kagame told me. Missing a shot is pardonable. Not trying hard enough is what he cannot stand.

There is always the urge to win, no doubt about it. I go for any ball. Sometimes I make problems for my partner, especially if he simply lets a ball go by. He should go for it! It's all right to fail to succeed, but not to fail to try. I just want to try.

What Kagame is trying, above all, is to pull Rwanda out of poverty. This is his obsession. He has made an amazingly successful start, impressing many who have been in the poverty-fighting business all their lives. Development, though, is not Rwanda's only challenge. Its leaders must also shape an inclusive political system in a country where everyone is used to exclusionary politics. That will require striking an exceedingly delicate balance between freedom and security.

Rwanda is a society on the edge. The genocide is fresh in everyone's mind, and with it the specter of another one. One day while I was in Kigali, someone called a radio talk show and began screaming that he and other Hutu would soon pick up their *pangas* again and "finish the job." A friend of mine returned from a late-night party at a safari lodge and told me she had overheard a handful of drunken Tutsi guests cursing the Hutu and vowing to do whatever possible to keep them down forever. Students in a secondary school math class were asked how many Tutsi would remain if there were 108 to start with "and you kill ninety-eight?" In January of 2007 the mayor of Nyagatare called genocide ideology "a contagious disease" and lamented, "The majority of the population is infected with this ideology." Two months later *New Times* reported that dozens of *gacaca* witnesses and judges had been murdered "in the recent past." That same week, a genocide memorial near Lake Kivu was bombed, apparently by a Hutu militia squad that had infiltrated from the Congo.

It would take only half a dozen high-profile attacks or bombings to send donors and expatriates fleeing from Rwanda. That would wipe away many of the gains the country has made and devastate its future prospects. Only a potent security apparatus can prevent such attacks. With his years of training and experience as an intelligence agent, President Kagame knows as well as any head of state in the world how to build, direct, and use that kind of apparatus. No one was surprised, for example, when the man who telephoned a radio station to call for a renewed genocide was arrested within a couple of hours.

Whether this level of security and social control is reasonable or excessive is the subject of furious debate. Behind it lies a larger argument over whether President Kagame is a prudent leader who limits freedom only to the extent necessary to safeguard his people or an instinctively repressive one who overstates threats in order to protect his own personal power. In no other country does the opinion of Western human rights groups clash so directly with that of diplomats and antipoverty activists.

"There is a huge difference between what people here think and what our bosses back home think," a European diplomat told me over lunch in Kigali one day.

This conflict is a staple of life for Westerners in Rwanda. During one of my visits, the diplomatic corps was abuzz with rumors that the American ambassador, Michael Arietti, was engaged in a fierce battle with the State Department over a forthcoming human rights report on Rwanda. Officials in Washington were said to have written paragraphs that portrayed Rwanda as repressive, but Ambassador Arietti refused to approve them because they did not jibe with what he was seeing around him. Other Western ambassadors have also spent much time trying, often in vain, to persuade colleagues at home that Rwanda is as free as it can be under its explosive circumstances.

"If you apply general Western standards and ask whether Rwandans will have the opportunity to replace the current government with a completely new team when the next election comes around, then no, it isn't a democracy," the British ambassador, a portly and reflective Scot named Jeremy Macadie, told me over tea one afternoon as we sat in his office beneath a portrait of Queen Elizabeth. "If, on the other hand, you ask, 'Is this government working for the benefit of the general population? Is it working to assure that people have enough to eat? Does it have a vision to lift this country out of poverty?'—then the answer is yes. It's the definition of democracy that's critical. In this country, the primary problem is peace and security. Giving people food, clean water, health care, and education is also very important. Are Rwandan leaders trying the best they can at all levels to improve conditions for the most needy people in this country? Yes. Are they trying to build a country in which all Rwandans can enjoy long-term peace and progress? Yes. Are they encouraging political opposition to their ideas? No. Is there an opportunity for people who have different ideas than the president's to express them? Yes, but not in ways with which we are familiar."

During my visits to Rwanda, I met diplomats from nearly every country that maintains an embassy there. Every one of them—even the French ambassador, before his expulsion—lavishly praised President Kagame and his government. One told me Rwandan society is "a very volatile broth," and that "interim measures are going to be necessary for the next generation, until people train themselves to think of themselves as Rwandans." Another told me Rwandan leaders "are doing some great things." A third complained that "enormous misinformation" about Rwanda circulates in foreign capitals.

"Some people, for one reason or another, hate Kagame and describe his government as a murderous bunch of people," this ambassador said. "The human rights situation here is not so good, but as I see it, it is improving. This is not a paradise, but it is not the hell some people are painting it to be."

By "some people," he meant human rights groups based in the United States and Europe. They reject the view of Rwanda held by nearly every foreigner who lives there. Instead of a country full of hope and promise, they see a fear-ridden land where tyrants rule, people dare not speak their minds, and the regime enforces its will by every means including murderous violence.

Some people keep making stupid and unfair noises about us. They don't know what we prevented from happening. That it did not happen is what they should really be trying to tell people. That's why I'm really full of contempt, in some cases, for some of these people who try to put themselves in roles where they know better than others about observance of human rights, democracy, and good governance. I don't know what they are thinking about. I have contempt for them. I really have a lot of it.

Amnesty International asserts that although the world has begun "to depict Rwanda as a success story," in fact it is a place where journalists face "intimidation, harassment and violence," and human rights advocates are "forced to flee the country for fear of being persecuted or arbitrarily arrested." Freedom House says "transitional justice has been largely one-sided in Rwanda" and sees a "downward trend" in respect for civil liberties. Reporters Without Borders, which ranks countries according to their level of press freedom, places Rwanda in the bottom fourth of the 167 countries it surveys. Human Rights Watch asserts that anyone who criticizes the government risks being charged with promoting "genocidal ideology."

Human Rights Watch is high on the list of organizations Rwandan leaders detest. They believe it is embarked on a mindless, fanatical crusade against President Kagame and his government. Part of the reason for this disdain is that the chief Rwanda specialist at Human Rights Watch, Alison Des Forges, is an outspoken critic of the regime. She travels among world capitals to warn policymakers and legislators that glowing reports about Rwanda's antipoverty efforts mask dark deeds and repression. Her deep knowledge and long connection to Rwanda make her one of the government's most effective adversaries. In the corridors of Urugwiro Village, the presidential compound, her name is a curse word.

"The last time I met her, I told her we should stop fighting and try to work together," the chief of the Rwandan security service, Emmanuel Ndahiro, told me in 2007. "She said, 'Very difficult.' Then I said, 'Alison, whatever differences we have over the human rights situation in Rwanda, wouldn't you at least agree that by any standard, we are improving?' And she said, 'No.'"

Alison Des Forges is a petite bundle of focused energy who is, depending on whom you ask, a relentless human rights defender motivated by passionate love for Rwanda or a deranged obsessive with an irrational hatred for President Kagame. When I met her in the United States, she told me she was worried that Kagame's government is leading Rwanda back toward conflagration. "The justice system is completely skewed," she said. "You have 818,000 Hutu accused of genocide and no one accused of war crimes. When you ask the RPF about that, they say, 'We've taken care of all the war crimes charges, it's all done.' They say, 'Anybody with a complaint should bring it forward, we're happy to investigate.' But people are obviously afraid to do that. A very dangerous process is going on in some people's minds. They are saying to themselves, 'There is no justice for the Hutu.' In the absence of dealing with the situation honestly and saying, 'Our guys did bad things but there are reasons,' they are sitting on it and refusing to act. What does that lead to? Frustration festers and grows. It leads to the idea of 'double genocide,' the feeling that what the Tutsi did was worse than what the Hutu did. This is nonsense, but more and more people believe it. The failure to deal with it gives a gift of inestimable value to the extremists. Imagine the long-term future of Rwanda if the Hutu believe there is no justice. What kind of reconciliation is it if justice is only for one side? But some of them don't care about justice. Justice is not at the top of their list. Development is at the top of their list, and justice is seen as a nuisance. They do not understand the level of bitterness and anger that people are feeling just ten miles from their offices. They have created a sense of inequality and unfairness on the part of the Hutu, and that's very dangerous."

Many countries restrict free speech in order to maintain a measure of harmony and national unity. Ireland bans "threatening, abusive or insulting" language if it is aimed against people "on account of their race, color, nationality, religion [or] ethnic or national origin." In Britain, incitement to racial hatred is punishable by up to seven years in prison. India forbids public statements that promote "disharmony or feelings of enmity, hatred or ill will" among religious groups. Hitler's *Mein Kampf* may not be sold in Germany. France forbids the public expression of anti-Semitism. Swedes may not utter "threats or expressions of contempt for a national, ethnic or other such group."

In none of these countries is the danger of conflagration as great as it is in Rwanda. Opponents of the regime who live outside the country, along with some human rights advocates, charge that Rwanda's laws against "divisionism" and "genocide ideology" prevent open debate and feed potentially explosive resentments. Those charges outrage some Rwandans. They see Western human rights activists as ignorant utopians who are divorced from the real world, blinded by cultural prejudices, and obsessed with the rights of individuals. What, they ask, about the rights of society? Doesn't a government promote human rights when it raises people's living standards, guarantees their personal safety, and assures that their children can go to school instead of having to spend their days in toil? Some human rights advocates reply that these are questions of development, not human rights. Others, like my friend Solange Katarebe, bitterly disagree.

"It drives me nuts when Westerners come to the restaurant and ask me, 'Aren't you oppressed?'" she railed one day. "People need to understand that if there are controls in terms of security, it's because of what happened in 1994. We need it. We want it. We're happy, so leave us alone. I'm not even remotely political, but Rwanda is free and secure. That's all I require, so who is human-rights-whatever to tell me I'm not free?"

Almost every non-Rwandan in Rwanda agrees with Solange. "Contrary to what I had heard, which is that this is a very closed and repressive place, I found the opposite," one of them told me. I found the same. The Rwanda that foreigners who live there see is the real one. Human Rights Watch, Amnesty International, and other human rights groups do a great service when they expose very real abuses that occur in Rwanda, but they fail to place these abuses in a wider context and thus judge the government too harshly.

Rwandan leaders have sought to shape a governing system that meets their country's unique needs in an unimaginably delicate period. Under the umbrella of authoritarian rule, they have stabilized their country and set it on a path toward a better future. That is what ordinary Rwandans care about. They have little interest in politics or ideology. Most sense that their lives are slowly improving. They are happy that President Kagame has centralized so much power in his own hands and are not fearful that he is becoming a dictator.

Yet even if one agrees that reports on Rwanda produced by Western human rights groups do not tell the country's full story, they are still worth considering. President Kagame could respond to them by saying he is dubious but will investigate every allegation. Instead he angrily condemns and rejects them. After Human Rights Watch issued a report listing twenty cases of Rwandans who allegedly died in police custody, for example, Kagame told reporters in Kigali that anyone who would make such charges had "probably consumed drugs."

In 2004 Rwanda won much praise by volunteering to be one of the first countries to submit to the new African Peer Review

Mechanism, an ambitious project that aims to give Africans a chance to assess themselves rather than allowing Westerners to do it. After an exhaustive study, investigators published a highly positive two-hundred-page report that praised Rwanda for its "dramatic recovery." It also concluded, though, that "the independence of the judiciary is compromised," that there were "serious concerns" about the legitimacy of *gacaca* tribunals, and that it was time for the government to consider "the opening up of political space for competition of ideas and power." Rather than reflect soberly on these conclusions, President Kagame dismissed them as "simplistic" and based on "generic and oversimplified modes of analysis."

The same thing happened a couple of years later, when the United Nations Development Program published a trenchant and deeply researched report called "Turning Vision 2020 into Reality." The report praised Rwanda for its "very favorable institutional and policy environments," and said it had laid "foundations of lasting peace" by achieving one of the highest growth rates in the region and a better anticorruption record than any other country in East or Central Africa. It also, however, listed "key structural bottlenecks" in Rwanda's economy, said the country had "low levels of political freedom," and urged the government to focus its efforts on promoting agriculture, limiting population growth, and improving income distribution—not on encouraging private enterprise, building infrastructure, or developing computer technology. So rather than embrace this report, the cabinet passed a resolution condemning it. The state minister for finance was sent out to declare that it contained "grave errors that completely misrepresent the facts."

Leaders of guerrilla armies must have unlimited self-confidence. They train themselves to see the world through an "us-versus-them" lens and are deeply suspicious of everyone outside their own inner circles. Without these qualities, Kagame could not have won his war or begun resurrecting a country many believed was beyond resurrection. Yet considering the generally corrupting tendencies of power, especially in a political system where there are no countervailing checks and balances, this mind-set can also lead to trouble. Successful heads of state see critics as useful allies. Half-way through his first presidential term, Kagame had still not made that transition.

"Whatever he wants for Rwanda is right," one of his former aides shrugged. "Everyone must toe the line or you're an enemy."

Authoritarian modernizers like Singapore's Lee Kwan Yew and Malaysia's Mohammad Mahatir are among Kagame's role models. The limits on democracy those leaders imposed while transforming their countries may indeed be appropriate for Rwanda. They cannot remain in place forever, though. If Kagame serves two seven-year terms in the presidency—that is all the constitution allows, and he has publicly denounced African leaders who try to change constitutions to extend their terms—he will be in power until 2017. His every waking moment is devoted to assuring that by then, Rwandans will live richer and more fulfilling lives than they do today. But if he cannot guide a transition to a more open political system, his achievements and legacy may be in danger.

Kagame is well positioned to direct a calibrated opening of Rwandan society. He dominates the political scene and has absolute control over the military. Even if he concludes that truly free elections would lead Rwanda back toward genocide, which may well be true, he could democratize the RPF and broaden the base of his government.

"Otherwise, at some point there will be a conflict," one former cabinet minister told me. "It will be violent and radical, and it's not sure that Kagame will emerge from it as the victor, as he did from the last one. . . . Hutu resistance has floundered up to now for reasons related to the genocide. It's easy to say, 'Those *genocidaires*!' But with time, that will seem a flimsy argument. There is intense resistance in Rwanda—not publicly, but in the minds of people. If avenues are closed, there will be violent change at some time."

One of President Kagame's favorite themes is the need for Rwanda to develop strong institutions. If such institutions emerge, though, they will inevitably challenge him. There is no prospect of that happening soon. From lowly submayors to generals and

Supreme Court justices, officials in Rwanda tremble at the prospect of his wrath.

That is because Rwandans are used to quaking before the powerful and because of Kagame's demanding personality. There may also be another reason that institutions have been slow to develop in Rwanda. If Rwandan journalists, human rights advocates, lawyers, prosecutors, and judges were allowed to act with complete freedom, some would investigate past killings and unsolved disappearances. At least a few of those investigations would undoubtedly suggest the guilt of figures in the government or RPF. If indicted, some might testify that their acts were sanctioned or ordered by high officials, perhaps even the president himself.

That may be why Rwandan leaders promote "unity and reconciliation" rather than, like their counterparts in South Africa, "truth and reconciliation."

This issue of accountability hangs over Rwanda's future. As long as the RPF fails to confront its own past, fear of a reckoning will prevent it from allowing truly independent institutions to emerge. The same fear could also distort political life. If a future presidential candidate, for example, were to promise to investigate every charge against the RPF dating back to 1994, the RPF would have to decide whether it could afford to allow that candidate to win.

"You never know what the next guy will do," one of Kagame's longtime confidantes told me. "It becomes very intense, even life or death."

Even if no one in Rwanda manages to force the issue of accountability to the fore, foreigners might. Several countries have adopted laws allowing judges to investigate human rights abuses anywhere in the world. In 2008 a judge in Spain, which has the most sweeping such law, issued a stunning indictment of forty Rwandan officers, including the military chief of staff, General James Kabarebe, for atrocities they allegedly committed after the RPF seized power in 1994. Although President Kagame is immune from prosecution because he is a head of state, the judge said there was also damning evidence against him.

Some who have watched President Kagame over the years say that his personality and approach to governing are still evolving. "At the beginning he was very angry and not fit to be a unifying president," one of his admirers told me. Another observed that in the first couple of years after Kagame was elected president in 2003, he "developed as a statesman and raised his eyes to the horizon."

"There's been a distillation in his thinking," this analyst said. "As a man matures, so do his ideas. He's taken more time to think about things, and he's surrounded himself with people who have read a lot and had experiences in the wider world."

History, however, suggests that Kagame will continue to centralize power in his own hands, not give it away to others. That is what leaders normally do. Even those who are constrained by laws, institutions, and traditions fight relentlessly to increase their power. In Rwanda, there are no such constraints. President Kagame can be as powerful as he wants. It would be almost unnatural for him not to take advantage of this reality. Why, after all, allow vital decisions to be made by someone else if you are sure your choices are right?

The reason Africa remains so far behind the developed world is not simply bad leadership. It is also that the challenges facing African countries are overwhelming. Uniting deeply divided societies and radically changing the mentality of entire populations are immensely difficult tasks. Rwanda is an indigent society, crippled by generations of misrule. Turning it into a happy, stable, prosperous place is a task of Herculean dimensions.

Rwanda is not without assets as it pushes toward a better future. It counts on visionary leadership, a vibrant returning diaspora, and a remarkable constellation of support from the outside world. Its small size, often seen as a curse, also helps. A compact country seems fixable. No one would dare to suggest that even the most brilliantly conceived development plan could pull huge and staggeringly diverse countries like Nigeria or the Congo out of poverty within a generation or two. In tiny Rwanda, that seems at least possible.

Rwanda benefits from what some call "the genocide credit." Because Rwandans suffered such horror in the recent past, its leaders have developed a quiet but palpable sense of moral superiority. The "genocide credit" gives them a free pass. It allows them to reject criticism by saying, "You outsiders allowed our people to be slaughtered, so you have no right to judge us." This silences some critics, but it does not help build a happy or peaceful society.

It may be unfortunate that so much of Rwanda's future—and with it the future of a development project that could reshape Africa—depends so fully on one individual. Given that reality, though, the fact that this individual is Paul Kagame could prove providential. He earned a place in history by overthrowing a dictatorship and stopping a genocide. That he followed this triumph by stabilizing Rwanda and setting it on the path toward prosperity is even more remarkable. These achievements set the stage for his greatest challenge.

Rwanda cannot have the majority of its people living on less than one dollar a day. It is simply unacceptable. You cannot have progress or a future when most of your people are barely living. Yet apart from the mistakes of governance, leadership, and politics, we have within us what we need to develop. We aspire to be like others, like the developed world. There are countries that forty or fifty years ago were at the same level of development as our country. They have moved forward and left us behind. Why can't we achieve that? That's a question I constantly ask myself.

Kagame has set out to do something that has never been done before: pull an African country from misery to prosperity in the space of a generation. To accomplish this, he must hack a path through his country's century-old social and political overgrowth. Because that overgrowth is so dense, because he is working without a model, and because like all human beings he is the product of his past experiences, this is as great a challenge as faces any leader in the world.

Can Rwanda, within the lifetime of anyone now alive, rise from poverty and enjoy the long-term stability that comes with prosperity and majority rule? No prudent outsider would dare to venture an answer. Whether President Kagame can put aside his autocratic tendencies is even more uncertain. He and his country are both works in progress. A rational person, coldly considering the odds, might not want to wager on their success. It would take a mean spirit, though, not to hope for it.

Two things about President Kagame are evident to all who consider his situation honestly. First, he has accomplished something truly remarkable. The contrast between where Rwanda is today and where most people would have guessed it would be today in the wake of the 1994 genocide is astonishing.

Second, Kagame is the man of the hour in modern Africa. The eyes of all who hope for a better Africa are upon him. No other leader has made so much out of so little, and none offers such encouraging hope for the continent's future.

Beside these two great achievements lie two daunting challenges.

The first comes from the unique nature of postgenocide Rwanda. Huge numbers of onetime killers and their supporters live there. Just across the border in the Congo, and in other places farther away, lie forces eager to destroy what Kagame's government is building. In this climate, permitting European-style democracy would be folly. It might well lead to another genocide. Most Rwandans realize this. Their understanding, coupled with their appreciation for the stability and the beginnings of prosperity they see around them, leads them to support their government. How long this special period must last, and what sort of transition lies in the future, remains uncertain.

The second challenge that lies ahead has to do not with Rwanda but with human nature. Rwanda has no democratic or constitutional tradition, nor has such a tradition developed in the surrounding region. In climates like this, leaders tend to become corrupted in one way or another. For Kagame, resisting this tendency is almost as great an imperative as finding the proper balance between development and individual rights.

No road map exists to guide this extraordinary man through the dense web of challenges he and his nation face. Modern Rwanda is a thrilling place, but its story is still unfolding. That is part of what makes it so exciting.

If Kagame can achieve half of what he has set out to do, he will go down in African history. If he can achieve it all, leaders of every poor country on earth will look to Rwanda for lessons, and bands of angels will sing in heaven. How much of what he dreams is really possible? That was the last question I asked him.

Seeing everything, we can do it. We can reduce the number of people below the poverty line, reduce the level of dependence on donor funds, and truly develop our country. We can and we want to. We are convinced—very, very convinced. We want to do it, and we will.

NOTES

INTRODUCTION

5   Yoweri Museveni, the Ugandan leader   Bill Berkeley, *The Graves Are Not Yet Full: Race, Tribe and Power in the Heart of Africa* (New York: Basic Books, 2001), 237.

5   In 2003 an American lawyer   Lester Hyman, *U.S. Policy toward Liberia 1922 to 2003: Unexpected Consequences* (Cherry Hill, N.J.: African Homestead Legacy, 2005), xii.

5   "Kagame has been a good person"   Confidential source, author's interview.

8   "We want to be first"   Boniface Rucagu (provincial governor), author's interview.

1. YOU CAN'T JUST PRETEND NOTHING HAPPENED

11   This "practice genocide,"   Josias Semujanga, *Origins of the Rwandan Genocide* (Amherst, N.Y.: Humanity, 2003), 181.

11   "In the morning the grim"   Meg Guillebaud, *Rwanda: The Land God Forgot* (London: Monarch, 2002), 142.

14   "If I dig"   Asteria Rutagambwa, author's interview.

14   "He was a measured person"   Emmanuel Ndahiro, author's interview.

17   Waves of pogroms   Gérard Prunier, *The Rwanda Crisis: History of a Genocide* (New York: Columbia University Press, 1995), 61–62.

2. ELEGANT GOLDEN-RED BEAUTIES

22   Scholars agree, however   Dixon Kamukama, *Rwanda Conflict: Its Roots and Regional Implications* (Kampala, Uganda: Fountain, 1993), 8–24; also, Jacques J. Maquet, *The Premise of Inequality in Ruanda: A Study of Political Relations in a Central African Kingdom* (Oxford, U.K.: International African Institute, 1961); Audrey Richards, *Economic Development and Tribal Change* (Cambridge, Mass.: EAISR, 1954); Rachel Van der Meeren, "Three Decades in Exile: Rwandan Refugees 1960–1990," *Journal of Refugee Studies* 9, no. 3

(1996), 253–256; and Jan Vansina, *Antecedents to Modern Rwanda: The Nyigi-nya Kingdom* (Madison: University of Wisconsin Press, 2004).

22   The symbol of national power   Prunier, *The Rwanda Crisis*, 10.

23   The first European to reach Rwanda   Learthen Dorsey, *Historical Dictionary of Rwanda* (Lanham, Md.: Scarecrow, 1994), 42.

24   Like the Europeans who came   John Bale, *Imagined Olympians: Body Culture and Colonial Representation in Rwanda* (Minneapolis: University of Minnesota Press, 2002), 17; also, Prunier, *The Rwanda Crisis*, 6–11.

25   To resolve this contradiction   Mahmood Mamdani, *When Victims Become Killers: Colonialism, Nativism, and the Genocide in Rwanda* (Princeton, N.J.: Princeton University Press, 2001), 99.

25   One Catholic priest   Prunier, *The Rwanda Crisis*, 6–8, 11.

26   The Tutsi reveled in the power   Prunier, *The Rwanda Crisis*, 9.

27   This system, in the words   Prunier, *The Rwanda Crisis*, 9.

27   In 1930, one of the first Catholics   Dorsey, *Historical Dictionary of Rwanda*, 196–197; also, Semujanga, *Origins of the Rwandan Genocide*, 141–145.

27   Within months after the 1930 agreement   Prunier, *The Rwanda Crisis*, 31.

28   The Belgians reacted by deposing   Prunier, ibid., 30; also, Dorsey, *Historical Dictionary of Rwanda*, 197.

28   Later he even followed the example   Prunier, ibid., 31.

28   Some Rwandans called him   Prunier, ibid., 31.

28   "Catholicism, after Mutara III Rudahigwa"   Prunier, ibid., 34.

30   Marxist ideas were spreading   U.S. Committee for Refugees, *Exile from Rwanda: Background to an Invasion* (New York: U.S. Committee for Refugees, 1991), 4.

30   The signers and their supporters   Mamdani, *When Victims Become Killers*, 112.

30   A Catholic press in northern Rwanda   Carol Rittner, et al., eds., *Genocide in Rwanda: Complicity of the Churches?* (St. Paul, Minn.: Paragon House, 2004), 152–153.

30   Kayibanda, a seminary graduate   Semujanga, *Origins of the Rwandan Genocide*, 174.

31   The UN Trusteeship Council protested   Richard F. Nyrop, et al., *Rwanda: A Country Study* (Washington, D.C.: U.S. Government Printing Office, 1982), 21.

32   The decisive episode   Dorsey, *Historical Dictionary of Rwanda*, 214–215; also, Mamdani, *When Victims Become Killers*, 124.

32   "The developments of these last eighteen months"   Michael Barnett, *Eyewitness to a Genocide: The United Nations and Rwanda* (Ithaca, N.Y.: Cornell University Press, 2002), 53.

33   "Between one thousand and two thousand Tutsi"   U.S. Committee for Refugees, *Exile from Rwanda*, 5.

33   Rampages like these   Mamdani, *When Victims Become Killers*, 130; also, Semujanga, *Origins of the Rwandan Genocide*, 187; Henry Kwami Anyidoho, *Guns over Kigali* (Kampala, Uganda: Fountain, 1998), 2.

34   He drew up a list   Mamdani, *When Victims Become Killers*, 130.
34   Vatican Radio reported   Colin M. Waugh, *Paul Kagame and Rwanda: Power, Genocide and the Rwandan Patriotic Front* (Jefferson, N.C.: McFarland, 2004), 28.
35   By the 1970s, nearly half   Waugh, ibid., 9–10; Prunier, *The Rwanda Crisis*, 63.
35   Falling suddenly from stable prosperity   U.S. Committee on Refugees, *Exile from Rwanda*, 9.
35   "Most refugees in Uganda"   Ibid.
36   This disturbed government leaders   Mamdani, *When Victims Become Killers*, 137; also, Prunier, *The Rwanda Crisis*, 61.
36   He ordered many officials   Semujanga, *Origins of the Rwandan Genocide*, 31.
36   Instead he chose to surround   Linda Melvern, *Conspiracy to Murder: The Rwandan Genocide* (London: Verso, 2004), 11; also, Linda Melvern, *A People Betrayed: The Role of the West in Rwanda's Genocide* (London: Zed, 2000), 25; Prunier, *The Rwanda Crisis*, 82; and author's interviews.
37   Rwanda became a pillar   Melvern, *A People Betrayed*, 41; also, Andrew Wallis, *Silent Accomplice: The Untold Story of France's Role in the Rwandan Genocide* (London: I. B. Tauris, 2006), 14–19, 22–26; Waugh, *Paul Kagame and Rwanda*, 10–11.
37   Members of the *akazu*   Alison Des Forges, et al., *Leave None to Tell the Story: Genocide in Rwanda* (New York: Human Rights Watch, 1999), 44.
37   An American living in Rwanda   Guillebaud, *Rwanda: The Land God Forgot*, 206.
37   The *akazu*'s guiding force   Prunier, *The Rwanda Crisis*, 86–87; also, Waugh, *Paul Kagame and Rwanda*, 21; Wallis, *Silent Accomplice*, 52.
38   By this time there were more than eighty thousand   Jason W. Clay, *The Eviction of Banyarwanda: The Story behind the Refugee Crisis in Southwest Uganda* (Cambridge, Mass.: Cultural Survival, 1984), 16.
40   Both admired Museveni   Prunier, *The Rwanda Crisis*, 68.

3. That's Why I Survived

44   "The NRA was a different kind of rebel army"   Waugh, *Paul Kagame and Rwanda*, 30–31.
44   Later, he would insist   Waugh, ibid., 25.
45   "There were killings"   U.S. Committee for Refugees, *Exile from Rwanda*, 11.
46   Most of them, according to   U.S. Committee for Refugees, ibid., 13.
47   By the time they captured Kampala   Pecos Kutesa, *Uganda's Revolution 1979–1986: How I Saw It* (Kampala, Uganda: Fountain, 2006).
47   "He came out of the bush"   Richard Sezibera, author's interview.
49   "There was a desire"   Tito Rutaremara, author's interview.
50   They became the Rwandan Patriotic Front   Dorsey, *Historical Dictionary of Rwanda*, 360–361; also, Hildegard Schürings, ed., *Ein Volk Verlässt sein Land: Krieg und Völkermord in Ruanda* (Cologne, Germany: ISP, 1994), 168–183;

William Cyrus Reed, "Exile, Reform and the Rise of the Rwandan Patriotic Front," *Journal of Modern African Studies*, 34, no. 3 (1996), 479–501.

50   Their declaration committed the RPF   Waugh, *Paul Kagame and Rwanda*, 38.

52   "Rwanda is full"   Emmanuel Ndahiro, author's interview.

52   Refugees repeatedly asked Habyarimana   Rakiya Omaar, *Rwanda: Death, Despair and Defiance* (London: African Rights, 1995), 26–27.

54   Given his charisma   Christopher Clapham, ed., *African Guerrillas* (Oxford, U.K.: James Currey, 1998), 128.

54   There were three thousand Rwandans   Prunier, *The Rwanda Crisis*, 71.

56   "The two camp rivalries"   Howard Adelman and Astri Suhrke, eds., *The Path of a Genocide: The Rwanda Crisis from Uganda to Zaire* (New Brunswick, N.J.: Transaction, 1999), 35.

56   At the same time, the regime   Prunier, *The Rwanda Crisis*, 160.

56   This was not true   Prunier, ibid., 68–69; also, Schürings, *Ein Volk Verlässt sein Land*, 171.

57   "Mobilize and invade"   Adelman and Subrke, *The Path of a Genocide*, 35–37.

4. A Glass of Milk

60   In fact, a relative had told her   Jeannette Nyiramongi, author's interview.

5. Devastation

74   "Are you alone?"   Jeannette Kagame, author's interview.

77   To dramatize the urgency   Prunier, *The Rwanda Crisis*, 102; also, Wallis, *Silent Accomplice*, 25.

77   "We are going to send him"   Prunier, *The Rwanda Crisis*, 100–101.

77   According to the flamboyant French mercenary   Wallis, *Silent Accomplice*, 28.

78   France took over management   Wallis, ibid., 32–39.

78   "France's official special services"   Wallis, ibid., 28–29.

78   "There was not a house"   Colonel George Rwigamba, author's interview.

79   "It was the logical choice"   Richard Sezibera, author's interview.

79   "Nobody at that time"   Ibid.

80   "Our most important support"   Tito Rutaremara, author's interview.

81   "The aggressors were not even"   Bill Weber and Amy Vedder, *In the Kingdom of Gorillas: Fragile Species in a Dangerous Land* (New York: Simon & Schuster, 2001), 312.

81   "Seeing soldiers dying"   Joseph Karamera, author's interview.

82   "It's not for an army"   Aloisea Inyumba, author's interview.

82   "If you had an order"   author's confidential interview.

83   "Seeing young people"   Joseph Karamera, author's interview.

83   By early 1991, the RPF force   Prunier, *The Rwanda Crisis*, 117; also, Catharine Watson, "War and Waiting," *Africa Report*, Nov.–Dec. 1992, 51–55.

83   Once there, they were organized   Paul Kagame, *The Rwandese Patriotic Army Operation Code of* Conduct: (Rwanda: Photocopy, 1991).

84   "In the way we fight"   *Major General Paul Kagame: What Is He Like?* Video produced by the Rwanda Bureau of Information and Broadcasting, 2000.

6. Creatures from Another World

88   Only later, when fifteen French paratroopers   Wallis, *Silent Accomplice*, 49.

88   A terrible massacre   Prunier, *The Rwanda Crisis*, 120; also, Melvern, *Conspiracy to Murder*, 16–17; Dorsey, *Historical Dictionary of Rwanda*, 130.

89   "The rebels remained hidden"   Rosamond Halsey Carr, with Ann Howard Halsey, *Land of a Thousand Hills: My Life in Rwanda* (New York: Viking, 1999), 203.

90   The army responded in a way   Melvern, *Conspiracy to Murder*, 17.

90   Hundreds were slaughtered   Wallis, *Silent Accomplice*, 59.

90   "President Habyarimana"   Omaar, *Rwanda: Death, Despair and Defiance*, 28.

92   It opposed any accommodation   Prunier, *The Rwanda Crisis*, 108.

92   Rwanda's foreign minister told   Mamdani, *When Victims Become Killers*, 189.

92   Members of the *akazu*   Hugh McCullum, *The Angels Have Left Us: The Rwanda Tragedy and the Churches* (Geneva: World Council of Churches, 2004), 10.

92   "We will never allow them"   *Financial Times*, June 27, 1994.

93   Perhaps coincidentally, the edition   Wallis, *Silent Accomplice*, 43.

93   "Every Hutu should know"   Omaar, *Rwanda: Death, Despair and Defiance*, 42–43.

94   During the early 1990s   Melvern, *A People Betrayed*, 66; also, Melvern, *Conspiracy to Murder*, 58; Prunier, *The Rwanda Crisis*, 113; Wallis, *Silent Accomplice*, 32.

94   When Egyptian financiers hesitated   Melvern, *A People Betrayed*, 66.

94   That allowed Rwanda to buy   Wallis, *Silent Accomplice*, 30.

94   "Africa is the only continent"   Adelman and Suhrke, *The Path of a Genocide*, 166.

95   "In President Mitterrand's analysis"   Wallis, *Silent Accomplice*, 27.

95   This prospect deeply alarmed   Prunier, *The Rwanda Crisis*, 107.

96   They went into a variety of businesses   John A. Berry and Carol Pott Berry, eds., *Genocide in Rwanda: A Collective Memory* (Washington, D.C.: Howard University Press, 1999), 45.

96   By night, according to a *New York Times* correspondent   Wallis, *Silent Accomplice*, 21.

98   They embodied, by one account   Prunier, *The Rwanda Crisis*, 129.

98   In their newspapers and radio broadcasts   Prunier, ibid., 142.

98   Most important, they portrayed every Tutsi   Melvern, *Conspiracy to Murder*, 51.

98   "Unaccountable before the law"   Berry and Berry, *Genocide in Rwanda*, 3.

99   "You want power?"   Prunier, *The Rwanda Crisis*, 156.

99   Together these "practice genocides"   Mamdani, *When Victims Become Killers*, 192.

99   "In the episodes of violence"   Des Forges et al., *Leave None to Tell the Story*, 95.

100   Here developed the vocabulary   Mamdani, *When Victims Become Killers*, 194.

101   Members not only learned paramilitary tactics   Waugh, *Paul Kagame and Rwanda*, 59.

101   "We were woken up"   Prunier, *The Rwanda Crisis*, 100.

102   "Kagame, a secretive"   Melvern, *Conspiracy to Murder*, 16.

102   According to one scholarly survey   Clapham, *African Guerrillas*, 131.

103   In March he announced   Dorsey, *Historical Dictionary of Rwanda*, 193; also, Prunier, *The Rwanda Crisis*, 145.

103   Soldiers, who had gone unpaid   Waugh, *Paul Kagame and Rwanda*, 60.

104   "We have to wipe out"   Melvern, *Conspiracy to Murder*, 37.

104   More than one thousand were killed   Alain Destexhe, *Rwanda and Genocide in the Twentieth Century* (London: Pluto, 1995), 46; also, Dorsey, *Historical Dictionary of Rwanda*, 179.

105   President Mitterrand, alarmed by news   Wallis, *Silent Accomplice*, 63.

105   "We had made our way"   General Jean-Bosco Kazura, author's interview.

105   By the time it was over   Mamdani, *When Victims Become Killers*, 204.

107   Thirteen months later   Adelman and Suhrke, *The Path of a Genocide*, 131–156.

108   The reality was that the French military   Wallis, *Silent Accomplice*, 45–46.

108   All understood that President Habyarimana   Prunier, *The Rwanda Crisis*, 194–195.

108   It is a political truism   Machiavelli, *The Discourses*, vol. 2, chapter 13, www.oll.libertyfund.org/index.

109   "Between the roots of the conflict"   Bruce D. Jones, "Civil War, the Peace Process, and Genocide in Rwanda," in Taisier, M. Ali, and Robert O. Matthews, eds., *Civil Wars in Africa: Roots and Resolution* (Montreal: McGill-Queen's University Press, 1999), 54.

109   Chanting slogans denouncing the "sell-out,"   Wallis, *Silent Accomplice*, 46.

109   It offered a snappy mix   Adelman and Suhrke, *The Path of a Genocide*, 93–107; also, McCullum, *The Angels Have Left Us*, 17; Melvern, *Conspiracy to Murder*, 52–56.

110   "It was the endless"   McCullum, *The Angels Have Left Us*, 18.

110   They directed the importation   Melvern, *Conspiracy to Murder*, 56.

110   In mid-1993, the United States   United States Department of Defense and Department of State, *Congressional Presentation for Security Assistance Programs, Fiscal Year 1993* (Washington, D.C.: U.S. Government Printing Office, 1993), 291.

110   Several months later, President Habyarimana   Melvern, *Conspiracy to Murder*, 56.

110   While he was there a Belgian scholar   Melvern, ibid., 28.

110   Bagosora, popularly known as "the colonel of death,"   Adelman, *The Path of a Genocide*, 148.

110 Part of his power came from   Wallis, *Silent Accomplice*, 52.

111 "He had a quick and nervous temper,"   Melvern, *Conspiracy to Murder*, 83.

111 Back to Kigali, he replied   Melvern, *A People Betrayed*, 54.

7. We Just Didn't Get It

113 "That's somewhere in Africa, right?"   Roméo Dallaire, *Shake Hands with the Devil: The Failure of Humanity in Rwanda* (New York: Carroll & Graf, 2003), 42.

114 "Pencil out a front tooth"   Louise Mushikiwabo and Jack Kramer, *Rwanda Means the Universe: A Native's Memoir of Blood and Bloodlines* (New York: St. Martin's, 2006), 39.

114 A UN diplomat described him   Barnett, *Eyewitness to a Genocide*, 64.

114 Friends had warned him, he later wrote   Dallaire, *Shake Hands with the Devil*, 49.

114 No one briefed him   Barnett, *Eyewitness to a Genocide*, 65; also, Melvern, *Conspiracy to Murder*, 65.

115 He never even saw public reports   David Waller, *Rwanda: Which Way Now?* (Oxford, U.K.: Oxfam, 1993).

115 Dallaire was told repeatedly   Dallaire, *Shake Hands with the Devil*, 50.

115 "This thing has to be"   Dallaire, ibid., 56.

116 The dynamic new prime minister   McCullum, *The Angels Have Left Us*, 23.

116 Rwanda's future hung in the balance   Dallaire, *Shake Hands with the Devil*, 60.

116 On the way, they stopped at a hellish camp   Dallaire, ibid., 64.

117 "Almost stereotypically Tutsi"   Dallaire, ibid., 66.

117 "This was a combat-proven"   Dallaire, ibid., 67.

117 He found it full of "poorly trained recruits"   Dallaire, ibid., 68.

118 "I did not understand"   Dallaire, ibid., 79.

118 Reluctantly he cut his request   Dallaire, ibid., 75.

118 The Americans never took Rwanda or me seriously"   Dallaire, ibid., 84.

118 He was Paris-educated   Melvern, *Conspiracy to Murder*, 87.

118 Among the favors he had done   Wallis, *Silent Accomplice,* 32–33.

119 Dallaire and his force   Anyidoho, *Guns over Kigali*, 4.

119 "UNAMIR was deployed naively"   Barnett, *Eyewitness to a Genocide*, 72.

120 Without an inkling of the horror   Dallaire, *Shake Hands with the Devil*, 93.

120 "All Hutu are one power!"   Melvern, *Conspiracy to Murder*, 72.

120 Dallaire and his handful of aides   Dallaire, *Shake Hands with the Devil*, 106.

120 By his own account he enjoyed   Dallaire, ibid., 103.

121 Dallaire reported that the mood   Dallaire, ibid., 110.

121 "The swiftness, the callous efficiency"   Melvern, *Conspiracy to Murder*, 75.

121 Their only effect in New York   Dallaire, *Shake Hands with the Devil*, 147; also, Alan J. Kuperman, *The Limits of Humanitarian Intervention: Genocide in Rwanda* (Washington, D.C.: Brookings, 2001), 88.

121   Peacekeeping soldiers who began arriving   Anyidoho, *Guns over Kigali*, 41; also, Dallaire, *Shake Hands with the Devil*, 203.

122   Dallaire requested twenty armored personnel carriers   Dallaire, ibid., 181.

122   Fax paper was doled out   Dallaire, ibid., 135.

122   Dallaire later estimated   Dallaire, ibid., 107; also, Melvern, *A People Betrayed*, 86.

122   "We had next to nothing"   Dallaire, ibid., 136.

122   This, he saw immediately   Melvern, *Conspiracy to Murder*, 84.

122   With no analysts to tell him   Dallaire, *Shake Hands with the Devil*, 90.

122   Dallaire's other great handicap   Melvern, *Conspiracy to Murder*, 103.

122   "The general public still"   Dallaire, *Shake Hands with the Devil*, 172.

124   "As we moved through the streets"   Dallaire, ibid., 130.

124   "I had to admire the moxie"   Dallaire, ibid., 127.

124   "The *inyenzi* have invaded the capital!"   Colonel Luc Marchal, *Rwanda, La Descente aux Enfers: Témoinage d'un Peacekeeper Decembre 1993–Avril 1994* (Brussels: Labor, 2001), 105.

125   Dallaire was chilled   Dallaire, *Shake Hands with the Devil*, 139.

125   He had found a high-ranking informant   Dallaire, ibid., 142; also, Melvern, *Conspiracy to Murder*, 95–100; *The New Yorker*, May 11, 1998.

125   "I was silent"   Dallaire, *Shake Hands with the Devil*, 142–143.

126   As he wrote, he felt himself   Dallaire, ibid., 146.

126   It ordered him to suspend his planned raid   Barnett, *Eyewitness to a Genocide*, 79.

126   "I was absolutely"   Dallaire, *Shake Hands with the Devil*, 146–147.

126   Dallaire reacted by sending a series of cables   Dallaire, ibid., 167.

126   He correctly sensed a "total disconnect"   Dallaire, ibid., 147.

127   That cable was   Barnett, *Eyewitness to a Genocide*, 80.

127   "We were cautious"   Barnett, ibid., 86.

127   Assuring that the one in Rwanda   Barnett, ibid., 95.

128   "People tried to tell us"   Joyce Leader, in PBS, "Ghosts of Rwanda," *Frontline*, 2004.

128   The first months of 1994   Barnett, *Eyewitness to a Genocide*, 94.

128   "I myself saw a group"   Colonel George Rwigamba, author's interview.

128   Tutsi families in several parts of the country   Anyidoho, *Guns over Kigali*, 19.

128   "Arusha was certainly"   Anyidoho, ibid., 17, 19.

129   It had been amazing to see   Dallaire, *Shake Hands with the Devil*, 154–156.

129   Death squads roamed   Dallaire, ibid., 161.

130   If once restrained by the fear   Barnett, *Eyewitness to a Genocide*, 90.

131   "The grave is only"   Mamdani, *When Victims Become Killers*, 212.

131   Soon afterward, an outspoken Hutu   Dallaire, *Shake Hands with the Devil*, 187.

131   Thirty-five died in the ensuing riots   Melvern, *Conspiracy to Murder*, 111.

131   Dallaire promised to provide them.   Dallaire, *Shake Hands with the Devil*, 190.

131 "The president drove in"   Anyidoho, *Guns over Kigali*, 16.

132 "The story of the Arusha process"   Bruce D. Jones, *Peacemaking in Rwanda: The Dynamics* of Failure (Boulder, Colo.: Lynne Rienner, 2004), 54, 66.

132 One sees the root of the slaughter   Barnett, *Eyewitness to a Genocide*, 51.

132 Another finds it in "the longstanding   Mamdani, *When Victims Become Killers*, 199–200.

133 Dallaire wrote in a cable to New York   Melvern, *Conspiracy to Murder*, 109.

133 "You will hear the sound of many bullets"   Philip Gourevitch, *We Wish to Inform You That Tomorrow We Will Be Killed with Our Families: Stories from Rwanda* (New York: Farrar, Straus and Giroux, 1998), 110.

133 "Even Habyarimana himself"   Berry and Berry, *Genocide in Rwanda*, 118–120; also Melvern, *Conspiracy to Murder*, 125.

133 For weeks, Dallaire had been sending   Melvern, *A People Betrayed*, 107.

133 "We knew nothing of the true reality"   Barnett, *Eyewitness to a Genocide*, 70.

133 By the luck of the diplomatic draw   Dallaire, *Shake Hands with the Devil*, 209; also, Wallis, *Silent Accomplice*, 105, 106.

134 In a perverse speech   Melvern, *A People Betrayed*, 113.

134 "Nobody said 'Stop it'"   Michael Barnett, quoted in Carol Off, *The Lion, the Fox & the Eagle: A Story of Generals and Justice in Rwanda and Yugoslavia* (Toronto: Random House Canada, 2000), 71.

135 "Now is the time"   Wallis, *Silent Accomplice*, 78.

8. This Is a Coup

137 He had agreed   Melvern, *Conspiracy to Murder*, 131.

138 It exploded in a ball of fire   Melvern, ibid., 133–136.

138 Announcers broadcast the names and addresses   Berry and Berry, *Genocide in Rwanda*, 15.

138 "There was little"   Prunier, *The Rwanda Crisis*, 224.

138 "Don't worry"   Prunier, ibid., 225.

140 Bagosora snapped back   Dallaire, *Shake Hands with the Devil*, 223–224; also, Melvern, *Conspiracy to Murder*, 137–141.

141 "I have to leave"   Dallaire, *Shake Hands with the Devil*, 245–246; also, Shaharyar M. Khan, *The Shallow Graves of Rwanda* (London: I. B. Tauris, 2006), 17; Melvern, *Conspiracy to Murder*, 151–153.

141 "We heard her screaming"   Melvern, ibid., 152.

141 A few hours later it was announced   Melvern, *A People Betrayed*, 129.

141 An RTLM announcer speculated   Melvern, ibid., 130.

142 "Rwanda was no"   McCullum, *The Angels Have Left Us*, 14.

143 He played the mediator   Dallaire, *Shake Hands with the Devil*, 250.

143 "His face contorted"   Dallaire, ibid., 251–252.

144 "I saw what seemed"   Dallaire, ibid., 240.

144 Afterward their bodies were mutilated.   Berry and Berry, *Genocide in Rwanda*, 14; also, Melvern, *Conspiracy to Murder*, 153.

144 They knew that Western nations   Dallaire, *Shake Hands with the Devil*, 240.

145 "I went through"   Dallaire, ibid., 260.

145 Twagiramungu told him   Dallaire, ibid., 261.

145 "What moderates?"   Dallaire, ibid., 266.

145 That evening Dallaire stopped   Dallaire, ibid., 268.

9. MADAM, THEY'RE KILLING MY PEOPLE

149 The sight of carnage   Anyidoho, *Guns over Kigali*, 29, 36–37.

151 Rebel fighters took up positions   Jones, *Peacemaking in Rwanda*, 42.

151 General Anyidoho found their march   Anyidoho, *Guns over Kigali*, 32.

151 He had already come to admire   Dallaire, *Shake Hands with the Devil*, 272.

152 It also led him to conclude   Dallaire, ibid., 288.

152 Within a few days, thirty-nine hundred people   Melvern, *Conspiracy to Murder*, 186–187.

153 "I saw how aggressively"   Dallaire, *Shake Hands with the Devil*, 188, 291.

153 Soon afterward the French government   Dallaire, ibid., 262; also, Wallis, *Silent Accomplice*, 101.

154 That left Dallaire   Dallaire, *Shake Hands with the Devil*, 320.

154 He asked Dallaire to "consider future options"   Dallaire, ibid., 293–294.

154 When Prudence Bushnell called from Washington   PBS, "Ghosts of Rwanda."

155 "A crime of genocide"   Melvern, *Conspiracy to Murder*, 198–199.

155 Over the next few days, Dallaire   Dallaire, *Shake Hands with the Devil*, 314.

155 That dissonance left him   Dallaire, ibid., 318.

155 "As Canadian soldiers"   Dallaire, ibid., 318.

155 "The Rwandan Patriotic Front"   Barnett, *Eyewitness to a Genocide*, 15.

156 The message Boutros-Ghali sent   Barnett, ibid., 20.

157 After hanging up, he fell into a chair   Anyidoho, *Guns over Kigali*, 29.

157 "Henry," he said after his rage had passed   Anyidoho, ibid., 50.

157 "Ultimately, led by the"   Dallaire, *Shake Hands with the Devil*, 322–323.

157 "We had a job to do"   Anyidoho, *Guns over Kigali*, 51.

158 "The more the *inkotanyi*"   Jean Hatzfeld, *Machete Season: The Killers in Rwanda Speak* (New York: Farrar, Straus & Giroux, 2005), 177.

159 In the western district of Kibuye   Melvern, *Conspiracy to Murder*, 224.

159 "Whole families are exterminated"   International Committee of the Red Cross, *Cri d'alarme du CICR au Nom des Victims de la Tragédie Rwandaise* (Geneva: ICRC, 1994).

159 Another warned that if Tutsi rebels   Adelman and Suhrke, *The Path of a Genocide*, 93–107; also, Melvern, *Conspiracy to Murder*, 207.

159 The Americans found reasons to refuse   Adelman and Suhrke, *The Path of a Genocide*, 101–103; also, Dallaire, *Shake Hands with the Devil*, 375.

160 A few days after the genocide began   Des Forges et al., *Leave None to Tell the Story*, 43–44, 245–246; also, Rittner et al., *Genocide in Rwanda*, 73–74.

160 "By not issuing a prompt, firm condemnation"   Des Forges et al., *Leave None to Tell the Story*, 246.

160 In the western town of Nyange   *New York Times*, Dec. 14, 2006; also, Rittner et al., *Genocide in Rwanda*, 196.

160 At a church complex   Rittner et al., *Genocide in Rwanda*, 192–195; also, McCullum, *The Angels Have Left Us*, 44–45.

161 In nearby Ntarama, militia men   Rittner et al., *Genocide in Rwanda*, 188.

161 It was one of the worst RPF atrocities   Dallaire, *Shake Hands with the Devil*, 414.

161 Moments after the last truckload   Wallis, *Silent Accomplice*, 96–98; this episode is also the subject of the feature film *Shooting Dogs*, released in the United States as *Beyond the Gates*.

162 They had to fight their way back   Melvern, *Conspiracy to Murder*, 26–27; also, Bonaventure Niyibizi, author's interview.

162 "The mission began as a clandestine operation"   Dallaire, *Shake Hands with the Devil*, 421.

162 All made it to safety   Dallaire, ibid., 347.

162 One of the most extraordinary dramas   Dallaire, ibid., 350; also, Melvern, *Conspiracy to Murder*, 227; Wallis, *Silent Accomplice*, 100–101.

163 Dallaire saw them as "live bait"   Dallaire, *Shake Hands with the Devil*, 382.

163 "There was so much concern"   Anyidoho, *Guns over Kigali*, 64.

163 General Anyidoho gave much credit   Anyidoho, ibid., 67.

164 "It's a war"   *The Observer* (London), July 3, 1994.

164 If one million people were slaughtered   *New Times* (Kigali), July 7, 2006.

165 "It was terrifying"   Dallaire, *Shake Hands with the Devil*, 231.

165 "These arms shipments"   Christian Jennings, *Across the Red River* (London: Phoenix, 2001), 113.

165 During the week they were in South Africa   Melvern, *Conspiracy to Murder*, 232.

165 A rabble that Gérard Prunier described   Prunier, *Genocide in Rwanda*, 231–232.

166 His features were indeed similar   Hatzfeld, *Machete Season*, 24.

166 For example, when he shows you   Hatzfeld, ibid., 10, 71.

167 The death of our president   Hatzfeld, ibid., 56.

167 We are an unfortunate generation.   Hatzfeld, ibid., 173.

10. What a Farce

169 "Everybody knew"   PBS, "Ghosts of Rwanda."

169 Those with the power   *Le Nouvel Observateur*, May 19, 1994.

170 "The fact of willful"   Barnett, *Eyewitness to a Genocide*, 2.

170 During the entire three-month period   Howard W. French, *A Continent for the Taking: The Tragedy and Hope of Africa* (New York: Vintage, 2004), 127.

170   "If we should ever falter"   *International Herald Tribune*, June 7, 1994.

170   "As a responsible government"   *New York Times*, June 10, 1994.

171   "How would you describe"   *State Department Briefing,* April 29, 1994 (Washington, D.C.: Federal News Service), 1–4.

172   "Considerable political and geo-strategic"   Prunier, *The Rwanda Crisis*, 278–279.

172   In mid-June, he dispatched   Wallis, *Silent Accomplice*, 115.

172   "The force was very cohesive"   Anyidoho, *Guns over Kigali*, 113.

172   This was another effort to portray   Wallis, *Silent Accomplice*, 106.

173   A Czech diplomat at the United Nations   Wallis, ibid., 109.

173   "What a farce"   Dallaire, *Shake Hands with the Devil*, 412, 414.

173   Huge masses of Hutu   Dallaire, ibid., 388.

174   "Then he floored me"   Dallaire, ibid., 422, 425–426.

175   People ran ecstatically through the streets   Dallaire, ibid., 437.

175   With them, they brought   Dallaire, ibid., 449.

175   They wanted to make the Turquoise Zone   Adelman and Suhrke, *The Path of a Genocide*, 281–307; also, Wallis, *Silent Accomplice*, 122–145.

175   "The French," one European reporter wrote   Scott Peterson, *Me against My Brother: At War in Somalia, Sudan and Rwanda* (London: Routledge, 2), 284.

175   Over the next several weeks   Wallis, *Silent Accomplice*, 176.

176   "While I was talking"   Dallaire, *Shake Hands with the Devil*, 450–151.

176   In the weeks after the Turquoise Zone   Wallis, *Silent Accomplice*, 159.

176   "If such a scenario came to pass"   Dallaire, *Shake Hands with the Devil*, 395.

176   They met in a conference room   Dallaire, ibid., 399.

177   Later, he was told   Dallaire, ibid., 403.

177   "There were corpses"   Khan, *The Shallow Graves of Rwanda*, 14.

178   General Dallaire's military assistant   Dallaire, *Shake Hands with the Devil*, 340.

178   "I would just sneak away"   Dallaire, ibid., 500.

178   "They said nothing"   Dallaire, ibid., 501.

11. SOMETHING REALLY FILLS UP IN YOUR MIND

182   Even Kigali's fleet of green-and-white municipal buses   McCullum, *The Angels Have Left Us*, 97; also, author's interviews.

182   "The first time most of the world"   John Rucyahana, with James Riordan, *Bishop of Rwanda: Finding Forgiveness amidst a Pile of Bones* (Nashville: Thomas Nelson, 2007), 138.

183   Another called it "the exodus of a nation."   McCullum, *The Angels Have Left Us*, 52.

183   "It was a staggering sight"   McCullum, ibid., 52–53.

184   "On the 17th of July"   Waugh, *Paul Kagame and Rwanda*, 101.

184 "Foreign staffers from UNHCR" French, *A Continent for the Taking*, 140.

185 On July 21, the United States Dallaire, *Shake Hands with the Devil*, 480.

185 They spread out through the camps Melvern, *Conspiracy to Murder*, 245.

185 Through this confusion *Liberation* (Paris), July 27, 1994.

186 "Must we get cholera" Waugh, *Paul Kagame and Rwanda*, 103.

186 "Nothing moved or breathed" Fergal Keane, *Season of Blood: A Rwandan Journey* (London: Penguin, 1995), 49.

187 The defeated army, settled into camps Khan, *The Shallow Graves of Rwanda*, 142.

188 "Former soldiers and militia men" Prunier, *The Rwanda Crisis*, 316.

188 "They are said to be recruiting" McCullum, *The Angels Have Left Us*, 55–56, 101.

188 She blocked a Security Council effort McCullum, ibid., 100.

189 "It is now ethically impossible for us" *New York Times*, Nov. 15, 1994; also, Waugh, *Paul Kagame and Rwanda*, 105.

189 In the weeks after the war ended African Rights, *Rwanda: The Insurgency in the Northwest* (London: African Rights, 1998), 264; also, author's interviews.

189 "There was not time" *Independent on Sunday* (London), Aug. 17, 1994.

189 "Most of our soldiers" *Los Angeles Times*, Aug. 17, 1994.

190 They doubt that attacks Khan, *The Shallow Graves of Rwanda*, 104–119; also, Thomas P. Odom, *Journey into Darkness: Genocide in Rwanda* (College Station: Texas A&M University Press, 2005), 223–230.

190 "It was never RPF policy" author's confidential interview.

190 Evidence suggests that many were Nigel Eltringham, *Accounting for Horror: Post-Genocide Debates in Rwanda* (London: Pluto, 2004), 108; Odom, *Journey into Darkness*, 255; Omaar, *Rwanda: Death, Despair and Defiance*, 644–651.

190 When an American diplomat asked for information Odom, ibid., 256–257.

191 The American military attaché in Kigali Rick Orth, "Rwanda's Hutu Extremist Genocidal Insurgency: An Eyewitness Perspective," *Small Wars and Insurgencies* 12, no. 1 (Spring 2001), 91.

191 "When these start to accumulate" *The Independent* (London), Jan. 5, 1995.

191 "We cannot go on lying" Khan, *The Shallow Graves of Rwanda*, 100–101.

191 That did not sit well with Sendashonga Dallaire, *Shake Hands with the Devil*, 250.

192 Rwanda's official news agency denounced Robert E. Gribbin, *In the Aftermath of Genocide: The U.S. Role in Rwanda* (New York: iUniverse, 2005), 156–157.

193 "Buses would be stopped" Waugh, *Paul Kagame and Rwanda*, 122.

193 In the border village of Kanama Khan, *The Shallow Graves of Rwanda*, 150–151; also, Johan Pottier, *Re-Imagining Rwanda: Conflict, Survival and Disinformation in the Twentieth Century* (Cambridge, U.K.: Cambridge University Press, 2002), 40.

193   "The army can only halfway"   *Christian Science Monitor*, Nov. 28, 1995.

193   Ultimately, the number reached 130,000.   Gribbin, *In the Aftermath of Genocide*, 107.

194   At one point, ten were dying every day   *Baltimore Sun*, May 26, 1980; also, Khan, *The Shallow Graves of Rwanda*, 119–121.

195   "The tribunal was created"   Waugh, *Paul Kagame and Rwanda*, 170.

195   As the process of accounting for genocide began   Human Rights Watch, *Rearming with Impunity: International Support for the Perpetrators of the Rwandan Genocide* (New York: Human Rights Watch Arms Project, 1995).

195   "We must find a solution"   Gribbin, *In the Aftermath of Genocide*, 163.

12. Rwanda Doesn't Matter

197   One American official later wrote   Gribbin, *In the Aftermath of Genocide*, 175.

198   One of them, Lieutenant Colonel Thomas Odom   Odom, *Journey into Darkness*, 188.

198   Once they were there   Mamdani, *When Victims Become Killers*, 254.

199   "Kagame is not expected"   McCullum, *The Angels Have Left Us*, 101.

200   "The larger responsibility"   Mamdani, *When Victims Become Killers*, 254–255.

202   One American report described him   Gribbin, *In the Aftermath of Genocide*, 194.

203   "I flagged such reports"   Gribbin, ibid., 176.

203   "All of them"   Gribbin, ibid., 195.

203   "The bulk of the refugees"   Waugh, *Paul Kagame and Rwanda*, 112–113; also, Elizabeth Neuffer, *The Key to My Neighbor's House: Seeking Justice in Bosnia and Rwanda* (New York: Picador, 2001), 253–256; also, Prunier, *The Rwanda Crisis*, 384.

205   Finally, after facing plagues   French, *A Continent for the Taking*, 140; also, Gribbin, *In the Aftermath of Genocide*, 213.

205   One of his last acts before fleeing   Berry and Berry, *Genocide in Rwanda*, xxix.

205   "There are not many people"   *Washington Post*, June 6, 1997.

206   Some also bridled under the influence   Eltringham, *Accounting for Horror*, 119; also Schürings, *Ein Volk Verlässt sein Land*, 169; Vansina, *Antecedents to Modern Rwanda*, 11; Waugh, *Paul Kagame and Rwanda*, 129.

206   Less than a year after Kabila took power   John F. Clark, ed., *The African Stakes of the Congo War* (New York: Palgrave Macmillan, 2002), 132.

206   In one of those raids   Clark, ibid., 133.

206   General Kabarebe, who owed   Waugh, *Paul Kagame and Rwanda*, 132.

206   "There were a lot of strong"   Rick Orth, author's interview.

13. The Tricky Part

209   one morning in the summer of 1997   Omaar, *Rwanda: Death, Despair and Defiance*, 146.

209   Insurgents who infiltrated   Orth, "Rwanda's Hutu Extremist Genocidal Insurgency," 89.

210   "The insurgency was"   African Rights, *The Insurgency in the Northwest*, 7–12.

210   In July of 1998, Kabila fired his Rwandan-born chief of staff   African Rights, ibid., 114.

211   Most unexpectedly, allied Rwandan and Ugandan forces   Waugh, *Paul Kagame and Rwanda*, 134–136; also, author's interviews.

212   The reports also recounted episodes   Clark, *The African Stakes of the Congo War*, 136–137; also, United Nations Security Council, *Final Report of the Panel of Experts on the Illegal Exploitation of Natural Resources and Other Forms of Wealth in the Democratic Republic of the Congo* (New York: United Nations, 2002); Waugh, *Paul Kagame and Rwanda*, 139.

212   "The *interahamwe* hid out"   Carr, *Land of a Thousand Hills*, 230, 233.

213   On April 25, 1998, they were brought   Gribbin, *In the Aftermath of Genocide*, 265; also, Waugh, *Paul Kagame and Rwanda*, 173.

213   "Painful medicine was necessary"   Eltringham, *Accounting for Horror*, 145.

214   "I told him he was too close"   Paul Rusesabagina, author's interview.

214   "General Kagame was the"   *Globe and Mail* (Toronto), May 25, 1996.

216   About four thousand of them eventually joined   Waugh, *Paul Kagame and Rwanda*, 120.

218   "The government apparently"   Orth, "Rwanda's Hutu Extremist Genocidal Insurgency," 104.

219   "The consequence of French policy"   Wallis, *Silent Accomplice*, 191.

219   They were, as *New York Times* correspondent   French, *A Continent for the Taking*, 141.

221   When Kagame visited Washington   *Washington Post*, July 31, 1996.

223   "The government of Rwanda"   Waugh, *Paul Kagame and Rwanda*, 98.

224   "He always considered"   author's confidential interview.

224   This purge was   Gribbin, *In the Aftermath of Genocide*, 306.

224   "The façade of multi-ethnicity crumbled"   Waugh, *Paul Kagame and Rwanda*, 149.

225   "If the current state of affairs"   *Jeune Afrique*, July 3, 2001.

227   "I returned to Kigali"   Rick Orth, author's interview.

228   "The Rwandan people"   Waugh, *Paul Kagame and Rwanda*, 190.

228   Several of them, including Léonard Hitimana   Dina Temple-Raston, *Justice on the Grass: Three Rwandan Journalists, Their Trial for War Crimes, and a Nation's Quest for Redemption* (New York: Free Press, 2005), 219; Thierry Cruvelier, et al., eds., *Augustin Cyiza: Un Homme Libre au Rwanda* (Paris: Karthala, 2004).

228　Kagame began lacing some of his speeches　Temple-Raston, *Justice on the Grass*, 219–220.

230　"Rwanda's key dilemma"　Mamdani, *When Victims Become Killers*, 266.

14. When You're Not Serious, You Can't Be Correct

234　Around the same time, an even more ambitious inspector　*New Times* (Kigali) July 13, 2006.

234　Then the education ministry　Ibid., July 12, 2006.

235　"We shall continue arresting them"　Ibid.

235　They just announce　author's confidential interview.

238　Once in a great while, protests　*New Times* (Kigali), Aug. 20, 2006, and Aug. 22, 2006.

238　At first, he dismissed their protests　Ibid., Aug. 16, 2006.

239　"Rwandans developed the practice"　National Curriculum Development Centre, *A Guide to Civic Education: Life Skills for Rwandan Primary Schools* (Kigali, Rwanda: National Curriculum Development Centre, 2004), 34.

239　Rwanda was represented by a handful of baskets　Tom Phillips, ed., *Africa: The Art of a Continent* (London: Prestel, 1999).

239　"Rwanda is one of the"　Dr. Cassing Hammond, author's interview.

241　During my visits I saw stories　*Newsline* (Kigali), May 12–18, 2006; July 12–18, 2006; Jan. 10–17, 2007; and Jan. 25–Feb. 2, 2007.

241　At the beginning of 2007　*Umurabyo* (Kigali), Dec. 8–22, 2006, and Feb. 5, 2007; also, Government Press Council (Kigali) press release, Dec. 15, 2006.

241　"This is not a democracy"　author's confidential interview.

242　Rwanda's sweeping development plan, Vision 2020　Republic of Rwanda, *2020 Vision* (Kigali, Rwanda: Ministry of Finance and Economic Planning, 2002).

243　They arrived to shoot a film version　Mushikiwabo and Kramer, *Rwanda Means the Universe*, 42–43.

244　America's ignorance was so complete　Jared Cohen, *One Hundred Days of Silence: America and the Rwandan Genocide* (Lanham, Md.: Rowman and Littlefield, 2007), 121.

245　The official Rwandan daily *New Times*　*New Times* (Kigali), June 29, 2006; Aug. 22, 2006; Dec. 21, 2006; and Jan. 16, 2007.

245　The film was wrong, *New Times* asserted　Ibid., June 29, 2006.

245　Antagonism between the world's two best-known Rwandans　Reuters, April 4, 2007.

246　"His DNA rebels"　author's confidential interview.

247　I told him I had just read his memoir　Paul Rusesabagina, with Tom Zoellner, *An Ordinary Man: The True Story behind "Hotel Rwanda"* (London: Bloomsbury, 2006), 254.

247　"In places and in danger"　Rusesabagina, ibid., 252.

247　Rusesabagina's memoir　Rusesabagina, ibid., 260.

248 By 1969, it was 3.6 million   Nyrop et al., *Rwanda: A Country Study*, vii.

251 *New Times* published a weekend supplement   *New Times* (Kigali), Dec. 19, 2007.

15. BREATHLESS WITH FEAR

253 She is one of many survivors   JAM International, *Voices of Rwanda* (Nairobi: Camerapix, 2003).

253 Eighty-seven percent saw dead bodies   Janice Booth and Philip Briggs, *Rwanda: The Bradt Travel Guide* (London: Bradt, 2006), 18.

254 Many struggle alone   D. C. Henderson et al., *The Crisis in Rwanda: Mental Health in the Service of Justice and Healing* (Cambridge, Mass.: Harvard Program in Refugee Trauma, 1996).

254 A study published in *World Psychiatry*   Frank G. Njerga et al., "War and Mental Disorders in Rwanda," Feb. 2006, vol. 5, no. 1.

258 Uvin found that the system   Peter Uvin, *The Introduction of a Modernized Gacaca for Judging Suspects of Participation in the Genocide and the Massacres of 1994 in Rwanda: A Discussion Paper* (Brussels: Belgian Secretary of State for Development Cooperation, 2000).

259 "They are doing this"   author's confidential s interview.

269 Four years after the Rwandan genocide   Khan, *The Shallow Graves of Rwanda*, 128–140; also, Waugh, *Paul Kagame and Rwanda*, 115–118.

270 "numbed in their incredulity"   Waugh, *Paul Kagame and Rwanda*, 117.

272 "I was not realizing"   PBS, "Ghosts of Rwanda."

272 "We, the international community   *Los Angeles Times*, Dec. 10, 1997.

272 A few months later   *New York Times*, March 26, 1998.

272 "I confirm that the"   *Toronto Star*, July 12, 2007.

273 In 1998 Doctors Without Borders   Wallis, *Silent Accomplice*, 202.

273 Foreign Minister Alain Juppé replied indignantly   Wallis, ibid., 203.

273 "I reject the question"   Wallis, ibid., 212.

273 "France, the country of light"   Wallis, ibid., 216.

275 France's foreign minister, Philippe Douste-Blazy   www.news.com.au, accessed Nov. 27, 2006.

276 "I was the commander"   PBS, "Ghosts of Rwanda."

276 Whenever he saw an article of clothing   Dallaire, *Shake Hands with the Devil*, 325.

276 "I became suicidal"   *Ottawa Citizen*, Dec. 13, 1998.

277 In a letter to the Canadian Broadcasting Corporation   Samantha Power, *"A Problem from Hell": America and the Age of Genocide* (New York: Basic, 2002), 389.

279 He predicted that the trip   Peter Raymont, dir., *Shake Hands with the Devil: The Journey of Roméo Dallaire* (White Pine Pictures, 2004).

279 "A bunch of them"   Dallaire speech at Chicago Public Library, Chicago, Nov. 28, 2006.

279 "You cannot even imagine"   Power, *"A Problem from Hell,"* 386.

16. FAMOUS FOR JUST ONE THING

281   Five years later, a second edition appeared   Booth, *Rwanda: The Bradt Travel Guide*, 2001 and 2006 editions.

282   Her book about them, *Gorillas in the Mist*   Dian Fossey, "The Imperiled Mountain Gorilla: A Grim Struggle for Survival," in *National Geographic*, April 1981; also, Harold T. P. Hayes, *The Dark Romance of Dian Fossey* (New York: Simon & Schuster, 1980); Jack Roberts, *The Importance of Dian Fossey* (San Diego: Lucent, 1995); Weber and Vedder, *In the Kingdom of Gorillas*, 237–255.

283   "In pursuit of her singular goal"   Roberts, *The Importance of Dian Fossey*, 99.

283   Some evidence suggested   Berkeley, *The Graves Are Not Yet Full*, 261.

285   "I always wondered"   Off, *The Lion, the Fox and the Eagle*, 82.

286   "It turns out"   *Sunday Times* (Kigali), May 7, 2006.

291   Some in the RPF   *African Research Bulletin* (London), Oct. 1990, no. 9874; also, Dorsey, *Historical Dictionary of Rwanda*, 31 and 361–362; Karrim Essack, *Civil War in Rwanda* (Dar es Salaam, Tanzania: Forem, 1991), 32–36; Jones, "Civil War," 83; Kamukama, *Rwanda Conflict*, 46.

291   "created a lot tension"   author's confidential interview.

294   Most remarkably, Nyamirambo was the only place   *Christian Century*, Dec. 13, 2005.

297   A year later three explorers   *Telegraph* (London), April 1, 2006; also, Reuters, April 1, 2006.

298   But was the mystery really solved?   *New Times* (Kigali), June 18, 2006.

298   A specialist at the Nile Basin Initiative   Ibid., Aug. 8, 2006.

298   He insisted that no doubt remained   Ibid., Aug. 14, 2006.

17. THE WEB GROWS BIG

305   In 2005 students at the Sonrise School   www.mustardseedproject.org.

307   They return from visits to Rwanda   *Christian Century*, March 31, 2004.

308   "I fell in love"   *New Yorker*, Sept. 12, 2005.

308   "God is going to use you"   *Los Angeles Times*, April 18, 2005.

308   Two years later, Kagame was able to say   *Houston Chronicle*, Jan. 6, 2007.

309   "Those who publicly proclaim"   *Focus* (Kigali), June 21–July 6, 2006.

309   Their admiration has spilled into the business press   *Fortune* online, March 29, 2007.

309   Andrew Young visited in 2005   *Atlanta Journal & Constitution*, Aug. 22, 2006.

309   Representative Donald Payne of New Jersey   Payne speech at Third Annual Rwanda Conference, Morristown, N.J., Sept. 23, 2006.

309   Quincy Jones, responding to an inquiry   *Vanity Fair*, July 2007.

316   Our visitor turned out to be Eugénie Musayidire   Eugénie Musayidire, *Mein Stein Spricht: Texte der Trauer, der Verzweiflung, des Zorns, der Anklage und des*

Protests über die Ermording Meiner Mutter Während des Völkermords in Rwanda 1994 (Bad Honnef, Germany: Horlemann, 1999).

18. WE ASPIRE TO BE LIKE OTHERS

325 "If you miss a shot" Confidential source, author's interview.

326 Students in a secondary school math class *New Times* (Kigali), June 27, 2006.

326 In January of 2007, the mayor of Nyagatare Ibid., Jan. 27, 2007.

326 Two months later *New Times* reported Ibid., Jan. 16, 2007.

326 That same week, a genocide memorial Ibid., March 26, 2007.

328 Amnesty International asserts *Country Report* (London: Amnesty International, 2006).

328 Freedom House says Sara Rakita, ed., *Countries at the Crossroads 2006* (New York: Freedom House, 2005).

328 Reporters Without Borders *Annual Report*, Reporters Without Borders, 2007.

328 Human Rights Watch asserts *World Report* (New York: Human Rights Watch, 2006).

331 After Human Rights Watch issued a report Human Rights Watch, *"There Will Be No Trial": Police Killings of Detainees and the Imposition of Collective Punishments*, July 2007; also, *New Times* (Kigali), Aug. 15, 2007.

332 After an exhaustive study African Peer Review Mechanism, *Country Review Report of the Republic of Rwanda* (Midrand, South Africa: 2005).

332 The same thing happened a couple of years later United Nations Development Program, *Turning Vision 2020 into Reality: From Recovery to Sustainable Human Development* (New York: UNDP, 2007).

332 The state minister for finance *New Times* (Kigali), Aug. 15, 2007.

333 "Whatever he wants for Rwanda" author's confidential interview.

333 If Kagame serves two seven-year terms *The Monitor* (Kampala, Uganda), July 5, 2006.

333 "Otherwise, at some point" author's confidential interview.

334 "You never know" author's confidential interview.

334 Even if no one *Los Angeles Times*, Feb. 7, 2008.

335 "There's been distillation" author's confidential interview.

335 Rwanda benefits from what some call André, Sibomana, *Hope for Rwanda: Conversations with Laure Guilbert and Hervé Deguine* (London: Pluto, 1999), 118–120.

BIBLIOGRAPHY

Aardema, Verna. *Sebugugu the Glutton: A Bantu Tale from Rwanda*. Grand Rapids, Mich.: William B. Eerdmans, 1993.

Adelman, Howard, and Astri Suhrke, eds. *The Path of a Genocide: The Rwanda Crisis from Uganda to Zaire*. New Brunswick, N.J.: Transaction, 1999.

Adolph, Frederick, Duke of Mecklenburg-Schwerin. *In the Heart of Africa*. London: Cassell, 1910.

African Peer Review Mechanism. *Country Review Report of the Republic of Rwanda*. Midrand, South Africa: 2005.

African Rights. *Father Hormisdas Nsengimana: Accused of Genocide, Sheltered by the Church*. London: African Rights, 2001.

———. *The Gisimba Memorial Center: No Place to Fear: A Tribute to Damas Mutezintare Gisimba*. London: African Rights, 2003.

———. *Joseph Ruyenzi: Witness to Genocide*. London: African Rights, 1997.

———. *Rwanda: Broken Bodies, Torn Spirits: Living with Genocide, Rape and HIV/AIDS*. London: African Rights, 2004.

———. *Rwanda: The Insurgency in the Northwest*. London: African Rights, 1998.

———. *Rwanda: Not So Innocent: When Women Become Killers*. London: African Rights, 1995.

———. *Witness to Genocide: John Yusufu Munyakazi, the Killer behind the Refugee*. London: African Rights, 1997.

Aguilar, Mario I. *The Rwanda Genocide and the Call to Deepen Christianity in Africa*. Nairobi, Kenya: Amecea Gaba, 1998.

Albright, Madeleine. *Madam Secretary: A Memoir*. New York: Miramax, 2005.

Amnesty International. *Report 2007: The State of the World's Human Rights* (May 2007).

———. *Rwanda: Amnesty International's Concerns since the Beginning of the Insurgency in October 1990* (March 1991).

———. *Rwanda: Arming the Perpetrators of Genocide* (June 1995).

———. *Rwanda: Ending the Silence* (Sept. 25, 1997).

———. *Rwanda: Gacaca: A Question of Justice* (Dec. 17, 2002).

————. *Rwanda: The Hidden Violence: "Disappearances" and Killings Continue* (June 1998).

————. *Rwanda: Mass Murder by Government Supporters and Troops in May 1994* (May 23, 1994).

————. *Rwanda: Persecution of Tutsi Minority and Repression of Government Critics 1990–1992* (May 1992).

————. *Rwanda: Reports of Killings and Abductions by the Rwandese Patriotic Army, April–August 1994* (Oct. 20, 1994).

Anyidoho, Henry Kwami. *Guns over Kigali*. Kampala, Uganda: Fountain, 1998.

Bale, John. *Imagined Olympians: Body Culture and Colonial Representation in Rwanda*. Minneapolis: University of Minnesota, 2002.

Barnett, Michael. *Eyewitness to a Genocide: The United Nations and Rwanda*. Ithaca, N.Y.: Cornell University, 2002.

————. "The UN Security Council, Indifference, and Genocide in Rwanda." *Cultural Anthropology* 12, no. 4 (1997).

Berkeley, Bill. *The Graves Are Not Yet Full: Race, Tribe and Power in the Heart of Africa*. New York: Basic Books, 2001.

Berry, John A., and Carol Pott Berry, eds. *Genocide in Rwanda: A Collective Memory*. Washington, D.C.: Howard University, 1999.

Bilinda, Lesley. *With What Remains: A Widow's Quest for Truth in Rwanda*. London: Hodder & Stoughton, 2006.

Bodnarchuk, Kari. *Rwanda: Country Torn Apart*. Minneapolis, Minn.: Lerner, 2000.

Bond, Patrick. *Looting Africa: The Economics of Exploitation*. London: Zed, 2006.

Booth, Janice, and Philip Briggs. *Rwanda: The Bradt Travel Guide*. London: Bradt, 2001 and 2006.

Braeckman, Colette. *Rwanda: Histoire d'un Genocide*. Paris: Fayard, 1994.

Burleson, Derick. *Ejo: Poems, Rwanda 1991–1994*. Madison: University of Wisconsin, 2000.

Calderisi, Robert. *The Trouble with Africa: Why Foreign Aid Isn't Working*. New York: Palgrave Macmillan, 2006.

Carr, Rosamond Halsey, with Ann Howard Halsey. *Land of a Thousand Hills: My Life in Rwanda*. New York: Viking, 1999.

Chrétien, Jean-Pierre. *The Great Lakes of Africa: Two Thousand Years of History*. New York: Zone, 2003.

Church, J. E. *Forgive Them: The Story of an African Martyr*. Chicago: Moody, 1967.

Clapham, Christopher, ed. *African Guerrillas*. Oxford, U.K.: James Currey, 1998.

Clark, John F., ed. *The African Stakes of the Congo War*. New York: Palgrave Macmillan, 2002.

Clay, Jason W. *The Eviction of Banyaruanda: The Story behind the Refugee Crisis in Southwest Uganda*. Cambridge, Mass.: Cultural Survival, 1984.

Cohen, Jared. *One Hundred Days of Silence: American and the Rwandan Genocide*. Lanham, Md.: Rowman and Littlefield, 2007.

Commission of Inquiry in the DRC. *International Non-Governmental Commission of Inquiry into the Massive Violations of Human Rights Committed in the Democratic*

Republic of the Congo—Former Zaire—1996–1997. Montreal: International Centre for Human Rights and Democratic Development, 1988.

Courtemanche, Gil. *A Sunday at the Pool in Rwanda*. New York: Alfred A. Knopf, 2003.

Crawford, Barry. "From Arusha to Goma: How the West Started the War in Rwanda." *Africa Direct*, Feb. 17, 1995.

Cruvelier, Thierry, et al., eds. *Augustin Cyiza: Un Homme Libre au Rwanda*. Paris: Karthala, 2004.

Dallaire, Roméo. *Shake Hands with the Devil: The Failure of Humanity in Rwanda*. New York: Carroll & Graf, 2003.

De Lame, Danielle. *A Hill among a Thousand: Transformations and Ruptures in Rural Rwanda*. Madison: University of Wisconsin, 2005.

Des Forges, Alison, et al. *Leave None to Tell the Story: Genocide in Rwanda*. New York: Human Rights Watch, 1999.

Destexhe, Alain. *Rwanda and Genocide in the Twentieth Century*. London: Pluto, 1995.

Dorsey, Learthen. *Historical Dictionary of Rwanda*. Lanham, Md.: Scarecrow, 1994.

Durch, William J., ed. *UN Peacekeeping: American Politics and the Uncivil Wars of the 1990s*. New York: St. Martin's, 1996.

Easterly, William. *The White Man's Burden: How the West's Efforts to Aid the Rest Have Done So Much Ill and So Little Good*. New York: Penguin, 2006.

Eltringham, Nigel. *Accounting for Horror: Post-Genocide Debates in Rwanda*. London: Pluto, 2004.

Essack, Karim. *Civil War in Rwanda*. Dar es Salaam, Tanzania: Forem, 1991.

———. *Rwanda: The International Significance of the Liberation Struggle*. Dar es Salaam, Tanzania: Thackers, 1996.

Feil, Scott R. *Preventing Genocide: How the Early Use of Force Might Have Succeeded in Rwanda*. New York: Carnegie Corporation, 1998.

Fossey, Dian. "The Imperiled Mountain Gorilla: A Grim Struggle for Survival." *National Geographic*, April 1981.

Freeman, Charles. *Crisis in Rwanda*. Austin, Tex.: Raintree Steck-Vaughn, 1999.

French, Howard W. *A Continent for the Taking: The Tragedy and Hope of Africa*. New York: Vintage, 2004.

George, Terry, ed. *Hotel Rwanda: Bringing the True Story of an African Hero to Film*. New York: Newmarket, 2005.

Gourevitch, Philip. *We Wish to Inform You That Tomorrow We Will Be Killed with Our Families: Stories from Rwanda*. New York: Farrar, Straus & Giroux, 1998.

Greenberg, Keith. *Rwanda: Fierce Clashes in Central Africa*. Woodbridge, Conn.: Blackbirch, 1997.

Gribbin, Robert E. *In the Aftermath of Genocide: The U.S. Role in Rwanda*. New York: iUniverse, 2005.

Guillebaud, Meg. *Rwanda: The Land God Forgot*. London: Monarch, 2002.

Hatzfeld, Jean. *Life Laid Bare: The Survivors in Rwanda Speak*. New York: Farrar, Straus & Giroux, 2007.

———. *Machete Season: The Killers in Rwanda Speak*. New York: Farrar, Straus & Giroux, 2005.

Hayes, Harold T. P. *The Dark Romance of Dian Fossey*. New York: Simon & Schuster, 1990.

Heremans, Rogers. *Introduction à l'Histoire du Rwanda*. Kigali, Rwanda: Editions Rwandaises, 1973.

History Channel. *Rwanda: Do Scars Ever Fade?* 2004.

Hochschild, Adam. *King Leopold's Ghost: A Story of Greed, Terror and Heroism in Colonial Africa*. Boston: Houghton Mifflin, 1998.

Human Rights Watch. *Beyond the Rhetoric: Continuing Human Rights Abuse in Rwanda* (June 1993).

———. *Genocide in Rwanda April–May 1994* (May 1994).

———. *Rearming with Impunity: International Support for the Perpetrators of the Rwandan Genocide*. New York: Human Rights Watch Arms Project, 1995.

———. *Rwanda: A New Catastrophe?* (Dec. 1994).

———. *Rwanda: Talking Peace and Waging War* (Feb. 27, 1992).

———. *"There Will Be No Trial": Police Killings of Detainees and the Imposition of Collective Punishments* (July 2007).

———. *Uprooting the Rural Poor in Rwanda* (May 2001).

Human Rights Watch Arms Project. *Arming Rwanda: The Arms Trade and Human Rights Abuses in the Rwandan War* (Jan. 1994).

Hyman, Lester. *U.S. Policy toward Liberia 1922 to 2003: Unexpected Consequences*. Cherry Hill, N.J.: African Homestead Legacy, 2005.

Ilibagiza, Immaculée. *Left to Tell: Discovering God amidst the Rwandan Holocaust*. (Carlsbad, Calif.: Hay House 2007).

International Committee of the Red Cross. *Cri d'alarme du CICR au Nom des Victims de la Tragédie Rwandaise*. Geneva: ICRC, 1994.

International Crisis Group. *Five Years after the Genocide in Rwanda: Justice in Question* (April 7, 1999).

———. *International Criminal Tribunal for Rwanda: Justice Delayed* (June 7, 2001).

———. *Uganda and Rwanda: Friends or Enemies?* (May 4, 2000).

JAM International. *Voices of Rwanda*. Nairobi: Camerapix, 2003.

Jefremovas, Villia. *Brickyards to Graveyards: From Production to Genocide in Rwanda*. Albany: State University of New York, 2002.

Jennings, Christian. *Across the Red River*. London: Phoenix, 2001.

Jones, Bruce D. "Civil War, the Peace Process, and Genocide in Rwanda," in Taisier M. Ali and Robert O. Matthews, eds., *Civil Wars in Africa: Roots and Resolution*. Montreal: McGill-Queen's University Press, 1999.

Jones, Bruce D. *Peacemaking in Rwanda: The Dynamics of Failure*. Boulder, Colo.: Lynne Rienner, 2004.

Kagame, Paul. *The Rwandese Patriotic Army Operation Code of Conduct*. Photocopy, 1991.

Kamukama, Dixon. *Rwanda Conflict: Its Roots and Regional Implications*. Kampala, Uganda: Fountain, 1993.

Keane, Fergal. *Season of Blood: A Rwandan Journey*. London: Penguin, 1995.

Khan, Shaharyar M. *The Shallow Graves of Rwanda*. London: I. B. Tauris, 2006.

Kinghoffer, Arthur Jay. *The International Dimension of Genocide in Rwanda*. London: Macmillan, 1998.

Koff, Clea. *The Bone Woman: Among the Dead in Rwanda, Bosnia, Croatia and Kosovo*. London: Atlantic, 2004.

Kuperman, Alan J. *The Limits of Humanitarian Intervention: Genocide in Rwanda*. Washington, D.C.: Brookings, 2001.

Kutesa, Pecos. *Uganda's Revolution 1979–1986: How I Saw It*. Kampala, Uganda: Fountain, 2006.

Lawrence, Carl. *Rwanda: A Walk through Darkness . . . into Light*. Gresham, Ore.: Vision House, 1995.

Lebor, Adam. *"Complicity with Evil": The United Nations in the Age of Modern Genocide*. New Haven, Conn.: Yale University, 2006.

Lemarchand, René. *Rwanda and Burundi*. London: Pall Mall, 1970.

———. "Rwanda: The Rationality of Genocide." *Issue: A Journal of Opinion* 23, no. 2 (1995).

Leonard, David K., and Scott Strauss. *Africa's Stalled Development: International Causes and Cures*. Boulder, Colo.: Lynne Rienner 2003.

Linden, Ian, and Jane Linden. *Church and Revolution in Rwanda*. New York: Manchester University, 1977.

Madsden, Wayne. *Genocide and Covert Actions in Africa, 1993–1999*. New York: Edwin Mellen, 1999.

Mamdani, Mahmood. *When Victims Become Killers: Colonialism, Nativism and the Genocide in Rwanda*. Princeton, N.J.: Princeton University, 2001.

Maquet, Jacques J. *The Premise of Inequality in Rwanda: A Study of Political Relations in a Central African Kingdom*. Oxford, U.K.: International African Institute, 1961.

Marchal, Colonel Luc. *Rwanda, La Descente aux Enfers: Témoinage d'un Peacekeeper Decembre 1993–Avril 1994*. Brussels: Labor, 2001.

McCullum, Hugh. *The Angels Have Left Us: The Rwanda Tragedy and the Churches*. Geneva: World Council of Churches, 2004.

McEvedy, Colin. *The Penguin Atlas of African History*. London: Penguin, 1995.

Melvern, Linda. *Conspiracy to Murder: The Rwandan Genocide*. London: Verso, 2004.

———. *A People Betrayed: The Role of the West in Rwanda's Genocide*. London: Zed, 2000.

Misser, Franois. *Vers un Nouveau Rwanda? Entretiens avec Paul Kagame*. Brussels: Luc Pire, 1995.

Mowat, Farley. *Woman in the Mists: The Story of Dian Fossey and the Mountain Gorillas of Africa*. New York: Warner, 1987.

Mujawiyera, Eugenie. *The Rwanda Tutsis: A Tutsi Woman's Account of the Hidden Causes of the Rwandan Tragedy*. London: Adonis & Abbey, 2006.

Musayidire, Eugénie. *Mein Stein Spricht: Texte der Trauer, der Verzweiflung, des Zorns, der Anklage und des Protests über die Ermording Meiner Mutter Während des Völkermords in Rwanda, 1994*. Bad Honnef, Germany: Horlemann, 1999.

Museveni, Yoweri. *Sowing the Mustard Seed: The Struggle for Freedom and Democracy in Uganda*. London: Macmillan, 1997.

Mushikiwabo, Louise, and Jack Kramer. *Rwanda Means the Universe: A Native's Memoir of Blood and Bloodlines*. New York: St. Martin's, 2006.

National Curriculum Development Centre. *A Guide to Civic Education: Life Skills for Rwandan Primary Schools*. Kigali, Rwanda: National Curriculum Development Centre, 2004.

Neuffer, Elizabeth. *The Key to My Neighbor's House: Seeking Justice in Bosnia and Rwanda*. New York: Picador, 2001.

Neumann, Hildegard. *Kennen Sie Ruanda? Das Vergessene Paradies im Herzen von Afrika*. Munich: Sebstverlag, 1978.

Newbury, Catherine M. *The Cohesion of Oppression: Clientship and Ethnicity in Rwanda 1860–1960*. New York: Columbia University, 1988.

Njera, Frank, et al."War and Mental Disorders in Rwanda." *World Psychiatry*, 5 no. 1 (February 2006).

Nyrop, Richard F., et al. *Rwanda: A Country Study*. Washington, D.C: U.S. Government Printing Office, 1982.

Odom, Thomas P. *Journey into Darkness: Genocide in Rwanda*. College Station: Texas A&M University Press, 2005.

Off, Carol. *The Lion, the Fox and the Eagle: A Story of Generals and Justice in Rwanda and Yugoslavia*. Toronto: Random House Canada, 2000.

Omaar, Rakiya. *Rwanda: Death, Despair and Defiance*. London: African Rights, 1995.

Orth, Rick. "Rwanda's Hutu Extremist Genocidal Insurgency: An Eyewitness Perspective." *Small Wars and Insurgencies* 12, no. 1 (Spring 2001).

PBS. "Ghosts of Rwanda." *Frontline*. 2004.

Péan, Pierre. *Noires Fureurs, Blancs Menteurs: Rwanda, 1990–1994*. Paris: Mille et Une Nuits, 2005.

Peterson, Scott. *Me against My Brother: At War in Somalia, Sudan and Rwanda*. London: Routledge, 2000.

Phillips, Tom, ed. *Africa: The Art of a Continent*. London: Prestel, 1999.

Pierce, Julian R. *Speak Rwanda*. New York: Picador, 1999.

Pottier, Johan. *Re-Imagining Rwanda: Conflict, Survival and Disinformation in the Late Twentieth Century*. Cambridge, England: Cambridge University, 2002.

Power, Samantha. *"A Problem from Hell": America and the Age of Genocide*. New York: Basic Books, 2002.

Pro Mundi Vita. *Ruanda: Strength and Weakness of the Christian Centre of Africa*. Brussels: Pro Mundi Vita, 1963.

Prunier, Gérard. *The Rwanda Crisis: History of a Genocide*. New York: Columbia University, 1995.

Rakita, Sara, ed. *Countries at the Crossroads 2006*. New York: Freedom House, 2005.

Raymont, Peter, dir. *Shake Hands with the Devil: The Journey of Roméo Dallaire*. White Pine Pictures, 2004.

Reader, John. *Africa: A Biography of the Continent*. New York: Alfred A. Knopf, 1998.

Reed, William Cyrus. "Exile, Reform and the Rise of the Rwandan Patriotic Front." *Journal of Modern African Studies* 34, no. 3 (1996).

Republic of Rwanda. *2020 Vision*. Kigali, Rwanda: Ministry of Finance and Economic Planning, 2002.

———. National Curriculum Development Centre. *A Guide to Civic Education: Life Skills for Rwandan Primary Schools*. Kigali, Rwanda: NCDC, 2004.

Reyntjens, Filip. *Again at the Crossroads: Rwanda and Burundi, 2000–2001*. Uppsala, Sweden: Nordic Africa Institute, 2001.

Richards, Audrey. *Economic Development and Tribal Change*. Cambridge, Mass.: EAISR, 1954.

Rieff, David. *A Bed for the Night: Humanitarianism in Crisis*. New York: Simon & Schuster, 2002.

Rittner, Carol, et al., eds. *Genocide in Rwanda: Complicity of the Churches?* St. Paul, Minn.: Paragon House, 2004.

Roberts, Jack. *The Importance of Dian Fossey*. San Diego: Lucent, 1995.

Rucyahana, John, with James Riordan. *Bishop of Rwanda: Finding Forgiveness amidst a Pile of Bones*. Nashville: Thomas Nelson, 2007.

Rusesabagina, Paul, with Tom Zoellner. *An Ordinary Man: The True Story behind "Hotel Rwanda."* London: Bloomsbury, 2006.

Sachs, Jeffrey D. *The End of Poverty: Economic Possibilities for Our Time*. New York: Penguin, 2005.

Schürings, Hildegard, ed. *Ein Volk Verlässt sein Land: Krieg und Völkermord in Ruanda*. Cologne, Germany: ISP, 1994.

Semujanga, Josias. *Origins of the Rwandan Genocide*. Amherst, N.Y.: Humanity, 2003.

Shawcross, William. *Deliver Us from Evil: Peacekeepers, Warlords and a World of Endless Conflict*. New York: Simon & Schuster, 2000.

Shyaka, Anastase. *Conflits en Afrique des Grand Lacs et Esquisse de leur Résolution*. Warsaw: Dialog, 2003.

———. *The Rwandan Conflict: Origin, Development, Exit Strategies*. Kigali, Rwanda: National Unity and Reconciliation Commission, 2005.

Sibomana, André. *Hope for Rwanda: Conversations with Laure Guilbert and Hervé Deguine*. London: Pluto, 1999.

Snyder, C. Albert, *On a Hill Far Away: Journal of a Missionary Doctor in Rwanda*. Indianapolis, Ind.: Light and Life, 1999.

Stassen, Jean-Philippe. *Deogratias: A Tale of Rwanda*. New York: First Second, 2006.

Strauss, Scott. *The Order of Genocide: Race, Power, and War in Rwanda*. Ithaca, N.Y.: Cornell University, 2006.

Tadjo, Veronique. *The Shadow of Imana: Reflections on the Rwandan Genocide*. London: Adonis & Abbey, 2006.

Temple-Raston, Dina. *Justice on the Grass: Three Rwandan Journalists, Their Trial for War Crimes, and a Nation's Quest for Redemption*. New York: Free Press, 2005.

United Nations. *Comprehensive Report on Lessons Learned from United Nations Assistance Mission for Rwanda (UNAMIR), October 1993–April 1996* (Dec. 1996).

———. *Final Report of the Commission of Experts Established Pursuant to Security Council Resolution 935* (Dec. 9, 1994).

———. *Interim Report of the Commission of Experts Established in Accordance with Security Council Resolution 935* (Oct. 4, 1994).

———. *Report of the Independent Inquiry into the Actions of the United Nations during the 1994 Genocide in Rwanda* (Dec. 15, 1999).

United Nations Development Program. *Turning Vision 2020 into Reality: From Recovery to Sustainable Human Development*. New York: UNDP, 2007.

United Nations Security Council. *Final Report of the Panel of Experts on the Illegal Exploitation of Natural Resources and Other Forms of Wealth in the Democratic Republic of the Congo*. New York: UNSC, 2002.

U.S. Committee for Refugees. *Exile from Rwanda: Background to an Invasion*. Washington, D.C.: U.S. Committee for Refugees, 1991.

U.S. Department of Defense and Department of State. *Congressional Presentation for Security Assistance Programs, Fiscal Year 1993*. Washington, D.C.: U.S. Government Printing Office, 1993.

U.S. Department of State. *Briefing*. Washington, D.C.: Federal News Service, 1994.

Uvin, Peter. *Aiding Violence: The Development Enterprise in Rwanda*. West Hartford, Conn.: Kumarian, 1998.

———. *Human Rights and Development*. West Hartford, Conn.: Kumarian, 2005.

———. *The Introduction of a Modernized Gacaca for Judging Suspects of Participation in the Genocide and the Massacres of 1994 in Rwanda: A Discussion Paper*. Brussels: Belgian Secretary of State for Development Cooperation, 2000.

Van der Meeren, Rachel. "Three Decades in Exile: Rwandan Refugees 1960–1990." *Journal of Refugee Studies* 9, no. 3 (1996), 253–256.

Vanderweff, Corrine. *Kill Thy Neighbor: One Man's Incredible Story of Loss and Deliverance in Rwanda*. Boise, Idaho: Pacific, 1996.

Vansina, Jan. *Antecedents to Modern Rwanda: The Nyiginya Kingdom*. Madison: University of Wisconsin, 2004.

Waller, David. *Rwanda: Which Way Now?* Oxford, U.K.: Oxfam, 1997.

Wallis, Andrew. *Silent Accomplice: The Untold Story of France's Role in the Rwandan Genocide*. London: I. B. Tauris, 2006.

Watson, Catharine. "War and Waiting." *Africa Report*, Nov.–Dec.1992, 51–55.

Waugh, Colin M. *Paul Kagame and Rwanda: Power, Genocide and the Rwandan Patriotic Front*. Jefferson, N. C.: McFarland, 2004.

Weber, Bill, and Amy Vedder. *In the Kingdom of Gorillas: Fragile Species in a Dangerous Land*. New York: Simon & Schuster, 2001.

INDEX